E. C. Blakeslee, S. H. Hughes, Emma Leslie

**The Compendium of Cookery and Reliable Recipes**

Two complete volumes in one

E. C. Blakeslee, S. H. Hughes, Emma Leslie

**The Compendium of Cookery and Reliable Recipes**
*Two complete volumes in one*

ISBN/EAN: 9783337092252

Printed in Europe, USA, Canada, Australia, Japan

Cover: Foto ©Lupo / pixelio.de

More available books at **www.hansebooks.com**

# THE COMPENDIUM OF COOKERY

AND

## RELIABLE RECIPES

TWO COMPLETE VOLUMES IN ONE

CONTAINING THE ENTIRE COMPILATION OF RULES
FOR COOKING AND CONFECTIONERY,

TOGETHER WITH

## THE BOOK OF KNOWLEDGE,

OR 1,000 WAYS OF GETTING RICH.

AS PREPARED BY

**MRS. E. C. BLAKESLEE,**
OF CHICAGO

**MISS EMMA LESLIE,**
OF PHILADELPHIA,

AND

**DR. S. H. HUGHES,**
CHEMIST, OF BOSTON.

## REVISED, ENLARGED AND ILLUSTRATED

CHICAGO:
THE MERCHANTS' SPECIALTY CO., PUBLISHERS.
1890.

# PREFACE.

Perhaps one can say that the subject of Cookery has never received so much and so intelligent attention as at the present time. Not that more people have deliberately concluded that the wisdom of the ages is to "live to eat," but a great many careful observers and close thinkers are convinced that the height of human wisdom is to "eat to live." Famous Cooks receive higher salaries than learned College Professors. The convictions of the older philosophers, and the rythm of earth's sweetest poet's are alike forgotten when placed side by side with the attractions of a fragrant roast, or an appetizing joint. A new and improved recipe, tested and approved by a noted cook, recieves more attention than the discovery of an asteroid, or a theory of creation. And there is reason for the choice. The perfection of brain and body are equally dependend on the perfection of the food consumed, and its method of preparation. The vast number of dyspeptics who make a travesty of life and living are proof positive that there is still room for improvement in cooking.

And so it is that there are Cook Books, and Cook Books of all sizes, shapes, claims and pretentions—Cook Books everywhere—and at prices that range from "Take one," to figures that startle the would be purchaser. Amidst this vast number of books we trust there is a place for the present volume and that it will receive a friendly greeting from a goodly number of the careful intelligent cooks who are so intimately associated with the health and happiness of our homes. Never was there a time when so much attention has been given to the plain practical demands of every day life, and a cook book designed for the people at large, containing the theories of no "cranks," nor the death dealing concoctions of any embryo professionals, ought to be, and we believe will be acceptable in any intelligent household.

The present volume is made up of tested recipes and is designed for use. Herein will be found much information that will interest every house-keeper. For those who desire, full directions are given for making the best Bread, Pastry, Soups, Preserves, Pickles, Sauces, and Condiments. The most approved methods for cooking all kinds of Meats, Fish, Fowls and Vegetables are clearly explained, and the secrets of making delicious Confectionery and the richest Ice Creams are herein open to all who will read.

The subject of carving is very carefully treated and very fully illustrated. No subject connected with house-hold manners and accomplishments deserves so much attention, and scarcely any one receives so little attention as carving. The instruction and the illustrations herein given, if carefully heeded, will transform the most awkward wielder of the knife and fork, into a personation of ease and elegance.

The Book of Knowledge and Reliable Recipes—which is a part of this volume, gives more than a thousand ways of getting rich. These recipes are of the highest interest alike to the Matron and Maid, whether looking for the useful and the pleasing in the home, or for beauty and attraction in form and feature, to the Man who is searching for dollars, and the Boy who is interested in fish and game, or in business experiments.

This is perhaps the most valuable compilation of Recipes ever given to the public.

# INDEX.

## BREAD AND BREAKFAST DISHES.

| | PAGE. |
|---|---|
| Yeast | 130 |
| Plain White Family Bread | 130 |
| Graham Bread | 131 |
| Boston Brown Bread | 131 |
| Corn Bread | 132 |
| Steamed Brown Bread | 132 |
| Parker House Rolls | 132 |
| French Rolls | 132 |
| Buns | 133 |
| Biscuits | 133 |
| To Make Rusks | 133 |
| Sweet Milk Gems | 134 |
| Breakfast Gems | 134 |
| Graham Breakfast Cakes | 134 |
| Buckwheat Cakes | 134 |
| Flannel Cakes | 135 |
| Rice Griddle Cakes | 136 |
| French Pancakes | 136 |
| Pancakes | 136 |
| Bread Fritters | 136 |
| Quick Sally Lunn | 137 |
| Breakfast Cake | 137 |
| Quick Waffles | 137 |
| Johnny Cake | 137 |
| Mush | 137 |
| Corn Mush | 138 |
| Graham Mush | 138 |

## CAKES.

| | PAGE. |
|---|---|
| White Lady Cake | 130 |
| Macaroons | 130 |
| Almond Icing | 131 |
| To Make Icing for Cakes | 131 |
| Loaf Cake | 132 |
| Rich Bride Cake | 132 |
| Lady-Fingers | 132 |
| Queen Cake | 133 |
| Chocolate Macaroons | 133 |
| Caramel Cake | 133 |
| Pound Cake | 134 |
| Cocoanut Sponge Cake | 134 |
| Cocoanut Pound Cake | 135 |

| | PAGE. |
|---|---|
| Cocoanut Cup Cake | 185 |
| Cocoanut Drops | 185 |
| Citron Heart Cakes | 186 |
| Imperial Cakes | 186 |
| Plum Cakes | 126 |
| Gold and Silver Cakes | 187 |
| To Make Small Sponge Cakes | 187 |
| Lemon Cheese Cakes | 188 |
| Snow Cakes | 188 |
| Tilden Cakes | 188 |
| Corn Starch Cakes | 188 |
| Birthday Cakes | 189 |
| Naples Biscuit | 189 |
| Cake Trifles | 189 |
| Savoy Cake | 189 |
| Composition Cake | 190 |
| Almond Cream Cake | 190 |
| Ice-Cream Cake | 190 |
| Economical Cake | 191 |
| Delicate Cake | 191 |
| Orange Cake | 191 |
| Jelly Kisses | 192 |
| Fig Cake | 192 |
| Fried Cake | 192 |
| Cocoanut Kisses | 192 |
| California Cake | 193 |
| White Mountain Cake | 193 |
| Lemon Cake | 193 |
| Strawberry Short Cake | 193 |
| Marble Cake | 194 |
| White Pound Cake | 194 |
| Nelly's Chocolate Cake | 194 |
| Rice Cake | 195 |
| Cream Cake | 195 |
| Sponge Cake | 195 |
| Doughnuts | 195 |
| Coffee Cake | 196 |
| Spice Cake | 196 |
| Soft Ginger Bread | 196 |
| Sweet Strawberry Short Cake | 196 |
| Ginger Nuts | 196 |
| Ribbon Cake | 197 |
| Jelly Roll | 197 |
| Delicate Crullers | 198 |

## COSMETIQUES

|  | PAGE |
|---|---|
| Complexion Wash | 245 |
| To Clear a Tanned Skin | 245 |
| Oil to Make the Hair Curl | 245 |
| Wrinkles in the Skin | 245 |
| Pearl Water for the Face | 246 |
| Pearl Dentifrice | 246 |
| Wash for a Blotched Face | 246 |
| Face Powder | 246 |
| Bandoline | 246 |
| A Good Wash for the Hair | 247 |

## DRINKS

| To Make Green Tea | 232 |
|---|---|
| To Make Black Tea—Make as directed for Green | 232 |
| Iced Tea | 232 |
| Coffee | 232 |
| Chocolate | 233 |
| Lemon Syrup | 233 |
| Strawberry Syrup | 234 |
| Raspberry Syrup | 234 |
| Strawberry Sherbet | 234 |
| Raspberry Vinegar | 235 |
| Lemonade | 235 |
| Egg-Nog | 235 |
| Raisin Wine | 235 |
| Currant Wine | 236 |
| Ginger Wine | 236 |
| Fine Milk Punch | 236 |
| Claret Cup | 237 |
| Roman Punch | 237 |
| Cream Nectar | 237 |
| Red Currant Cordial | 237 |
| Elderberry Syrup | 238 |

## DESSERT AND TEA DISHES

| Boiled Custard | 199 |
|---|---|
| Lemon Custard | 199 |
| Snow Custard | 199 |
| Tapioca Custard | 200 |
| Blanc Mange | 201 |
| Rice Blanc Mange | 201 |
| Apple Trifle | 202 |
| Lemon Trifle | 202 |
| Floating Island | 203 |
| Apple Snow | 203 |
| Tropical Snow | 203 |
| Swiss Cream | 204 |
| Italian Cream | 204 |
| Whipped Cream | 204 |
| Tipsy Cake | 205 |
| Snow Pyramids | 205 |

| An Excellent Dessert | 205 |
|---|---|
| Apple Fritters | 206 |
| Jelly Cake Fritters | 206 |
| Black Meringue | 206 |
| Charlotte Russe | 207 |
| Jellied Grapes | 207 |
| Jelly and Custard | 207 |
| Lemon Toast | 207 |
| Dish of Snow whipped Cream | 208 |
| Omelet for Dessert | 208 |
| Jelly Fritters | 209 |

## FISH

| Boiled Salmon | 34 |
|---|---|
| Broiled Salmon | 34 |
| Baked Salmon | 34 |
| Salmon Trout | 35 |
| Spiced Salmon (Pickled) | 35 |
| Salmon and Caper Sauce | 36 |
| Salmon Cutlets | 36 |
| Dried or Smoked Salmon | 36 |
| Boiled Cod | 37 |
| Cod Pie | 37 |
| Dried Codfish | 37 |
| Stewed Salt Cod | 37 |
| Codfish Cakes | 38 |
| Boiled Bass | 38 |
| Fried Bass | 38 |
| To Fry or Boil Fish Properly | 39 |
| Baked Black Bass | 39 |
| Broiled Mackerel | 39 |
| Salt Mackerel with Cream Sauce | 40 |
| Boiled Eels | 41 |
| Fricasseed Eels | 41 |
| Fried Eels | 41 |
| Collared Eels | 41 |
| Fried Trout | 42 |
| Trout in Jelly (or other Fish) | 42 |
| Boiled Trout | 42 |
| Broiled Trout | 43 |
| Baked Haddock | 43 |
| Curried Haddock | 43 |
| Fricaseed Haddock | 44 |
| Broiled White Fish (Fresh) | 44 |
| Baked White Fish | 44 |
| To Choose Lobsters | 45 |
| Boiled Lobsters | 45 |
| Curried Lobsters | 45 |
| Lobster Chowder | 45 |
| Chowder | 46 |
| To Fry Smelts | 46 |
| Red Herrings or Yarmouth Bloaters | 47 |
| Boiled Fish | 47 |
| Oysters on the Shell | 48 |

## INDEX.

| | PAGE. |
|---|---|
| Oysters Stewed with Milk | 48 |
| Oysters Fried in Butter | 48 |
| Oysters Scalloped | 48 |
| Oysters Fried | 49 |
| Oyster Patties | 49 |
| Oysters Broiled | 50 |
| Clam Fritters | 50 |
| Clams, Soft Shelled | 50 |
| To Broil Soft Shell Clams | 50 |
| Clam Chowder | 51 |

### ICES, ICE-CREAM, CANDY.

| | |
|---|---|
| Currant Ice | 226 |
| Strawberry or Raspberry Ice | 226 |
| Orange and Lemon Ices | 226 |
| Ice-Cream | 226 |
| Vanilla or Lemon Ice-cream | 227 |
| Strawberry Ice-cream | 227 |
| Chocolate Ice-cream | 227 |
| Cream Candies | 228 |
| Pineapple Ice-cream | 228 |
| Italian Cream | 229 |
| To Make Barley Sugar | 229 |
| To Make Everton Toffy | 230 |
| Cocoanut Drops | 230 |
| Molasses Candy | 230 |
| Chocolate Caramels | 230 |
| Lemon Candy | 231 |

### INVALID COOKERY.

| | |
|---|---|
| Port Wine Jelly | 239 |
| Tapioca Jelly | 239 |
| Arrowroot Wine Jelly | 239 |
| Jellied Chicken | 239 |
| Chicken Broth | 240 |
| To Make Gruel | 240 |
| Barley Water | 241 |
| Arrowroot Blanc Mange | 241 |
| Lemonade for Invalids | 241 |
| Mutton Broth | 242 |
| Flax Seed Lemonade | 242 |
| Arrowroot | 242 |
| Stewed Rabbits in Milk | 243 |
| Slippery Elm Bark Tea | 243 |
| Beef Tea | 243 |
| Egg Wine | 243 |
| Toast Water | 244 |
| Onion Gruel | 244 |

### MEATS.

| | |
|---|---|
| Roast Beef | 52 |
| Round of Beef Boiled | 52 |
| Beef Salted, or Corned Beef | 53 |

| | PAGE. |
|---|---|
| To Boil Corned Beef | 54 |
| A Nice Way to Serve Cold Beef | 54 |
| Spiced Beef | 54 |
| Broiled Beefsteak | 55 |
| Fried Beefsteak | 55 |
| Beefsteak Pie | 56 |
| Boiled Leg of Mutton | 56 |
| Roast Loin of Mutton | 57 |
| Broiled Mutton Chops | 57 |
| Mutton Chop, Fried | 57 |
| Roast Forequarter of Lamb | 57 |
| Lambs' Sweet Breads | 58 |
| To Roast Veal | 59 |
| Veal Cutlets | 60 |
| Stuffed Fillet of Veal with Bacon | 60 |
| Veal Cake | 61 |
| Veal Pie | 61 |
| Boiled Calf's Head | 62 |
| Calf's Head Cheese | 63 |
| Boiled Calf's Feet, Parsley and Butter | 63 |
| Calf's Liver and Bacon | 63 |
| Sweet Breads | 64 |
| Egged Veal Hash | 64 |
| Roast Beef with Yorkshire Pudding | 65 |
| Beef Heart, Baked or Roasted | 65 |
| Beef Kidney | 66 |
| Rolled Beef | 66 |
| Boiled Tongue | 67 |
| Fricassed Tripe | 67 |
| Broiled Tripe | 67 |
| Roast Rabbit | 68 |
| Stewed Rabbit, Larded | 68 |
| Fricassed Rabbit | 69 |
| A Pretty Dish of Venison | 69 |
| To Boil Venison Steaks | 69 |
| Beefsteak and Kidney Pudding | 70 |

### BREAKFAST DISHES.

| | |
|---|---|
| Hashed Cold Meat | 71 |
| Potato and Beef Hash | 71 |
| Dried Beef | 72 |
| Chicken Cutlets | 72 |
| Beef Patties | 73 |
| Jellied Veal | 73 |
| Rice and Meat Croquettes | 74 |
| American Toast | 74 |
| Meat and Potatoes | 74 |
| Breaded Sausages | 74 |
| Ham Croquettes | 74 |
| A Nice Breakfast Dish | 75 |
| Chicken in Jelly | 75 |
| A Good Dish | 75 |

## MISCELLANEOUS.

| | PAGE |
|---|---|
| An Excellent Hard Soap | 248 |
| To Wash Woolen Blankets | 248 |
| For Clothes that Fade | 249 |
| Lamp Wicks | 249 |
| To Make Old Crape Look Nearly Equal to New | 249 |
| A Cement for Stoves | 249 |
| To Clean Kid Gloves | 250 |
| Stains and Spots | 250 |
| To Remove Grease Spots | 251 |
| Stains on Marble | 251 |
| Paint or Varnish | 252 |
| To Remove Ink from Carpets | 252 |
| To Remove Ink from Paper | 252 |
| Feed for Canary Birds | 252 |
| Ink on Rosewood or Mahogany | 253 |
| Coal Fire | 253 |
| Polish for Bright Stoves and Steel Articles | 253 |
| To Prevent Pumps from Freezing | 253 |
| To Keep Starch from Sticking | 253 |
| To Keep off Mosquitoes | 254 |
| To Brighten Gilt Frames | 254 |
| To Make Hens Lay in Winter | 254 |
| To Preserve Steel Pens | 254 |
| Mice | 254 |
| Camphor | 255 |
| To Clean Combs | 255 |
| For Cleaning Jewelry | 255 |
| For Washing Silver and Silverware | 255 |
| For Washing Glass and Glassware | 256 |
| Insects and Vermin | 256 |
| Moths in Carpets | 257 |
| Smooth Sad Irons | 257 |
| To Sweeten Meat | 257 |
| Stove Polish | 257 |
| Cleaning White Paint | 258 |
| To Cleanse the Inside of Jars | 258 |
| Furniture Polish | 258 |
| Squeaking Doors | 258 |
| For Cleaning Mirrors | 258 |
| To Soften Putty | 258 |
| To Remove Stains from Mattresses | 259 |
| Kalsomining | 259 |
| Papering Whitewashed Walls | 259 |
| How to Clean Corsets | 260 |
| To Clean Hairbrushes | 260 |
| How to Wash Flannels | 260 |
| Cleaning Lace | 261 |
| New Kettles | 261 |
| To Keep Flies off Gilt Frames | 261 |
| To Prevent Knives from Rusting | 261 |

| | PAGE |
|---|---|
| Cement for Glassware | 262 |
| Waterproof Paper | 262 |
| Recipe for Violet Ink | 262 |
| Perspiration | 262 |
| Renewing Old Kid Gloves | 263 |
| Cologne Water | 263 |
| To Cleanse a Sponge | 263 |
| Icy Windows | 263 |
| To Remove Blood from Cloth | 263 |
| Camphor Ice | 264 |
| Starch Polish | 264 |
| To Clean Feathers | 264 |
| To Test Nutmegs | 264 |
| To Clean Mica | 264 |
| To Soften Hard Water | 264 |
| To Destroy Vermin in the Hair | 265 |
| To Remove Bruises from Furniture | 265 |
| Pearl Smelling Salts | 265 |
| Pounded Glass | 265 |
| Polish for Boots | 265 |
| To Clean Plate | 266 |
| To Clean Decanters | 266 |
| Spots on Towels and Hosiery | 266 |
| Croup | 267 |
| Poison Ivy or Oak | 267 |
| Convulsion Fits | 268 |
| Burns and Scalds | 268 |
| Cuts | 268 |
| Cold on the Chest | 268 |
| Bleeding from the Nose | 268 |
| Chilblains | 269 |
| To Cure a Sting of Bee or Wasp | 270 |
| For Toothache | 270 |
| Choking | 270 |
| Excellent Carminative Powder for Flatulent Infants | 270 |
| Cubeb Berries for Catarrh | 271 |
| Diarrhœa | 271 |
| For Sick Room | 271 |
| Bites of Dogs | 272 |
| Measles and Scarlatina | 272 |
| Stye in the Eye | 273 |
| For Constipation | 273 |
| Leanness | 273 |
| Superfluous Hairs | 273 |
| The Breath | 274 |
| The Quinine Cure for Drunkenness | 274 |
| For Sore Throat | 274 |
| A Good Cure for Colds | 274 |
| To Stop Bleeding | 275 |
| A Health Appetizer | 275 |
| To Remove Discoloration from Bruises | 275 |

## INDEX.

| | PAGE |
|---|---|
| Earache | 275 |
| To Cure Toothache | 276 |
| For Felon | 276 |
| Excellent Deodorizers | 276 |
| To Cure a Boil | 276 |
| To Cure a Whitlow | 277 |
| Tape Worms | 277 |
| For a Caked Breast | 277 |
| Remedy for Blistered Feet | 277 |
| Relief for Asthma | 277 |
| Chapped Hands | 278 |
| Lunar Caustic | 278 |
| Rheumatism and Headache | 278 |
| Fever and Ague | 278 |
| For a Fainting Fit | 278 |
| To Restore from Stroke of Lightning | 279 |
| Relief for Inflamed Feet | 279 |
| Warm Water | 279 |
| Cleaning House, Sitting and Dining Room | 279 |
| How to Dust a Room | 282 |
| Girls Learn to Cook | 283 |
| Teach the Little Ones | 283 |
| Children Love Games | 284 |
| Teach Your Own Children | 285 |
| Cultivating Selfishness in Children | 285 |
| Packing Away Furs | 287 |
| Courage | 287 |
| The Art of Beauty in Dress | 288 |
| Home Dressmaking | 290 |
| A Woman's Skirts | 292 |
| To Make Sleeves | 293 |
| All About Kitchen Work | 294 |
| A Nice Clothes Frame | 296 |
| Sunlit Rooms | 297 |
| Pleasant Homes | 298 |
| How to be Handsome | 299 |
| Headache | 305 |
| High-Heeled Boots | 306 |
| Make Home Pleasant | 309 |
| Dinner Table Fancies | 310 |
| The Use of Ammonia | 311 |
| Laughter | 312 |
| Items Worth Remembering | 312 |
| Those Ungraceful Habits | 313 |

### PUDDINGS.

| | PAGE |
|---|---|
| Remarks | 153 |
| Christmas Plum Pudding | 154 |
| Boiled Batter Pudding | 155 |
| Batter Pudding | 155 |
| Madeira Pudding | 156 |

| | PAGE |
|---|---|
| Apple Sauce Pudding | 156 |
| Queen of Puddings | 156 |
| Orange Pudding | 157 |
| Corn Starch Pudding | 157 |
| French Pudding | 158 |
| Belle's Pudding | 158 |
| Cream Tapioca Pudding | 159 |
| A Bachelor's Pudding | 159 |
| Macaroni Pudding | 159 |
| Baked Indian Pudding | 160 |
| Boiled Indian Pudding | 160 |
| Marmalade Pudding | 160 |
| Boiled Apple Pudding | 161 |
| Nelly's Pudding | 161 |
| Rich Baked Apple Pudding | 162 |
| Snow Balls | 162 |
| Rice Pudding | 162 |
| Apple Charlotte | 163 |
| Ground Rice Pudding | 163 |
| Fig Pudding | 163 |
| Bread and Butter Pudding | 164 |
| Cabinet Pudding | 164 |
| Snow Pudding | 164 |
| Carrot Pudding | 165 |
| Lemon Pudding | 165 |
| Roly-Poly Pudding | 165 |
| Cottage Pudding | 165 |
| Cocoanut Pudding | 166 |
| Cream Pudding | 166 |
| Tapioca Pudding | 166 |
| Common Custard | 166 |

### PUDDING SAUCES.

| | PAGE |
|---|---|
| Rich Wine Sauce | 168 |
| Whipped Cream Sauce | 168 |
| Lemon Sauce | 168 |
| Jelly Sauce | 168 |
| Cabinet Pudding Sauce | 169 |
| Foaming Sauce | 169 |
| Spanish Sauce | 169 |
| Hard Sauce | 169 |
| Pudding Sauce | 169 |
| Sauce for Plum Pudding | 170 |
| Vanilla Sauce | 170 |

### PASTRY.

| | PAGE |
|---|---|
| Very Good Puff Paste | 171 |
| Plainer Paste | 172 |
| Suet Crusts for Pies or Puddings | 172 |
| To Ice Pastry | 172 |
| To Graze Pastry | 173 |
| Mince Meat | 173 |
| Mock Mince Pie | 174 |

|  | PAGE |
|---|---|
| Apple Custard Pie | 174 |
| Apple Meringue Pie | 174 |
| Apple Pie | 175 |
| Lemon Pie | 175 |
| Custard Pie | 175 |
| Cocoanut Pie | 176 |
| Lemon Tarts | 176 |
| Pastry Sandwiches | 176 |
| Cherry Pie | 177 |
| Squash Pie | 177 |
| Cream Pie | 177 |
| Tartlets | 177 |
| Peach Pie | 178 |
| Pumpkin Pie | 178 |
| Tart Shells | 178 |
| Mince Pies | 179 |

## PRESERVES, CANNED FRUITS, JELLY.

|  |  |
|---|---|
| To Preserve Plums Without the Skins | 210 |
| To Preserve Purple Plums | 210 |
| Preserved Greengages in Syrup | 211 |
| Preserved Cherries in Syrup | 211 |
| Preserved Pears | 212 |
| Preserved Peaches | 212 |
| Preserved Citron | 213 |
| Crab Apples Preserved | 213 |
| Pineapples Preserved | 213 |
| Gooseberry Jam | 213 |
| Black Currant Jam | 214 |
| Raspberry Jam | 214 |
| Quince Preserve | 214 |
| Red Currant Jelly | 215 |
| Apple Jelly | 216 |
| Black Currant Jelly | 216 |
| Crab Apple Jelly | 217 |
| Other Jellies | 217 |
| Wine Jelly | 217 |
| Calves' Feet Jelly | 217 |
| Orange Marmalade | 218 |
| Lemon Marmalade | 218 |
| Quince Marmalade | 218 |
| Peach Marmalade | 219 |
| Apple Butter | 219 |
| Lemon Butter | 219 |
| Peach Butter | 220 |

## PRESERVED AND CANNED FRUITS.

|  |  |
|---|---|
| Apple Ginger (A Dessert Dish) | 220 |
| Iced Currants | 220 |
| To Bottle Fresh Fruit | 221 |

|  | PAGE |
|---|---|
| To Green Fruit for Preserving in Sugar or Vinegar | 221 |
| To Color Preserves Pink | 222 |
| To Color Fruit Yellow | 222 |
| Canned Peaches | 222 |
| Canned Strawberries | 223 |
| Canned Pears | 223 |
| Canned Plums | 223 |
| Canned Currants | 223 |
| Canned Pineapple | 224 |
| Canned Quinces | 224 |
| Canned Tomatoes | 224 |
| Canned Corn | 224 |

## POULTRY, GAME, ETC.

|  |  |
|---|---|
| Roast Turkey | 77 |
| Boiled Turkey | 78 |
| To Roast a Fowl or Chicken | 79 |
| Boiled Chicken | 80 |
| Broiled Chicken | 80 |
| Fried Chicken | 80 |
| Fricassee of Chicken | 81 |
| To Curry Chicken | 81 |
| Pressed Chicken | 81 |
| Chicken Pot-Pie | 82 |
| Chicken Salad | 82 |
| Chicken, Jellied | 83 |
| Chicken Patés | 83 |
| Sage and Onion Stuffing for Geese, Ducks and Pork | 84 |
| To Roast a Goose | 84 |
| Roast Ducks | 85 |
| Roast Pigeons | 85 |
| To Make a Bird's Nest | 86 |
| Pigeons in Jelly | 86 |
| Pigeon Pie | 87 |
| Wild Ducks | 88 |
| Roast Wild Duck | 88 |
| Wild Turkey | 88 |
| To Roast Snipe, Woodcock, and Plover | 89 |
| Roast Partridge | 90 |
| Roast Quail | 90 |
| Roast Prairie Chicken | 90 |
| Larded Grouse | 91 |

## PORK, HAM AND EGGS.

|  |  |
|---|---|
| To Choose Pork | 92 |
| Curing Hams | 92 |
| To Roast a Leg of Pork | 92 |
| Pork and Beans | 93 |
| Pork Sausages | 93 |
| Pork Chops, Steaks and Cutlets | 93 |

## INDEX.

| | PAGE. |
|---|---|
| Roast Pig | 94 |
| Pigs' Check | 95 |
| Roast Spare Rib | 95 |
| Pork Fritters | 96 |
| Baked Ham | 96 |
| To Boil a Ham | 96 |
| To Broil a Ham | 97 |
| Fried Ham and Eggs | 97 |
| Ham Toast | 97 |
| Head Cheese | 98 |
| Pigs' Feet Soused | 99 |
| To Make Lard | 99 |
| To Tell Good Eggs | 100 |
| Keeping Eggs Fresh | 100 |
| Poached Eggs | 101 |
| Dropped Eggs | 101 |
| Stuffed Eggs | 101 |
| Eggs a la Suisse | 102 |
| Eggs Brouille | 102 |
| Eggs Curried | 102 |
| Eggs Creamed | 103 |
| Soft Boiled Eggs | 103 |
| Eggs Upon Toast | 103 |
| Dutch Omelet | 103 |
| Eggs Poached in Balls | 104 |
| Omelet au Natural | 104 |
| Omelet in Batter | 104 |
| Scrambled Eggs | 105 |
| Omelet (Splendid) | 105 |

### SOUPS.

| | |
|---|---|
| Remarks on Soups | 20 |
| Stock Soups | 22 |
| White Stock | 22 |
| Shin of Beef | 23 |
| Mutton with Tapioca | 24 |
| Veal | 25 |
| Ox Tail | 25 |
| Vegetable | 25 |
| Macaroni | 26 |
| Vermicelli | 26 |
| Chicken Cream | 26 |
| Mock Turtle | 27 |
| Hard Pea | 27 |
| Green Pea | 28 |
| Potato | 29 |
| Tomato | 29 |
| Game | 30 |
| Celery | 30 |
| Oyster | 30 |
| Lobster | 31 |
| Egg Balls for Soup | 31 |
| Noodles | 31 |

| | PAGE. |
|---|---|
| Irish Stew | 32 |
| To get up Soup in Haste | 36 |
| To Color Soups | 33 |

### SAUCES FOR MEATS, ETC.

| | |
|---|---|
| To Make Drawn Butter | 123 |
| Parsley Sauce | 123 |
| Egg Sauce | 123 |
| Onion Sauce | 124 |
| Anchovy Sauce | 124 |
| Bread Sauce | 124 |
| Tomato Sauce | 124 |
| Tomato Mustard | 125 |
| Mint Sauce | 125 |
| Celery Sauce | 125 |
| Governor's Sauce | 125 |
| Cream Sauce | 126 |
| Russian Sauce | 126 |
| Mayonnaise Sauce | 126 |
| Oyster Sauce | 127 |
| Lobster Sauce | 127 |
| Caper Sauce | 127 |
| Mustard Sauce | 127 |
| Curry Sauce | 128 |
| Cranberry Sauce | 128 |
| Port Wine Sauce for Game | 129 |
| Currant Jelly Sauce | 129 |
| Apple Sauce | 129 |

### SALADS, PICKLES AND CATSUP.

| | |
|---|---|
| Lettuce | 139 |
| Lettuce Salad | 139 |
| Salmon Salad | 140 |
| Lobster Salad | 140 |
| Tomato Salad | 141 |
| Sardine Salad | 141 |
| Salad Dressing | 141 |
| French Salad Dressing | 141 |
| Cream Dressing for Cold Slaw | 142 |
| Chicken Salad | 142 |
| Red Vegetable Salad | 142 |
| Celery Salad | 143 |
| Cold Slaw | 143 |
| Salad Dressing (Excellent) | 143 |
| Pickled Cucumbers | 144 |
| To Pickle Onions | 144 |
| Pickled Cauliflowers | 144 |
| Red Cabbage | 144 |
| To Pickle Tomatoes | 145 |
| Ripe Tomato Pickles | 145 |
| Chopped Pickle | 145 |

# INDEX.

| | PAGE | | PAGE |
|---|---|---|---|
| Chow-Chow | 146 | Turnips | |
| Piccalilli | 146 | Spinach | |
| Pickled Walnuts (very good) | 146 | Beets | |
| Green Tomato Pickle | 147 | To Preserve Vegetables for Winter | |
| Chili Sauce | 147 | Delicate Cabbage | |
| Mixed Pickles | 147 | Red Cabbage | |
| Pickled Mushrooms | 148 | Cauliflowers | |
| Favorite Pickles | 148 | Mashed Carrots | |
| Tomato Mustard | 149 | Boiled Green Corn | |
| Indian Chutney | 149 | Green Peas | |
| Pickled Cherries | 149 | To Boil Onions | |
| Pickled Plums | 150 | Fried Onions | |
| Spiced Plums | 150 | Boiled Parsnips | |
| Peaches, Pears and Sweet Apples | 150 | Parsnips Fried in Butter | |
| Tomato Catsup | 150 | Parsnips Creamed | |
| Walnut Catsup | 151 | Parsnip Fritters | |
| Mushroom Catsup | 151 | Salsify, or Vegetable Oyster | |
| Brine that Preserves Butter a Year | 152 | Broiled Vegetable Marrow | |
| Butter in Haste | 152 | Stewed Tomatoes | |
| | | Baked Tomatoes | |
| | | Stuffed Tomatoes | |

## VEGETABLES.

| | PAGE | | PAGE |
|---|---|---|---|
| Boiled Potatoes | 106 | Scalloped Tomatoes | |
| Mashed Potatoes | 106 | To Peel Tomatoes | |
| Fried Potatoes | 107 | Baked Beans | |
| Broiled Potatoes | 107 | String Beans | |
| Potatoes and Cream | 107 | Butter Beans | |
| Potato Puffs | 108 | Asparagus with Eggs | |
| Potato Snow | 108 | Asparagus upon Toast | |
| Potato Border | 108 | Mushrooms, Stewed | |
| Potatoes, Whipped | 108 | Mushrooms, Fried | |
| Potatoes, Scalloped | 109 | Mushrooms, Baked | |
| Potato Croquettes | 109 | Mushrooms, Broiled | |
| Potatoes a la Cream | 109 | Mashed Squash | |
| To Boil Sweet Potatoes | 109 | Baked Squash | |
| Roasted Sweet Potatoes | 110 | Fried Squash | |
| Baked Sweet Potatoes | 110 | Stewed Celery | |
| French Fried | 110 | Stuffed Egg Plant | |

# THE EVERYDAY COOK-BOOK.

Of all the arts upon which the physical well-being of man, in his social state, is dependent, none has been more neglected than that of cookery, though none is more important, for it supplies the very fountain of life. The preparation of human food, so as to make it at once wholesome, nutritive, and agreeable to the palate, has hitherto been beset by imaginary difficulties and strong prejudices.

Many persons associate the idea of wealth with culinary perfection; others consider unwholesome, as well as expensive, everything that goes beyond the categories of boiling, roasting, and the gridiron. All are aware that wholesome and luxurious cookery is by no means incompatible with limited pecuniary means; whilst in roasted, boiled, and broiled meats which constitute what is termed true American fare, much that is nutritive and agreeable is often lost for want of skill in preparing them. Food of every description is wholesome and digestible in proportion as it approaches nearer to the state of complete digestion, or, in other words, to that state termed *chyme*, whence the chyle or milky juice that afterwards forms blood is absorbed, and conveyed to the heart. Now nothing is further from this state than raw meat and raw vegetables. Fire is therefore necessary to soften them, and thereby begin that elaboration which is consummated in the stomach. The preparatory process, which forms the cook's art, is more or less perfect in proportion as the aliment is softened, without losing any of its juices or flavor—for flavor is not only an agreeable but a necessary accompaniment to wholesome food. Hence it follows, that meat very much underdone, whether roasted or boiled, is not so wholesome as meat well done but retaining all its juices. And here comes the necessity for the cook's skill, which is so often at fault even in these simple modes of preparing human nourishment.

Pork, veal, lamb, and all young meats, when not thoroughly cooked, are absolute poison to the stomach; and if half-raw beef or mutton are often eaten with impunity, it must not be inferred that they are unwholesome in their semi-crude state, but only less wholesome than the young meats.

Vegetables, also, half done, which is the state in which they are often sent to the table, are productive of great gastric derangement, often of a predisposition to cholera.

A great variety of relishing, nutritive, and even elegant dishes, may be prepared from the most homely materials, which may not only be rendered more nourishing, but be made to go much farther in a large family than they usually do. The great secret of all cookery, except in roasting and broiling, is a judicious use of butter, flour, and herbs, and the application of a very slow fire—for good cooking requires only gentle simmering, but no boiling up, which only renders the meat hard. Good roasting can only be acquired by practice, and the perfection lies in cooking the whole joint thoroughly without drying up the juice of any part of it. This is also the case with broiling; while a joint under process of broiling, as we have said, should be allowed to simmer gently.

With regard to *made-dishes*, as the horrible imitations of French cookery prevalent in America are termed, we must admit that they are very unwholesome. All the juices are boiled out of the meat which is swimming in a heterogeneous compound, disgusting to the sight, and seasoned so strongly with spice and Cayenne pepper enough to inflame the stomach of an ostrich.

French cookery is generally mild in seasoning, and free from grease; it is formed upon the above-stated principle of reducing the aliment as near to the state of chyme as possible, without injury to its nutritive qualities, rendering it at once easy of digestion and pleasant to the taste.

## HINTS ON MARKETING.

In the first place, the housewife ought, where it is possible, to do her marketing herself, *and pay ready money for everything she purchases.* This is the only way in which she can be sure of getting the best goods at the lowest price. We repeat that this is the only way compatible with economy; because, if a servant be entrusted with the buying, she will, if she is not a good judge of the quality of articles, bring home those she can get for the least money (and these are seldom the cheapest); and even if she is a good judge, it is ten to one against her taking the trouble to make a careful selection.

When the ready-money system is found inconvenient, and an account is run with a dealer, the mistress of the house ought to have a pass-book in which she should write down all the orders herself, leaving the dealer to fill in only the prices. Where this is not done, and the mistress neglects to compare the pass-book with the goods ordered every time they are brought in, it sometimes happens, either by mistake, or the dishonesty of the dealer, or the servant, that goods are entered which were never ordered, perhaps never had, and that those which were ordered are overcharged; and if these errors are not detected at the time, they are sure to be difficult of adjustment afterwards. For these and other economic reasons, the housewife should avoid running accounts, and pay ready money.

## RULES FOR EATING.

Dr. Hall, on this important subject, gives the following advice:

1. Never sit down to table with an anxious or disturbed mind; better a hundred times intermit that meal, for there will then be that much more food in the world for hungrier stomachs than yours; and besides, eating under such circumstances can only, and will always, prolong and aggravate the condition of things.

2. Never sit down to a meal after any intense mental effort, for physical and mental injury are inevitable, and no one has a right to deliberately injure body, mind, or estate.

3. Never go to a full table during bodily exhaustion—designated by some as being worn out, tired to death, used up, over done, and the like. The wisest thing to be done under such circumstances is to take a cracker and a cup of warm tea, either black or green, and no more. In ten minutes you will feel a degree of refreshment and liveliness which will be pleasantly surprising to you; not of the transient kind which a glass of liquor affords, but permanent; but the tea gives present stimulus and a little strength, and before it subsides, nutriment begins to draw from the sugar, and cream, and bread, thus allowing the body gradually, and by safe degrees, to regain its usual vigor. Then, in a couple of hours, a full meal may be taken, provided that it does not bring it later than two hours before sundown; if later, then take nothing for that day in addition to the cracker and tea, and the next day you will feel a freshness and vigor not recently known.

No lady will require to be advised a second time, who will conform to the above rules; while it is a fact of no unusual observation among intelligent physicians, that eating heartily and under bodily exhaustion, is not unfrequently the cause of alarming and painful illness, and sometimes sudden death. These things being so, let every family make it a point to assemble around the table with kindly feelings—with a cheerful humor, and a courteous spirit; and let that member of it be sent from it in disgrace who presumes to mar the reunion by sullen silence, or impatient look, or angry tone, or complaining tongue. Eat ever in thankful gladness, or away with you to the kitchen, you "ill-tempered thing, that you are." There was good philosophy in the old-time custom of having a buffoon or music at the dinner-table.

## HOW TO CHOOSE MEAT.

Ox-BEEF, when it is young, will have a fine open grain, and a good red color; the fat should be white, for when it is of a deep yellow color, the meat is seldom very good. The grain of cow-beef is closer, the fat whiter, and the lean scarcely so red as that of ox-beef. When you see beef, of which the fat is hard and skinny, and the lean of a deep red, you may be sure that it is of an inferior kind; and when the meat is old, you may know it by a line of horny texture running through the meat of the ribs.

MUTTON must be chosen by the firmness and fineness of the grain, its good color, and firm white fat. It is not considered prime until the sheep is about five years old.

LAMB will not keep long after it is killed. It can be discovered by the neck end in the fore-quarter if it has been killed too long, the veins in the neck being bluish when the meat is fresh, but green when it is stale. In the hind quarter, the same discovery may be made by examining the kidney and the knuckle, for the former has a slight smell, and the knuckle is not firm when the meat has been killed too long.

PORK should have a thin rind; and when it is fresh, the

meat is smooth and cool; but, when it looks flabby, and is clammy to the touch, it is not good; and pork, above all meat, is disagreeable when it is stale. If you perceive many enlarged glands, or, as they are usually termed, kernels, in the fat of the pork, you may conclude that the pork cannot be wholesome.

VEAL is generally preferred of a delicate whiteness, but it is more juicy and well-flavored when of a deeper color. Butchers bleed calves profusely in order to produce this white meat; but this practice must certainly deprive the meat of some of its nourishment and flavor. When you choose veal, endeavor to look at the loin, which affords the best means of judging of the veal generally, for if the kidney, which may be found on the under side of one end of the loin, be deeply enveloped in white and firm-looking fat, the meat will certainly be good; and the same appearance will enable you to judge if it has been recently killed. The kidney is the part which changes the first; and then the suet around it becomes soft, and the meat flabby and spotted.

BACON, like pork, should have a thin rind; the fat should be firm, and inclined to a reddish color; and the lean should firmly adhere to the bone, and have no yellow streak in it. When you are purchasing a ham, have a knife stuck into it to the bone, which, if the ham be well cured, may be drawn out again without having any of the meat adhering to it, and without your perceiving any disagreeable smell. A short ham is reckoned the best.

## ROAST SIRLOIN OF BEEF.

Take a piece of sirloin, comprising the best part of the fillet; saw off the chine bone; flatten the flap and tie it under to the fillet; trim the joint; tie a layer of suet over the fillet and cover the sirloin with buttered paper; tie it up, and put it on the spit, to roast before an even fire; ten minutes before the meat is done, take off the paper and sprinkle the joint with salt.

## ROAST LEG OF MUTTON.

Take a 6-lb. leg of mutton; saw off the shank bone one and a half inches below the knuckle; put it on the spit to roast before an even fire for an hour and a half; put two gills of broth in the dripping-pan, and baste well during cooking; sprinkle with two pinches of salt five minutes before taken from the fire.

VEAL.—CALF'S HEAD AND FEET.

The pieces of veal used for roasting are: the neck, loin, and chump end of the loin; never buy any but very white veal, with clear, transparent fat. Avoid lean veal of a reddish tint, and the kidney of which is surrounded by red-looking fat.

FISH.—CARP—EEL—PIKE.

A fresh fish is recognizable by the redness of the gills, the brightness of the eyes, and the firmness of the flesh. It is not enough to be guided by the smell; it may have laid days on ice without acquiring any noticeable smell; but the flesh, in such a case, will be dull and flaccid, and care should be taken not to use fish in that condition.

## HOW TO CHOOSE FISH.

TURBOT, which is in season the greater part of the year should have the underside of a yellowish white, for when it is very transparent, blue, or thin, it is not good; the whole fish should be thick and firm.

SALMON should have a fine red flesh and gills; the scales should be bright, and the whole fish firm. Many persons think that salmon is improved by keeping a day or two.

COD should be judged by the redness of the gills, the whiteness, stiffness, and firmness of the flesh, and the clear freshness of the eyes; these are the infallible proofs of its being good. The whole fish should be thick and firm.

WHITE-FISH may be had good almost throughout the year; but the time in which they are in their prime is early in the year. The white-fish is light and delicate, and in choosing it you must examine whether the fins and flesh be firm.

FRESH-WATER FISH may be chosen by similar observations respecting the firmness of the flesh, and the clear appearance of the eyes, as salt-water fish.

In a LOBSTER lately caught, you may put the claws in motion by pressing the eyes; but when it has been long caught, the muscular action is not excited. The freshness of boiled lobsters may be determined by the elasticity of the tail, which is flaccid when they have lost any of their wholesomeness. Their goodness, independent of freshness, is determined by their weight.

CRABS, too, must be judged of by their weight, for when they prove light, the flesh is generally found to be wasted and watery. If in perfection, the joints of the legs will be stiff, and the body will have an agreeable smell. The eyes, by a dull appearance, betray that the crab has been long caught.

## HOW TO CHOOSE POULTRY.

IN the choice of poultry the age of the bird is the chief point to which you should attend.

A young TURKEY has a smooth black leg; in an old one the legs are rough and reddish. If the bird be fresh killed the eyes will be full and fresh, and the feet moist.

FOWLS, when they are young, the combs and the legs will be smooth, and rough when they are old.

In GEESE, when they are young, the bills and the feet are yellow and have a few hairs upon them, but they are red if the bird be old. The feet of a goose are pliable when the bird is fresh killed, and dry and stiff when it has been killed some time. Geese are called green till they are two or three months old.

DUCKS should be chosen by their feet, which should be supple; and they should also have a plump and hard breast. The feet of a tame duck are yellowish, those of a wild one, reddish.

PIGEONS should always be eaten while they are fresh; when they look flabby and discolored about the under part, they have been kept too long. The feet, like those of poultry, show the age of the bird; when they are supple, it is young; when stiff, it is old. Tame pigeons are larger than wild ones.

## HOW TO CHOOSE GAME.

VENISON, when young, will have the fat clear and bright, and this ought also to be of a considerable thickness. When you do not wish to have it in a very high state, a knife plunged into either haunch or the shoulder, and drawn out, will by the smell enable you to judge if the venison is sufficiently fresh.

With regard to venison, which, as it is not an every-day

article of diet, it may be convenient to keep for some time after it has begun to get high or tainted, it is useful to know that the animal putrefaction is checked by fresh burnt charcoal; by means of which, therefore, the venison may be prevented from getting worse, although it cannot be restored to its original freshness. The meat should be placed in a hollow dish, and the charcoal powder strewed over it until it covers the joint to the thickness of half an inch.

HARES and RABBITS, when the ears are dry and tough, the haunch thick, and the claws blunt and rugged, they are old. Smooth and sharp claws, ears that readily tear, and a narrow cleft in the lip, are the marks of a young hare. Hares may be kept for some time after they have been killed; indeed, many people think they are not fit for the table until the inside begins to turn a little. Care, however, should be taken to prevent the inside from becoming musty, which would spoil the flavor of the stuffing.

PARTRIDGES have yellow legs and a dark-colored bill when young. They are not in season till after the first of September.

## HOW TO CHOOSE EGGS.

In putting the hand round the egg, and presenting to the light, the end which is not covered, it should be transparent. If you can detect some tiny spots, it is not newly laid, but may be very good for all ordinary purposes except boiling soft. If you see a large spot near the shell, it is bad, and should not be used on any account. The white of a newly-laid egg boiled soft is like milk; that of an egg a day old, is like rice boiled in milk; and that of an old egg, compact, tough, and difficult to digest. A cook ought not to give eggs two or three days old to people who really care for fresh eggs, under the delusion that they will not find any difference; for an amateur will find it out in a moment, not only by the appearance, but also by the taste.

## CARVING.

The seat for the carver should be somewhat elevated above the other chairs; it is extremely ungraceful to carve standing, and it is rarely done by any person accustomed to the business. Carving depends more on skill than on strength. We have seen very small women carve admirably sitting down; and very tall men who knew not how to cut a piece of beefsteak without rising on their feet to do it.

The carving-knife should be very sharp, and not heavy; and it should be held firmly in the hand; also the dish should not be too far from the carver. It is customary to help the fish with a fish-trowel, and not with a knife. The middle part of a fish is generally considered the best. In helping it, avoid breaking the flakes, as that will give it a mangled appearance.

In carving ribs or sirloin of beef begin by cutting thin slices off the side next to you. Afterwards you may cut from the tenderloin, or cross-part near the lower end. Do not send anyone the outside piece, unless you know they particularly wish it.

In helping beefsteak put none of the bone on the plate. In cutting a round of corned beef begin at the top; but lay aside the first cut or outside piece, and send it to no one, as it is always dry and hard. In a round of *beef a-la mode* the outside is frequently preferred.

A leg of mutton begin across the middle, cutting the slices quite down to the bone. The same with a leg of pork or a ham. The latter should be cut in very thin slices, as its flavor is spoiled when cut thick.

To taste well, tongue should be cut crossways in round slices. Cutting it lengthwise (though the practice at many tables) injures the flavor. The middle part of the tongue is the best. Do not help anyone to a piece of the root; that, being by no means a favored part, is generally left in the dish.

In carving a fore-quarter of lamb first separate the shoulder part from the breast and ribs by passing the knife under, and then divide the ribs. If the lamb is large, have another dish brought to put the shoulder in.

For a loin of veal begin near the smallest end, and separate the ribs; helping a part of the kidney (as far as it will go) with each piece. Carve a loin of pork or mutton in the same manner.

In carving a fillet of veal begin at the top. Many persons prefer the first cut or outside piece. Help a portion of the stuffing with each slice.

In a breast of veal there are two parts very different in quality, the ribs and the brisket. You will easily perceive the division; enter your knife as it and cut through, which will separate the two parts. Ask the person you are going to help whether they prefer a rib or a piece of the brisket.

For a haunch of venison first make a deep incision by passing your knife all along the side, cutting quite down to the bone. This is to let out the gravy. Then turn the broad end of the haunch toward you, and cut it as deep as you can in thin slices, allowing some of the fat to each person.

For a saddle of venison, or of mutton, cut from the tail to the other end on each side of the backbone, making very thin slices, and sending some fat with each. Venison and roast mutton chill very soon. Currant jelly is an indispensable appendage to venison, and to roast mutton, and to ducks.

A young pig is most generally divided before it comes to table, in which case it is not customary to send in the head, as to many persons it is a revolting spectacle after it is cut off. When served up whole, first separate the head from the shoulders, then cut off the limbs, and then divide the ribs. Help some of the stuffing with each piece.

To carve a fowl, begin by sticking your fork in the pinion, and draw it towards the leg; and then passing your knife underneath take off the wing at the joint. Next, slip your knife between the leg and the body, to cut through the joint; and with the fork turn the leg back, and the joint will give way. Then take off the other wing and leg. If the fowl has been trussed (as it ought to be) with the liver and gizzard, help the liver with one wing, and the gizzard with the other. The liver-wing is considered the best. After the limbs are taken off enter your knife into the top of the breast, and cut under the merry-thought, so as to loosen it, lifting it with your fork. Afterwards cut slices from both sides of the breast. Next take off the collar-bones, which lie on each side of the merry-thought, and then separate the side-bones from the back. The breast and wings are considered the most delicate part of the fowl; the back, as the least desirable, is generally left in the dish. Some persons, in carving a fowl, find it more convenient to take it on a plate, and as they separate it return each part to the dish, but this is not the usual way.

A turkey is carved in the same manner as a fowl; except that the legs and wings, being larger, are separated at the lower joint. The lower part of the leg (or drum-stick, as it is called), being hard, tough, and stringy, is never helped to any one, but allowed to remain in the dish. First cut off the wing, leg, and breast from one side; then turn the turkey over, and cut them off from the other.

To carve a goose, separate the leg from the body, by putting the fork into the small end of the limb; pressing it close to the body, and then passing the knife under, and turning the leg back, as you cut through the joint. To take off the wing, put your fork into the small end of the pinion, and press it closely to the body; then slip the knife under, and separate the joint. Next cut under the merry-thought, and take it off; and then cut slices from the breast. Then turn the goose, and dismember the other side. Take off the two upper side-bones that are next to the wings, and then the two lower side-bones. The breast and legs of a goose afford the finest pieces. If a goose is old there is no fowl so tough; and, if difficult to carve, it will be still more difficult to eat.

Partridges, pheasants, grouse, etc., are carved in the same manner as fowls. Quails, woodcocks, and snipes are merely split down the back; so also are pigeons, giving a half to each person.

In helping any one to gravy, or to melted butter, do not pour it *over* their meat, fowl, or fish, but put it to one side on a vacant part of the plate, that they may use just as much of it as they like. In filling a plate never heap one thing on another.

In helping vegetables, do not plunge the spoon down to the bottom of the dish, in case they should not have been perfectly well drained, and the water should have settled there.

By observing carefully how it is done you may acquire a knowledge of the joints, and of the process of carving, which a little daily practice will soon convert into dexterity. If a young lady is ignorant of this useful art, it will be well for her to take lessons of her father, or her brother, and a married lady can easily learn from her husband. Domestics who wait at table may soon, from looking on daily, become so expert that, when necessary, they can take a dish to the side-table and carve it perfectly well.

At a dinner-party, if the hostess is quite young, she is frequently glad to be relieved of the trouble of carving by the gentleman who sits nearest to her; but if she is familiar with the business, she usually prefers doing it herself.

The following Engraving represents the method of dividing an Ox for the table, in England, and in most of the southern cities of the United States. The method in Boston varies considerably, dividing into smaller pieces, and this plan we pursue in the following tables but the manner of cooking each is nearly the same.

1. Sirloin.
2. Rump.
3. Edge Bone.
4. Buttock.
5. Mouse Buttock.
6. Veiny Piece.
7. Thick Flank.
8. Thin Flank.
9. Leg.
10. Fore rib: Five ribs.
11. Middle rib: Four ribs.
12. Chuck: Three ribs.
13. Shoulder or leg-of-mutton p 
14. Brisket.
15. Clod.
16. Neck, or Sticking Piece.
17. Shin.
18. Cheek.

## CARVING.

### MACKEREL.

In helping, first cut off the head, at 1, as that part is very inferior and unsavory then divide down the back, and give a side to each; if less is asked for, the thickest end, which is the most choice, should be served. Inquire if the roe is liked; it may be found between 1 and 2. That of the female is hard, of the male soft.

### CARP, PERCH, HADDOCK, ETC.,

will be easily helped by attending to the foregoing directions. The head of the Carp is esteemed a delicacy, which should be borne in mind.

### COD'S HEAD AND SHOULDERS.

Introduce the fish-slice at 1, and cut quite through the back, as far as 2, then help pieces from between 3 and 4, and with each slice give a portion of the sound, which lines the under side of the back bone. It is thin, and of a darker color than the other part of the fish, and is esteemed a delicacy.

Some persons are partial to the tongue and palate, for which you must insert a spoon into the mouth. The jelly part is about the jaw, the firm part within the head, on which are some other delicate pickings; the finest portions may be found about the shoulders.

### TURBOT.

The under side of this fish is the most esteemed, and is placed uppermost on the dish. The fish-slice must be introduced at 1, and an incision made as far as 2; then cut from the middle, which is the primest part. After helping the whole of that side, the upper part must be attacked, and as it is difficult to divide the back bone, raise it with the fork, while you separate a portion with the fish-slice; this part is more solid, and is preferred by some, though it is less delicate than the under side. The fins are esteemed a nicety, and should be attended to accordingly.

### BRILL, SOLES, PLAICE,

and flat fish in general, may be served in the same manner as a Turbot.

## SECTION II.

### JOINTS.

In helping the more fleshy joints, such as a Sirloin of Beef, Leg of Mutton, Fillet of Veal, cut thin smooth slices, and let the knife pass through to the bones of Mutton and Beef.

It would prevent much trouble, if the joints of the loin, neck, and breast, were cut through by the butcher previous to the cooking, so that when sent to table they may easily be severed. Should the whole of the meat belonging to each bone be too thick, one or more slices may be taken off from between every two bones.

In some boiled joints, round and aitch-bone of beef for instance, the water renders the outsides vapid, and of course unfit to be eaten; you will therefore be particular to cut off and lay aside a thick slice from the top, before you begin to serve.

### SHOULDER OF MUTTON.

Cut in to the bone at the line 1, and help thin slices of lean from each side of the incision; the prime part of the fat lies at the outer edge, at 2.

Should more meat be required than can be got from that part, cut on either side of the line, 3, which represents the blade bone, and some good and delicate slices may be procured. By cutting horizontally from the under side, many "nice bits" will be obtained.

### LEG OF MUTTON.

The finest part is situated in the centre, at 1, between the knuckle and farther end; insert the knife there, and cut thin, deep slices each way, as far in as 2. The outside rarely being very fat, some neat cuts may be obtained off the broad end, at 3. The knuckle of a fine leg is tender, though dry, and many prefer it, although the other is the most juicy. There are some good cuts on the broad end of the back of the leg, from which slices may be procured lengthways.

The cramp bone is by some esteemed a delicacy; to get it out, cut down to the thighbone, at 4, and pass the knife under it in a semicircular course, to 5.

### HAUNCH OF MUTTON

consists of the leg and part of the loin, cut so as to resemble a Haunch of Venison. It must be helped at table in a similar manner.

# CARVING.

## SADDLE OF MUTTON.

This is an excellent joint, and produces many nice bits. Cut the whole length of it close to the back bone, and take off some long thin slices in that direction. The upper division consists of lean; the fat may be easily got at by cutting from the left side.

## LOIN OF MUTTON.

As the bones of this joint are divided, it is very easily managed. Begin at the narrow end and take off the chops; when the joints are cut through, some slices of meat may be obtained between the bones.

### FORE QUARTER OF LAMB.

First divide the shoulder from the scoven, which consists of the breast and ribs, by passing the knife under the knuckle, in the direction of 1, 2, 3, and cutting so as to leave a fair portion of meat on the ribs; lay it on a separate dish, and squeeze the juice of half a Seville orange over the other part, which, after being sprinkled with pepper and salt, should be divided in the line 3-4. This will separate the ribs from the gristly part, and you may help from either, as may be chosen, cutting as directed by the lines 5, 6.

### SHOULDER OF LAMB

must be carved like a shoulder of mutton, of which it is a miniature edition.

### LEG OF LAMB.

Follow the directions given for leg of mutton, at page xli.

### LOIN OF LAMB

may be helped similar to a loin of mutton. (See LOIN OF MUTTON.) This, and the two foregoing, being small joints, should be helped sparingly, as there is very little meat on them, especially when first in season.

### AITCH-BONE OF BEEF.

Cut off and lay aside a thick slice from the entire surface, as marked 1-2, then help. There are two sorts of fat to this joint, and, as tastes differ, it is necessary to learn which is preferred. The solid fat will be found at 3, and must be cut horizontally; the softer, which resembles marrow, at the back of the bone, below 4.

A silver skewer should be substituted for the one which keeps the meat properly together while boiling, and it may be withdrawn when you cut down to it.

## CARVING.

#### SIRLOIN OF BEEF.

There are two modes of helping this meat. The better way is by carving long thin slices from 1 to 2; the other way is by cutting it across, which, however, spoils it. The most tender and prime part is in the direction of the line 3; there will also be found some delicate fat, part of which should be given with each piece.

#### RIBS OF BEEF.

may be carved similar to the Sirloin, always commencing at the thin end of the joint, and cutting long slices so as to give fat and lean together.

#### AITCH OF BEEF.

This joint is so very easy to attend to, that we have not deemed it necessary to give a drawing of it; it only requires a steady hand and a sharp knife. The upper surface being removed, as directed for the aitch-bone of beef, carve thin slices, and give a portion of fat with each.

You must cut the meat as even as possible, as it is of consequence to preserve the beauty of its appearance.

#### A TONGUE.

Cut nearly through the middle, at the line 1, and take thin slices from each side. The fat is situated underneath, at the root of the tongue.

#### A CALF'S HEAD.

Cut thin slices from 1 to 2, and let the knife penetrate to the bone. At the thick part of the neck end, 3, the throat sweetbread is situated; carve slices from 3 to 4, and help with the other part. Should the eye be asked for, it must be extracted with the point of the knife, and a portion given. The palate, esteemed a delicacy, is situated under the head, and some fine lean may be found by removing the jaw-bone; portions of each of these should be helped round.

## CARVING.

### A LOIN OF VEAL

should be jointed previous to being sent to table, when each division may be easily cut through with a knife. The fat surrounds the kidney, and portions of each should be given with the other parts.

### A BREAST OF VEAL

is composed of the ribs and brisket, which must be separated by cutting through the line 1-2; the latter is the thickest and has gristles. Divide each portion into convenient pieces, and proceed to help.

### FILLET OF VEAL

resembles a round of beef, and should be carved similar to it, in thin and very smooth slices, off the top; cut deep into the flap, between 1 and 2, for the stuffing, and help a portion of it to each person.
Slices of lemon are always served with this dish.

### HAND OF PORK.

Cut thin slices from this delicate joint, either across near the knuckle, or from the blade bone, as directed for a shoulder of mutton. This forms a nice dish for a tete-a-tete dinner; there is not sufficient for a third person.

### ROAST PIG.

As this is usually divided as above, before sent to table, little remains to be done by the carver. First separate a shoulder from the body, and then the leg; divide the ribs into convenient portions, and send round with a sufficiency of the stuffing and gravy. Many prefer the neck end between the shoulders, although the ribs are considered the finest part; but as this all depends on taste, the question should be put. The ear is reckoned a delicacy.
Should the head not be divided, it must be done, and the brains taken out, and mixed with the gravy and stuffing.

### A LOIN OF PORK

is cut up in the same manner as a loin of Mutton. See page xli

## CARVING.

### LEG OF PORK.

Commence carving about midway, between the knuckle and farther end, and cut thin deep slices from either side of the line 1. For the seasoning in a roast leg, lift it up, and it will be found under the skin at the large end.

### HAM.

The usual mode of carving this joint, is by long delicate slices, through the thick fat, in the direction 1-2, laying open the bone at each cut, which brings you to the prime part at once. A more saving way is to commence at the knuckle and proceed onwards.

Some persons take out a round piece at 3, and enlarge the hole, by cutting thin circular slices with a sharp knife. This keeps the meat moist, and preserves the gravy, but seldom looks handsome.

## SECTION III.

### POULTRY, GAME, ETC.

The carving-knife for poultry is smaller and lighter than the meat carver; the point is more peaked and the handle longer.

In cutting up a Turkey, Goose, Duck, or Wild Fowl, more prime pieces may be obtained by carving slices from pinion to pinion, without making wings; this is an advantage when your party is large, as it makes the bird go farther.

### A FOWL.

It will be more convenient in carving this to take it on your plate, and lay the joints, as divided, neatly on the dish. Fix your fork in the middle of the breast, and take the wing off in the direction of 1-2; divide the joint at 1, lift up the pinion with your fork and draw the wing towards the leg, which will separate the fleshy part more naturally than by the knife; cut between the leg and body at 3 to the bone, 2,

## CARVING.

give the blade a sudden turn, and the joint will break if the fowl is not old. When a similar operation is performed on the other side, take off the merrythought, by cutting in to the bone at 4, and turning it back, which will detach it; next remove the neck bones and divide the breast from the back, by cutting through the whole of the ribs, close to the breast. Turn up the back, press the point of the knife about half way between the neck and rump, and on raising the lower end it will separate easily. Turn the rump from you, take off the sidesmen, and the operation is complete.

The breast and wings are the most delicate parts, but the leg is more juicy in a young bird. Great care should be taken to cut the wings as handsome as possible.

### A TURKEY.

The finest parts of this bird are the breast and wings; the latter will bear some delicate slices being taken off. After the fore quarters are severed, the thighs must be divided from the drumsticks, which, being tough, should be reserved till last. In other respects, a turkey must be dealt with exactly as recommended for a fowl, except that it has no merrythought.

Give a portion of the stuffing or forced-meat, which is inside the breast, to each person.

### A PARTRIDGE

is cut up in the same manner as a fowl, only, on account of the smallness of the bird, the merrythought is seldom divided from the breast. The wings, breast, and merrythought, are the finest parts of it, but the wing is considered the best, and the tip of it is reckoned the most delicious morsel of the whole.

### A PHEASANT.

Fix your fork in the centre of the breast, and make incisions to the bone at 1-2, then take off the leg in the line 3-4, and the wing at 3-5; serve the other side in the same manner, and separate the slices you had previously divided on the breast. In taking off the wings, be careful not to venture too near the neck, or you will hit on the neck bone, from which the wing should be divided. Pass the knife through the line 6, and under the merrythought towards the neck, which will detach it. The other parts may be served as directed for a fowl.

The breast, wings, and merrythought, are the most delicate parts, although the leg has a higher flavor.

### WOODCOCKS, GROUSE, ETC.

are carved similar to a fowl, if not too small, when they may be cut in quarters and helped.

Snipes, being smaller, should be divided in halves.

### PIGEONS

The usual way of carving these birds is to insert the knife at 1, and cut to 2 and 3, when each portion may be divided into two pieces and helped; sometimes they are cut in halves, either across or down the middle, but as the lower part is thought the best, the first mode is the fairest.

Should they be very large and fine, they may be served like fowls.

## SOUPS.

### GENERAL REMARKS.

BE careful to proportion the quantity of water to that of the meat. Somewhat less than a quart of water to a pound of meat is a good rule for common soups. Rich soups, intended for company, may have a still smaller allowance of water.

Soup should always be made entirely of fresh meat that has not been previously cooked. An exception to this rule may sometimes be made in favor of the remains of a piece of roast beef that has been *very much* under-done in roasting. This may be *added* to a good piece of raw meat. Cold ham, also, may be occasionally put into white soups.

Soup, however, that has been originally made of raw meat entirely is frequently better the second day than the first, provided it is reboiled only for a very short time, and that no additional water is added to it.

Unless it has been allowed to boil too hard, so as to exhaust the water, the soup-pot will not require replenishing. When it is found absolutely necessary to do so, the additional water must be boiling-hot when poured in; if lukewarm or cold, it will entirely spoil the soup.

Every particle of fat should be carefully skimmed from the surface. Greasy soup is disgusting and unwholesome. The lean of meat is much better for soup than the fat.

Long and slow boiling is necessary to extract the strength from the meat. If boiled fast over a large fire, the meat becomes hard and tough, and will not give out its juices.

Potatoes, if boiled in the soup, are thought by some to render it unwholesome, from the opinion that the water in which potatoes have been cooked is almost a poison. As potatoes are a part of every dinner, it is very easy to take a few out of the pots in which they have been boiled by themselves, and to cut them up and add them to the soup just before it goes to table. Remove all shreds of meat and bone.

The cook should season the soup but very slightly with salt and pepper. If she puts in too much it may spoil it for the taste of most of those who are to eat it; but if too little it is easy to add more to your own plate.

## SOUPS.

### STOCK.

Four pounds of shin of beef, or four pounds of knuckle of veal, or two pounds of each; any bones, trimmings of poultry, or fresh meat, quarter pound of lean bacon or ham, two ounces of butter, two large onions, each stuck with cloves; one turnip, three carrots, one head of celery, three lumps of sugar, two ounces of salt, half a teaspoonful of whole pepper, one large blade of mace, one bunch of savory herbs, four quarts and half pint of cold water.

Cut up the meat and bacon, or ham, into pieces of about three inches square; rub the butter on the bottom of the stewpan; put in half a pint of water, the meat, and all the other ingredients. Cover the stewpan, and place it on a sharp fire, occasionally stirring its contents. When the bottom of the pan becomes covered with a pale, jelly-like substance, add the four quarts of cold water, and simmer very gently for five hours. As we have said before, do not let it boil quickly. Remove every particle of scum while it is doing, and strain it through a fine hair sieve.

This stock is the basis of many of the soups afterwards mentioned, and will be found quite strong enough for ordinary purposes.

Time: five and one-half hours. Average cost, twenty-five cents per quart.

### WHITE STOCK SOUP.

Six pounds knuckle of veal, half pound lean bacon, two tablespoonfuls of butter rubbed in one of flour, two onions, two carrots, two turnips, three cloves stuck in an onion, one blade of mace, bunch of herbs, six quarts of water, pepper and salt, one cup of boiling milk.

Cut up the meat and crack the bones. Slice carrots, turnips, and one onion, leaving that with the cloves whole. Put on with mace, and all the herbs except the parsley, in two quarts of cold water. Bring to a slow boil; take off the scum, as it rises, and at the end of an hour's stewing, add the rest of the cold water—one gallon. Cover and cook steadily, always gently, four hours. Strain off the liquor, of which there should be about five quarts; rub the vegetables through the colander, and pick out bones and meat. Season these highly and put, as is your Saturday custom, into a wide-mouth jar, or a large bowl. Add to them three quarts of stock, well salted, and, when cold, keep on ice. Cool to-day's stock; remove the fat, season, put in chopped parsley, and put over the fire. Heat in a saucepan a cup of milk, stir in the floured butter; cook three minutes. When the soup has simmered ten minutes after the last boil, and been carefully skimmed, pour into the tureen, and stir in the hot, thickened milk.

## SHIN OF BEEF SOUP.

Get a shin-bone of beef weighing four or five pounds; let the butcher saw it in pieces about two inches long, that the marrow may become the better incorporated with the soup, and so give it greater richness.

Wash the meat in cold water; mix together of salt and pepper each a tablespoonful, rub this well into the meat, then put into a soup-pot; put to it as many quarts of water as there are pounds of meat, and set it over a moderate fire, until it comes to a boil, then take off whatever scum may have risen, after which cover it close, and set it where it will boil very gently for two hours longer, then skim it again, and add to it the proper vegetables, which are these—

one large carrot grated, one large turnip cut in slices (the yellow or ruta baga is best), one leek cut in slices, one bunch of parsley cut small, six small potatoes peeled and cut in half, and a teacupful of pearl barley well washed, then cover it and let it boil gently for one hour, at which time add another tablesponful of salt and a thickening made of a tablespoonful of wheat flour and a gill of water, stir it in by the spoonful; cover it for fifteen minutes and it is done.

Three hours and a half is required to make this soup; it is the best for cold weather. Should any remain over the first day, it may be heated with the addition of a little boiling water, and served again.

Take the meat from the soup, and if to be served with it, take out the bones, and lay it closely and neatly on a dish, and garnish with sprigs of parsley; serve made mustard and catsup with it. It is very nice pressed and eaten with mustard and vinegar or catsup.

## MUTTON SOUP WITH TAPIOCA.

Three pounds perfectly lean mutton. The scrag makes good soup and costs little. Two or three pounds of bones, well pounded, one onion, two turnips, two carrots, two stalks of celery, a few sprigs of parsley; if you have any tomatoes left from yesterday, add them, four tablespoonfuls of pearl or granulated tapioca (not heaping spoonfuls), four quarts of water.

Put on the meat, cut in small pieces, with the bones, in two quarts of cold water. Heat very slowly, and when it boils, pour in two quarts of hot water from the kettle. Chop the vegetables, cover with cold water. So soon as they begin to simmer, throw off the first water, replenishing with hot, and stew until they are boiled to pieces. The meat should cook steadily, never fast, five hours, keeping the pot-lid on. Strain into a great bowl; let it cool to throw the fat to the surface; skim and return to the fire. Season with pepper and salt, boil up, take off the scum; add the vegetables with their liquor. Heat together ten minutes, strain again, and bring to a slow boil before the tapioca goes in. This should have been soaked for one hour in cold water, then cooked in the same within another vessel of boiling water until each grain is clear. It is necessary to stir up often from the bottom while cooking. Stir gradually into the soup until the tapioca is dissolved.

Send around grated cheese with this soup.

## VEAL SOUP.

To about three pounds of a joint of veal, which must be well broken up, put four quarts of water and set it over to boil. Prepare one-fourth pound of macaroni by boiling it by itself, with sufficient water to cover it; add a little butter to the macaroni when it is tender, strain the soup and season to taste with salt and pepper, then add the macaroni in the water in which it is boiled. The addition of a pint of rich milk or cream and celery flavor is relished by many.

## OX-TAIL SOUP.

Take two ox tails and two whole onions, two carrots, a small turnip, two tablespoonfuls of flour, and a little white pepper, add a gallon of water, let all boil for two hours; then take out the tails and cut the meat into small pieces, return the bones to the pot, for a short time, boil for another hour, then strain the soup, and rinse two spoonfuls of arrowroot to add to it with the meat cut from the bones, and 'et all boil for a quarter of an hour.

## VEGETABLE SOUP.

Two pounds of coarse, lean beef, cut into strips, two pounds of knuckle of veal chopped to pieces, two pounds of mutton bones, and the bones left from your cold veal cracked to splinters, pound of lean ham, four large carrots, two turnips, two onions, bunch of herbs, three tablespoonfuls of butter, and two of flour, one tablespoonful of sugar, salt and pepper, seven quarts of water.

Put on meat, bones, herbs and water, and cook slowly five hours. Strain the soup, of which there should be five quarts. Season meat and bones, and put into the stock-pot with three quarts of liquor. Save this for days to come. While the soup for to-day is cooling that you may take off the fat, put the butter into a frying pan with sliced carrots, turnips and onions, and fry to a light brown. Now, add a pint of the skimmed stock, and stew the vegetables tender, stir in the flour wet with water, and put all, with your cooled stock, over the fire in the soup-kettle. Season with sugar, Cayenne and salt, boil five minutes, rub through a colander, then a soup-sieve, heat almost to boiling, and serve.

## MACARONI SOUP.

To a rich beef or other soup, in which there is no seasoning other than pepper or salt, take half a pound of small pipe macaroni, boil it in clear water until it is tender, then drain it and cut it in pieces of an inch in length, boil it for fifteen minutes in the soup and serve.

## VERMICELLI SOUP.

Swell quarter of a pound of vermicelli in a quart of warm water, then add it to a good beef, veal, lamb or chicken soup or broth with quarter of a pound of sweet butter; let the soup boil for fifteen minutes after it is added.

## CHICKEN CREAM SOUP.

Boil an old fowl, with an onion, in four quarts of cold water, until there remain but two quarts. Take it out and let it get cold. Cut off the whole of the breast, and chop very fine. Mix with the pounded yolks of two hard-boiled eggs, and rub through a colander. Cool, skim, and strain the soup into a soup-pot. Season, add the chicken-and-egg mixture, simmer ten minutes, and pour into the tureen. Then add a small cup of boiling milk.

## MOCK-TURTLE SOUP.

Clean and wash a calf's head, split it in two, save the brains, boil the head until tender in plenty of water; put a slice of fat ham, a bunch of parsley cut small, a sprig of thyme, two leeks cut small, six cloves, a teaspoonful of pepper, and three ounces of butter, into a stew-pan, and fry them a nice brown; then add the water in which the head was boiled, cut the meat from the head in neat square pieces, and put them to the soup; add a pint of Madeira and one lemon sliced thin, and Cayenne pepper and salt to taste; let it simmer gently for two hours, then skim it clear and serve.

Make a forcemeat of the brains as follows: put them in a stew-pan, pour hot water over, and set it over the fire for a few minutes, then take them up, chop them small, with a sprig of parsley, a saltspoonful of salt and pepper each, a tablespoonful of wheat flour, the same of butter, and one well-beaten egg; make it in small balls, and drop them in the soup fifteen minutes before it is taken from the fire; in making the balls, a little more flour may be necessary. Egg-balls may also be added.

## HARD PEA SOUP.

Many persons keep the bones of their roast in order to convert them into stock for pea soup, which is, to my taste, one of the most relishable of all soups, and a famous dish for cold weather, with this advantage in its favor, that it may be made from almost anything. Capital stock for pea soup can be made from a kuckle of ham or from a piece of pickled-pork. Supposing that some such stock is at hand to the extent of about two quarts, procure, say, two pounds of split peas, wash them well, and then soak them for a night in water to which a very little piece of soda has been added (the floating peas should be all thrown away), strain out the peas and place them in the stock, adding a head of celery, a cut-down carrot and a large onion or two, and season with a pinch of curry powder, or half an eggspoonful of Cayenne pepper. Boil with a lid on the pot till all is soft, skimming off the scum occasionally, and then carefully strain into a well-warmed tureen, beating the pulp through the strainer with a spoon. Serve as hot as possible, placing a breakfastcupful of crumbled toast (bread) into the tureen before the soup is dished. Much of the success in preparing this soup lies in the "straining," which ought to be carefully attended to. A wire sieve is best; but an active housewife must never stick. If she has not a sieve made for the purpose, she can fold a piece of net two or three times, and use that. When a knuckle of ham has been used to make the stock it should form a part of the dinner, with potatoes, or it may be used as a breakfast or supper relish.

## GREEN PEA SOUP.

Wash a small quarter of lamb in cold water, and put it into a soup-pot with six quarts of cold water; add to it two tablespoonfuls of salt, and set it over a moderate fire—let it boil gently for two hours, then skim it clear, add a quart of shelled peas, and a teaspoonful of pepper; cover it, and let it boil for half an hour, then having scraped the skins from a quart of small young potatoes, add them to the soup; cover the pot, and let it boil for half an hour longer; work quarter of a pound of butter, and a dessert spoonful of flour together, and add them to the soup ten or twelve minutes before taking it off the fire.

Serve the meat on a dish with parsley sauce over, and the soup in a tureen.

## POTATO SOUP.

Potato soup is suitable for a cold day. **Make it in the following manner:** Get as many beef or ham bones as you can, and smash them into fragments. Add a little bit of lean ham to give flavor. Boil the bone and ham for two hours and a half at least. The bone of a roast beef is excellent. Strain off the liquor carefully, empty the bones and *debris* of the ham, restore the liquor to the pot, and place again on the fire. Having selected, washed, and pared some nice potatoes, cut them into small pieces, and boil them in the stock till they melt away. An onion or two may also be boiled among the bones to help the flavor. I do not like thick potato soup, and I usually strain it through a hair sieve, after doing so placing it again on the fire, seasoning it with pepper and salt to taste. A stick of celery boiled with the bones is an improvement. Make only the quantity required for the day, as potato soup is best when it is newly made.

## TOMATO SOUP.

Tomato soup is a much relished American dish, and is prepared as follows: Steam, or rather stew slowly, a mess of turnips, carrots, and onions, also a stalk of celery, with half a pound of lean ham and a *little bit* of fresh butter over a slow fire for an hour or so. Then add two quarts of diluted stock or of other liquor in which meat has been boiled, as also eight or ten ripe tomatoes. Stew the whole for an hour and a half, then pass through the sieve into the pan again; add a little pepper and salt, boil for **ten minutes and serve hot**

## GAME SOUP.

Two grouse or partridges, or if you have neither, use a pair of rabits; half a pound of lean ham; two medium-sized onions; one pound of lean beef; fried bread; butter for frying; pepper, salt, and two stalks of white celery cut into inch lengths; three quarts of water.

Joint your game neatly; cut the ham and onions into small pieces, and fry all in butter to a light brown. Put into a soup-pot with the beef, cut into strips, and a little pepper. Pour on the water; heat slowly, and stew gently two hours. Take out the pieces of bird, and cover in a bowl; cook the soup an hour longer; strain; cool; drop in the celery, and simmer ten minutes. Pour upon fried bread in the tureen.

## CELERY SOUP.

Celery soup may be made with *white stock*. Cut down the white of half a dozen heads of celery into little pieces and boil it in four pints of white stock, with a quarter of a pound of lean ham and two ounces of butter. Simmer gently for a full hour, then drain through a sieve, return the liquor to pan and stir in a few spoonfuls of cream with great care. Serve with toasted bread, and, if liked, thicken with a little flour. Season to taste.

## OYSTER SOUP.

Two quarts of oysters, one quart of milk, two tablespoonfuls of butter, one teacupful hot water; pepper, salt.

Strain all the liquor from the oysters; add the water and heat. When near the boil, add the seasoning, then the oysters. Cook about five minutes from the time they begin to simmer, until they "ruffle." Stir in the butter, cook one minute and pour into the tureen. Stir in the boiling milk, and send to table.

## LOBSTER SOUP.

Procure a large hen fish, boiled, and with all its coral, if possible. Cut away from it all the meat in neat little pieces; beat up the fins and minor claws in a mortar, then stew the results in a stew-pan, slowly, along with a little white stock; season this with a bunch of sweet herbs; a small onion, a little bit of celery, and a carrot may be placed in the stock as also the toasted crust of a French roll. Season to taste with salt and a little Cayenne. Simmer the whole for about an hour; then strain and return the liquor to the saucepan; place in it the pieces of lobster, and having beat up the coral in a little flour and gravy, stir it in. Let the soup remain on the fire for a few minutes without boiling and serve hot. A small strip of the rind of a lemon may be boiled in the stock, and a little nutmeg may be added to the seasoning. This is a troublesome soup to prepare, but there are many who like it when it is well made.

## EGG BALLS FOR SOUP.

Boil four eggs; put into cold water; mash yolks with yolk of one raw egg, and one teaspoonful of flour, pepper, salt and parsley; make into balls and boil two minutes.

## NOODLES FOR SOUP.

Rub into two eggs as much sifted flour as they will absorb; then roll out until thin as a wafer; dust over a little flour, and then roll over and over into a roll, cut off thin slices from the edge of the roll, and shake out into long strips; put them into the soup lightly and boil for ten minutes; salt should be added while mixing with the flour—about a saltspoonful.

## IRISH STEW.—STOVED POTATOES.

These form excellent and nutritious dishes. The former dish can be made from a portion of the back ribs or neck of mutton, the fleshy part of which must be cut into cutlets. Flatten these pieces of meat with a roller, and dip them in a composition of pepper, salt and flour. Peel potatoes and slice them to the extent of two pounds of potatoes for every pound of meat. An onion or two sliced into small bits will be required. Before building the materials into a goblet, melt a little suet or dripping in it, then commence by laying in the pot a layer of potatoes, which dust well with pepper and salt, then a layer of meat sprinkled with the chopped onions, and so on till the goblet is pretty full. Fill in about a breakfast-cupful of gravy, if there be any in the house; if not, water will do. Finish off with a treble row of potatoes on the top. Let the mess stew slowly for about three hours, taking great care to keep the lid so tight that none of the virtue can escape—letting away the steam is just letting away the flavor. Shake the pot occasionally with some force, to prevent burning. Some cooks in preparing this dish, boil the potatoes for some time, and then pour and dry them well; others add a portion of kidney to the stew; while extravagent people throw in a few oysters, a slice or two of lean ham, or a ham shank. Irish stew should be served as hot as possible. It is a savory and inexpensive dish for cold weather.—*Stoved potatoes* are prepared much in the same way. Cut down what of the Sunday's roast is left, and proceed with it just as you would with the neck of mutton. Some cooks would stew the bones of the roast, in order to make a gravy in which to stove the meat and potatoes, but the bones will make excellent potato soup. Irish stew is an excellent dish for skaters and curlers. It is sometimes known as "hot pot."

### VEGETABLES.

The first consideration in the purchase of vegetables is to have due regard to the variations of taste and appearance which the same vegetables undergo in different seasons. Spring carrots, for instance, are very different from those of Autumn and Winter.

### FRUIT.

Some fruits are of the highest value as articles of food, whilst others are generally regarded as articles of luxury. The coolness of succulent fruits renders them peculiarly grateful in warm climates, and are always welcome and refreshing as a dessert.

HORS-D'ŒUVRE.

A selected list of the Hors-D'Œuvre comprises the following: Radishes, Gherkins, Olives, Anchovies, Cucumber, Artichokes, Pickled Herrings, Pickled Oysters, Mixed Pickles.

PASTES.

Pastes are comprised as follows: Maccaroni, Rice, Sago, Tapioca, &c., and are made into numerous delectable dishes, the preparation of which is fully described in this volume.

## TO GET UP A SOUP IN HASTE.

Chop some cold cooked meat fine, and put a pint into a stew-pan with some gravy, season with pepper and salt and a little butter if the gravy is not rich, add a little flour moistened with cold water, and three pints boiling water, boil moderately half an hour. Strain over some rice or nicely toasted bread, and serve. Uncooked meat may be used by using one quart of cold water to a pound of chopped meat, and letting it stand half before boiling. Celery root may be grated in as seasoning, or a bunch of parsley thrown in.

## TO COLOR SOUPS.

A fine amber color is obtained by adding finely-grated carrot to the clear stock when it is quite free from scum.

Red is obtained by using red skinned tomatoes from which the skin and seeds have been strained out.

Only white vegetables should be used in white soups, as chicken.

Spinach leaves, pounded in a mortar, and the juice expressed, and added to the soups, will give a green color.

Black beans make an excellent brown soup. The same color can be gotten by adding burnt sugar or browned flour to clear stock.

# FISH.

Fish are good, when the gills are red, eyes are full, and the body of the fish is firm and stiff. After washing them well, they should be allowed to remain for a short time in salt water sufficient to cover them; before cooking wipe them dry, dredge lightly with flour, and season with salt and pepper. Salmon trout and other small fish are usually fried or broiled; all large fish should be put in a cloth, tied closely with twine, and placed in cold water, when they may be put over the fire to boil. When fish are baked, prepare the fish the same as for boiling, and put in the oven on a wire gridiron, over a dripping pan.

## BOILED SALMON.

The middle slice of salmon is the best. Sew up neatly in a mosquito-net bag, and boil a quarter of an hour to the pound in hot, salted water. When done, unwrap with care, and lay upon a hot dish, taking care not to break it. Have ready a large cupful of drawn butter, very rich, in which has been stirred a tablespoonful of minced parsley and the juice of a lemon. Pour half upon the salmon, and serve the rest in a boat. Garnish with parsley and sliced eggs.

Here is a recipe for a nice *pickle for cold salmon* made out of the liquor in which the fish has been boiled, of which take as much as you wish, say three breakfast-cupfuls, to which add vinegar to taste (perhaps a teacupful will be enough), a good pinch of pepper, a dessert-spoonful of salt. Boil for a few minutes with a sprig or two of parsley and a little thyme. After it has become quite cold, pour it over the fish.

## BROILED SALMON.

Cut some slices about an inch thick, and broil them over a gentle bright fire of coals, for ten or twelve minutes. When both sides are done, take them on to a hot dish; butter each slice well with sweet butter; strew over each a very little salt and pepper to taste, and serve.

## BAKED SALMON.

Clean the fish, rinse it, and wipe it dry; rub it well outside and in. with a mixture of pepper and salt, and fill it

with a stuffing made with slices of bread, buttered freely
and moistened with hot milk or water (add sage or thyme
to the seasoning if liked); tie a thread around the fish so
as to keep the stuffing in (take off the thread before serving); lay muffin-rings, or a trivet in a dripping-pan, lay bits
of butter over the fish, dredge flour over, and put it on the
rings; put a pint of hot water in the pan, to baste with; bake
one hour if a large fish, in a quick oven; baste frequently.
When the fish is taken up, having cut a lemon in very
thin slices, put them in the pan, and let them fry a little;
then dredge in a teaspoonful of wheat flour; add a small bit
of butter; stir it about, and let it brown without burning
for a little while then add half a teacupful or more of boiling water stir it smooth, take the slices of lemon into the
gravy boat, and strain the gravy over. Serve with boiled
potatoes. The lemon may be omitted if preferred, although
generally it will be liked.

## SALMON-TROUT.

Dressed the same as salmon.

## SPICED SALMON (PICKLED).

Boil a salmon, and after wiping it dry, set it to cool;
take of the water in which it was boiled, and good vinegar
each equal parts, enough to cover it; add to it one dozen
cloves, as many small blades of mace, or sliced nutmeg, one
teaspoonful of whole pepper, and the same of alspice; make
it boiling hot, skim it clear, add a small bit of butter (the
size of a small egg), and pour it over the fish; set it in a cool
place. When cold, it is fit for use, and will keep for a long
time, covered close, in a cool place. Serve instead of pickled oysters for supper.

A fresh cod is very nice, done in the same manner, as is
also a striped sea bass.

## SALMON AND CAPER SAUCE.

Two slices of salmon, one quarter pound butter, one half teaspoonful of chopped parsley, one shalot; salt, pepper and grated nutmeg to taste.

*Mode:* Lay the salmon in a baking-dish, place pieces of butter over it, and add the other ingredients, rubbing a little of the seasoning into the fish; baste it frequently; when done, take it out and drain for a minute or two; lay it in a dish; pour caper sauce over it, and serve; salmon dressed in this way, with tomato sauce, is very delicious.

## SALMON CUTLETS.

Cut the slices one inch thick, and season them with pepper and salt; butter a sheet of white paper, lay each slice on a separate piece, with their ends twisted; boil gently over a clear fire, and serve with anchovy or caper sauce. When higher seasoning is required, add a few chopped herbs and a little spice.

## DRIED OR SMOKED SALMON.

Cut the fish down the back, take out the entrails, and roe, scale it, and rub the outside and in with common salt, and hang it to drain for twenty-four hours.

Pound three ounces of saltpetre, two ounces of coarse salt and two of coarse brown sugar; mix these well together, and rub the salmon over every part with it; then lay it on a large dish for two days; then rub it over with common salt, and in twenty-four hours it will be fit to dry. Wipe it well, stretch it open with two sticks, and hang it in a chimney, with a smothered wood fire, or in a smoke house, or in a dry, cool place.

Shad done in this manner are very fine.

## BOILED COD.

Lay the fish in cold water, a little salt, for half an hour. Wipe dry, and sew up in a linen cloth, coarse and clean fitted to the shape of the piece of cod. Have but one fold over each part. Lay in the fish-kettle, cover with boiling water, salted at discretion. Allow nearly an hour for a piece weighing four pounds.

## COD PIE.

Any remains of cold cod, twelve oysters, sufficint melted butter to moisten it; mashed potatoes enough to fill up the dish.

*Mode:* Flake the fish from the bone, and carefully take away all the skin. Lay it in a pie-dish, pour over the melted butter and oysters (or oyster sauce, if there is any left), and cover with mashed potatoes. Bake for half an hour, and send to table of a nice brown color.

## DRIED CODFISH.

This should always be laid in soak at least one night before it is wanted; then take off the skin and put it in plenty of cold water; boil it gently (skimming it meanwhile) for one hour, or tie it in a cloth and boil it.

Serve with egg sauce; garnish with hard-boiled eggs cut in slices, and sprigs of parsley. Serve plain boiled or mashed potatoes with it.

## STEWED SALT COD.

Scald some soaked cod by putting it over the fire in boiling water for ten minutes; then scrape it white, pick it in flakes, and put it in a stew-pan, with a tablespoonful of butter worked into the same of flour, and as much milk as will moisten it; let it stew gently for ten minutes; add pepper to taste, and serve hot; put it in a deep dish, slice hard-boiled eggs over, and sprigs of parsley around the edge.

This is a nice relish for breakfast, with coffe and tea, and rolls or toast.

## CODFISH CAKES.

First boil soaked cod, then chop it fine, put to it an equal quantity of potatoes boiled and mashed; moisten it with beaten eggs or milk, and a bit of butter and a little pepper; form it in small, round cakes, rather more than a half inch thick; flour the outside, and fry in hot lard or beef drippings until they are a delicate brown; like fish, these must be fried gently, the lard being boiling hot when they are put in; when one side is done turn the other. Serve for breakfast.

## BOILED BASS.

Put enough water in the pot for the fish to swim in, easily. Add half a cup of vinegar, a teaspoonful of salt, an onion, a dozen black peppers, and a blade of mace. Sew up the fish in a piece of clean net, fitted to its shape. Heat slowly for the first half hour, then boil eight minutes, at least, to the pound, quite fast. Unwrap, and pour over it a cup of drawn butter, based upon the liquor in which the fish was boiled, with the juice of half a lemon stirred into it. Garnish with sliced lemon.

## FRIED BASS.

Clean, wipe dry, inside and out, dredge with flour, and season with salt. Fry in hot butter, beef-dripping, or sweet lard. Half-butter, half-lard is a good mixture for frying fish. The moment the fish are done to a good brown, take them from the fat and drain in a hot colander. Garnish with parsley.

## TO FRY OR BROIL FISH PROPERLY.

After the fish is well cleansed, lay it on a folded towel and  out all the water. When well wiped and dry, roll it in wheat flour, rolled crackers, grated stale bread, or Indian meal, whichever may be preferred; wheat flour will generally be liked.

Have a thick-bottomed frying-pan or spider, with plenty of sweet lard salted (a tablespoonful of salt to each pound of lard), for fresh fish which have not been previously salted; let it become boiling not, then lay the fish in and let it fry gently, until one side is a fine delicate brown, then turn the other; when both are done, take it up carefully and serve quickly, or keep it covered with a tin cover, and set the dish where it will keep hot.

## BAKED BLACK BASS.

Eight good-sized onions chopped fine; half that quantity of bread-crumbs; butter size of hen's egg; plenty of pepper and salt, mix thoroughly with anchovy sauce until quite red. Stuff your fish with this compound and pour the rest over it, previously sprinkling it with a little red pepper. Shad, pickerel, and trout are good the same way. Tomatoes can be used instead of anchovies, and are more economical. If using them take pork in place of butter and chop fine.

## BROILED MACKEREL.

Pepper and salt to taste, a small quantity of oil. Mackerel should never be washed when intended to be broiled, but merely wiped very clean and dry after taking out the gills and inside. Open the back, and put in a little pepper, salt, and oil; broil it over a clear fire, turn it over on both sides, and also on the back. When sufficiently cooked, the flesh can be detached from the bone, which will be in about ten minutes for a small mackerel. Chop a little parsley, work it up in the butter, with pepper and salt to taste, and a squeeze of lemon-juice, and put it in the back. Serve before the butter is quite melted.

*Mode:* Scale and clean the pike, and fasten the tail in its mouth by means of a skewer. Lay it in cold water, and when it boils, throw in the salt and vinegar. The time for boiling depends, of course, on the size of the fish; but a middling-sized pike will take about half an hour. Serve with Dutch or anchovy sauce, and plain melted butter.

Mackerel baked will be found palatable. Clean and trim the fish nicely, say four large ones, or half a dozen small ones, bone them and lay neatly in a baking dish, or a bed of potato chips well dusted with a mixture of pepper and salt; on the potatoes place a few pieces of butter. Dust the fish separately with pepper and salt, and sprinkle slightly with a diluted mixture of anchovy sauce and catsup. Bake three quarters of an hour.

## SALT MACKEREL WITH CREAM SAUCE.

Soak over night in lukewarm water, changing this in the morning for ice-cold. Rub all the salt off, and wipe dry. Grease your gridiron with butter, and rub the fish on both sides with the same, melted. Then broil quickly over a clear fire, turning with a cake-turner so as not to break it. Lay upon a hot water dish, and cover until the sauce is ready.

Heat a small cup of milk to scalding. Stir into it a teaspoonful of corn-starch wet up with a little water. When this thickens, add two tablespoonfuls of butter, pepper, salt, and chopped parsley. Beat an egg light, pour the sauce gradually over it, put the mixture again over the fire, and stir one minute, not more. Pour upon the fish, and let all stand, covered, over the hot water in the chafing dish.

Put fresh boiling water under the dish before sending to table.

### BOILED EELS.

Four small eels, sufficient water to cover them; a large bunch of parsley.

Choose small eels for boiling, put them on a stewpan with the parsley, and just sufficient water to cover them; simmer till tender. Take them out, pour a little parsley and butter over them, and serve some in a tureen.

### FRICASSEED EELS.

After skinning, clearing, and cutting five or six eels in pieces of two inches in length, boil them in water nearly to cover them, until tender; then add a good-sized bit of butter, with a teaspoonful of wheat flour or rolled cracker, worked into it, and a little scalded and chopped parsley; add salt and pepper to taste, and a wine-glass of vinegar if liked; let them simmer for ten minutes and serve hot.

### FRIED EELS.

After cleaning the eels well, cut them in pieces two inches long; wash them and wipe them dry; roll them in wheat flour or rolled cracker, and fry as directed for other fish, in hot lard or beef dripping, salted. They should be browned all over and thoroughly done,

Eels may be prepared in the same manner and broiled.

### COLLARED EELS.

One large eel, pepper and salt to taste; two blades of mace, two cloves, a little allspice very finely pounded, six leaves of sage, and a small bunch of herbs minced very small.

*Mode:* Bone the eel and skin it; split it, and sprinkle it over with the ingredients, taking care that the spices are very finely pounded, and the herbs chopped very small. Roll it up and bind with a broad piece of tape, and boil it in water, mixed with a little salt and vinegar, till tender. It may either be served whole or cut in slices; and when cold, the eel should be kept in the liquor it was boiled in but with a little more vinegar put to it.

## FRIED TROUT.

They must, of course, be nicely cleaned and trimmed all round, but do not cut off their heads. Dredge them well with flour, and fry in a pan of boiling hot fat or oil. Turn them from side to side till they are nicely browned, and quite ready. Drain off all the fat before sending the fish to table; garnish them with a few sprigs of parsley, and provide plain melted butter. If preferred, the trout can be larded with beaten egg, and be then dipped in bread crumb. The frying will occupy from five to eight minutes, according to size. Very large trout can be cut in pieces.

## TROUT IN JELLY (or other Fish).

This is a beautiful supper dish, and may be arranged as follows: Turn the fish into rings, with tail in mouth, prepare a seasoned water in which to boil the trout; the water should have a little vinegar and salt in it, and may be flavored with a shallot or clove or garlic. When the water is cold, place the trout in it, and boil them very gently, so as not to hash or break them. When done, lift out and drain. Baste with fish jelly, for which a recipe is given elsewhere, coat ofter coat, as each coat hardens. Arrange neatly, and serve.

## BOILED TROUT.

Let the water be thoroughly a-boil before you put in the fish. See that it is salt, and that a dash of vinegar has been put in it. Remove all scum as it rises, and boil the fish till their eyes protrude. Lift them without breaking, drain off the liquor, and serve on a napkin if you like. To be eaten with a sauce according to taste, that is, if it can be made of either anchovies or shrimps.

### BROILED TROUT.

Clean and split them open, season with a little salt and Cayenne; dip in whipped egg, dredge with flour and brander over a clear fire. Serve with sauce.

### BAKED HADDOCK.

Choose a nice fish of about six pounds, which trim and scrape nicely, gutting it carefully, fill the vacuum with a stuffing of veal, chopped ham, and bread-crumbs, sew up with strong thread, and shape the fish round, putting its tail into its mouth, or, if two are required, lay them along the dish reversed—that is, tail to head; rub over with plenty of butter, or a batter of eggs and flour, and then sprinkle with bread-crumbs. Let the oven be pretty hot when put in. In about on hour the fish will be ready. Serve on the tin or aisset in which they have been baked, placing them on a larger dish for that purpose. Mussel sauce is a good accompaniment.

### CURRIED HADDOCK.

Curried haddock is excellent. Fillet the fish and curry it in a pint of beef stock slightly diluted with water, and thickened with a tablespoonful of curry powder. Some cooks chop up an onion to place in the stew. It will take an hour to ready this fish. If preferred, fry the fish for a few minutes in clean lard oil before stewing it in the curry.

## RIZZARED HADDOCK.

First, of course, procure your fish, clean them thoroughly, rub them well with salt, and let them lie for one night, after which hang them in the open air, to dry, in a shady place. In two days they will be ready for the gridiron. Before cooking them take out the backbone and skin them, if desired (I never do *skin* them), broil till ready, eat with a little fresh butter.

Haddocks can be boiled with advantage: all that is necessary is plenty of salt in the water, and not to serve them till they are well done. As a general rule, it may be ascertained when fish is sufficiently cooked by the readiness with which the flesh lifts from the bone. Stick a fork into the shoulder of a cod or haddock and try it. If living sufficiently near the sea, procure sea water in which to boil your haddocks.

## BROILED WHITE-FISH—FRESH.

Wash and drain the fish; sprinkle with pepper and lay with the inside down upon the gridiron, and broil over fresh bright coals. When a nice brown, turn for a moment on the other side, then take up and spread with butter. This is a very nice way of broiling all kinds of fish, fresh or salted. A little smoke under the fish adds to its flavor. This may be made by putting two or three cobs under the gridiron.

## BAKED WHITE-FISH.

Fill the fish with a stuffing of fine bread-crumbs and a little butter; sew up the fish; sprinkle with butter, pepper and salt. Dredge with flour and bake one hour, basting often and serving with parsley sauce or egg sauce

## TO CHOOSE LOBSTERS.

These are chosen more by weight than size, the heaviest are best; a good, small-sized one will not unfrequently be found to weigh as heavily as one much larger. If fresh, a lobster will be lively and the claws have a strong motion when the eyes are pressed with the finger.

The male is best for boiling; the flesh is firmer, and the shell a brighter red; it may be readily distinguished from the female; the tail is narrower, and the two uppermost fins within the tail are stiff and hard. Those of the hen lobster are not so, and the tail is broader.

Hen lobsters are preferred for sauce or salad, on account of their coral. The head and small claws are never used.

## BOILED LOBSTER.

These crustaceans are usually sold ready-boiled. When served, crack the claws and cut open the body, lay neatly on a napkin-covered dish, and garnish with a few sprigs of parsley. Lobster so served is usually eaten cold.

## CURRIED LOBSTER.

Pick out the meat of two *red* lobsters from the shells into a shallow sauce-pan, in the bottom of which has been placed a thin slice of tasty ham, with a little Cayenne pepper and a teaspoonful of salt. Mix up half a cupful of white soup and half a cupful of cream and pour over the meat. Put it on the fire and let it simmer for about an hour, when you will add a dessert-spoonful of curry, and another of flour rubbed smooth in a little of the liquor taken out of the pot; in three minutes the curry will be ready to dish. Some add a dash of lemon to this curry (I don't), and the cream can be dispensed with, if necessary. Put a rim of well-boiled rice round the dish if you like, or serve the rice separately.

## LOBSTER CHOWDER.

Four or five pounds of lobster, chopped fine; take the green part and add to it four pounded crackers; stir this into one quart of boiling milk; then add the lobster, a piece of butter one-half the size of an egg, a little pepper and salt, and bring it to a boil.

## CHOWDER.

Cut some slices of pork very thin, and fry them out dry in the dinner-pot; then put in a layer of fish cut in slices on the pork, then a layer of onions, and then potatoes, all cut in exceedingly thin slices; then fish, onions, potatoes again, till your materials are all in, putting some salt and pepper on each layer of onions; split some hard biscuits, dip them in water, and put them round the sides and over the top; put in water enough to come up in sight; stew for over half an hour, till the potatoes are done; add half a pint of milk, or a teacup of sweet cream, five minutes before you take it up.

## TO FRY SMELTS.

Egg and bread-crumbs, a little flour, boiling lard. Smelts should be very fresh, and not washed more than is necessary to clean them. Dry them in a cloth, lightly flour, dip them in egg, and sprinkle over with very fine bread-crumbs, and put them into boiling lard. Fry of a nice pale brown, and be careful not to take off the light roughness of the crumbs, or their beauty will be spoiled. Dry them before the fire on a drainer, and serve with plain melted butter.

## TO BAKE SMELTS.

Smelts, bread-crumbs, one-quarter pound of fresh butter, two blades of pounded mace; salt and Cayenne to taste

Wash, and dry the fish thorougly in a cloth, and arrange them nicely in a flat baking-dish. Cover them with fine bread-crumbs, and place little pieces of butter all over them. Season and bake for fifteen minutes. But before serving, add a squeeze of lemon-juice, and garnish with fried parsley and cut lemon.

## RED HERRINGS or YARMOUTH BLOATERS.

The best way to cook these is to make incisions in the skin across the fish, because they do not then require to be so long on the fire, and will be far better than when cut open. The hard roe makes a nice relish by pounding it in a mortar, with a little anchovy, and spreading it on toast.

If very dry, soak in warm water, one hour before dressing.

## POTTED FISH.

Take out the backbone of the fish; for one weighing two pounds take a tablespoonful of allspice and cloves mixed; these spices should be put into little bags of not too thick muslin; put sufficient salt directly upon each fish; then roll in a cloth, over which sprinkle a little Cayenne pepper; put alternate layers of fish, spice and sago in an earthen jar; cover with the best cider-vinegar; cover the jar closely with a plate and over this put a covering of dough, rolled out to twice the thickness of pie crust. Make the edges of paste, to adhere closely to the sides of the jar, so as to make it air-tight. Put the jar into a pot of cold water and let it boil from three to five hours, according to quantity. Ready when cold.

## OYSTERS ON THE SHELL.

Wash the shells and put them on hot coals or upon the top of a hot stove, or bake them in a hot oven; open the shells with an oyster-knife, taking care to lose none of the liquor, and serve quickly on hot plates, with toast. Oysters may be steamed in the shells, and are excellent eaten in the same manner.

## OYSTERS STEWED WITH MILK.

Take a pint of fine oysters, put them with their own liquor, and a gill of milk into a stew pan, and if liked, a blade of mace, set it over the fire, take off any scum which may rise; when they are plump and white turn them into a deep plate; add a bit of butter, and pepper to taste. Serve crackers and dressed celery with them. Oysters may be stewed in their own liquor without milk.

## OYSTERS FRIED IN BATTER.

Half pint of oysters, two eggs, half pint of milk, sufficient flour to make the batter; pepper and salt to taste; when liked, a little nutmeg; hot lard. Scald the oysters in their own liquor, beard them, and lay them on a cloth, to drain thoroughly. Break the eggs into a basin, mix the flour with them, add the milk gradually, with nutmeg and seasoning, and put the oysters in a batter. Make some lard hot in a deep frying-pan, put in the oysters, one at a time; when done, take them up with a sharp-pointed skewer, and dish them on a napkin. Fried oysters are frequently used for garnishing boiled fish, and then a few bread-crumbs should be added to the flour.

## SCALLOPED OYSTERS.

Two tablespoonfuls of white stock, two tablesponfuls of cream; pepper and salt to taste; bread-crumbs, oiled butter. Scald the oysters in their own liquor, take them out, beard them, and strain the liquor free from grit. Put one ounce of butter into a stewpan; when melted, dredge in sufficient flour to dry it up; add the stock, cream and strained liquor, and give one boil. Put in the oysters and seasoning; let them gradually heat through, but not boil. Have ready the scallop-shells buttered; lay in the oysters, and as much of the liquid as they will hold; cover them over with bread-crumbs, over which drop a little oiled butter. Brown them in the oven, or before the fire, and serve quickly, and very hot.

## FRIED OYSTERS.

Take large oysters from their own liquor on to a thickly folded napkin to dry them off; then make a tablespoonful of lard or beef fat hot, in a thick bottomed frying-pan, add to it half a saltspoonful of salt; dip each oyster in wheat flour, or cracker rolled fine, until it will take up no more, then lay them in the pan, hold it over a gentle fire until one side is a delicate brown; turn the other by sliding a fork under it; five minutes will fry them after they are in the pan. Oysters may be fried in butter but it is not so good, lard and butter half and half is very nice for frying. Some persons like a very little of the oyster liquid poured in the pan after the oysters are done; let it boil up, then put it in the dish with the oysters; when wanted for breakfast, this should be done.

Oysters to be fried, after drying as directed, may be dipped into beaten egg first, then into rolled cracker.

## OYSTER PATTIES.

Make some rich puff paste and bake it in very small tin patty pans; when cool, turn them out upon a large dish; stew some large fresh oysters with a few cloves, a little mace and nutmeg; then add the yolk of one egg, boiled hard and grated; add a little butter, and as much of the oyster liquid as will cover them. When they have stewed a little while take them out of the pan and let them be cool

When quite cold, lay two or three oysters in each shell of puff paste.

### BROILED OYSTERS.

Drain the oysters well and dry them with a napkin. Have ready a griddle hot and well buttered; season the oysters; lay them to griddle and brown them on both sides. Serve them on a hot plate with plenty of butter.

### CLAM FRITTERS.

Take fifty small or twenty-five large sand clams from their shells; if large, cut each in two, lay them on a thickly folded napkin; put a pint bowl of wheat flour into a basin, add to it two well-beaten eggs, half a pint of sweet milk, and nearly as much of their own liquor; beat the batter until it is smooth and perfectly free from lumps; then stir in the clams. Put plenty of lard or beef fat into a thick-bottomed frying pan, let it become boiling hot; put in the batter by the spoonful; let them fry gently; when one side is a delicate brown, turn the other.

### SOFT-SHELLED CLAMS.

These are very fine if properly prepared. They are good only during cold weather and must be perfectly fresh.

Soft-shelled clams may be boiled from the shells, and served with butter, pepper and salt over.

### TO BOIL SOFT-SHELL CLAMS.

Wash the shells clean, and put the clams, the edges downwards, in a kettle; then pour about a quart of boiling water over them; cover the pot and set it over a brisk fire for three quarters of an hour; pouring boiling water on them causes the shells to open quickly and let out out the sand which may be in them.

Take them up when done, take off the black skin which covers the hard part, trim them clean, and put them into a stew-pan; put to them some of the liquor in which they were boiled; put to it a good bit of butter and pepper and salt to taste; make them hot; serve with cold butter and rolls.

## CLAM CHOWDER.

Butter a deep tin basin, strew it thickly with grated bread-crumbs, or soaked cracker; sprinkle some pepper over and bits of butter the size of a hickory nut, and, if liked, some finely chopped parsley; then put a double layer of clams, season with pepper, put bits of butter over, then another layer of soaked cracker; after that clams and bits of butter; sprinkle pepper over; add a cup of milk or water, and lastly a layer of soaked crackers. Turn a plate over the basin, and bake in a hot oven for three-quarters of an hour; use half a pound of soda biscuit, and quarter of a pound of butter with **fifty clams.**

## MEATS.

### ROAST BEEF.

Prepare for the oven by dredging lightly with flour, and seasoning with salt and pepper; place in the oven, and baste frequently while roasting. Allow a quarter of an hour for a pound of meat, if you like it rare; longer if you like it well done. Serve with a sauce made from the drippings in the pan, to which has been added a tablespoon of Harvey or Worcestershire sauce, and a tablespoon of tomato catsup.

### ROUND OF BEEF BOILED.

See that it is not too large, and that it is tightly bound all round. About twelve pounds or fourteen pounds form a convenient size, and a joint of that weight will require from three hours to three hours and a quarter to boil. Put on with cold water—as the liquor is valuable for making pea-soup—and let it come slowly to the boil. Boil carefully but not rapidly, and skim frequently; as a rule, keep the lid of the pot well fixed. The meat may be all the better if taken out once or twice in the process of cooking. Carrots and turnips may be boiled to serve with the round; they will, of course, cook in about a third of the time necessary to boil the beef.

### BEEF SALTED, OR CORNED, RED,
#### To Keep for Years.

Cut up a quarter of beef. For each hundredweight take half a peck of coarse salt, quarter of a pound of saltpetre, the same weight of saleratus, and a quart of molasses, or two pounds of coarse brown sugar. Mace, cloves and allspice may be added for spiced beef.

Strew some of the salt in the bottom of a pickle-tub or barrel; then put in a layer of meat, strew this with salt, then add another layer of meat, and salt and meat alternately, until all is used. Let it remain one night. Dissolve the saleratus and saltpetre in a little warm water, and put it to the molasses or sugar; then put it over the meat, add water enough to cover the meat, lay a board on it to keep it under the brine. The meat is fit for use after ten days. This receipt is for winter beef. Rather more salt may be used in warm weather.

Towards spring take the brine from the meat, make it boiling hot, skim it clear, and when it is cooled, return it to the meat.

Beef tongues and smoking pieces are fine pickled in this brine. Beef liver put in this brine for ten days and then wiped dry and smoked, is very fine. Cut it in slices, and fry or broil it. The brisket of beef, after being corned, may be smoked, and is very fine for boiling.

Lean pieces of beef, cut properly from the hind quarter, are the proper pieces for being smoked. There may be some fine pieces cut from the fore-quarter.

After the beef has been in brine ten days or more wipe it dry, and hang it in a chimney where wood is burnt, or make a smothered fire of sawdust or chips, and keep it smoking for ten days; then rub fine black pepper over every part, to keep the flies from it, and hang it in a dry, dark, cool place. After a week it is fit for use. A strong, coarse brown paper, folded around beef, and fastened with paste, keeps it nicely.

Tongues are smoked in the same manner. Hang them by a string put through the root end. Spiced brine for smoked beef or tongues will be generally liked.

For convenience make a pickle as mentioned for beef, keep it in the cellar, ready for pickling beef at any time. Beef may remain in three or four or more days.

## TO BOIL CORNED BEEF.

Put the beef in water enough to cover it, and let it heat slowly, and boil slowly, and be careful to take off the grease. Many think it much improved by boiling potatoes, turnips, and cabbages with it. In this case the vegetables must be peeled and *all* the grease carefully skimmed as fast as it rises. Allow about twenty minutes of boiling for each pound of meat.

## A NICE WAY TO SERVE COLD BEEF.

Cut cold roast beef in slices, put gravy enough to cover them, and a wineglass of catsup or wine, or a lemon sliced thin; if you have not gravy, put hot water and a good bit of butter, with a teaspoonful or more of browned flour; put it in a closely covered stew-pan, and let it simmer gently for half an hour. If you choose, when the meat is down, cut a leek in thin slices, and chop a bunch of parsley small, and add it; serve boiled or mashed potatoes with it. This is equal to beef-a-la-mode.

Or, cold beef may be served cut in neat slices, garnished with sprigs of parsley, and made mustard, and tomato catsup in the castor; serve mashed, if not new potatoes, with it, and ripe fruit, or pie, or both, for dessert, for a small family dinner.

## SPICED BEEF.

Four pounds of round of beef chopped fine; take from it all fat; add to it three dozen small crackers rolled fine, four eggs, one cup of milk, one tablespoon ground mace, two tablespoons of black pepper, one tablespoon melted butter; mix well and put in any tin pan that it will just fill, packing it well; baste with butter and water, and bake two hours in a slow oven.

## BROILED BEEFSTEAK.

Lay a thick tender steak upon a gridiron over hot coals, having greased the bars with butter before the steak has been put upon it (a steel gridiron with slender bars is to be preferred, the broad flat iron bars of gridirons commonly used fry and scorch the meat, imparting a disagreeable flavor). When done on one side, have ready your platter warmed, with a little butter on it; lay the steak upon the platter with the cooked side down, that the juices which have gathered may run on the platter, but do not press the meat; then lay your beefsteak again upon the gridiron quickly and cook the other side. When done to your liking, put again on the platter, spread lightly with butter, place where it will keep warm for a few moments, but not to let the butter become oily (over boiling steam is best); and then serve on hot plates. Beefsteak should never be seasoned with salt and pepper while cooking. If your meat is tough, pound *well* with a steak mallet on both sides.

## FRIED BEEFSTEAKS.

Cut some of the fat from the steak, and put it in a frying pan and set it over the fire; if the steaks are not very tender, beat them with a rolling pin, and when the fat is boiling hot, put the steak evenly in, cover the pan and let it fry briskly until one side is done, sprinkle a little pepper and salt over, and turn the other; let it be rare or well done as may be liked; take the steak on a hot dish, add a wineglass or less of boiling water or catsup to the gravy; let it boil up once, and pour it in the dish with the steak.

## BEEFSTEAK PIE.

Take some fine tender steaks, beat them a little, season with a saltspoonful of pepper and a teaspoonful of salt to a two-pound steak; put bits of butter, the size of a hickory nut, over the whole surface, dredge a teaspoonful of flour over, then roll it up and cut it in pieces two inches long; put a rich pie paste around the sides and bottom of a tin basin; put in the pieces of steak, nearly fill the basin with water, add a piece of butter the size of a large egg, cut small, dredge in a teaspoonful of flour, add a little pepper and salt, lay skewers across the basin, roll a top crust to half an inch thickness, cut a slit in the center; dip your fingers in flour and neatly pinch the top and side crust together all around the edge. Bake one hour in a quick oven.

## BOILED LEG OF MUTTON.

Mutton, water, salt. A leg of mutton for boiling should not hang too long, as it will not look a good color when dressed. Cut off the shank-bone, trim the knuckle and wash and wipe it very clean; plunge it into sufficient boiling water to cover it; let it boil up, then draw the saucepan to the side of the fire, where it should remain till the finger can be borne in the water. Then place it sufficiently near the fire, that the water may gently simmer, and be very careful that it does not boil fast, or the meat will be hard. Skim well, add a little salt, and in about two and one quarter hours after the water begins to simmer, a moderate-sized leg of mutton will be done. Serve with carrots and mashed turnips, which may be boiled with the meat, and send caper sauce to table with it in a tureen.

## ROAST LOIN OF MUTTON.

Loin of mutton, a little salt. Cut and trim off the superfluous fat, and see that the butcher joints the meat properly, as thereby much annoyance is saved to the carver, when it comes to table. Have ready a nice clear fire (it need not be a very wide, large one), put down the meat, dredge with flour, and baste well until it is done.

## BROILED MUTTON CHOPS.

Loin of mutton, pepper and salt, a small piece of butter. Cut the chops from a well-hung, tender loin of mutton, remove a portion of the fat, and trim them into a nice shape; slightly beat and level them; place the gridiron over a bright, clear fire, rub the bars with a little fat, and lay on the chops. While broiling, frequently turn them, and in about eight minutes they will be done. Season with pepper and salt, dish them on a very hot dish, rub a small piece of butter on each chop, and serve very hot and expeditiously.

## MUTTON CHOP FRIED.

Cut some fine mutton chops without much fat, rub over both sides with a mixture of salt and pepper, dip them in wheat flour or rolled crackers, and fry in hot lard or beef drippings; when both sides are a fine brown, take them on a hot dish, put a wineglass of hot water in the pan, let it become hot, stir in a teaspoonful of browned flour, let it boil up at once, and serve in the pan with the meat.

## ROAST FORE-QUARTER OF LAMB.

Lamb, a little salt. To obtain the flavor of lamb in perfection it should not be long kept; three to four is all that is required; and though the meat may be somewhat thready, the juices and flavor will be infinitely superior to that of lamb that has been killed two or three days. Make up the fire in good time, that it may be clear and brisk when the joint is put down. Place it at sufficient distance to prevent the fat from burning, and baste it constantly till the moment of serving. Lamb should be very thoroughly done without being dried up, and not the slightest appearance of red gravy should be visible, as in roast mutton; this rule is applicable to all young white meats. Serve with a little gravy made in the dripping-pan, the same as for other roasts, and send to table with a tureen of mint sauce.

## LAMBS' SWEETBREADS.

Two or three sweetbreads, one-half pint of veal stock, white pepper and salt to taste, a small bunch of green onions, one blade of pounded mace, thickening of butter and flour, two eggs, nearly one-half pint of cream, one teaspoonful of minced parsley, a very little grated nutmeg.

*Mode:* Soak the sweetbreads in lukewarm water, and put them into a saucepan with sufficient boiling water to cover them, and let them simmer for ten minutes; then take them out and put them into cold water. Now lard them, lay them in a stewpan, add the stock, seasoning, onions, mace, and a thickening of butter and flour, and stew gently for one-quarter of an hour or twenty minutes. Beat up the egg with the cream, to which add the minced parsley and very little grated nutmeg. Put this to the other ingredients; stir it well till quite hot, but do not let it boil after the cream is added, or it will curdle. Have ready some asparagus-tops, boiled; add these to the sweetbreads, and serve.

Lamb Steak dipped in egg, and then in biscuit or bread-crumbs, and fried until it is brown, helps to make variety for the breakfast table. With baked sweet potatoes, good coffee, and buttered toast or corn muffins, one may begin the day with courage.

## TO ROAST VEAL.

Rinse the meat in cold water; if any part is bloody, wash it off; make a mixture of pepper and salt, allowing a large teaspoonful of salt and a saltspoonful of pepper for each pound of meat; wipe the meat dry; then rub the seasoning into every part, shape it neatly, and fasten it with skewers, and put it on a spit, or set it on a trivet or muffin rings, in a pan; stick bits of butter over the whole upper surface; dredge a little flour over, put a pint of water in the pan to baste with, and roast it before the fire in a Dutch oven or reflector, or put it into a hot oven; baste it occasionally, turn it if necessary that every part may be done; if the water wastes add more, that the gravy may not burn; allow fifteen minutes for each pound of meat; a piece weighing four or five pounds will then require one hour, or an hour and a quarter.

## VEAL CHOPS.

Cut veal chops about an inch thick; beat them flat with a rolling-pin, put them in a pan, pour boiling water over them, and set them over the fire for five minutes; then take them up and wipe them dry; mix a tablespoonful of salt and a teaspoonful of pepper for each pound of meat; rub each chop over with this, then dip them, first into beaten egg, then into rolled crackers as much as they will take up; then finish by frying in hot lard or beef drippings; or broil them. For the broil have some sweet butter on a steak dish; broil the chops until well done, over a bright clear fire of coals; (let them do gently that they may be well done,) then take them on to the butter, turn them carefully once or twice in it, and serve. Or dip the chops into a batter, made of one egg beaten with half a teacup of milk and as much wheat flour as may be necessary. Or simply dip the chops without parboiling into wheat flour; make some lard or beef fat hot in a frying-pan; lay the chops in, and when one side is a fine delicate brown, turn the other. When all are done, take them up, put a very little hot water into the pan, then put it in the dish with the chops.

Or make a flour gravy thus: After frying them as last directed, add a tablespoonful more of fat to that in the pan, let it become boiling hot; make a thin batter, of a small tablespoonful of wheat flour and cold water; add a little more salt and pepper to the gravy, then gradually stir in the batter; stir it until it is cooked and a nice brown; then put it over the meat, or in the dish with it; if it is thicker than is liked, add a little boiling water.

## VEAL CUTLETS.

Two or three pounds of veal cutlets, egg and bread-crumbs, two tablespoonfuls of minced savory herbs, salt and pepper to taste, a little grated nutmeg.

Cut the cutlets about three-quarters of an inch in thickness, flatten them, and brush them over with the yolk of an egg; dip them into bread-crumbs and minced herbs, season with pepper and salt and grated nutmeg, and fold each cutlet in a piece of buttered paper. Broil them, and send them to table with melted butter or a good gravy.

## STUFFED FILLET OF VEAL WITH BACON.

Take out the bone from the meat, and pin into a round with skewers. Bind securely with soft tapes. Fill the cavity left by the bone with a force-meat of crumbs, chopped pork, thyme, and parsley, seasoned with pepper, salt, nutmeg and a pinch of lemon-peel. Cover the top of the fillet with thin slices of cold *cooked*, fat bacon or salt pork, tying them in place with twines crossing the meat in all directions. Put into a pot with two cups of boiling water, and cook slowly and steadily two hours. Then take from the pot and put into a dripping-pan. Undo the strings and tapes. Brush the meat all over with raw egg, sift rolled cracker thickly over it, and set in the oven for half an hour, basting often with gravy from the pot. When it is well browned, lay upon a hot dish with the pork about it. Strain and thicken the gravy, and serve in a boat.

If your fillet be large, cook twice as long in the pot. The time given above is for one weighing five pounds.

### VEAL CAKE (a Convenient Dish for a Picnic).

A few slices of cold roast veal, a few slices of cold ham, two hard boiled eggs, two tablespoonfuls of minced parsley, a little pepper, good gravy, or stock No. 109.

Cut off all the brown outside from the veal, and cut the eggs into slices. Procure a pretty mold; lay veal, ham, eggs, and parsley in layers, with a little pepper between each, and when the mold is full, get some *strong* stock, and fill up the shape. Bake for one half-hour, and when cold, turn it out.

### VEAL PIE.

Cut a breast of veal small, and put it in a stewpan, with hot water to cover it; add to it a tablespoonful of salt, and set it over the fire; take off the scum as it rises; when the meat is tender, turn it into a dish to cool; take out all the small bones, butter a tin or earthen basin or pudding-pan, line it with a pie paste, lay some of the parboiled meat in to half fill it; put bits of butter the size of a hickory nut all over the meat; shake pepper over, dredge wheat flour over until it looks white; then fill it nearly to the top with some of the water in which the meat was boiled; roll a cover for the top of the crust, puff paste it, giving it two or three turns, and roll it to nearly half an inch thickness; cut a slit in the center, and make several small incisions on either side of it; lay some skewers across the pie, put the crust on, trim the edges neatly with a knife; bake one hour in a quick oven. A breast of veal will make two two-quart basin pies; half a pound of nice corned pork, cut in thin slices and parboiled with the meat, will make it very nice, and very little, if any butter, will be required for the pie; when pork is used, no other salt will be necessary.

### BOILED CALF HEAD (without the skin).

Calf's head, water, a little salt, four tablespoonfuls of melted butter, one tablespoonful of minced parsley, pepper and salt to taste, one tablespoonful of lemon-juice.

After the head has been thoroughly cleaned, and the brains removed, soak it in warm water to blanch it. Lay the brains also into warm water to soak, and let them remain for about an hour. Put the head into a stewpan, with sufficient cold water to cover it, and when it boils, add a little salt; take off every particle of scum as it rises, and boil the head until perfectly tender. Boil the brains, chop them, and mix with them melted butter, minced parsley, pepper, salt, and lemon-juice in the above proportion. Take up the head, skin the tongue, and put it on a small dish with the brains round it. Have ready some parsley and butter, smother the head with it, and the remainder send to table in a tureen. Bacon, ham, pickled pork, or a pig's cheek are indispensable with calf's head. The brains are sometimes chopped with hard-boiled eggs.

## CALF'S HEAD CHEESE.

Boil a calf's head in water enough to cover it, until the meat leaves the bones, then take it with a skimmer into a wooden bowl or tray; take from it every particle of bone; chop it small; season with pepper and salt; a heaping tablespoonful of salt, and a teaspoonful of pepper will be sufficient; if liked, add a tablespoonful of finely chopped sweet herbs; lay a cloth in a colander, put the minced meat into it, then fold the cloth closely over it, lay a plate over, and on it a gentle weight. When cold it may be sliced thin for supper or sandwiches. Spread each slice with made mustard.

## BOILED CALF'S FEET AND PARSLEY BUTTER.

Two calf's feet, two slices of bacon, two ounces of butter, two tablespoonfuls of lemon-juice, salt and whole pepper to taste, one onion, a bunch of savory herbs, four cloves, one blade of mace, water, parsley and butter.

Procure two white calf's feet; bone them as far as the first joint, and put them into warm water to soak for two hours. Then put the bacon, butter, lemon-juice, onion, herbs, spices, and seasoning into a stewpan; lay in the feet, and pour in just sufficient water to cover the whole. Stew gently for about three hours; take out the feet, dish them, and cover with parsley and butter.

The liquor they were boiled in should be strained and put by in a clean basin for use; it will be found very good as an addition to gravies, etc., etc.

## CALF'S LIVER AND BACON.

Two or three pounds of liver, bacon, pepper and salt to taste, a small piece of butter, flour, two tablespoonfuls of lemon-juice, one-quarter pint of water.

Cut the liver in thin slices, and cut as many slices of bacon as there are of liver; fry the bacon first, then put that on a hot dish before the fire. Fry the liver in the fat which comes from the bacon, after seasoning it with pepper and salt, and dredging over it a very little flour. Turn the liver occasionally to prevent its burning, and when done, lay it round the dish with a piece of bacon between each. Pour away the bacon fat, put in a small piece of butter, dredge in a little flour, add the lemon-juice and water, give one boil, and pour it in the *middle* of the dish.

## SWEETBREAD.

Three sweetbreads, egg, and bread-crumbs, oiled butter, three slices of toast, brown gravy.

Choose large white sweetbreads; put them into warm water to draw out the blood, and to improve the color; let them remain for rather more than one hour; then put them into boiling water, and allow them to simmer for about ten minutes, which renders them firm. Take them up, drain them, brush over the egg, sprinkle with bread-crumbs; dip them in egg again, and then into more bread-crumbs. Drop on them a little oiled butter, and put the sweetbreads into a moderately heated oven, and let them bake for nearly three-quarters of an hour. Make three pieces of toast; place the sweetbreads on the toast, and pour round but not over them, a good brown gravy.

## EGGED VEAL HASH.

Chop fine remnants of cold roast veal. Moisten with the gravy or water. When hot, break into it three or four eggs, according to the quantity of veal. When the eggs are cooked, stir into it a spoonful of butter, and serve quickly. If to your taste, shake in a little parsley. Should you lack quantity, half a cup of fine stale bread-crumbs are no disadvantage.

## ROAST BEEF, WITH YORKSHIRE PUDDING.

Have your meat ready for roasting on Saturday, always. Roast upon a grating of several clean sticks (not pine) laid over the dripping-pan. Dash a cup of boiling water over the beef when it goes into the oven; baste often, and see that the fat does not scorch. About three-quarters of an hour before it is done, mix the pudding.

## YORKSHIRE PUDDING.

One pint of milk, four eggs, whites and yolks beaten separately; two cups of flour—prepared flour is best; one teaspoonful of salt.

Use less flour if the batter grows too stiff. Mix quickly; pour off the fat from the top of the gravy in the dripping pan, leaving just enough to prevent the pudding from sticking to the bottom. Pour in the batter and continue to roast the beef, letting the dripping fall upon the pudding below. The oven should be brisk by this time. Baste the meat with the gravy you have taken out to make room for the batter. In serving, cut the pudding into squares and lay about the meat in the dish. It is very delicious.

## BEEF HEART BAKED OR ROASTED.

Cut a beef heart in two, take out the strings from the inside; wash it with warm water, rub the inside with pepper and salt, and fill it with a stuffing made of bread and butter moistened with water, and seasoned with pepper and salt, and, if liked, a sprig of thyme made fine; put it together and tie a string around it, rub the outside with pepper and salt; stick bits of butter on, then dredge flour over and set it on a trivet, or muffin rings, in a dripping-pan; put a pint of water in to baste with, then roast it before a hot fire, or in a hot oven; turn it around and baste frequently. One hour will roast or bake it; when done, take it up, cut a lemon in thick slices, and put it in the pan with a bit of butter, dredged in a teaspoonful of flour; let it brown; add a small teacup of boiling water, stir it smooth, and serve in a gravy tureen.

## BEEF KIDNEY.

Cut the kidney into thin slices, flour them, and fry of a nice brown. When done, make a gravy in the pan by pouring away the fat, putting in a small piece of butter, one-quarter pint of boiling water, pepper and salt, and a tablespoonful of mushroom catsup. Let the gravy just boil up, pour over the kidney, and serve.

## POTTED BEEF.

Two pounds of lean beef, one tablespoonful of water, one-quarter pound of butter, a seasoning to taste of salt, Cayenne, pounded mace, and black pepper. Procure a nice piece of lean beef, as free as possible from gristle, skin, etc., and put it into a jar (if at hand, one with a lid) with one teaspoonful of water. Cover it *closely*, and put the jar into a saucepan of boiling water, letting the water come within two inches of the top of the jar. Boil gently for three and a half hours, then take the beef, chop it very small with a chopping-knife, and pound it thoroughly in a mortar. Mix with it by degrees, all, or a portion of the gravy that will have run from it, and a little clarified butter; add the seasoning, put it in small pots for use, and cover with a little butter just warmed and poured over. If much gravy is added to it, it will keep but a short time; on the contrary, if a large proportion of butter is used, it may be preserved for some time.

## BOILED TONGUE.

One tongue, a bunch of savory herbs, water. In choosing a tongue, ascertain how long it has been dried or pickled, and select one with a smooth skin, which denotes its being young and tender. If a dried one, and rather hard, soak it at least for twelve hours previous to cooking it; if, however, it is fresh from the pickle, two or three hours will be sufficient for it to remain in soak. Put the tongue into a stewpan with plenty of cold water and a bunch of savory herbs; let it gradually come to a boil, skim well, and simmer very gently until tender. Peel off the skin, garnish with tufts of cauliflowers or Brussels sprouts, and serve. Boiled tongue is frequently sent to table with boiled poultry, instead of ham, and is, by many persons, preferred. If to serve cold, peel it, fasten it down to a piece of board by sticking a fork through the root, and another through the top, to straighten it. When cold, glaze it, and put a paper ruche round the root, and garnish with tufts of parsley.

## FRICASSEED TRIPE.

Cut a pound of tripe in narrow strips, put a small cup of water or milk to it, add a bit of butter the size of an egg; dredge in a large teaspoonful of flour, or work it with the butter; season with pepper and salt, let it simmer gently for half an hour, serve hot. A bunch of parsley cut small and put with it is an improvement.

## BROILED TRIPE.

Prepare tripe as for frying; lay it on a gridiron over a clear fire of coals, let it broil gently; when one side is a fine brown, turn the other side (it must be nearly done through before turning); take it up on a hot dish, butter it, and if liked, add a little catsup or vinegar to the gravy.

## ROAST RABBIT.

Empty, skin, and thoroughly wash the rabbit; wipe it dry, line the inside with sausage-meat and force-meat (the latter of bread-crumbs, well-seasoned, and worked up). Sew the stuffing inside, skewer back the head between the shoulders, cut off the fore joints of the shoulders and legs, bring them close to the body, and secure them by means of a skewer. Wrap the rabbit in buttered paper, keep it well basted, and a few minutes before it is done remove the paper, flour and froth it, and let it acquire a nice brown color. It should be done in three-quarters of an hour. Take out the skewers, and serve with brown gravy and red-currant jelly. To bake the rabbit, proceed in the same manner as above; in a good oven it will take about the same time as roasting. Most cooks garnish the rabbit with slices of lemon and serve up with currant jelly. Sometimes the head is cut off before sending to the table; but this is a matter of individual taste.

## STEWED RABBIT, Larded.

One rabbit, a few strips of bacon, rather more than one pint of good broth or stock, a bunch of savory herbs, salt and pepper to taste, thickening of butter and flour, one glass of sherry. Well wash the rabbit, cut it into quarters, lard them with slips of bacon, and fry them; then put them into a stewpan with the broth, herbs, and a seasoning of pepper and salt; simmer gently until the rabbit is tender, then strain the gravy, thicken it with butter and flour, add the sherry, give one boil, pour it over the rabbit, and serve. Garnish with slices of cut lemon.

## FRICASSEED RABBITS.

The best way of cooking rabbits is to fricassee them. Cut them up, or disjoint them. Put them into a stewpan; season them with Cayenne pepper, salt and some chopped parsley. Pour in a pint of warm water (or of veal broth, if you have it) and stew it over a slow fire till the rabbits are quite tender; adding (when they are about half done) some bits of butter rolled in flour. Just before you take it from the fire, enrich the gravy with a gill or more of thick cream with some nutmeg grated into it. Stir the gravy well, but take care not to let it boil after the cream is in, lest it curdle. Put the pieces of rabbit on a hot dish, and pour the gravy over them.

## A PRETTY DISH OF VENISON.

Cut a breast of venison in steaks, make quarter of a pound of butter hot, in a pan, rub the steaks over with a mixture of a little salt and pepper, dip them in wheat flour, or rolled crackers, and fry a rich brown; when both sides are done, take them up on a dish, and put a tin cover over; dredge a heaping teaspoonful of flour into the butter in the pan, stir it with a spoon until it is brown, without burning, put to it a small teacup of boiling water, with a tablespoonful of currant jelly dissolved into it, stir it for a few minutes, then strain it over the meat and serve. A glass of wine, with a tablespoonful of white sugar dissolved in it, may be used for the gravy, instead of the jelly and water. Venison may be boiled, and served with boiled vegetables, pickled beets, etc., and sauce.

## TO BOIL VENISON STEAKS.

Let the gridiron become hot, rub the bars with a bit of suet, then lay on the steaks, having dipped them in rolled crackers or wheat flour, and set it over a bright, clear, but not fierce fire of coals; when one side is done, take the steak carefully over the steak dish, and hold it so that the blood may fall into the dish, then turn them on the gridiron, let it broil nicely; set a steak dish where it will become hot, put on a bit of butter the size of an egg for each pound of venison, put to it a saltspoon of salt, and the same of black pepper, put to it a tablespoonful of currant jelly, made liquid with a tablespoonful of hot water or wine, lay the steaks on, turn them once or twice in the gravy, and serve hot. Or they may be simply broiled, and served with butter, pepper, and salt; or having broiled one side, and turned the steaks, lay thin slices of lemon over, and serve in the dish with the steaks.

## BEEFSTEAK AND KIDNEY PUDDING.

Two pounds of rump-steak, two kidneys, seasoning to taste of salt and black pepper, suet crust made with milk (*see* PASTRY), in the proportion of six ounces of suet to each one pound of flour.

*Mode:* Procure some tender rump-steak (that which has been hung a little time), and divide it into pieces about an inch square, and cut each kidney into eight pieces. Line the dish (of which we have given an engraving) with crust made with suet and flour in the above proportion, leaving a small piece of crust to overlap the edge. Then cover the bottom with a portion of the steak and a few pieces of kidney; season with salt and pepper (some add a little flour to thicken the gravy, but it is not necessary), and then add another layer of steak kidney, and seasoning. Proceed in this manner till the dish is full, when pour in sufficient water to come within two inches of the top of the basin. Moisten the edges of the crust, cover the pudding over, press the two crusts together, that the gravy may not escape, and turn up the overhanging paste. Wring out a cloth in hot water, flour it, and tie up the pudding; put it into boiling water, and let it boil for at least four hours. If the water diminishes, always replenish with some, hot in a jug, as the pudding should be kept covered all the time, and not allowed to stop boiling. When the cloth is removed, cut a round piece in the top of the crust, to prevent the pudding bursting, and send it to table in the basin, either in an ornamental dish, or with a napkin pinned round it. Serve quickly.

## BREAKFAST DISHES.

### HASHED COLD MEAT.

Take your bones, and stew them in a little water with an onion, some salt and pepper, and, if you like, a little savory herbs; when the goodness is all out of the bones, and it tastes nice, thicken the gravy with a teaspoonful of corn starch, and if it is not very strong put in a bit of butter, then place your stewpan on the hot hearth, and put in your slices of meat. Warm but not boil. Serve with toasted bread.

### POTATO AND BEEF HASH.

Mince some cold beef, a little fat with the lean, put to it as much cold boiled potatoes chopped as you like, (the quantity as of meat or twice as much), season with pepper and salt; add as much gravy or hot water as will make it moist, then put in a stewpan over a gentle fire; dredge in a small quantity of wheat flour; stir it about with a spoon, cover the stewpan, and let it simmer for half an hour—take care that it does not burn. Dish it with or without a slice of toast under it, for breakfast. This hash may be made without potatoes, if water is used instead of gravy, a bit of butter may be added, more or less, according to the proportion of fat with the lean meat.

## DRIED BEEF.

The most common way of serving dried or smoked beef is to shave it into thin slices or chips, raw; but a more savory relish may be made of it with little trouble. Put the slices of uncooked beef into a frying pan with just enough boiling water to cover them; set them over the fire for ten minutes, drain off all the water, and with a knife and fork cut the meat into small bits. Return to the pan, which should be hot, with a tablespoonful of butter and a little pepper. Have ready some well-beaten eggs, allowing four to a half pound of beef; stir them into the pan with the minced meat and toss and stir the mixture for about two minutes. Send to table in a covered dish.

## CHICKEN CUTLETS.

Season pieces of cold chicken or turkey with salt and pepper. Dip in melted butter; let this cool on the meat, and dip in beaten egg and in fine bread-crumbs. Fry in butter till a delicate brown. Serve on slices of hot toast, with either a white or curry sauce poured around. Pieces of cold veal make a nice dish, if prepared in this manner.

## BEEF PATTIES.

Chop fine some cold beef; beat two eggs and mix with the meat and add a little milk, melted butter, and salt and pepper. Make into rolls and fry.

## JELLIED VEAL.

Boil the veal tender, pick it up fine, put in a mold, add the water it was boiled in, and set it in a cold place; season with salt and pepper to taste; a layer of hard-boiled eggs improves it.

### RICE AND MEAT CROQUETTES.

One cupful of boiled rice, one cupful of finely-chopped cooked meat—any kind; one teaspoonful of salt, a little pepper, two tablespoonfuls of butter, half a cupful of milk, one egg. Put the milk on to boil, and add the meat, rice and seasoning. When this boils, add the egg, well beaten; stir one minute. After cooling, shape, dip in egg and crumbs, and fry as before directed.

### AMERICAN TOAST.

To one egg thoroughly beaten, put one cup of sweet milk and a little salt. Slice light bread and dip into the mixture, allowing each slice to absorb some of the milk; then brown on a hot buttered griddle; spread with butter, and serve hot.

### MEAT AND POTATOES.

Mince beef or mutton, small, with onions, pepper and salt; add a little gravy, put into scalloped shells or small cups, making them three parts full, and fill them up with potatoes mashed with a little cream, put a bit of butter on the top and brown them in an oven.

### BREADED SAUSAGES.

Wipe the sausages dry. Dip them in beaten egg and bread-crumbs. Put them in the frying-basket and plunge into boiling fat. Cook ten minutes. Serve with a garnish of toasted bread and parsley.

### HAM CROQUETTES.

One cupful of finely-chopped cooked ham, one of bread-crumbs, two of hot mashed potatoes, one large tablespoonful of butter, three eggs, a speck of Cayenne. Beat the ham, Cayenne, butter, and two of the eggs into the potato. Let the mixture cool slightly, and shape it like croquettes. Roll in the bread-crumbs, dip in beaten egg and again in crumbs, put in the frying-basket and plunge into boiling fat. Cook two minutes. Drain, and serve.

## A NICE BREAKFAST DISH.

Chopped cold meat well seasoned; wet with gravy, if convenient, put it on a platter; then take cold rice made moist with milk and one egg, seasoned with pepper and salt; if not sufficient rice, add powdered bread-crumbs; place this around the platter quite thick; set in oven to heat and brown.

## CHICKEN IN JELLY.

A little cold chicken (about one pint), one cupful of water or stock, one-fifth of a box of gelatine, half a teaspoonful of curry powder, salt, pepper. Cut the meat from the bones of a chicken left from dinner. Put the bones on with water to cover, and boil down to one cupful. Put the gelatine to soak in one-fourth of a cupful of cold water. When the stock is reduced as much as is necessary, strain and season. Add the curry and chicken. Season and simmer ten minutes; then add the gelatine, and stir on the table until it is dissolved. Turn all into a mold, and set away to harden. This makes a nice relish for tea or lunch. If you have mushrooms, omit the curry, and cut four of them into dice. Stir into the mixture while cooking. This dish can be varied by using the whites of hard-boiled eggs, or bits of boiled ham. To serve: Dip the mold in warm water, and turn out on the dish. Garnish with parsley.

## A GOOD DISH.

Minced cold beef or lamb; if beef put in a pinch of pulverized cloves; if lamb, a pinch of summer savory to season it, very little pepper and some salt, and put it in a baking-dish; mash potatoes and mix them with cream and butter and a little salt, and spread them over the meat; beat up an egg with cream or milk, a very little, spread it over the potatoes, and bake it a short time, sufficient to warm it through and brown the potatoes.

## POULTRY, GAME, ETC.

In choosing poultry, the best way to determine whether it is young, is to try the skin under the leg or wing; if it is easily broken, it is young; or, turn the wing backwards; if the joint yields readily, it is tender; a fat fowl is best for any purpose.

After a chicken or fowl is killed, plunge it into a pot of scalding hot water; then pluck off the feathers, taking care not to tear the skin; when it is picked clean, roll up a sheet of white wrapping paper, set fire to it, singe off all the hairs. Poultry should be carefully picked, and nicely singed.

If a fowl is fresh killed, the vent will be close, and the flesh have a pleasant smell.

### ROAST TURKEY.

Carefully pluck the bird, singe it with white paper, and wipe it thoroughly with a cloth; draw it, preserve the liver and gizzard, and be particular not to break the gall-bag, as no washing will remove the bitter taste it imparts where it once touches. Wash it *inside* well, and wipe it thoroughly with a dry cloth; the *outside* merely requires wiping nicely. Cut off the neck close to the back, but leave enough of the crop-skin to turn over; break the leg-bones close below the knee; draw out the strings from the thighs, and flatten the breast-bone to make it look plump. Have ready your dressing of bread-crumbs, mixed with butter, pepper, salt, thyme or sweet marjoram; fill the breast with this, and sew the neck over to the back. Be particular that the turkey is firmly trussed. Dredge it lightly with flour, and put a piece of butter into the basting-ladle; as the butter melts, baste the bird with it. When of a nice brown and well-frothed, serve with a tureen of good brown gravy and one of bread-sauce. The liver should be put under one pinion, and the gizzard under the other. Fried sausages are a favorite addition to roast turkey; they make a pretty garnish, besides adding much to the flavor. When these are not at hand, a few force-meat balls should be placed round the dish as a garnish. Turkey may also be stuffed with sausage-meat, and a chestnut force-meat with the same sauce is, by many persons, much esteemed as an accompaniment to this favorite dish.

SECOND RECIPE.—After drawing and cleansing the turkey, prepare a dressing of chopped sausage and bread-crumbs, mixing in butter, pepper, salt and thyme to flavor. Fill the craw and the body of the turkey with this, and sew up carefully. Dredge with flour and put in the oven to roast, basting freely first with butter and water, then with the gravy from the pan. The time it takes to roast will depend both on the age and the weight of the turkey. If you have a good fire, you will be safe to allow ten minutes or so to the pound. Roast to a fine brown, and serve with the chopped giblets, which should be well stewed; add cranberry sauce.

## BOILED TURKEY.

Hen turkeys are the best for boiling. They are the whitest, and if nicely kept, tenderest. Of course the sinews must be drawn, and they ought to be trussed with the legs out, so as to be easily carved. Take care to clean the ani-

TURKEY TRUSSED FOR BRAIZING.
A good turkey will be recognized by the whiteness of the flesh and fat. Beware of those with long hairs, and whose flesh, on the legs and back, is of a violet tinge.

GAME.
Pheasants should be selected with the spur but little developed; the tenderness of the bird is known by trying the flesh of the pinion. Wood-cocks, as well as water-fowl (such as wild ducks, teal, widgeon, &c.), can be tried by pinching the pinion and breast. The age of partridges can be ascertained by examining the long feathers of the wing: round at the tip in an old bird, and pointed in a young.

### THE TABLE LAID—THE SOUP SERVED.

A dinner party should consist of an equal number of gentlemen and ladies, those being invited who it is thought will like to meet. It is not necessary to introduce all the members of the party to each other; in a friend's house all talk to each other without introduction, and without this forming any subsequent acquaintance, unless such is desired by both parties.

### DESSERT.

All the dishes for dessert are now usually placed down the centre of the table, dried and fresh fruit alternately, the former being arranged on small round or oval glass plates, and the latter on the dishes with stems. The fruit should always be gathered on the same day that it is required for the table, and should be tastefully arranged on the dishes, with leaves between and around it. Cheese, plain and grated, is very often served at dessert.

mal well after it has been singed. Place the fowl in a sufficiently large pot with clean water sufficient to cover it, and little more; let the fire be a clear one, but not too fierce, as the slower the turkey boils the plumper it will be. Skim carefully and constantly, and simmer for two hours and a half in the case of a large fowl, and two hours for a smaller beast, and from an hour and ten to forty minutes for still smaller turkeys. Some people boil their turkeys in a floured cloth. I don't; the whiteness being mostly in the animal itself. My stuffing for a boiled turkey is thought good. I prepare it of crumbs of stale bread, with a little marrow or butter, some finely-shred parsley, and two dozen of small oysters, minus their beards, of course, and neatly trimmed. Stuff with this and a little chopped ham in addition, if desired.

## TO ROAST A FOWL OR CHICKEN.

Have a bright, clear, and steady fire for roasting poultry; prepare it as directed; spit it, put a pint of hot water in the dripping-pan, add to it a small tablespoonful of salt, and a small teaspoonful of pepper, baste frequently, and let it roast quickly, without scorching; when nearly done, put a piece of butter the size of a large egg to the water in the pan; when it melts, baste with it, dredge a little flour over, baste again, and let it finish; half an hour will roast a full grown chicken, if the fire is right. When done take it up, let the giblets (heart, liver, and gizzard) boil tender, and chop them very fine, and put them in the gravy; add a tablespoonful of browned flour and a bit of butter, stir it over the fire for a few minutes, then serve in a gravy tureen. Or put the giblets in the pan and let them roast.

## BOILED CHICKENS.

Clean, wash, and stuff as for roasting. Baste a floured cloth around each, and put into a pot with enough boiling water to cover them well. The hot water cooks the skin at once, and prevents the escape of the juices. The broth will not be so rich as if the fowls are put on in cold water, but this is proof that the meat will be more nutritious and better flavored. Stew very slowly, for the first half hour especially. Boil an hour or more, guiding yourself by size and tougness. Serve with egg or bread sauce.

## BROILED CHICKEN.

Prepare in the same way as for boiling, cut them in two through the back, and flatten them; place on a cold gridiron over a nice red fire. After a little time, when they have become thoroughly hot, set them on a plate or other dish, and lard them well with a piece of butter; pepper and salt them to taste, chiefly on the inside, then place them on the brander and continue turning till done—they will take fully twenty minutes. Serve hot, with a little dab of butter and plenty of stewed mushrooms—a delightful dish.

## FRIED CHICKEN.

Cut the chicken in pieces, lay it in salt and water, which change several times; roll each piece in flour; fry in very hot lard or butter; season with salt and pepper; fry parsley with them also. Make a gravy of cream seasoned with salt, pepper, and a little mace, thickened with a little flour in the pan in which the chickens were fried, pouring off the lard.

## FRICASSEE OF CHICKEN.

Cut into joints, scald and skin, place in a stewpan, with two raw onions cut into eight parts, a little chopped parsley, salt and pepper, and the least squeeze of lemon-juice. Add a bit of butter as large as an egg, and fill in a pint of water. Stew for an hour under a very close lid, then lift and strain off the gravy, into which beat gradually a teacupful of cream and the yolks of two eggs; heat up the gravy, taking care that it does not boil, and pour it over the fricassee.

## TO CURRY CHICKEN.

Slice an onion and brown in a little butter; add a spoonful of curry powder; allow it to remain covered for a few minutes to cook; add a little more butter and put in chicken, veal, etc., etc.; cut up small, thicken with a little flour. This is excellent.

## PRESSED CHICKEN.

Cut up the fowls and place in a kettle with a tight cover, so as to retain the steam; put about two teacups of water and plenty of salt and pepper over the chicken, then let it cook until the meat cleaves easily from the bones; cut or chop all the meat (freed from skin, bone and gristle) about as for chicken salad; season well, put into a dish and pour the remnant of the juice in which it was cooked over it. This will jelly when cold, and can then be sliced or set on the table in shape. Nice for tea or lunch. The knack of making this simple dish is not having too much water; it will not jelly if too weak, or if the water is allowed to boil away entirely while cooking.

## CHICKEN POT-PIE.

Skin and cut up the fowls into joints, and put the neck, legs and back bones in a stew pan, with a little water, an onion, a bunch of savory herbs, and a blade of mace; let these stew for an hour, and, when done, strain off the liquor; this is for gravy. Put a layer of fowl at the bottom of a pie-dish, then a layer of ham, then one of force-meat and hard-boiled eggs, cut in rings; between the layers put a seasoning of pounded mace, nutmeg, pepper and salt. Pour in about half a pint of water, border the edge of dish with puff-crust, put on the cover, ornament the top and glaze it by brushing over it the yolk of an egg. Bake for about an hour and a half, and, when done, pour in at the top the gravy made from the bones.

## A CHICKEN SALAD.

Take a fine white bunch of celery (four or five heads), scrape and wash it white; reserve the delicate green leaves; shred the white part like straws, lay this in a glass, or white china dish, in the form of a nest. Mince all the white meat of a boiled, or white stewed fowl, without the skin, and put it in the nest.

Make a salad dressing thus: Rub the yolks of two hard-boiled eggs to a smooth paste, with a dessertspoonful of salad oil, or melted butter; add to it two teaspoonfuls of made mustard, and a small teaspoonful of fine white sugar, and put to it gradually (stirring it in) a large cup of strong vinegar.

Make a wreath of the most delicate leaves of the celery, around the edge of the nest, between it and the chicken; pour the dressing over the chicken, when ready to serve; if the dressing is poured over too soon it will discolor the celery.

White heart lettuce may be used for the nest instead of celery.

## JELLIED CHICKEN.

Boil a fowl until it will slip easily from the bones; let the water be reduced to about one pint in boiling; pick the meat from the bones in good sized pieces, taking out all gristle, fat, and bones; place in a wet mold; skim the fat from the liquor; a little butter; pepper and salt to the taste, and one-half ounce of gelatine. When this dissolves, pour it hot over the chicken. The liquor must be seasoned pretty high, for the chicken absorbes.

## CHICKEN PATES.

Mince chicken that has been previously roasted or boiled, and season well; stir into this a sauce made of half a pint of milk, into which while boiling a teaspoonful of corn starch has been added to thicken, season with butter, about a teaspoonful, and salt and pepper to taste. Have ready small pate pans lined with a good puff paste. Bake the crust in a brisk oven; then fill the pans and set in the oven a few minutes to brown very slightly.

## SAGE-AND-ONION STUFFING, FOR GEESE, DUCKS AND PORK.

Four large onions, ten sage-leaves, one-quarter pound of bread-crumbs, one and one-half ounce of butter, salt and pepper to taste, one egg. Peel the onions, put them into boiling water, let them simmer for five minutes or rather longer, and, just before they are taken out, put in the sage-leaves for a minute or two to take off their rawness. Chop both these very fine, add the bread, seasoning, and butter, and work the whole together with the yolk of an egg, when the stuffing will be ready for use. It should be rather highly seasoned, and the sage-leaves should be very finely chopped. Many cooks do not parboil the onions in the manner just stated, but merely use them raw. The stuffing then, however, is not nearly so mild, and, to many tastes, its strong flavor would be very objectionable. When made for goose, a portion of the liver of the bird, simmered for a few minutes and very finely minced, is frequently added to this stuffing; and where economy is studied, the egg may be dispensed with.

## TO ROAST A GOOSE.

Having drawn and singed the goose, wipe out the inside with a cloth, and sprinkle in some pepper and salt. Make a stuffing of four good-sized onions, minced fine, and half their quantity of green sage-leaves, minced also, a large tea-cupful of grated bread-crumbs, a piece of butter the size of a walnut, and the beaten yolks of two eggs, with a little pepper and salt. Mix the whole together, and incorporate them well. Put the stuffing into the goose, and press it in hard; but do not entirely fill up the cavity, as the mixture will swell in cooking. Tie the goose securely round with a greased or wetted string; and paper the breast to prevent it from scorching. The fire must be brisk and well kept up. It will require from two hours to two and a half to roast. Baste it at first with a little salt and water, and then with its own gravy. Take off the paper when the goose is about half done, and dredge it with a little flour towards the last. Having parboiled the liver and heart, chop them and put them into the gravy, which must be skimmed well and thickened with a little brown flour.

Send apple sauce to table with the goose; also mashed potatoes.

A goose may be stuffed entirely with potatoes, boiled and mashed with milk, butter, pepper and salt.

You may make a gravy of the giblets, that is the neck, pinions, liver, heart and gizzard, stewed in a little water, thickened with butter, rolled in flour, and seasoned with pepper and salt. Before you send it to table, take out all but the liver and heart; mince them and leave them in the gravy. This gravy is by many preferred to that which comes from the goose in roasting. It is well to have both.

If a goose is old it is useless to cook it, as when hard and tough it cannot be eaten.

## ROAST DUCKS.

Wash and dry the ducks carefully. Make a stuffing of sage and onion; insert, and sew up completely that the seasoning may not escape. If tender, ducks do not require more than an hour to roast. Keep them well basted, and a few minutes before serving, dredge lightly with flour, to make them froth and look plump. Send to table hot, with a good brown gravy poured not *round* but *over* them. Accompany with currant jelly, and, if in season, green peas.

## ROAST PIGEONS.

Clean the pigeons, and stuff them the same as chickens; leave the feet on, dip them into scalding water, strip off the skin, cross them, and tie them together below the breast-bone; or cut them off; the head may remain on; if so, dip it in scalding water, and pick it clean; twist the wings back, put the liver between the right wing and the body, and turn the head under the other; rub the outside of each bird with a mixture of pepper and salt; spit them, and put some water in the dripping-pan; for each bird put a bit of butter the size of a small egg, put them before a hot fire, and let them roast quickly; baste frequently; half an hour will do them; when nearly done, dredge them with wheat flour and baste with the butter in the pan; turn them, that they may be nicely and easily browned; when done, take them up, set the pan over the fire, make a thin batter of a teaspoonful of wheat flour, and cold water; when the gravy is boiling hot, stir it in; continue to stir it for a few minutes, until it is brown, then pour it through a gravy sieve into a tureen, and serve with the pigeons.

## TO MAKE A BIRD'S NEST.

Boil some yellow macaroni gently, until it is quite swelled out and tender, then cut it in pieces, the length of a finger, and lay them on a dish like a straw nest.

Truss pigeons with the heads on, (having scalded and picked them clean), turned under the left wing, leave the feet on, and having stewed them, arrange them as in a nest; pour the gravy over and serve.

The nest may be made of boiled rice, or bread cut in pieces, the length and thickness of a finger, and fried a nice brown in hot lard, seasoned with pepper and salt. Or, make it of bread, toasted a yellow brown. Any small birds may be stewed or roasted, and served in this way.

## PIGEONS IN JELLY.

Wash and truss one dozen pigeons. Put them in a kettle with four pounds of the shank of veal, six cloves, twenty-five pepper-corns, an onion that has been fried in one spoonful of butter, one stalk of celery, a bouquet of sweet herbs and four and a half quarts of water. Have the veal shank broken in small pieces. As soon as the contents of the kettle come to a boil, skim carefully, and set for three hours where they will just simmer. After they have been cooking one hour, add two tablespoonfuls of salt. When the pigeons are done, take them up, being careful not to break them, and remove the strings. Draw the kettle forward, where it will boil rapidly, and keep there for forty minutes; then strain the liquor through a napkin, and taste to see if seasoned enough. The water should have boiled down to two and a half quarts. Have two molds that will each hold six pigeons. Put a thin layer of the jelly in these, and set on ice to harden. When hard, arrange the pigeons in them, and cover with the jelly, which must be cold, but liquid. Place in the ice-chest for six, or, better still, twelve hours. There should be only one layer of the pigeons in the mold.

To serve: Dip the mold in a basin of warm water for one minute, and turn on a cold dish. Garnish with pickled beets and parsley. A Tartare sauce can be served with this dish.

If squabs are used, two hours will cook them. All small birds, as well as partridge, grouse, etc., can be prepared in the same manner. Remember that the birds must be cooked tender, and that the liquor must be so reduced that it will become jellied.

### PIGEON PIE.

Clean and truss three or four pigeons, rub the outside and in with a mixture of pepper and salt; rub the inside with a bit of butter, and fill it with a bread-and-butter stuffing, or mashed potatoes; sew up the slit, butter the sides of a tin basin or pudding-dish, and line (the sides only) with pie paste, rolled to quarter of an inch thickness; lay the birds in; for three large tame pigeons, cut quarter of a pound of sweet butter and put it over them, strew over a large teaspoonful of salt, and a small teaspoonful of pepper, with a bunch of finely-cut parsley, if liked; dredge a large table-spoonful of wheat flour over; put in water to nearly fill the pie; lay skewers across the top, cover with a puff paste crust; cut a slit in the middle, ornament the edge with leaves, braids, or shells of paste, and put it in a moderately hot or quick oven, for one hour; when nearly done, brush the top over with the yolk of an egg beaten with a little milk, and finish. The pigeons for this pie may be cut in two or more pieces, if preferred.

Any small birds may be done in this manner.

## WILD DUCKS.

Nearly all wild ducks are liable to have a fishy flavor, and when handled by inexperienced cooks, are sometimes uneatable from this cause. Before roasting them guard against this by parboiling them with a small carrot, peeled, put within each. This will absorb the unpleasant taste. An onion will have the same effect; but unless you mean to use onion in the stuffing, the carrot is preferable. In my own kitchen, I usually put in the onion, considering a suspicion of garlic a desideratum in roast duck, whether wild or tame.

## ROAST WILD DUCK.

Parboil as above directed; throw away the carrot or onion, lay in fresh water half an hour; stuff with breadcrumbs seasoned with pepper, salt, sage, and onion, and roast until brown and tender, basting for half the time with butter and water, then with the drippings. Add to the gravy, when you have taken up the ducks, a teaspoonful of currant jelly, and a pinch of Cayenne. Thicken with browned flour and serve in a tureen.

## WILD TURKEY.

Draw and wash the inside very carefully, as with all game. Domestic fowls are, or should be, put up without eating for at least twelve hours before they are killed; but we must shoot wild when we can get the chance, and of course it often happens that their crops are distended by a recent hearty meal of rank or green food. Wipe the cavity with a dry, soft cloth before you stuff. Have a rich force-meat, breadcrumbs, some bits of fat pork, chopped fine, pepper and salt. Moisten with milk, and beat in an egg and a couple of tablespoonfuls of melted butter. Baste with butter and water for the first hour, then three or four times with gravy; lastly, five or six times with melted butter. A generous and able housekeeper told me once that she always allowed a pound of butter for basting a large wild turkey. This was an extravagant quantity, but the meat is drier than that of the domestic fowl, and not nearly so fat. Dredge with flour at the last, froth with butter, and when he is of a tempting brown, serve. Skim the gravy, add a little hot water, pepper, thicken with the giblets chopped fine and browned flour, boil up, and pour into a tureen. At the South the giblets are not put in the gravy, but laid whole, one under each wing, when the turkey is dished. Garnish with small fried sausages, not larger than a dollar, crisped parsley between them. Send around currant jelly and cranberry sauce with it.

## TO ROAST SNIPES, WOODCOCKS, OR PLOVERS.

Pick them immediately; wipe them, and season them slightly with pepper and salt. Cut as many slices of bread as you have birds. Toast them brown, butter them, and lay them in the pan. Dredge the birds with flour, and put them in the oven with a brisk fire. Baste them with lard or fresh butter. They will be done in twenty or thirty minutes. Serve them up laid on the toast, and garnish with sliced orange, or with orange jelly.

## ROAST PARTRIDGE.

Choose young birds, with dark-colored bills and yellowish legs, and let them hang a few days, or there will be no flavor to the flesh, nor will it be tender. The time they should be kept entirely depends on the taste of those for whom they are intended, as what some persons would consider delicious, would be to others disgusting and offensive. They may be trussed with or without the head, the latter mode is now considered the most fashionable. Pluck, draw, and wipe the partridge carefully inside and out; cut off the head, leaving sufficient skin on the neck to skewer back; bring the legs close to the breast, between it and the side-bones, and pass a skewer through the pinions and thick part of the thighs. When the head is left on, it should be brought round and fixed on to the point of the skewer. When the bird is firmly and plumply trussed, roast it before a nice bright fire; keep it well basted, and a few minutes before serving, flour and froth it well. Dish it, and serve with gravy and bread-sauce, and send to table hot and quickly. A little of the gravy should be poured over the bird.

## ROAST QUAIL.

Pluck and draw the birds, rub a little butter over them, tie a strip of bacon over the breasts, and set them in the oven for twenty or twenty-five minutes.

## ROAST PRAIRIE CHICKEN.

The bird being a little strong, and its flesh when cooked a little dry, it should be either larded or wide strips of bacon or pork placed over its breast. A mild seasoned stuffing will improve the flavor of old birds. Dust a little flour over them, baste occasionally, and serve. Pheasants may be managed in the same manner

## LARDED GROUSE.

Clean and wash the grouse. Lard the breast and legs. Put a small skewer into the legs and through the tail. Tie firmly with twine. Dredge with salt, and rub the breast with soft butter; then dredge thickly with flour. Put into a quick oven. If to be very rare, cook twenty minutes; if wished better done, thirty minutes. The former time, as a general thing, suits gentlemen better, but thirty minutes is preferred by ladies. If the birds are cooked in a tin-kitchen, it should be for thirty or thirty-five minutes. When done, place on a hot dish, on which has been spread bread-sauce. Sprinkle fried crumbs over both grouse and sauce. Garnish with parsley. The grouse may, instead, be served on a hot dish, with the parsley garnish, and the sauce and crumbs served in separate dishes. The first method is the better, however, as you get in the sauce all the gravy that comes from the birds.

## PORK, HAMS, ETC.

To Choose Pork.—If the rind of pork is tough and thick, and cannot easily be impressed with the finger, it is old.

If fresh, the flesh will look cool and smooth; when moist or clammy it is stale. The knuckle is the first to become tainted.

Pork is often what is called measly, and is then almost poisonous; measly pork may easily be detected, the fat being full of small kernels. Swill or still-fed pork is not fit for curing; either dairy or corn-fed is good.

Fresh pork is in season from October to April.

In cutting up a large hog, it is first cut in two down the back and belly. The chine or back-bone should be cut out from each side the whole length, and is either boiled or roasted. The chine is considered the prime part. The sides of the hog are made into bacon, and the inside or ribs is cut with very little meat; this is the spare-rib.

## CURING HAMS.

Hang up the hams a week or ten days, the longer the tenderer and better, if kept perfectly sweet; mix for each good-sized ham, one teacup of salt, one tablespoon of molasses, one ounce of saltpetre; lay the hams in a clean dry tub; heat the mixture and rub well into the hams, especially around the bones and recesses; repeat the process once or twice, or until all the mixture is used; then let the hams lie two or three days, when they must be put for three weeks in brine strong enough to bear an egg; then soak eight hours in cold water; hang up to dry in the kitchen or other more convenient place for a week or more; smoke from three to five days, being careful not to heat the hams. Corn-cobs and apple-tree wood are good for smoking. The juices are better retained if smoked with the hock down. Tie up carefully in bags for the summer.

## TO ROAST A LEG OF PORK.

Take a sharp knife and score the skin across in narrow strips (you may cross it again so as to form diamonds) and rub in some powdered sage. Raise the skin at the knuckle and put in a stuffing of minced onion and sage, bread-crumbs, pepper, salt, and beaten yolk of egg. Fasten it down with a buttered string, or with skewers. You may make deep incisions in the meat of the large end of the leg, and stuff them also, pressing in the filling very hard Rub a little sweet oil all over the skin with a brush or a goose feather, to make it crisp and of a handsome brown. A leg of pork will require from three to four hours to roast

Moisten it all the time by brushing it with sweet oil, or with fresh butter tied in a rag. To baste it with its own drippings will make the skin tough and hard. Skim the fat carefully from the gravy, which should be thickened with a little flour.

A roast leg of pork should always be accompanied by apple sauce, and by mashed potatoes and mashed turnips.

## PORK AND BEANS.

Pick over carefully a quart of beans and let them soak over night; in the morning wash and drain in another water, put on to boil in cold water with half a teaspoon of soda; boil about thirty minutes (when done, the skin of a bean will crack if taken out and blown upon), drain, and put in an earthen pot first a slice of pork and then the beans, with two or three tablespoons of molasses. When the beans are in the pot, put in the centre half or three-fourths of a pound of well-washed salt pork with the rind scored in slices or squares, and uppermost; season with pepper and salt if needed; cover all over with hot water, and bake six hours or longer in a moderate oven, adding hot water as needed; they cannot be baked too long. Keep covered so that they will not burn on the top, but remove cover an hour or two before serving, to brown the top and crisp the pork.

## PORK SAUSAGES.

Take such a proportion of fat and lean pork as you like; chop it quite fine, and for every ten pounds of meat take four ounces of fine salt, and one of fine pepper; dried sage, or lemon thyme, finely powdered, may be added if liked; a teaspoonful of sage, and the same of ground allspice and cloves, to each ten pounds of meat. Mix the seasoning through the meat; pack it down in stone pots or put in muslin bags. Or fill the hog's or ox's guts, having first made them perfectly clean, thus: empty them, cut them in lengths, and lay them three or four days in salt and water, or weak lime water; turn them inside out once or twice, scrape them; then rinse them, and fill with the meat.

If you do not use the skins or guts, make the sausage meat up to the size and shape of sausages, dip them in beaten egg, and then into wheat flour, or rolled crackers, or simply into wheat flour, and fry in hot lard. Turn them, that every side may be a fine color. Serve hot, with boiled potatoes or hominy; either taken from the gravy, or after they are fried, pour a little boiling water into the gravy in the pan, and pour it over them; or first dredge in a teaspoonful of wheat flour, stir it until it is smooth and brown; then add a little boiling water, let it boil up once, then put it in the dish with the sausages.

Chopped onion and green parsley may be added to the sausage meat, when making ready to fry.

Or sausage meat may be tied in a muslin bag, and boiled, and served with vegetables; or let it become cold, and cut in slices.

### PORK CHOPS, STEAKS AND CUTLETS.

Fry or stew pork chops, after taking off the rind or skin, the same as for veal.

Cutlets and steaks are also fried, broiled, or stewed, the same as veal.

### ROAST PIG.

Thoroughly clean the pig, then rinse it in cold water, wipe it dry; then rub the inside with a mixture of salt and pepper, and if liked, a little pounded and sifted sage; make a stuffing thus: cut some wheat bread in slices half an inch thick, spread butter on to half its thickness, sprinkled with pepper and salt, and if liked, a little pounded sage and minced onion; pour enough hot water over the bread to make it moist or soft, then fill the body with it and sew it together, or tie a cord around it to keep the dressing in, then spit it; put a pint of water in the dripping-pan, put into it a tablespoonful of salt, and a teaspoonful of pepper, let the fire be hotter at each end than in the middle, put the pig down at a little distance from the fire, baste it as it begins to roast, and gradually draw it nearer; continue to baste occasionally; turn it that it may be evenly cooked; when the eyes drop out it is done; or a better rule is to judge by the weight, fifteen minutes for each pound of meat, if the fire is right.

Have a bright clear fire, with a bed of coals at the bottom; first put the roast at a little distance, and gradually draw it nearer; when the pig is done stir up the fire, take a coarse cloth with a good bit of butter in it, and wet the pig all over with it, and when the crackling is crisp take it up; dredge a little flour into the gravy, let it boil up once, and having boiled the heart, liver, etc., tender, and chopped it fine, add it to the gravy, give it one boil, then serve.

## PIG'S CHEEK,

Is smoked and boiled like ham with vegetables; boiled cabbage or fried parsnips may be served with it.

## ROAST SPARE-RIB.

Trim off the rough ends neatly, crack the ribs across the middle, rub with salt and sprinkle with pepper, fold over, stuff with turkey-dressing, sew up tightly, place in dripping-pan with pint of water, baste frequently, turning over once so as to bake both sides equally until a rich brown.

## PORK FRITTERS.

Have at hand a thick batter of Indian meal and flour; cut a few slices of pork and fry them in the frying-pan until the fat is fried out; cut a few more slices of the pork, dip them in the batter, and drop them in the bubbling fat, seasoning with salt and pepper; cook until light brown, and eat while hot.

## BAKED HAM.

Cover your ham with cold water, and simmer gently just long enough to loosen the skin, so that it can be pulled off. This will probably be from two to three hours, according to the size of your ham. When skinned, put in a dripping-pan in the oven, pour over it a teacup of vinegar and one of hot water, in which dissolve a teaspoonful of English mustard, bake slowly, basting with the liquid, for two hours. Then cover the ham all over to the depth of one inch with coarse brown sugar, press it down firmly, and do not baste again until the sugar has formed a thick crust, which it will soon do in a very slow oven. Let it remain a full hour in, after covering with the sugar, until it becomes a rich golden brown. When done, drain from the liquor in the pan and put on a dish to cool. When it is cool, but not cold, press by turning another flat dish on top, with a weight over it. You will never want to eat ham cooked in any other way when you have tasted this, and the pressing makes it cut firmly for sandwiches or slicing.

## TO BOIL A HAM.

Wash thoroughly with a cloth. Select a small size to boil, put it in a large quantity of cold water, and boil twenty minutes for each pound, allowing it to boil slowly;

take off the rind while hot and put in the oven to brown half an hour; remove and trim.

## TO BROIL HAM.

Cut some slices of ham, quarter of an inch thick, lay them in hot water for half an hour, or give them a scalding in a pan over the fire; then take them up, and lay them on a gridiron, over bright coals; when the outside is browned, turn the other; then take the slices on a hot dish, butter them freely, sprinkle pepper over and serve. Or, after scalding them, wipe them dry, dip each slice in beaten egg, and then into rolled crackers, and fry or broil.

## FRIED HAM AND EGGS (a Breakfast Dish).

Cut the ham into slices, and take care that they are of the same thickness in every part. Cut off the rind, and if the ham should be particularly hard and salt, it will be found an improvement to soak it for about ten minutes in hot water, and then dry it in a cloth. Put it into a cold frying-pan, set it over the fire, and turn the slices three or four times whilst they are cooking. When done, place them on a dish, which should be kept hot in front of the fire during the time the eggs are being poached. Poach the eggs; slip them on to the slices of ham, and serve quickly.

## HAM TOAST.

Mince finely a quarter of a pound of cooked ham with an anchovy boned and washed; add a little Cayenne and pounded mace; beat up two eggs; mix with the mince, and add just sufficient milk to keep it moist; make it quite hot, and serve on small rounds of toast or fried bread.

## HEAD CHEESE.

**Having** thoroughly cleaned a hog's head or pig's head, split it in two with a sharp knife, take out the eyes, take out the brains, cut off the ears, and pour scalding water over them and the head, and scrape them clean. Cut off any part of the nose which may be discolored so as not to be scraped clean; then rinse all in cold water, and put it into a large kettle with hot (not boiling) water to cover it, and set the kettle (having covered it) over the fire; let it boil gently, taking off the scum as it rises; when boiled so that the bones leave the meat readily, take it from the water with a skimmer into a large wooden bowl or tray; take from it every particle of bone; chop the meat small and season to taste with salt and pepper, and if liked, a little chopped sage or thyme; spread a cloth in a colander or sieve; set it in a deep dish, and put the meat in, then fold the cloth closely over it, lay a weight on which may press equally the whole surface (a sufficiently large plate will serve). Let the weight be more or less heavy, according as you may wish the cheese to be fat or lean; a heavy weight by pressing out the fat will of course leave the cheese lean. When cold, take the weight off; take it from the colander or sieve, scrape off whatever fat may be found on the outside of the cloth, and keep the cheese in the cloth in a cool place, to be eaten sliced thin, with or without mustard, and vinegar or catsup. After the water is cold in which the head was boiled, take off the fat from it, and whatever may have drained from the sieve, or colander, and cloth; put it together in some clean water, give it one boil; then strain it through a cloth, and set it to become cold; then take off the cake of fat. It is fit for any use.

## PIGS' FEET SOUSED.

Scald and scrape clean the feet; if the covering of the toes will not come off without, singe them in hot embers, until they are loose, then take them off. Many persons lay them in weak lime water to whiten them. Having scraped them clean and white, wash them and put them in a pot of hot (not boiling) water, with a little salt, and let them boil gently, until by turning a fork in the flesh it will easily break and the bones are loosened. Take off the scum as it rises. When done, take them from the hot water into cold vinegar, enough to cover them, add to it one-third as much of the water in which they were boiled; add whole pepper and allspice, with cloves and mace if liked, put a cloth and a tight-fitting cover over the pot or jar. Soused feet may be eaten cold from the vinegar, split in two from top to toe, or having split them, dip them in wheat flour and fry in hot lard, or broil and butter them. In either case, let them be nicely browned.

## TO MAKE LARD.

Take the leaf fat from the inside of a bacon hog, cut it small, and put it in an iron kettle, which must be perfectly free from any musty taste; set it over a steady, moderate fire, until nothing but scraps remain of the meat; the heat must be kept up, but gentle, that it may not burn the lard; spread a coarse cloth in a wire sieve, and strain the liquid into tin basins which will hold two or three quarts; squeeze out all the fat from the scraps. When the lard in the pans is cold, press a piece of new muslin close upon it, trim it off at the edge of the pan, and keep it in a cold place. Or it may be kept in wooden kegs with close covers. Lard made with one-third as much beef suet as fat is supposed by many persons to keep better.

## TO TELL GOOD EGGS.

Put them in water—if the large end turns up, they are not fresh. This is an infallible rule to distinguish a good egg from a bad one.

## KEEPING EGGS FRESH.

"All it is necessary to do to keep eggs through summer is to procure small, clean wooden or tin vessels, holding from ten to twenty gallons, and a barrel, more or less, of common, fine-ground land plaster. Begin by putting on the bottom of the vessel two or three inches of plaster, and then, having fresh eggs, with the yolks unbroken, set them up, small end down, close to each other, but not crowding, and make the first layer. Then add more plaster and enough so the eggs will stand upright, and set up the second layer; then another deposit of plaster, followed by a layer of eggs, till the vessel is full, and finish by covering the top layer with plaster. Eggs so packed and subjected to a temperature of at least 85 degrees, if not 90 degrees, during August and September, came out fresh, and if one could be certain of not having a temperature of more than 75 degrees to contend with, I am confident eggs could be kept by these means all the year round. Observe that the eggs must be fresh laid, the yolks unbroken, the packing done in small vessels, and with clean, fine-ground land plaster, and care must be taken that no egg so presses on another as to break the shell."

Eggs may be kept good for a year in the following manner:

To a pail of water, put of unslacked lime and coarse salt each a pint; keep it in a cellar, or cool place, and put the eggs in, as fresh laid as possible.

It is well to keep a stone pot of this lime water ready to

receive the eggs as soon as laid; make a fresh supply every few months. This lime water is of exactly the proper strength; strong lime water will cook the eggs. Very strong lime water will eat the shell.

## POACHED EGGS.

Two eggs, two tablespoonfuls of milk, half a teaspoonful of salt, half a teaspoonful of butter. Beat the eggs, and add the salt and milk. Put the butter in a small saucepan, and when it melts, add the eggs. Stir over the fire until the mixture thickens, being careful not to let it cook hard. About two minutes will cook it. The eggs, when done, should be soft and creamy. Serve immediately.

## DROPPED EGGS.

Have one quart of boiling water and one tablespoonful of salt in a frying-pan. Break the eggs, one by one, into a saucer, and slide carefully into the salted water. Cook until the white is firm, and lift out with a griddle-cake turner and place on toasted bread. Serve immediately.

## STUFFED EGGS.

Six hard-boiled eggs cut in two, take out the yolks and mash fine; then add two teaspoonfuls of butter, one of cream, two or three drops of onion-juice, salt and pepper to taste. Mix all thoroughly and fill the eggs with this mixture; put them together. Then there will be a little of the filling left, to which add one well-beaten egg. Cover the eggs with this mixture, and then roll in cracker-crumbs. Fry a light brown in boiling fat. Plain baked eggs make a quite pretty breakfast dish. Take a round white-ware dish thick enough to stand the heat of the oven, put into it sufficient fresh butter, and break as many eggs in it as are desirable, putting a few bits of butter on the top, and set in a rather slow oven until they are cooked. Have a dish of nicely made buttered toast arranged symmetrically on a plate, and garnish it and the dish of eggs with small pieces of curled parsley.

## EGGS A LA SUISSE.

Spread the bottom of a dish with two ounces of fresh butter; cover this with grated cheese; break eight whole eggs upon the cheese without breaking the yolks. Season with red pepper and salt if necessary; pour a little cream on the surface, strew about two ounces of grated cheese on the top, and set the eggs in a moderate oven for about a quarter of an hour. Pass a hot salamander over the top to brown it.

## EGGS BROUILLE.

Six eggs, half a cupful of milk, or, better still, of cream; two mushrooms, one teaspoonful of salt, a little pepper, three tablespoonfuls of butter, a slight grating of nutmeg. Cut the mushrooms into dice, and fry them for one minute in one tablespoonful of the butter. Beat the eggs, salt, pepper, and cream together, and put them in a saucepan. Add the butter and mushrooms to these ingredients. Stir over a moderate heat until the mixture begins to thicken. Take from the fire and beat rapidly until the eggs become quite thick and creamy. Have slices of toast on a hot dish. Heap the mixture on these, and garnish with points of toast. Serve immediately.

## CURRIED EGGS.

Slice two onions and fry in butter, add a tablespoon curry-powder and one pint good broth or stock, stew till onions are quite tender, add a cup of cream thickened with arrowroot or rice flour, simmer a few moments, then add eight or ten hard-boiled eggs, cut in slices, and beat them well, but do not boil.

## CREAMED EGGS.

Boil six eggs twenty minutes. Make one pint of cream sauce. Have six slices of toast on a hot dish. Put a layer of sauce on each one, and then part of the whites of the eggs, cut in thin strips; and rub part of the yolks through a sieve on to the toast. Repeat this, and finish with a third layer of sauce. Place in the oven for about three minutes. Garnish with parsley, and serve.

## SOFT-BOILED EGGS.

Place the eggs in a warm saucepan, and cover with *boiling* water. Let them stand where they will keep hot, but *not* boil, for ten minutes. This method will cook both whites and yolks.

## EGGS UPON TOAST.

Put a good lump of butter into a frying-pan. When it is hot, stir in four or five well-beaten eggs, with pepper, salt, and a little parsley. Stir and toss for three minutes. Have ready to your hand some slices of buttered toast (cut round with a tin cake cutter before they are toasted); spread thickly with ground or minced tongue, chicken, or ham. Heap the stirred egg upon these in mounds, and set in a hot dish garnished with parsley and pickled beets.

## DUTCH OMELET.

Break eight eggs into a basin, season with pepper and salt, add two ounces of butter cut small, beat these well together, make an ounce of butter hot in a frying-pan, put the eggs in, continue to stir it, drawing it away from the sides, that it may be evenly done, shake it now and then to free it from the pan; when the under side is a little browned, turn the omelet into a dish, and serve; this must be done over a moderate fire.

### EGGS POACHED IN BALLS.

Put three pints of boiling water into a stewpan; set it on a hot stove or coals; stir the water with a stick until it runs rapidly around, then having broken an egg into a cup, taking care not to break the yolk, drop it into the whirling water; continue to stir it until the egg is cooked; then take it into a dish with a skimmer and set it over a pot of boiling water; boil one at a time, until you have enough. These will remain soft for a long time.

### OMELET AU NATURAL.

Break eight or ten eggs into a basin; add a small teaspoonful of salt and a little pepper, with a tablespoonful of cold water; beat the whole well with a spoon or whisk. In the meantime put some fresh sweet butter into an omelet pan, and when it is nearly hot, put in an omelet; while it is frying, with a skimmer spoon raise the edges from the pan that it may be properly done. When the eggs are set and one side is a fine brown, double it half over and serve hot. These omelets should be put quite thin in the pan; the butter required for each will be about the size of a small egg.

### OMELET IN BATTER.

Fry an omelet; when done, cut it in squares or diamonds; dip each piece in batter made of two eggs and a pint of milk, with enough wheat flour, and fry them in nice salted lard to a delicate brown. Serve hot.

## SCRAMBLED EGGS.

Four eggs, one tablespoonful of butter, half a teaspoonful of salt. Beat the eggs and add the salt to them. Melt the butter in a saucepan. Turn in the beaten eggs, stir quickly over a hot fire for one minute, and serve.

## OMELET (SPLENDID).

Six eggs, whites and yolks beaten separately; half pint milk, six teaspoons corn starch, one teaspoon baking powder, and a little salt; add the whites, beaten to stiff froth, last; cook in a little butter.

## VEGETABLES.

### BOILED POTATOES.

Old potatoes are better for being peeled and put in cold water an hour before being put over to boil. They should then be put into fresh cold water, when set over the fire. New potatoes should always be put in a boiling water, and it is best to prepare them just in time for cooking. Are better steamed than boiled.

### MASHED POTATOES.

Potatoes are not good for mashing until they are full grown; peel them, and lay them in water for an hour or more before boiling, for mashing.

Old potatoes, when unfit for plain boiling, may be served mashed; cut out all imperfections, take off all the skin, and lay them in cold water for one hour or more; then put them into a dinner-pot or stewpan, with a teaspoonful of salt; cover the stewpan, and let them boil for half an hour, unless they are large, when three-quarters of an hour will be required; when they are done, take them up with a skimmer into a wooden bowl or tray, and mash them fine with a potato beetle; melt a piece of butter, the size of a large egg, into half a pint of hot milk; mix it with the mashed potatoes until it is thoroughly incorporated, and a smooth mass; then put it in a deep dish, smooth the top over, and mark it neatly with a knife; put pepper over and serve. The quantity of milk used must be in proportion to the quantity of potatoes.

Mashed potatoes may be heaped on a flat dish; make it in a crown or pineapple; stick a sprig of green celery or parsley in the top; or first brown it before the fire or in an oven.

Mashed potatoes may be made a highly ornamental dish; after shaping it, as taste may direct, trim the edge of the plate with a wreath of celery leaves or green parsley; or first brown the outside in an oven or before the fire.

## FRIED POTATOES.

Peel and cut the potatoes into thin slices, as nearly the same size as possible; make some butter or dripping quite hot in a frying-pan; put in the potatoes, and fry them on both sides to a nice brown. When they are crisp and done, take them up, place them on a cloth before the fire to drain the grease from them, and serve very hot, after sprinkling them with salt. These are delicious with rump-steak, and in France are frequently served thus as a breakfast dish. The remains of cold potatoes may also be sliced and fried by the above recipe, but the slices must be cut a little thicker.

## BROILED POTATOES.

Cut cold boiled potatoes in slices lengthwise, quarter of an inch thick; dip each slice in wheat flour, and lay them on a gridiron over a bright fire of coals; when both sides are browned nicely, take them on a hot dish, put a bit of butter, pepper and salt to taste over, and serve hot.

## POTATOES AND CREAM.

Mince cold boiled potatoes fine; put them into a spider with melted butter in it; let them fry a little in the butter, well covered; then put in a fresh piece of butter, seasoned with salt and pepper, and pour over cream or rich milk; let it boil up once and serve.

## POTATO PUFFS.

Prepare the potatoes as directed for mashed potato. While *hot*, shape in balls about the size of an egg. Have a tin sheet well buttered, and place the balls on it. As soon as all are done, brush over with beaten egg. Brown in the oven. When done, slip a knife under them and slide them upon a hot platter. Garnish with parsley, and serve immediately.

## POTATO SNOW.

Choose large white potatoes, as free from spots as possible; boil them in their skin in salt and water until perfectly tender, drain and *dry them thoroughly* by the side of the fire, and peel them. Put a hot dish before the fire, rub the potatoes through a coarse sieve on to this dish; do not touch them afterwards, or the flakes will fall, and serve as hot as possible.

## POTATO BORDER.

Six potatoes, three eggs, one tablespoonful of butter, one of salt, half a cupful of boiling milk. Pare, boil and mash the potatoes. When fine and light, add the butter, salt and pepper and two well-beaten eggs. Butter the border mold and pack the potato in it. Let this stand on the kitchen table ten minutes; then turn out on a dish and brush over with one well-beaten egg. Brown in the oven.

## WHIPPED POTATOES.

Instead of mashing in the ordinary way whip with a fork until light and dry; then whip in a little melted butter, some milk, and salt to taste, whipping rapidly until creamy. Pile as lightly and irregularly as you can in a hot dish.

## SCALLOPED POTATOES.

Prepare in this proportion: Two cups of mashed potatoes, two tablespoonfuls of cream or milk, and one of melted butter; salt and pepper to taste. Stir the potatoes, butter, and cream together, adding one raw egg. If the potatoes seem too moist, beat in a few fine bread-crumbs. Bake in a hot oven for ten minutes, taking care to have the top a rich brown.

## POTATO CROQUETTES.

Pare, boil, and mash six good-sized potatoes. Add one tablespoonful of butter, two-thirds of a cupful of hot cream or milk, the whites of two eggs well beaten, salt and pepper to taste. When cool enough to handle, work into shape, roll in eggs and bread-crumbs, and fry in hot lard.

## POTATOES A LA CREME.

Heat a cupful of milk; stir in a heaping tablespoonful of butter cut up in as much flour. Stir until smooth and thick; pepper and salt, and add two cupfuls of cold boiled potatoes, sliced, and a little very finely-chopped parsley. Shake over the fire until the potatoes are hot all through, and pour into a deep dish.

## TO BOIL SWEET POTATOES.

Wash them perfectly clean, put them into a pot or stewpan, and pour boiling water over to cover them; cover the pot close, and boil fast for half an hour, or more if the potatoes are large; try them with a fork; when done, drain off the water, take off the skins, and serve.

Cold sweet potatoes may be cut in slices across or lengthwise, and fried or broiled as common potatoes; or they may be cut in half and served cold.

## ROASTED SWEET POTATOES.

Having washed them clean, and wiped them dry, roast them on a hot hearth as directed for common potatoes; or put them in a Dutch oven or tin reflector. Roasted or baked potatoes should not be cut, but broken open and eaten from the skin, as from a shell.

## TO BAKE SWEET POTATOES.

Wash them perfectly clean, wipe them dry, and bake in a quick oven, according to their size—half an hour for quite small size, three-quarters for larger, and a full hour for the largest. Let the oven have a good heat, and do not open it, unless it is necessary to turn them, until they are done.

## FRENCH FRIED SWEET POTATOES.

Prepare and fry the same as the white potatoes. Or they can first be boiled half an hour, and then pared, cut and fried as directed. The latter is the better way, as they are liable to be a little hard if fried when raw.

## TURNIPS.

Boil until tender; mash and season with butter, pepper, salt, and a little rich milk or cream.

## SPINACH.

An excellent way to serve spinach is to first look it over carefully; wash it in two or three waters. If the stalks are not perfectly tender, cut the leaves from the stalk. Boil for twenty minutes in water with enough salt dissolved in it to salt the spinach sufficiently. When done let it drain, then chop it fine, put it on the stove in a saucepan, with a lump of butter, salt, and pepper, and enough milk to moisten it. When the butter is melted and spinach steaming, take from the fire and put it in the dish in which it is going to the table. Garnish with hard-boiled eggs cut in slices or in rings—that is, with the yolk removed and rings of the white only left.

## BEETS.

Clean these nicely, but do not pare them, leaving on a short piece of the stalk. Then put over to boil in hot water. Young beets will cook tender in an hour; old beets require several hours' boiling. When done, skin quickly while hot, slice thin into your vegetable dish, put on salt, pepper, and a little butter, put over a little vinegar, and serve hot or cold.

## TO PRESERVE VEGETABLES FOR WINTER USE.

Green string beans must be picked when young; put a layer three inches deep in a small wooden keg or half barrel; sprinkle in salt an inch deep, then put another layer of beans, then salt, and beans and salt in alternate layers, until you have enough; let the last be salt; cover them with a piece of board which will fit the inside of the barrel or keg, and place a heavy weight upon it; they will make a brine.

When wanted for use, soak them one night or more in plenty of water, changing it once or twice, until the salt is out of them, then cut them, and boil the same as when fresh.

Carrots, beans, beet-roots, parsnips, and potatoes

keep best in dry sand or earth in a cellar; turnips keep best on a cellar bottom, or they may be kept the same as carrots, etc. Whatever earth remains about them when taken from the ground, should not be taken off.

When sprouts come on potatoes or other stored vegetables, they should be carefully cut off. The young sprouts from turnips are sometimes served as a salad, or boiled tender in salt and water, and served with butter and pepper over.

Celery may be kept all winter by setting it in boxes filled with earth; keep it in the cellar; it will grow and whiten in the dark; leeks may also be kept in this way.

Cabbage set out in earth, in a good cellar, will keep good and fresh all winter. Small close heads of cabbage may be kept many weeks by taking them before the frost comes, and laying them on a stone floor; this will whiten them, and make them tender.

Store onions are to be strung, and hung in a dry, cold place.

## DELICATE CABBAGE.

Remove all defective leaves, quarter and cut as for coarse slaw, cover well with cold water, and let remain several hours before cooking, then drain and put into pot with enough boiling water to cover; boil until thoroughly cooked (which will generally require about forty-five minutes), add salt ten or fifteen minutes before removing from fire, and when done, take up into a colander, press out the water well, and season with butter and pepper. This is a good dish to serve with corned meats, but should not be cooked with them; if preferred, however, it may be seasoned by adding some of the liquor and fat from the boiling meat to the cabbage while cooking. Drain, remove, and serve in a dish with drawn butter or a cream dressing poured over it.

### RED CABBAGE.

Select two small, solid heads of hard red cabbage; divide them in halves from crown to stem; lay the split side down, and cut downwards in thin slices. The cabbage will then be in narrow strips or shreds. Put into a saucepan a tablespoonful of clean drippings, butter, or any nice fat; when fat is hot, put in cabbage, a teaspoonful of salt, three tablespoonfuls vinegar (if the latter is very strong, use but two), and one onion, in which three or four cloves have been stuck, buried in the middle; boil two hours and a half; if it becomes too dry and is in danger of scorching, add a very *little* water. This is very nice.

### CAULIFLOWER.

Boil a fine cauliflower, tied up snugly in coarse tarlatan, in hot water, a little salt. Drain and lay in a deep dish, flower uppermost. Heat a cup of milk; thicken with two tablespoonfuls of butter, cut into bits, and rolled in flour. Add pepper, salt, the beaten white of an egg, and boil up one minute, stirring well. Take from the fire, squeeze the juice of a lemon through a hair sieve into the sauce, and pour half into a boat, the rest over the cauliflower.

### MASHED CARROTS.

Scrape, wash, lay in cold water half an hour; then cook tender in boiling water. Drain well, mash with a wooden spoon, or beetle, work in a good piece of butter, and season with pepper and salt. Heap up in a vegetable dish, and serve very hot.

### BOILED GREEN CORN.

Choose young sugar-corn, full grown, but not hard; test with the nail. When the grain is pierced, the milk should escape in a jet, and not be thick. Clean by stripping off the outer leaves, turn back the innermost covering carefully, pick off every thread of silk, and re-cover the ear with the thin husk that grew nearest it. Tie at the top with a bit of thread, put boiling water salted, and cook fast from twenty minutes to half an hour, in proportion to size and age. Cut off the stalks close to the cob, and send whole to table wrapped in a napkin.

Or you can cut from the cob while hot and season with butter, pepper, and salt. Send to table in a vegetable dish.

## GREEN PEAS.

Shell and lay in cold water fifteen minutes. Cook from twenty to twenty-five minutes in boiling salted water. Drain, put into a deep dish with a good lump of butter; pepper and salt to taste.

## TO BOIL ONIONS.

Take off the tops and tails, and the thin outer skin; but no more, lest the onions should go to pieces. Lay them on the bottom of a pan which is broad enough to contain them without piling one on another; just cover them with water, and let them simmer slowly till they are tender all through, but not till they break.

Serve them up with melted butter.

## FRIED ONIONS.

Cut them in thin slices and season them; have a piece of fat bacon frying to get the juice, take it out, and put the onions in and stir until a pretty brown.

## BOILED PARSNIPS.

Wash the parsnips, scrape them thoroughly, and with the point of a knife, remove any black spots about them, and should they be very large, cut the thick part into quarters. Put them into a saucepan of boiling water, salted in the above proportion, boil them rapidly until tender, which may be ascertained by thrusting a fork into them; take them up, drain them, and serve in a vegetable dish. This vegetable is usually served with salt fish, boiled pork, or boiled beef; when sent to table with the latter, a few should be placed alternately with carrots round the dish as a garnish.

### PARSNIPS FRIED IN BUTTER.

Scrape the parsnips and boil gently forty-five minutes. When cold, cut in long slices about one-third of an inch thick. Season with salt and pepper. Dip in melted butter and in flour. Have two tablespoonfuls of butter in the frying-pan, and as soon as hot, put in enough parsnips to cover the bottom. Fry brown on both sides and serve on a hot dish.

### CREAMED PARSNIPS.

Boil tender, scrape, and slice lengthwise. Put over the fire with two tablespoonfuls of butter, pepper, and salt, and a little minced parsley. Shake until the mixture boils. Dish the parsnips, add to the sauce three tablespoonfuls of cream in which has been stirred a quarter spoonful of flour. Boil once, and pour over the parsnips.

### PARSNIP FRITTERS.

Boil four or five parsnips; when tender, take off the skin and mash them fine, add to them a teaspoonful of wheat flour and a beaten egg; put a tablespoonful of lard or beef dripping in a frying-pan over the fire, add to it a saltspoonful of salt; when boiling hot, put in the parsnips, make it in small cakes with a spoon; when one side is a delicate brown, turn the other; when both are done, take them on a dish, put a very little of the fat in which they were fried over, and serve hot. These resemble very nearly the taste of the salsify or oyster plant, and will generally be preferred.

## SALSIFY, OR VEGETABLE OYSTER.

Boil and serve as directed for parsnips, either plain boiled, or fried, or made fritters.

## BOILED VEGETABLE MARROW.

Have ready a saucepan of boiling water, properly salted; put in the marrows after peeling them, and boil them until quite tender. Take them up with a slice; halve, and, should they be very large, quarter them. Dish them on toast, and send to table with them a tureen of melted butter, or, in lieu of this, a small pat of salt butter. Large vegetable marrows may be preserved throughout the winter by storing them in a dry place; when wanted for use, a few slices should be cut and boiled in the same manner as above; but, when once begun, the marrow must be eaten quickly, as it keeps but a short time after it is cut. Vegetable marrows are also very delicious mashed; they should be boiled, then drained, and mashed smoothly with a wooden spoon. Heat them in a saucepan, add a seasoning of salt and pepper, and a small piece of butter, and dish with a few snippets of toasted bread placed round as a garnish.

Vegetable marrows are delightful when sliced and fried for ten minutes in butter. Before being fried they may be dipped in a batter of flour and water, seasoned with a little salt. Vegetable marrows may also be dressed as follows: Boil one, and when it is about ready, cut it in pieces, which place in a fresh saucepan, covered with soup stock, either white or brown; add a little salt in stewing. Serve in a deep dish when thoroughly tender. Vegetable marrows are very nice plain boiled, and served upon buttered toast. Peel them and cut them so as to be able to remove the seeds. Marrows will take from twenty minutes to an hour to boil, according to size and age. After being parboiled, they may be sliced down, dipped in egg, and then rubbed among bread-crumbs, and fried; serve them as hot as possible.

Tomatoes may be sliced thin, and served with salt, pepper, and vinegar over, for breakfast; or sliced, and strewn with sugar and grated nutmeg, for tea; for dinner they may be stewed or broiled, or baked.

Tomatoes may be preserved in sugar, or as catsup, when out of season. Such as like them, declare them to be equally excellent in each and every form or dressing.

## STEWED TOMATOES.

Pour boiling water over six or eight large tomatoes, or a greater number of smaller ones; let them remain for a few minutes, then peel off the skins, squeeze out the seeds, and some of the juice, by pressing them gently in the hand; put them in a well-tinned stewpan, with a teaspoonful of salt, a saltspoonful of pepper, a bit of butter, half as large as an egg, and a tablespoonful of grated bread or rolled crackers; cover the stewpan close, and set it over the fire for nearly an hour; shake the stewpan occasionally, that they may not burn; serve hot.

This is decidedly the best manner of stewing tomatoes; they may be done without the bread-crumbs, and with less stewing if preferred.

## BAKED TOMATOES.

Wash five or six smooth tomatoes; cut a piece from the stem end, the size of a twenty-five cent piece; put a saltspoonful of salt, half as much pepper, and a bit of butter the size of a nutmeg, in each; set them in a dish or pan, and bake in a moderate oven for nearly one hour.

## STUFFED TOMATOES.

Twelve large, smooth tomatoes, one teaspoonful of salt, a little pepper, one tablespoonful of butter, one of sugar, one cupful of bread-crumbs, one teaspoonful of onion-juice. Arrange the tomatoes in a baking-pan. Cut a thin slice from the smooth end of each. With a small spoon, scoop out as much of the pulp and juice as possible without injuring the shape. When all have been treated in this way, mix the pulp and juice with the other ingredients, and fill the tomatoes with this mixture. Put on the tops, and bake slowly three-quarters of an hour. Slide the cake turner under the tomatoes and lift gently on to a flat dish. Garnish with parsley, and serve.

## SCALLOPED TOMATOES.

Turn nearly all the juice off from a can of tomatoes. Salt and pepper this, by the way, and put aside in a cool place for some other day's soup. Put a layer of bread-crumbs in the bottom of a buttered pie-dish; on them one of tomatoes; sprinkle with salt, pepper, and some bits of butter, also a little sugar. Another layer of crumbs, another of tomatoes —seasoned—then a top layer of very fine, dry crumbs. Bake covered until bubbling hot, and brown quickly.

## TO PEEL TOMATOES.

Put the tomatoes in a frying basket and plunge them into boiling water for about three minutes. Drain and peel.

## BAKED BEANS.

Pick one quart of beans free from stones and dirt. Wash and soak in cold water over night. In the morning pour off the water. Cover with hot water, put two pounds of corned beef with them, and boil until they begin to split open (the time depends upon the age of the beans, but it will be from thirty to sixty minutes). Turn them into the colander, and pour over them two or three quarts of cold water. Put about half of the beans in a deep earthen pot, then put in the beef, and finally the remainder of the beans. Mix one teaspoonful of mustard and one tablespoonful of molasses with a little water. Pour this over the beans, and then add boiling water to just cover. Bake *slowly* ten hours. Add a little water occasionally.

## STRING BEANS.

String, snap and wash two quarts beans, boil in plenty of water about fifteen minutes, drain off and put on again in about two quarts boiling water; boil an hour and a half, and add salt and pepper just before taking up, stirring in one and a half tablespoons butter, rubbed into two tablespoons flour and half pint sweet cream. Or boil a piece of salted pork one hour, then add beans and boil an hour and a half. For shelled beans boil half an hour in water enough to cover, and dress as above.

## BUTTER BEANS.

With a knife cut off the ends of pods and strings from both sides, being very careful to remove every shred; cut every bean lengthwise, in two or three strips, and leave them for half an hour in cold water. Much more than cover them with boiling water; boil till perfectly tender.

It is well to allow three hours for boiling. Grain well, return to kettle, and add a dressing of half a gill of cream, one and a half ounces butter, one even teaspoon salt, and half a teaspoon pepper. This is sufficient for a quart of cooked beans.

## ASPARAGUS WITH EGGS.

Boil a bunch of asparagus twenty minutes; cut off the tender tops and lay in a deep pie-plate, buttering, salting, and peppering well. Beat four eggs just enough to break up the yolks, add a tablespoonful of melted butter, with pepper and salt, and pour upon the asparagus. Bake eight minutes in a quick oven, and serve immediately.

## ASPARAGUS UPON TOAST.

Tie the bunch of asparagus up with soft string, when you have cut away the wood, and cook about twenty-five minutes in salted boiling water. Have ready some slices of crustless toast; dip each in the asparagus liquor; butter well while hot and lay upon a heated dish. Drain the asparagus, and arrange upon the toast. Pepper, salt, and butter generously.

## MUSHROOMS, STEWED.

If fresh, let them lie in salt and water about an hour, then put them in the stewpan, cover with water and let them cook two hours gently. Dress them with cream, butter and flour as oysters, and season to taste.

## MUSHROOMS, FRIED.

When peeled put them into hot butter and let them heat thoroughly through—too much cooking toughens them. Season well with butter, pepper and salt. Serve on buttered toast; a teaspoon of wine or vinegar on each mushroom is a choice method.

## BAKED MUSHROOMS.

Place some large flat ones nicely cleaned and trimmed on thin slices of well-buttered toast, putting a little nudgel of butter in each, as also a snuff of pepper and salt; lay them on a baking-tray, and cover them carefully; heap the hot ashes upon them, and let them bake on the hearth for fifteen or twenty minutes.

## BROILED MUSHROOMS.

Choose the largest sort, lay them on a small gridiron over bright coals; the stalk upwards. Broil quickly, and serve, with butter, pepper, and salt over.

## MASHED SQUASH.

Peel, seed and slice fresh summer squashes. Lay in cold water ten minutes; put into boiling water, a little salt, and cook tender. Twenty minutes will suffice if the squash be young. Mash in a colander, pressing out all the water; heap in a deep dish, seasoning with pepper, salt and butter. Serve hot.

## BAKED SQUASH.

Cut in pieces, scrape well, bake from one to one and a half hours, according to the thickness of the squash; to be eaten with salt and butter as sweet potatoes.

## FRIED SQUASHES.

Cut the squash into thin slices, and sprinkle it with salt; let it stand a few moments; then beat two eggs, and dip the squash into the egg; then fry it brown in butter.

## STEWED CELERY

Is an excellent winter dish, and is very easily cooked. Wash the stalks thoroughly, and boil in well-salted water till tender, which will be in about twenty minutes. After it is made ready as above, drain it thoroughly, place it on toasted bread, and pour over it a quantity of sauce. A sauce of cream, seasoned with a little mace, may be served over the celery. It may also be served with melted butter.

## STUFFED EGG-PLANT.

Cut the egg-plant in two; scrape out all the inside and put it in a saucepan with a little minced ham; cover with water and boil with salt; drain off the water; add two tablespoonfuls grated crumbs, tablespoonful butter, half a minced onion, salt and pepper; stuff each half of the hull with the mixture; add a small lump of butter to each, and bake fifteen minutes.

# SAUCES FOR MEATS, FISH, POULTRY OR VEGETABLES.

### TO MAKE DRAWN BUTTER.

Put half a pint of milk in a perfectly clean stewpan, and set it over a moderate fire; put into a pint bowl a heaping tablespoonful of wheat flour, quarter of a pound of sweet butter, and a saltspoonful of salt; work these well together with the back of a spoon, then pour into it, stirring it all the time, half a pint of boiling water; when it is smooth, stir it into the boiling milk, let it simmer for five minutes or more, and it is done.

Drawn butter made after this receipt will be found to be most excellent; it may be made less rich by using less butter.

### PARSLEY SAUCE.

Make a drawn butter as directed, dip a bunch of parsley into boiling water, then cut it fine, and stir into the drawn butter a few minutes before taking it up.

### EGG SAUCE.

Make a drawn butter; chop two hard-boiled eggs quite fine, the white and yolk separately, and stir it into the sauce before serving. This is used for boiled fish or vegetables.

## ONION SAUCE.

Peel some nice white onions, and boil them tender; press the water from them; chop them fine, and put them to a half pint of hot milk; add a bit of butter, and a teaspoonful of salt, and pepper to taste. Serve with boiled veal, or poultry, or mutton.

## ANCHOVY SAUCE.

Make the butter sauce, and stir into it four tablespoonfuls of essence of anchovy and one of lemon-juice.

## BREAD SAUCE.

One pint milk, one cup bread-crumbs (very fine), one onion, sliced, a pinch of mace, pepper and salt to taste, three tablespoonfuls butter. Simmer the sliced onion in the milk until tender; strain the milk and pour over the bread-crumbs, which should be put into a saucepan. Cover and soak half an hour; beat smooth with an egg-whip, add the seasoning and butter; stir in well, boil up once, and serve in a tureen. If it is too thick, add boiling water and more butter.

This sauce is for roast poultry. Some people add some of the gravy from the dripping-pan, first straining it and beating it well in with the sauce.

## TOMATO SAUCE

Can be cheaply made either from the fresh fruit or from the canned tomatoes, which are on sale in every grocer's shop. Squeeze as much as you require through a sieve, and then simmer slowly for a little time in a few tablespoonfuls of beef gravy, season with pepper and salt. Excellent for chops and cutlets, or for roasted beef.

## TOMATO MUSTARD.

One peck of ripe tomatoes; boiled with two onions, six red peppers, four cloves of garlic, for one hour; then add a half pint or half pound salt, three tablespoons black pepper, half ounce ginger, half ounce allspice, half ounce mace, half ounce cloves; then boil again for one hour longer, and when cold add one pint of vinegar and a quarter pound of mustard; and if you like it very hot, a tablespoonful of Cayenne.

## MINT SAUCE.

Mix one tablespoon of white sugar to half a teacup of good vinegar; add the mint and let it infuse for half an hour in a cool place before sending to the table. Serve with roast lamb or mutton.

## CELERY SAUCE.

Mix two tablespoons of flour with half a teacup of butter; have ready a pint of boiling milk; stir the flour and butter into the milk; take three heads of celery, cut into small bits, and boil for a few minutes in water, which strain off; put the celery into the melted butter, and keep stirred over the fire for five or ten minutes. This is very nice with boiled fowl or turkey.

## GOVERNOR'S SAUCE.

One peck green tomatoes, four large onions, six red peppers, one teacup grated horseradish, one teaspoon Cayenne and one of black pepper, one teaspoon mustard, half cup sugar; slice the tomatoes and sprinkle one teacup salt on, and lay all night; drain well in the morning, then simmer all together till cooked through.

## CREAM SAUCE.

**One** cupful of milk, a teaspoonful of flour and a tablespoonful of butter, salt and pepper. Put the butter in a small frying-pan, and when hot, but not brown, add the flour. Stir until smooth; then gradually add the milk. Let it boil up once. Season to taste with salt and pepper, and serve. This is nice to cut cold potatoes into and let them just heat through. They are then creamed potatoes. It also answers as a sauce for other vegetables, omelets, fish and sweetbreads, or, indeed, for anything that requires a white sauce. If you have plenty of cream, use it, and omit the butter.

## RUSSIAN SAUCE.

(Piquant) may be thus made: Grated horseradish, four tablespoonfuls, weak mustard, one spoonful, sugar, half a spoonful, a little salt, two or three grains of Cayenne, and a spoonful or two of vinegar. Mix thoroughly, and serve to cold meat. When wanted for fish, let it be added to melted butter—two parts butter to one of sauce.

## MAYONNAISE SAUCE.

**Mix** in a two-quart bowl one even teaspoon ground mustard, one of salt, and one and a half of vinegar; beat in the yolk of a raw egg, then add very gradually half a pint pure olive oil (or melted butter), beating briskly all the time. The mixture will become a very thick batter. Flavor with vinegar or fresh lemon-juice. Closely covered, it will keep for weeks in a cold place, and is delicious.

## OYSTER SAUCE.

Take a pint of oysters, and save out a little of their liquor. Put them with their remaining liquor, and some mace and nutmeg, into a covered saucepan, and simmer them on hot coals about ten minutes. Then drain them. Oysters for sauce should be large. Having prepared in a saucepan some drawn or melted butter (mixed with oyster liquid instead of water), pour it into a sauceboat, add the oysters to it, and serve it up with boiled poultry, or with boiled fresh fish. Celery, first boiled and then chopped, is an improvement to oyster sauce.

## LOBSTER SAUCE.

Put the coral and spawn of a boiled lobster into a mortar, with a tablespoonful of butter, pound it to a smooth mass, then rub it through a sieve; melt nearly a quarter of a pound of sweet butter, with a wineglass of water, or vinegar; add a teaspoonful of made mustard, stir in the coral and spawn, and a little salt and pepper; stir it until it is smooth, and serve. Some of the meat of the lobster may be chopped fine, and stirred into it.

## CAPER SAUCE.

Make a butter sauce, and stir into it one tablespoonful of lemon-juice, two of capers, and one of essence of anchovy.

## MUSTARD SAUCE.

Stir three tablespoonfuls of mixed mustard and a speck of Cayenne into a butter sauce. This is nice for devilled turkey and broiled smoked herrings.

## CURRY SAUCE.

One tablespoonful of butter, one of flour, one teaspoonful of curry powder, one large slice of onion, one large cupful of stock, salt and pepper to taste. Cut the onion fine, and fry brown in the butter. Add the flour and curry powder. Stir for one minute, add the stock, and season with salt and pepper. Simmer five minutes; then strain, and serve. This sauce can be served with a broil or *saute* of meat or fish.

## CRANBERRY SAUCE.

After removing all soft berries, wash thoroughly, place for about two minutes in scalding water, remove, and to every pound of fruit add three-quarters of a pound of granulated sugar and a half pint water; stew together over a moderate but steady fire. Be careful to *cover* and *not to stir* the fruit, but occasionally shake the vessel, or apply a gentler heat if in danger of sticking or burning. If attention to these particulars be given, the berries will retain their shape to a considerable extent, which adds greatly to their appearance on the table. Boil from five to seven minutes, remove from fire, turn into a deep dish, and set aside to cool. If to be kept, they can be put up at once in air-tight jars. Or, for strained sauce, one and a half pounds of fruit should be stewed in one pint of water for ten or twelve minutes, or until quite soft, then strained through a colander or fine wire sieve, and three-quarters of a pound of sugar thoroughly stirred into the pulp thus obtained, after cooling it is ready for use. Serve with roast turkey or game. When to be kept for a long time without sealing, more sugar may be added, but its too free use impairs the peculiar cranberry flavor. For dinner sauce half a pound is more economical, and really preferable to three-quarters, as given above. It is better, though not necessary, to use a porcelain kettle.

Some prefer not to add the sugar till the fruit is almost done, thinking this plan makes it more tender, and preserves the color better.

## PORT WINE SAUCE FOR GAME.

Half a tumbler of currant jelly, half a tumbler of port wine, half a tumbler of stock, half a teaspoonful of salt, two tablespoonfuls of lemon-juice, four cloves, a speck of Cayenne. Simmer the cloves and stock together for half an hour. Strain on the other ingredients, and let all melt together. Part of the gravy from the game may be added to it.

## CURRANT JELLY SAUCE.

Three tablespoonfuls of butter, one onion, one bay leaf, one sprig of celery, two tablespoonfuls of vinegar, half a cupful of currant jelly, one tablespoonful of flour, one pint of stock, salt, pepper. Cook the butter and onion until the latter begins to color. Add the flour, and herbs. Stir until brown; add the stock, and simmer twenty minutes. Strain, and skim off all the fat. Add the jelly, and stir over the fire until it is melted. Serve with game.

## APPLE SAUCE.

Peel, quarter, and core, rich tart apples; put to them a very little water, cover them, and set them over the fire; when tender, mash them smooth, and serve with roasted pork, goose, or any other gross meat.

## BREAD AND BREAKFAST CAKES.

### YEAST.

Put two quarts of water and two tablespoonfuls of hops on to boil. Pare and grate six large potatoes. When the hops and water *boil* strain the water on the grated potatoes, and stir well. Place on the stove and boil up once. Add half a cupful of sugar and one-fourth of a cupful of salt. Let the mixture get blood-warm; then add one cupful of yeast, or one cake of compressed yeast, and let it rise in a warm place five or six hours. When well-risen turn into a stone jug. Cork this tightly, and set in a cool place.

### PLAIN WHITE FAMILY BREAD.

Take one pint of flour and half a pint of good hop yeast and stir it together about five o'clock in the afternoon; at nine put one-half gallon of flour in a tray, put the sponge in the middle of the flour with a piece of lard as large as a walnut. Knead it all up with tepid water made salt with two teaspoonfuls or more to taste; work it well, and put it in a jar to rise. Next morning knead it over with a little flour; make it in two loaves; and set it in a warm place or oven until ready; then put it to bake, and when done, wrap it in a nice coarse towel. If you have no sugar in the yeast you use, stir a large teaspoonful in it before putting it in the flour.

## GRAHAM BREAD.

Take a little over a quart of warm water, one-half cup brown sugar or molasses, one-fourth cup hop yeast, and one and one-half teaspoons salt; thicken the water with unbolted flour to a thin batter; add sugar, salt and yeast, and stir in more flour until quite stiff. In the morning add a small teaspoon soda, and flour enough to made the batter stiff as can be stirred with a spoon, put it into pans and let rise again; then bake in even oven, not too hot at first; *keep warm while rising;* smooth over the loaves with a spoon or knife dipped in water.

## BOSTON BROWN BREAD.

One heaping coffee-cup each of corn, rye and Graham meal. The rye meal should be as fine as the Graham, or rye flour may be used. Sift the three kinds together as closely as possible, and beat together thoroughly with two cups New Orleans or Porto Rico molasses, two cups sweet milk, one cup sour milk, one dessertspoon soda, one teaspoon salt; pour into a tin form, place in a kettle of *cold* water, put on and boil four hours. Put on to cook as soon as mixed. It may appear to be too thin, but it is not, as this receipt has never been known to fail. Serve warm, with baked beans or Thanksgiving turkey. The bread should not quite fill the form (or a tin pail with a cover will answer), as it must have room to swell. See that the water does not boil up to the top of the form; also take care it does not boil entirely away or stop boiling. To serve it, remove the lid and set it a few moments into the open oven to dry the top, and it will then turn out in perfect shape. This bread can be used as a pudding, and served with a sauce made of thick sour cream, well sweetened and seasoned with nutmeg, or it is good toasted the next day.

## CORN BREAD.

Sift three quarts of corn meal, add a tablespoonful of salt, one teaspoonful baking powder, and mix sufficient water with it to make a thin batter. Cover it with a breadcloth and set it to rise. When ready to bake stir it well, pour it into a baking-pan, and bake slowly. Use cold water in summer and hot water in winter.

## STEAMED BROWN BREAD.

One quart each of milk and Indian meal, one pint rye meal, one cup of molasses, two tablespoonfuls of soda. Add a little salt and steam four hours.

## PARKER HOUSE ROLLS.

One teacup home-made yeast, a little salt, one tablespoon sugar, a piece of lard size of an egg, one pint milk, flour sufficient to mix. Put the milk on the stove to scald, with the lard in it. Prepare the flour with salt, sugar and yeast. Then add the milk, not too hot. Knead thoroughly when mixed at night; in the morning but very slight kneading is necessary. Then roll out and cut with large biscuit cutter. Spread a little butter on each roll and lap together. Let them rise very light, then bake in a quick oven.

## FRENCH ROLLS.

One pint of milk, scalded; put into it while hot half a cup of sugar and one tablespoon of butter. When the milk is cool, add a little salt and half a cup of yeast, or one compressed yeast cake; stir in flour to make a stiff sponge, and when light, mix as for bread. Let it rise until light, punch it down with the hand, and let it rise again—repeat two or three times, then turn the dough on to the molding-board and pound with the rolling-pin until thin enough to cut. Cut out with a tumbler, brush the surface of each one with melted butter, and fold over. Let the rolls rise on the tins; bake, and while warm brush over the surface with melted butter to make the crust tender.

## BUNS.

Break one egg into a cup and fill with sweet milk; mix with it half cup yeast, half cup butter, one cup sugar, enough flour to make a soft dough; flavor with nutmeg. Let it rise till very light, then mold into biscuits with a few currants. Let rise a second time in pan; bake, and when nearly done, glaze with a little molasses and milk. Use the same cup, no matter about the size, for each measure.

## BISCUIT.

Dissolve one and a half tablespoon of butter in a pint of hot milk, when lukewarm stir in one quart of flour, and one teaspoon soda, a little salt, and a teacup of yeast; work into dough cuts smooth. If winter, set in a warm place; if summer, a cool one to rise. In the morning work softly and roll out one-half inch and cut into biscuit and set to rise for thirty minutes, when they will be ready to bake. These are delicious.

## TO MAKE RUSKS.

To every pound of flour add two ounces of butter, one-quarter pint of milk, two ounces of loaf sugar, three eggs, one tablespoonful of yeast. Put the milk and butter into a saucepan, and keep shaking it round until the latter is melted. Put the flour into a basin with the sugar, mix these well together, and beat the eggs. Stir them with the yeast to the milk and butter, and with this liquid work the flour into a smooth dough. Cover a cloth over the basin, and leave the dough to rise by the side of the fire; then knead it, and divide it into twelve pieces; place them in a brisk oven, and bake for about twenty minutes. Take the rusks out, break them in half, and then set them in the oven to get crisp on the other side. When cold, they should be put into tin canisters to keep them dry; and, if intended for the cheese course, the sifted sugar should be omitted.

### SWEET MILK GEMS.

Beat an egg well, add a pint new milk, a little salt, and Graham flour until it will drop off the spoon nicely; heat and butter the gem-pans before dropping in the dough; bake in a hot oven twenty minutes.

### BREAKFAST GEMS.

One cup sweet milk, one and a half cups flour, one egg, one teaspoon salt, one teaspoon baking powder, beaten together five minutes; bake in hot gem-pans in a hot oven about fifteen minutes.

### GRAHAM BREAKFAST CAKES.

Two cups of Graham flour, one cup of wheat flour, two eggs well beaten; mix with sweet milk, to make a very thin batter; bake in gem-irons; have the irons hot, then set them on the upper grate in the oven; will bake in fifteen minutes.

### BUCKWHEAT CAKES.

One quart buckwheat flour; four tablespoonfuls yeast; one teaspoonful salt; one handful Indian meal; two tablespoonfuls molasses—*not* syrup. Warm water enough to make a thin batter. Beat very well and set to rise in a warm place. If the batter is in the least sour in the morning, stir in a very little soda dissolved in hot water. Mix in an earthen crock, and leave some in the bottom each morning—a cupful or so—to serve as sponge for the next night, instead of getting fresh yeast. In cold weather this plan can be successfully pursued for a week or ten days without setting a new supply. Of course you add the usual quantity of flour, etc., every night, and beat up well. Do not make your cakes too small. Buckwheats should be of generous size. Some put two-thirds buckwheat, one-third oat-meal, omitting the Indian.

## FLANNEL CAKES.

Beat six eggs very light, stir in them two pounds of flour, one gill of yeast, small spoonful of salt, and sufficient milk to make a thick batter. Make them at night for breakfast, and at ten in the morning for tea. Have your griddle hot, grease it well, and bake as buckwheat. Butter and send them hot to the table, commencing after the family are seated.

## RICE GRIDDLE-CAKES.

Boil half a cup rice; when cold, mix one quart sweet milk, the yolks of four eggs, and flour sufficient to make a stiff batter; beat the whites to a froth, stir in one teaspoon soda, and two of cream tartar; add a little salt, and lastly, the whites of eggs; bake on a griddle. A nice way to serve is to spread them while hot with butter, and almost any kind of preserves or jelly; roll them up neatly, cut off the ends, sprinkle them with sugar, and serve immediately.

## FRENCH PANCAKES.

Two eggs, two ounces of butter, two ounces of sifted sugar, two ounces of flour, half pint of new milk. Beat the eggs thoroughly, and put them into a basin with the butter, which should be beaten to a cream; stir in the sugar and flour, and when these ingredients are well mixed, add the milk; keep stirring and beating the mixture for a few minutes; put it on buttered plates, and bake in a quick oven for twenty minutes. Serve with a cut lemon and sifted sugar, or pile the pancakes high on a dish, with a layer of preserve or marmalade between each.

## PANCAKES.

Two cups of prepared flour; six eggs; one saltspoonful of salt; milk to make a thin batter. Beat the eggs light; add salt, two cups of milk, then the whites and flour alternately with milk, until the batter is of the right consistency. Run a teaspoonful of lard over the bottom of a hot frying-pan, pour in a large ladleful of batter and fry quickly. Roll the pancake up like a sheet of paper; lay upon a hot dish; put in more lard, and fry another pancake. Keep hot over boiling water, sending half a dozen to the table at a time.

## BREAD FRITTERS.

One quart milk—boiling hot; two cups fine bread-crumbs; three eggs; one teaspoonful nutmeg; one tablespoonful butter—melted; one saltspoonful salt, and the same of soda, dissolved in hot water. Soak the bread in the boiling milk ten minutes, in a covered bowl. Beat to a smooth paste; add the whipped yolks, the butter, salt, soda and finally the whites, whipped stiff.

## QUICK SALLY LUNN.

One cup of sugar, half cup of butter; stir well together, and then add one or two eggs; put in one good pint of sweet milk, and with sufficient flour to make a batter about as stiff as cake; put in three teaspoons of baking powder; bake and eat hot with butter, for tea or breakfast.

## BREAKFAST CAKE.

One pint of flour, three tablespoons of butter, three tablespoons of sugar, one egg, one cup sweet milk, one teaspoon cream tartar, half teaspoon soda; to be eaten with butter.

## QUICK WAFFLES.

Two pints sweet milk, one cup butter (melted), sifted flour to make a soft batter; add the well-beaten yolks of six eggs, then the beaten whites, and lastly (just before baking), four teaspoons baking powder, beating very hard and fast for a few minutes. These are very good with four or five eggs, but much better with more.

## JOHNNY CAKE.

Two-thirds teaspoon soda, three tablespoons sugar, one teaspoon cream tartar, one egg, one cup sweet milk, six tablespoons Indian meal, three tablespoonfuls flour, and a little salt. This makes a thin batter.

## MUSH.

Indian or oatmeal mush is best made in the following manner: Put fresh water in a kettle over the fire to boil, and put in some salt; when the water boils, stir in handful by handful corn or oatmeal until thick enough for use. In order to have excellent mush, the meal should be allowed to cook well and long as possible while thin and before the final handful is added. When desired to be fried for breakfast, turn into an earthen dish and set away to cool. Then cut in slices when you wish to fry; dip each piece in beaten eggs and fry on a hot griddle.

### CORN MUSH.

Put four quarts fresh water in a kettle to boil, salt to suit the taste; when it begins to boil stir in one and a half quarts meal, letting it sift through the fingers slowly to prevent lumps, adding it a little faster at the last, until as thick as can be conveniently stirred with one hand; set in the oven in the kettle, (or take out into a pan), bake an hour, and it will be thoroughly cooked. It takes corn meal so long to cook thoroughly that it is very difficult to boil it until done without burning. Excellent for frying when cold. Use a hard wood paddle, two feet long, with a blade two inches wide and seven inches long, to stir with. The thorough cooking and baking in oven afterwards takes away all the raw taste that mush is apt to have, and adds much to its sweetness and delicious flavor.

### GRAHAM MUSH.

Sift meal slowly into boiling salted water, stirring briskly until it is as thick as can be stirred with one hand; serve with milk, or cream and sugar, or butter and syrup. It is much improved by removing from the kettle to a pan as soon as thoroughly mixed, and steaming for three or four hours. It may also be eaten cold, or sliced and fried like corn mush.

## SALADS, PICKLES AND CATSUP.

### LETTUCE.

The early lettuce, and first fine salad, are five or six leaves in a cluster; their early appearance is their greatest recommendation; cabbage or white-heart lettuce is later and much more delicate; break the leaves apart one by one from the stalk and throw them into a pan of cold water; rinse them well, lay them into a salad bowl or a deep dish, lay the largest leaves first, put the next size upon them, then lay on the finest white leaves; cut hard-boiled eggs in slices or quarters and lay them at equal distances around the edge and over the salad; serve with vinegar, oil, and made mustard in the castor. Or, having picked and washed the lettuce, cut the leaves small; put the cut salad in a glass dish or bowl, pour a salad dressing over and serve; or, garnish with small red radishes, cut in halves or slices, and hard-boiled eggs cut in quarters or slices; pour a salad dressing over when ready to serve. Serve with boiled lobster, boiled fowls, or roasted lamb or veal.

### LETTUCE SALAD.

Take the yolks of three hard-boiled eggs, add salt and mustard to taste; mash it fine; make a paste by adding a dessertspoon of olive oil or melted butter (use butter always when it is difficult to get *fresh* oil); mix thoroughly, and then dilute by adding *gradually* a teacup of vinegar, and pour over the lettuce. Garnish by slicing another egg and laying over the lettuce. This is sufficient for a moderate-sized dish of lettuce.

## SALMON SALAD.

One quart of cooked salmon, two heads of lettuce, two tablespoonfuls of lemon-juice, one of vinegar, two of capers, one teaspoonful of salt, one-third of a teaspoonful of pepper, one cupful of mayonnaise dressing, or the French dressing. Break up the salmon with two silver forks. Add to it the salt, pepper, vinegar and lemon-juice. Put in the ice-chest or some other cold place, for two or three hours. Prepare the lettuce as directed for lobster salad. At serving time, pick out leaves enough to border the dish. Cut or tear the remainder in pieces, and arrange these in the centre of a flat dish. On them heap the salmon lightly, and cover with the dressing. Now sprinkle on the capers. Arrange the whole leaves at the base; and, if you choose, lay one-fourth of a thin slice of lemon on each leaf.

## LOBSTER SALAD.

Put a large lobster over the fire in boiling water slightly salted; boil rapidly for about twenty minutes; when done it will be of a bright red color, and should be removed, as if boiled too long it will be tough; when cold, crack the claws, after first disjointing, twist off the head (which is used in garnishing), split the body in two lengthwise, pick out the meat in bits not too fine, saving the coral separate; cut up a large head of lettuce slightly, and place on a dish over which lay the lobster, putting the coral around the outside. For dressing, take the yolks of three eggs, beat well, add four tablespoons salad oil, dropping it in very slowly, beating all the time; then add a little salt. Cayenne pepper, half teaspoon mixed mustard, and two tablespoons vinegar. Pour this over the lobster, just before sending to table.

## TOMATO SALAD.

Take the skin, juice and seeds from nice, fresh tomatoes, chop what remains with celery, and add a good salad-dressing.

## SALAD DRESSING.

Yolks of two hard-boiled eggs rubbed very fine and smooth, one teaspoon English mustard, one of salt, the yolks of two raw eggs beaten into the other, dessertspoon of fine sugar. Add very fresh sweet oil poured in by very small quantities, and beaten as long as the mixture continues to thicken, then add vinegar till as thin as desired. If not hot enough with mustard, add a little Cayenne pepper.

## SARDINE SALAD.

Arrange one quart of any kind of cooked fish on a bed of crisp lettuce. Split six sardines, and if there are any bones, remove them. Cover the fish with the sardine dressing. Over this put the sardines, having the ends meet in the center of the dish. At the base of the dish make a wreath of thin slices of lemon. Garnish with parsley or lettuce, and serve immediately.

## FRENCH SALAD DRESSING.

Three tablespoonfuls of oil, one of vinegar, one saltspoonful of salt, one-half a saltspoonful of pepper. Put the salt and pepper in a cup, and add one tablespoonful of the oil. When thoroughly mixed, add the remainder of the oil and the vinegar. This is dressing enough for a salad for six persons. If you like the flavor of onion, grate a little juice into the dressing. The juice is obtained by first peeling the onion, and then grating with a coarse grater, using a good deal of pressure. Two strokes will give about two drops of juice.

## CREAM DRESSING FOR COLD SLAW.

Two tablespoons whipped sweet cream, two of sugar, and four of vinegar; beat well and pour over cabbage, previously cut very fine and seasoned with salt.

## CHICKEN SALAD.

Boil one chicken tender; chop moderately fine the whites of twelve hard-boiled eggs and the chicken; add equal quantities of chopped celery and cabbage; mash the yolks fine, add two tablespoons butter, two of sugar, one teaspoon mustard; pepper and salt to taste; and lastly, one-half cup good cider vinegar; pour over the salad, and mix thoroughly. If no celery is at hand, use chopped pickled cucumbers or lettuce and celery seed. This may be mixed two or three days before using.

## RED VEGETABLE SALAD.

One pint of cold boiled potatoes, one pint of cold boiled beets, one pint of uncooked red cabbage, six tablespoonfuls of oil, eight of red vinegar (that in which beets have been pickled), two teaspoonfuls of salt (unless the vegetables have been cooked in salted water), half a teaspoonful of pepper. Cut the potatoes in *thin* slices and the beets fine, and slice the cabbage as thin as possible. Mix all the ingredients. Let stand in a cold place one hour; then serve. Red cabbage and celery may be used together.

## CELERY SALAD.

One boiled egg, one raw egg, one tablespoonful salad oil, one teaspoonful white sugar, one saltspoonful of salt, one saltspoon of pepper, four tablespoonfuls of vinegar, one teaspoonful made mustard. Prepare the dressing as for tomato salad; cut the celery into bits half an inch long, and season. Eat at once, before the vinegar injures the crispness of the vegetable.

## COLD SLAW.

Chop or shred a small white cabbage. Prepare a dressing in the proportion of one tablespoonful of oil to four of vinegar, a teaspoonful of made mustard, the same quantity of salt and sugar, and half as much pepper. Pour over the salad, adding, if you choose, three tablespoonfuls of minced celery; toss up well and put into a glass bowl.

## SALAD DRESSING (Excellent).

Four eggs, one teaspoonful of mixed mustard, one-quarter teaspoonful of white pepper, half that quantity of Cayenne, salt to taste, four tablespoonfuls of cream, vinegar.

Boil the eggs until hard, which will be in about one-quarter hour or twenty minutes; put them into cold water, take off the shells, and pound the yolks in a mortar to a smooth paste. Then add all the other ingredients, except the vinegar, and stir them well until the whole are thoroughly incorporated one with the other. Pour in sufficient vinegar to make it of the consistency of cream, taking care to add but little at a time. The mixture will then be ready for use.

## PICKLED CUCUMBERS.

Wash and wipe six hundred small cucumbers and two quarts of peppers. Put them in a tub with one and a half cupfuls of salt and a piece of alum as large as an egg. Heat to the boiling point three gallons of cider vinegar and three pints of water. Add a quarter of a pound each of whole cloves, whole allspice and stick cinnamon, and two ounces of white mustard seed, and pour over the pickles.

## TO PICKLE ONIONS.

Peel the onions until they are white, scald them in strong salt and water, then take them up with a skimmer; make vinegar enough to cover them, boiling hot; strew over the onions whole pepper and white mustard seed, pour the vinegar over to cover them; when cold, put them in wide-mouthed bottles, and cork them close. A tablespoonful of sweet oil may be put in the bottles before the cork. The best sort of onions for pickling are the small white buttons.

## PICKLED CAULIFLOWERS.

Two cauliflowers, cut up; one pint of small onions, three medium-sized red peppers. Dissolve half a pint of salt in water enough to cover the vegetables, and let these stand over night. In the morning drain them. Heat two quarts of vinegar with four tablespoonfuls of mustard, until it boils. Add the vegetables, and boil for about fifteen minutes, or until a fork can be thrust through the cauliflower.

## RED CABBAGE.

Procure a firm good-sized cabbage, and after taking off any straggling or soiled leaves, cut it in very thin slices, which, after you sprinkle them well with salt, lay aside for forty-eight hours. Next drain off the salt liquor which has formed, and pour over the cabbage a well-seasoned pickle of boiling hot vinegar; black pepper and ginger are best for seasoning. Cover the pickle jars till the cabbage is cold, and then cork.

## TO PICKLE TOMATOES.

Take the round, smooth green tomatoes, put them in salt and water, cover the vessel and put them over the fire to scald; that is, to let the water become boiling hot; then set the kettle off; take them from the pot into a basin of cold water; to enough cold vinegar to cover them, put whole pepper and mustard seed; when the tomatoes are cold take them from the water, cut each in two across, shake out the seeds and wipe the inside dry with a cloth, then put them into glass jars, and cover with the vinegar; cork them close or with a close-fitting tin cover.

## RIPE TOMATO PICKLES.

To seven pounds of ripe tomatoes add three pounds sugar, one quart vinegar; boil them together fifteen minutes, skim out the tomatoes and boil the syrup a few minutes longer. Spice to suit the taste with cloves and cinnamon.

## CHOPPED PICKLE.

One peck of green tomatoes, two quarts of onions and two of peppers. Chop all fine, separately, and mix, adding three cupfuls of salt. Let them stand over night, and in the morning drain well. Add half a pound of mustard seed, two tablespoonfuls of ground allspice, two of ground cloves and one cupful of grated horseradish. Pour over it three quarts of boiling vinegar.

## CHOW CHOW.

One peck of green tomatoes, half peck string beans, quarter peck small white onions, quarter pint green and red peppers mixed, two large heads cabbage, four tablespoons white mustard seed, two of white or black cloves, two of celery seed, two of allspice, one small box yellow mustard, pound brown sugar, one ounce of turmeric; slice the tomatoes and let stand over night in brine that will bear an egg; then squeeze out brine, chop cabbage, onions and beans; chop tomatoes separately, mix with the spices, put all in porcelain kettle, cover with vinegar and boil three hours.

## PICCALILLI.

One peck of green tomatoes; (if the flavor of onions is desired, take eight, but it is very nice without any); four green peppers; slice all, and put in layers, sprinkle on one cup of salt, and let them remain over night; in the morning press dry through a sieve, put it in a porcelain kettle and cover with vinegar; add one cup of sugar, a tablespoon of each kind of spice; put into a muslin bag; stew slowly about an hour, or until the tomatoes are as soft as you desire.

## PICKLED WALNUTS (Very Good).

One hundred walnuts, salt and water. To each quart of vinegar allow two ounces of whole black pepper, one ounce of allspice, one ounce of bruised ginger. Procure the walnuts while young; be careful they are not woody, and prick them well with a fork; prepare a strong brine of salt and water (four pounds of salt to each gallon of water), into which put the walnuts, letting them remain nine days, and changing the brine every third day; drain them off, put them on a dish, place it in the sun until they become perfectly black, which will be in two or three days; have ready dry jars, into which place the walnuts, and do not quite fill the jars. Boil sufficient vinegar to cover them, for ten minutes, with spices in the above proportion, and pour it hot over the walnuts, which must be quite covered with the pickle; tie down with bladder, and keep in dry place. They will be fit for use in a month, and will keep good two or three years.

## GREEN TOMATO PICKLE.

One peck green tomatoes sliced, six large onions sliced, one teacup of salt over both; mix thoroughly and let it remain over night; pour off liquor in the morning and throw it away; mix two quarts of water and one of vinegar, and boil twenty minutes; drain and throw liquor away; take three quarts of vinegar, two pounds of sugar, two tablespoons each of allspice, cloves, cinnamon, ginger, and mustard, and twelve green peppers chopped fine; boil from one to two hours. Put away in a stone crock.

## CHILI SAUCE.

Eight quarts tomatoes, three cups of peppers, two cups of onions, three cups of sugar, one cup of salt, one and a half quarts of vinegar, three teaspoonfuls of cloves; same quantity of cinnamon, two teaspoonfuls each of ginger and nutmeg; boil three hours; chop tomatoes, peppers, and onions very fine; bottle up and seal.

## MIXED PICKLES.

Three hundred small cucumbers, four green peppers sliced fine, two large or three small heads cauliflower, three heads white cabbage shaved fine, nine large onions sliced, one large root horseradish, one quart green beans cut one inch long, one quart green tomatoes sliced; put this mixture in a pretty strong brine twenty-four hours; drain three hours, then sprinkle in a quarter pound black and a quarter pound white mustard seed; also one tablespoon black ground pepper; let it come to a good boil in just vinegar enough to cover it, adding a little alum. Drain again, and when cold, mix in a half pint ground mustard; cover the whole with good cider vinegar; add turmeric enough to color, if you like.

### PICKLED MUSHROOMS.

Sufficient vinegar to cover the mushrooms, to each quart of mushrooms, two blades pounded mace, one ounce ground pepper; salt to taste. Choose some nice young button-mushrooms for pickling, and rub off the skin with a piece of flannel and salt, and cut off the stalks; if very large, take out the red inside, and reject the black ones, as they are too old. Put them in a stewpan, sprinkle salt over them, with pounded mace and pepper in the above proportion; shake them well over a clear fire until the liquor flows, and keep them there until it is all dried up again; then add as much vinegar as will cover them; just let it simmer for one minute, and store it away in stone jars for use. When cold, tie down with bladder, and keep in a dry place; they will remain good for a length of time, and are generally considered delicious.

### FAVORITE PICKLES.

One quart raw cabbage chopped fine; one quart boiled beets chopped fine; two cups sugar, tablespoon salt, one teaspoon black pepper, a quarter teaspoon red pepper one tea-cup grated horseradish; cover with cold vinegar and keep from the air.

## TOMATO MUSTARD.

Slice and boil for an hour, with six small red peppers, half bushel of ripe tomatoes; strain through a colander and boil for an hour with two tablespoonfuls of black pepper, two ounces of ginger, one ounce allspice, half ounce cloves, one-eighth ounce mace, quarter pound salt. When cold add two ounces mustard, two ounces curry powder, and one pint of vinegar.

## INDIAN CHETNEY.

Eight ounces of sharp, sour apples, pared and cored, eight ounces of tomatoes, eight ounces of salt, eight ounces of brown sugar, eight ounces of stoned raisins, four ounces of Cayenne, four ounces of powdered ginger, two ounces of garlic, two ounces of shalots, three quarts of vinegar, one quart of lemon-juice. Chop the apples in small square pieces, and add to them the other ingredients. Mix the whole well together, and put in a well-covered jar. Keep this in a warm place, and stir every day for a month, taking care to put on the lid after this operation; strain, but do not squeeze it dry; store it away in clean jars or bottles for use, and the liquor will serve as an excellent sauce for meat or fish.

## PICKLED CHERRIES.

Five pounds of cherries, stoned or not; one quart of vinegar, two pounds of sugar, one-half ounce of cinnamon, one-half ounce of cloves, one-half ounce of mace, boil the sugar and vinegar and spices together (grind the spices and tie them in a muslin bag), and pour hot over the cherries.

## PICKLED PLUMS.

To seven pounds plums, four pounds sugar, two ounces stick cinnamon, two ounces cloves, one quart vinegar, add a little mace; put in the jar first a layer of plums, then a layer of spices alternately; scald the vinegar and sugar together, pour it over the plums; repeat three times for plums (only once for cut apples and pears), the fourth time scald all together, put them into glass jars and they are ready for use.

## SPICED PLUMS.

Make a syrup, allowing one pound of sugar to one of plums, and to every three pounds of sugar a scant pint of vinegar. Allow one ounce each of ground cinnamon, cloves, mace, and allspice to a peck of plums. Prick the plums. Add the spices to the syrup, and pour, boiling, over the plums. Let these stand three days; then skim them out, and boil down the syrup until it is quite thick, and pour hot over the plums in the jar in which they are to be kept. Cover closely.

## PEACHES, PEARS, AND SWEET APPLES.

For six pounds of fruit use three of sugar, about five dozen cloves, and a pint of vinegar. Into each apple, pear, or peach, stick two cloves. Have the syrup hot, and cook until tender.

## TOMATO CATSUP.

Take one gallon of skinned tomatoes, four tablespoonfuls of salt, four ditto of whole black pepper, half a spoonful of allspice, eight pods of red pepper, and three spoonfuls of mustard, boil them together for one hour, then strain it through a sieve or coarse cloth, and when cold, bottle for use; have the best velvet corks.

## WALNUT CATSUP.

Bruise to a mass one hundred and twenty green walnuts, gathered when a pin could pierce one; put to it three-quarters of a pound of salt and a quart of good vinegar; stir them every day for a fortnight, then strain and squeeze the liquor from them through a cloth, and set it aside, put to the husks half a pint of vinegar, and let it stand all night, then strain and squeeze them as before; put the liquor from them to that which was put aside, add to it one ounce and a quarter of whole pepper, forty cloves, half an ounce of nutmeg sliced, and half an ounce of ginger, and boil it for half an hour closely covered, then strain it; when cold, bottle it for use. Secure the bottles with new corks, and dip them in melted rosin.

## MUSHROOM CATSUP.

To each peck of mushrooms one-half pound of salt; to each quart of mushroom liquor one-quarter ounce of Cayenne, one-half ounce of allspice, one-half ounce of ginger, two blades of pounded mace. Choose full-grown mushroom-flaps, and take care they are perfectly *fresh-gathered* when the weather is tolerably dry; for, if they are picked during very heavy rain the catsup from which they are made is liable to get musty, and will not keep long. Put a layer of them in a deep pan, sprinkle salt over them, and then another layer of mushrooms, and so on alternately. Let them remain for a few hours, then break them up with the hand; put them in a nice cool place for three days, occasionally stirring and mashing them well to extract from them as much juice as possible. Now measure the quantity of liquor without straining, and to each quart allow the above proportion of spices, etc. Put all into a stone jar, cover it up very closely, put it in a saucepan of boiling water, set it over the fire, and let it boil for three hours.

Have ready a nice clean stewpan; turn into it the contents of the jar, and let the whole simmer very gently for half an hour; pour into a jug, where it should stand in a cool place till next day; then pour it off into another jug, and strain it into very dry, clean bottles, and do not squeeze the mushrooms. To each pint of catsup add a few drops of brandy. Be careful not to shake the contents, but leave all the sediment behind in the jug; cork well, and either seal or rosin the cork, so as perfectly to exclude the air. When a very clear, bright catsup is wanted, the liquor must be strained through a very fine hair-sieve, or flannel bag, *after* it has been very gently poured off; if the operation is not successful, it must be repeated until you have quite a clear liquor. It should be examined occasionally, and if it is spoiling should be reboiled with a few peppercorns.

## BRINE THAT PRESERVES BUTTER A YEAR

To three gallons of brine strong enough to bear an egg, add one-quarter pound good loaf sugar, and one tablespoonful of saltpetre; boil the brine, and when it is cold strain carefully. Pack butter closely in small jars, and allow the brine to cover the butter to the depth of at least four inches. This completely excludes the air. If practicable make your butter into small rolls, wrap each carefully in a clean muslin cloth, tying up with a string; place a weight over the butter to keep it all submerged in the brine. This mode is most recommended by those who have tried both.

## BUTTER IN HASTE,

#### FROM WINTER CREAM, OR FROM THE MILK OF ONE COW.

Take milk fresh from the cow, strain it into clean pans, set it over a gentle fire until it is scalding hot; do not let it boil; then set it aside; when it is cold skim off the cream; the milk will still be fit for any ordinary use; when you have enough cream, put it into a clean earthen basin; beat it with a wooden spoon until the butter is made, which will not be long; then take it from the milk and work with a little cold water, until it is free from milk, then drain off the water, put a small tablespoonful of fine salt to each pound of butter, and work it in. A small teaspoonful of fine white sugar, worked in with the salt, will be found an improvement—sugar is a great preservative. Make the butter in a roll; cover with a bit of muslin, and keep it in a cool place.

This receipt was obtained from one who practiced it for several winters.

# PUDDINGS.

## GENERAL REMARKS.

*All boiled pudding* should be put on in *boiling water*, which must not be allowed to stop simmering, and the pudding must always be covered with the water; if requisite the saucepan should be kept filled up. To prevent a pudding boiled in a cloth from sticking to the bottom of the saucepan, place a small plate or saucer underneath it, if a mold is used, this precaution is not necessary; but care must be taken to keep the pudding well covered with water. For dishing a boiled pudding as soon as it comes out of the pot, dip it into a basin of cold water, and the cloth will then not adhere to it. Great expedition is necessary in sending puddings to table, as, by standing, they quickly become heavy, batter puddings particularly. For baked or boiled puddings, the molds, cups, or basins should be always buttered before the mixture is put into them, and they should be put into the saucepan directly they are filled.

## CHRISTMAS PLUM PUDDING.

One pound butter, one pound suet, freed from strings and chopped fine, one pound sugar, two and a half pounds flour, two pounds raisins, seeded, chopped and dredged with flour, two pounds currants, picked over carefully after they are washed, one-quarter pound citron, shred fine, twelve eggs, whites and yolks beaten separately, one pint milk, one cup brandy, one-half ounce cloves, one-half ounce mace, two grated nutmegs. Cream the butter and sugar, beat in the yolks when you have whipped them smooth and light; next put in the milk, then the flour, alternately with the beaten whites, then the brandy and spice, lastly the fruit, well dredged with flour. Mix all thoroughly wring out your pudding-cloth in hot water, flour well inside, pour in the mixture and boil five hours.

## BOILED BATTER PUDDING.

Three eggs, one ounce butter, one pint milk, three tablespoonfuls flour, a little salt. Put the flour into a basin, and add sufficient milk to moisten it; carefully rub down all the lumps with a spoon, then pour in the remainder of the milk, and stir in the butter, which should be previously melted; keep beating the mixture, add the eggs and a pinch of salt, and when the batter is quite smooth, put it into a well-buttered basin, tie it down very tightly, and put it into boiling water; move the basin about for a few minutes after it is put into the water, to prevent the flour settling in any part, and boil for one and one-quarter hours. This pudding may also be boiled in a floured cloth that has been wetted in hot water; it will then take a few minutes less than when boiled in a basin. Send these puddings very quickly to table, and serve with sweet sauce, wine sauce, stewed fruit, or jam of any kind; when the latter is used, a little of it may be placed round the dish in small quantities, as a garnish.

## BATTER PUDDING.

One quart milk, four eggs, six ounces flour, a little soda and salt. Mix the flour very carefully with a little milk so it will not be lumpy. Bake twenty minutes. Serve immediately.

## MADEIRA PUDDING.

One-half pound cheap suet, three-quarters of a pound bread-crumbs, six ounces moist sugar, one-quarter pound flour, two eggs, two wineglasses sherry; mix the suet, bread-crumbs, sugar and flour well together. When these ingredients are well-mixed, add the eggs and two glasses of sherry, to make a thick batter; boil three hours and a half. Serve with wine sauce.

## APPLE SAGO PUDDING.

One cup sago in a quart of tepid water, with a pinch of salt, soaked for one hour; six or eight apples, pared and cored, or quartered, and steamed tender, and put in the pudding dish; boil and stir the sago until clear, adding water to make it thin, and pour it over the apples; this is good hot with butter and sugar, or cold with cream and sugar.

## QUEEN OF PUDDINGS.

One large cup of fine bread-crumbs soaked in milk, three-quarters cup sugar, one lemon, juice and grated rind, six eggs, one-half pound stale sponge cake, one-half pound macaroons—almond, one-half cup jelly or jam, and one small tumbler sherry wine, one-half cup milk poured upon the bread-crumbs, one tablespoonful melted butter. Rub the butter and sugar together; put the beaten yolks in next, then the soaked bread-crumbs, the lemon, juice and rind, and beat to a smooth, light paste before adding the whites. Butter your mold very well, and put in the bottom a light layer of dry bread-crumbs, upon this one of macaroons, laid evenly and closely together. Wet this with wine, and cover with a layer of the mixture, then with slices of sponge cake, spread thickly with jelly or jam; next macaroons, wet with wine, more custard, sponge-cake and jam, and so on until the mold is full, putting a layer of the mixture at the top. Cover closely, and steam in the oven three-quarters of an hour; then remove the cover to brown the top. Turn out carefully into a dish, and pour over it a sauce made of currant jelly warmed, and beaten up with two tablespoonfuls melted butter and a glass of pale sherry.

## ORANGE PUDDING.

**Peel** and cut five sweet oranges into thin slices, taking out the seeds, pour over them a coffee-cup of white sugar; let a pint of milk get boiling hot, by setting it in a pot of boiling water; add the yolks of three eggs well beaten, one tablespoonful of corn starch, made smooth with a little cold milk: stir all the time; as soon as thickened pour over the fruit. Beat the whites to a stiff froth, adding a tablespoonful of sugar, and spread over the top for frosting; set it in the oven for a few minutes to harden; eat cold or hot (better cold), for dinner and supper. Berries or peaches can be substituted for oranges.

## CORN STARCH PUDDING.

One pint sweet milk, whites of three eggs, two tablespoons corn starch, three of sugar, a little salt. Put the milk in a pan or small bucket, set in a kettle of hot water on the stove, and when it reaches the boiling point add the sugar, then the starch dissolved in a little cold milk, and lastly the whites of eggs whipped to a stiff froth; beat it, and let cook for a few minutes, then pour into teacups, filling about half full, and set in cool place. For sauce, make a boiled custard as follows: Bring to boiling point one pint of milk, add three tablespoons sugar, then the beaten yolks thinned by adding one tablespoon milk, stirring all the time till it thickens; flavor with two teaspoons lemon or two of vanilla, and set to cool. In serving, put one of the molds in a saucedish for each person, and pour over it some of the boiled custard. Or the pudding may be made in one large mold.

To make a chocolate pudding, flavor the above pudding with vanilla, remove two-thirds of it, and add half a cake of chocolate softened, mashed, and dissolved in a little milk. Put a layer of half the white pudding into the mold, then the chocolate, then the rest of the white; or two layers of chocolate may be used with a white between; or the centre may be cocoa (made by adding half a cocoanut grated fine), and the outside chocolate; or pineapple chopped fine (if first cooked in a little water, the latter makes a nice dressing), or strawberries may be used.

## FRENCH PUDDING.

One quart of milk, three tablespoons of corn starch, yolks of four eggs, half cup sugar and a little salt; put part of the milk, salt and sugar on the stove and let it boil; dissolve the corn starch in the rest of the milk; stir into the milk, and while boiling add the yolks. Flavor with vanilla.

FROSTING.—Whites of four eggs beaten to a stiff froth, half a cup of sugar; flavor with lemon; spread it on the pudding, and put it into the oven to brown, saving a little of the frosting to moisten the top; then put on grated cocoanut to give it the appearance of snow-flake.

## BELLE'S PUDDING.

Soak for an hour in a pint of cold water one box of Cox's sparkling gelatine, and add one pint of boiling water, one pint of wine, the juice of four lemons, and three large cupfuls of sugar. Beat the whites of four eggs to a stiff froth, and stir into the jelly when it begins to thicken. Pour into a large mold, and set in ice-water in a cool place. When ready to serve, turn out as you would jelly, only have the pudding in a deep dish. Pour one quart of soft custard around it, and serve.

## CREAM TAPIOCA PUDDING.

Soak three tablespoons of tapioca in water over night; put the tapioca into a quart of boiling milk, and boil half an hour; beat the yolks of four eggs with a cup of sugar; add three tablespoons of prepared cocoanut; stir in and boil ten minutes longer; pour into a pudding-dish; beat the whites of four eggs to a stiff froth, stir in three tablespoons of sugar; put this over the top and sprinkle cocoanut over the top and brown for five minutes.

## A BACHELOR'S PUDDING.

Four ounces of grated bread, four ounces of currants, four ounces of apples, two ounces of sugar, three eggs, a few drops of essence of lemon, a little grated nutmeg. Pare, core, and mince the apples very finely, sufficient, when minced, to make four ounces; add to these the currants, which should be well washed, the grated bread, and sugar; whisk the eggs, beat these up with the remaining ingredients, and, when all is thoroughly mixed, put the pudding into a buttered basin, tie it down with a cloth, and boil for three hours.

## MACARONI PUDDING.

One-half pound macaroni broken into inch lengths, two cups boiling water, one teaspoonful butter, one large cup milk, two tablespoonfuls sugar, grated peel of half a lemon, a little cinnamon and salt. Boil the macaroni in the water until it is tender, and has soaked up the liquid. It must be cooked in a farina-kettle. Add the butter and salt. Cover for five minutes without cooking. Put in the rest of the ingredients. Simmer, after the boil begins, ten minutes longer, before serving in a deep dish. Be careful, in stirring, not to break the macaroni. Eat with butter and powdered sugar, or cream and sugar.

### BAKED INDIAN PUDDING.

Two quarts scalded milk with salt, one and one-half cups Indian meal (yellow); one tablespoon ginger, letting this stand twenty minutes; one cup molasses, two eggs (saleratus if no eggs), a piece of butter the size of a common walnut. Bake two hours. Splendid.

### BOILED INDIAN PUDDING.

Warm a pint of molasses and pint of milk, stir well together, beat four eggs, and stir gradually into molasses and milk; add a pound beef suet chopped fine, and Indian meal sufficient to make a thick batter; add a teaspoon pulverized cinnamon, nutmeg and a little grated lemon-peel, and stir all together thoroughly; dip cloth into boiling water, shake, flour a little, turn in the mixture, tie up, leaving room for the pudding to swell, and boil three hours; serve hot with sauce made of drawn butter, wine and nutmeg.

### MARMALADE PUDDINGS.

Half pound suet, half pound grated bread-crumbs, half pound sugar, three ounces orange marmalade; mix these ingredients together with four eggs; boil four hours. Lay a few raisins open in the bottom of the mold. Sauce: Two ounces butter, and two ounces white sugar; beat to a cream and flavor with brandy or lemon.

## BOILED APPLE DUMPLINGS.

Add to two cups sour milk one teaspoon soda, and one salt, half cup butter, lard, flour enough to make dough a little stiffer than for biscuit; or make a good baking powder crust; peel and core apples, roll out crust, place apples on dough, fill cavity of each with sugar, encase each apple in coating of the crust, press edges tight together, (it is nice to tie a cloth around each one), put into kettle of boiling water slighted salted, boil half an hour, taking care that the water covers the dumplings. They are also very nice steamed. To bake, make in same way, using a soft dough, place in a shallow pan, bake in a hot oven, and serve with cream and sugar, or place in a pan which is four or five inches deep (do not have the dumplings touch each other); then pour in hot water, just leaving top of dumplings uncovered. To a pan of four or five dumplings, add one teacup sugar and half a teacup butter; bake from half to three-quarters of an hour. If water cooks away too much, add more. Serve dumplings on platter and the liquid in sauce-boat for dressing. Fresh or canned peaches may be made in the same way.

## NELLY'S PUDDING.

Half pound flour, half pound treacle, half pound suet, the rind and juice of one lemon, a few strips of candied lemon-peel, three tablespoonfuls cream, two eggs. Chop the suet finely; mix with it the flour, treacle, lemon-peel minced, and candied lemon-peel; add the cream, lemon-juice, and two well-beaten eggs; beat the pudding well, put it into a buttered basin, tie it down with a cloth, and boil from three and a half to four hours.

### RICH BAKED APPLE PUDDING.

Half pound the pulp of apples, half pound loaf sugar, six ounces butter, the rind one lemon, six eggs, puff paste. Peel, core and cut the apples, as for sauce; put them into a stewpan, with only just sufficient water to prevent them from burning, and let them stew until reduced to a pulp. Weigh the pulp, and to every half pound add sifted sugar, grated lemon-rind, and six well-beaten eggs. Beat these ingredients well together; then melt the butter, stir it to the other things, put a border of puff paste round the dish, and bake for rather more than half an hour. The butter should not be added until the pudding is ready for the oven.

### SNOW BALLS.

Pick all imperfections from a half pint of rice, put it in water, and rub it between the hands; then pour that water off, put more on, stir it about in it, let the rice settle, then drain the water off; put the rice in a two-quart stewpan, with a teaspoonful of salt, and a quart of water; cover the stewpan, and set it where it will boil gently for one hour, or until the water is all absorbed; dip some teacups into cold water, fill them with the boiled rice, press it to their shape; then turn them out on a dish, and serve with butter and sugar, or wine sauce.

### RICE PUDDING.

One teacup rice, one teacup sugar, one teacup raisins, small piece butter, a little salt, two quarts milk. Bake from one hour and a half to two hours. Serve with sauce.

## APPLE CHARLOTTE.

Cut slices of wheat bread or rolls, and having rubbed the bottom and sides of a basin with a bit of butter, line it with the sliced bread or rolls; peel tart apples, cut them small, and nearly fill the pan, strewing bits of butter and sugar between the apples; grate a small nutmeg over; soak as many slices of bread or rolls as will cover it; over which put a plate, and a weight, to keep the bread close upon the apples; bake two hours in a quick oven, then turn it out. Quarter of a pound of butter, and half a pound of sugar, to half a peck of tart apples.

## GROUND RICE PUDDING.

This is an economical pudding, made with two pints of sweet milk, a teacupful of ground rice, two tablespoonfuls of sugar, three eggs, and a little ground nutmeg. Bring half the quantity of milk to the boiling point, with the nutmeg or any other flavoring matter, and sugar. In the other half of the milk beat up the rice flour into a thin batter, adding to it through a strainer the hot seasoned milk, stirring all the time. The eggs well-whisked should next be added. A sprinkling of salt is an improvement. Bake this mixture in a moderate oven for a little over an hour, say seventy minutes, or boil in a buttered basin or shape. Serve with apricot preserve, or marmalade, or indeed any kind of jam.

## FIG PUDDING.

One-half pound figs, one-quarter pound grated bread, two and a half ounces powdered sugar, three ounces butter, two eggs, one teacup of milk. Chop the figs small and mix first with the butter, then all the other ingredients by de-greens; butter a mold, sprinkle with bread-crumbs, cover it tight and boil for three hours.

## BREAD AND BUTTER PUDDING.

Place as many slices of thin cut bread and butter as you like in a pie-dish, say ten or twelve slices, sprinkle a few well-washed currants between the layers, beat up half a dozen of eggs in two pints of new milk, adding sugar to taste and a little flavoring, such as nutmeg or cinnamon, and pour over the bread and butter. Bake for an hour and ten minutes, and send it to table in the dish it has been baked in.

## CABINET PUDDING.

One quart of milk, four eggs, four tablespoonfuls of sugar, half a teaspoonful of salt, one tablespoonful of butter, three pints of stale sponge cake, one cupful of raisins, chopped citron and currants. Have a little more of the currants than of the two other fruits. Beat the eggs, sugar, and salt together, and add the milk. Butter a three-pint pudding mold (the melon shape is nice), sprinkle the sides and bottom with the fruit, and put in a layer of cake. Again sprinkle in fruit, and put in more cake. Continue this until all the materials are used. Gradually pour on the custard. Let the pudding stand two hours, and steam an hour and a quarter. Serve with wine or creamy sauce.

## SNOW PUDDING.

One half package Cox's gelatine; pour over it a cup of cold water and add one and one-half cups of sugar; when soft, add one cup boiling water, juice of one lemon and the whites of four well-beaten eggs; beat all together until very light; put in a glass dish and pour over it custard made as follows: One pint milk, yolks of four eggs, and grated rind of one lemon; boil. Splendid.

## CARROT PUDDING.

One pound grated carrots, three-fourths pound chopped suet, half pound each raisins and currants, four tablespoons sugar, eight tablespoons flour, and spices to suit the taste. Boil four hours, place in the oven for twenty minutes, and serve with wine sauce.

## LEMON PUDDING.

Half pound of sugar, half pound of butter, five eggs, half gill brandy, rind and juice of one large lemon; beat well the butter and sugar, whisk the eggs, add them to the lemon, grate the peel, line a dish with puff-paste, and bake in a moderate oven.

## ROLY-POLY.

Take one quart of flour; make good biscuit crust; roll out one-half inch thick and spread with any kind of fruit, fresh or preserved; fold so that the fruit will not run out; dip cloth into boiling water, and flour it and lay around the pudding closely, leaving room to swell; steam one and one-half hours; serve with boiled sauce; or lay in steamer without a cloth, and steam for one hour.

## COTTAGE PUDDING.

One-half cup of sugar, one cup of milk, one pint of flour, three tablespoonfuls of melted butter, one teaspoonful soda, two of cream of tartar, two eggs, a little salt; bake one-quarter of an hour in small pans.

## COCOANUT PUDDING.

Beat two eggs with one cupful of new milk; add one-quarter of a pound of grated cocoanut; mix with it three tablespoonfuls each of grated bread and powdered sugar, two ounces of melted butter, five ounces of raisins, and one teaspoonful of grated lemon-peel; beat the whole well together; pour the mixture into a buttered dish, and bake in a slow oven; then turn it out, dust sugar over it, and serve. This pudding may be either boiled or baked.

## CREAM PUDDING.

Stir together one pint cream, three ounces sugar, the yolks of three eggs, and a little grated nutmeg; add the well-beaten whites, stirring lightly, and pour into a buttered pie-plate on which has been sprinkled the crumbs of stale bread to about the thickness of an ordinary crust; sprinkle over the top a layer of bread-crumbs, and bake.

## TAPIOCA PUDDING.

Cover three tablespoons tapioca with water; stand over night; add one quart milk, a small piece of butter, a little salt, and boil; beat the yolks of three eggs with a cup of sugar, and boil the whole to a very thick custard, flavor with vanilla; when cold cover with whites of eggs beaten.

## COMMON CUSTARD.

Beat either four or five fresh eggs light; then stir them into a quart of milk; sweeten to taste; flavor with a teaspoonful of peach-water, or extract of lemon, or vanilla, and half a teaspoonful of salt; rub butter over the bottom and sides of a baking-dish or tin basin; pour in the custard, grate a little nutmeg over, and bake in a quick oven. Three-quarters of an hour is generally enough. Try whether it is done by putting a teaspoon handle into the middle of it; if it comes out clean, it is enough.

Or butter small cups; set them into a shallow pan of hot water, reaching nearly to the top of the cups; nearly fill them with the custard mixture; keep the water boiling until they are done. The pan may be set in an oven, or hot shovel.

## PUDDING SAUCES.

### RICH WINE SAUCE.

One cupful of butter, two of powdered sugar, half a cupful of wine. Beat the butter to a cream. Add the sugar gradually, and when very light add the wine, which has been made hot, a little at a time. Place the bowl in a basin of hot water and stir for two minutes. The sauce should be smooth and foamy.

### WHIPPED CREAM SAUCE.

Whip a pint of thick sweet cream, add the beaten whites of two eggs, sweeten to taste; place pudding in centre of dish, and surround with the sauce; or pile up in centre and surround with molded blanc-mange, or fruit puddings.

### LEMON SAUCE.

One cup of sugar, half a cup of butter, one egg, one lemon, juice and grated rind, three tablespoonfuls of boiling water; put in a tin pail and thicken over steam.

### JELLY SAUCE.

Melt one ounce of sugar and two tablespoons grape jelly over the fire in a half pint of boiling water, and stir into it half a teaspoon corn starch dissolved in a half cup cold water; let it come to a boil, and it will be ready for use. Any other fruit jelly may be used instead of grape.

## CABINET PUDDING SAUCE.

Take the yolks of five eggs and whip them lightly; express the juice of a lemon and grate down a little of the peel. The other ingredients are a tablespoon of butter, a cup of sugar, a glass of good wine, and a little spice. Mix the sugar and butter, adding the yolks, spice, and lemon-juice. Beat fifteen minutes, then add the wine, and stir hard. Immerse in a saucepan of boiling water, beating while it heats.

## FOAMING SAUCE.

Beat whites of three eggs to a stiff froth; melt teacup of sugar in a little water, let it boil, stir in one glass of wine, and then the whites of the three eggs; serve at once.

## SPANISH SAUCE.

One half cup of boiling water, one tablespoon corn starch, two tablespoonfuls vinegar, one tablespoonful of butter, one cup sugar, one-half nutmeg.

## HARD SAUCE.

Beat to a cream a quarter of a pound of butter, add gradually a quarter of a pound of sugar; beat it until very white; add a little lemon-juice, or grate nutmeg on top.

## PUDDING SAUCE

One cup of sugar, one-half cup of butter, yelks of three eggs; one teaspoon of corn starch or arrow-root; stir the whole until very light; add sufficient boiling water to make the consistency of thick cream; wine or brandy to suit the taste.

## SAUCE FOR PLUM PUDDING.

The yolks of three eggs, one tablespoonful of powdered sugar, one gill of milk, a very little grated lemon-rind, two small wineglassfuls of brandy. Separate the yolks from the whites of three eggs, and put the former into a stewpan; add the sugar, milk, and grated lemon-rind, and stir over the fire until the mixture thickens; but do *not* allow it to *boil*. Put in the brandy; let the sauce stand by the side of the fire, to get quite hot; keep stirring it, and serve in a boat or tureen separately, or pour it over the pudding.

## VANILLA SAUCE.

The whites of two eggs and the yolk of one, half a cupful of powdered sugar, one teaspoonful of vanilla, three tablespoonfuls of milk. Beat the whites of the eggs to a stiff froth, next beat in the sugar, and then the yolk of the egg and the seasoning. Serve immediately. This sauce is for light puddings.

## PASTRY.

### VERY GOOD PUFF-PASTE.

To every pound of flour allow one pound of butter, and not quite one-half pint of water. Carefully weigh the flour and butter, and have the exact proportion; squeeze the butter well, to extract the water from it, and afterwards wring it in a clean cloth, that no moisture may remain. Sift the flour; see that it is perfectly dry, and proceed in the following manner to make the paste, using a very *clean* paste-board and rolling-pin. Supposing the quantity to be one pound of flour, work the whole into a smooth paste, with not quite one-half pint of water, using a knife to mix it with; the proportion of this latter ingredient must be regulated by the discretion of the cook; if too much be added, the paste, when baked, will be tough. Roll it out until it is of an equal thickness of about an inch; break four ounces of the butter into small pieces; place these on the paste, sift over it a little flour, fold it over, roll out again, and put another four ounces of butter. Repeat the rolling and buttering until the paste has been rolled out four times, or equal quantities of flour and butter have been used. Do not omit, every time the paste is rolled out, to dredge a little flour over that and the rolling-pin, to prevent both from sticking. Handle the paste as lightly as possible, and do not press heavily upon it with the rolling-pin. The next thing to be considered is the oven, as the baking of pastry requires particular attention. Do not put it into the oven until it is sufficiently hot to raise the paste; for the best-prepared paste, if not properly baked, will be good for nothing. Brushing the paste as often as rolled out, and the pieces of butter placed thereon, with the white of an egg, assists it to rise in *leaves* or *flakes*. As this is the great beauty of puff-paste, it is as well to try this method.

## PLAINER PASTE.

One pound of flour, a little more for rolling-pin and board, and half a pound of butter and half a pound of lard. Cut the butter and lard through the flour (which should be sifted), and mix with sufficient ice-water to roll easily. Avoid kneading it, and use the hands as little as possible in mixing.

## SUET CRUST, FOR PIES OR PUDDINGS.

To every pound of flour allow five or six ounces of beef suet, one-half pint of water. Free the suet from skin and shreds; chop it extremely fine, and rub it well into the flour; work the whole to a smooth paste with the above proportion of water; roll it out, and it is ready for use. This crust is quite rich enough for ordinary purposes; but when a better one is desired, use from one-half to three-quarters pound of suet to every pound of flour. Some cooks, for rich crusts, pound the suet in a mortar, with a small quantity of butter. It should then be laid on the paste in small pieces, the same as for puff-crust, and will be found exceedingly nice for hot tarts. Five ounces of suet to every pound of flour will make a very good crust; and even one-quarter pound will answer very well for children, or where the crust is wanted very plain.

## TO ICE PASTRY.

To ice pastry, which is the usual method adopted for fruit tarts and sweet dishes of pastry, put the white of an egg on a plate, and with the blade of a knife beat it to a stiff froth. When the pastry is nearly baked, brush it over with this, and sift over some pounded sugar; put it back into the oven to set a glaze, and in a few minutes it will be done. Great care should be taken that the paste does not catch or burn in the oven, which it is very liable to do after the icing is laid on.

## TO GLAZE PASTRY.

To glaze pastry, which is the usual method adopted for meat or raised pies, break an egg, separate the yolk from the white, and beat the former for a short time. Then, when the pastry is nearly baked, take it out of the oven, brush it over with this beaten yolk of egg, and put it back in the oven to set the glaze.

## MINCE-MEAT.

Take five or six pounds scraggy beef—a neck piece will do—and put to boil in water enough to cover it; take off the scum that rises when it reaches the boiling point, add hot water from time to time until it is tender, then remove the lid from the pot, salt, let boil till almost dry, turning the meat over occasionally in the liquor, take from the fire, and let stand over night to get thoroughly cold; pick bones, gristle, or stringy bits from the meat, chop very fine, mincing at the same time three pounds of nice beef suet; seed and cut four pounds raisins, wash and dry four pounds currants, slice thin a pound of citron, chop fine four quarts good cooking tart apples; put into a large pan together, add two ounces cinnamon, one of cloves, one of ginger, four nutmegs, the juice and grated rind of two lemons, one tablespoon salt, one teaspoon pepper, and two pounds sugar. Put in a porcelain kettle one quart boiled cider, or, better still, one quart currant or grape-juice (canned when grapes are turning from green to purple), one quart nice molasses or syrup, also a good lump of butter; let it come to boiling point, and pour over the ingredients in the pan after having first mixed them well, then mix again thoroughly. Pack in jars and put in a cool place, and, when cold, pour molasses over the top an eighth of an inch in thickness, and cover tightly. This will keep two months. For baking, take some out of the jar; if not moist enough add a little hot water, and strew a few whole raisins over each pie. Instead of boiled beef, a beef's heart or roast meat may be used; and a good proportion for a few pies is one-third chopped meat and two-thirds apples, with a little suet, raisins, spices, butter, and salt.

## MOCK MINCE PIE.

One egg, three or four large crackers, or six or eight small ones, one-half cup of molasses, one-half cup sugar, one-half cup vinegar, one-half cup strong tea, one cup chopped raisins, a small piece butter, spice and salt.

## APPLE CUSTARD PIE.

Peel sour apples and stew until soft and not much water is left in them, and rub through a colander. Beat three eggs for each pie. Put in proportion of one cup butter and one of sugar for three pies. Season with nutmeg.

## APPLE MERINGUE PIE.

Pare, slice, stew and sweeten ripe, tart and juicy apples, mash and season with nutmeg (or stew lemon-peel with them for flavor), fill crust and bake till done; spread over the apple a thick meringue made by whipping to froth whites of three eggs for each pie, sweetening with three tablespoons powdered sugar; flavor with vanilla, beat until it will stand alone, and cover pie three-quarters of an inch thick. Set back in a quick oven till well "set," and eat cold. In their season substitute peaches for apples.

## APPLE PIE.

Stew green or ripe apples, when you have pared and cored them. Mash to a smooth compote, sweeten to taste, and, while hot, stir in a teaspoon butter for each pie. Season with nutmeg. When cool, fill your crust, and either cross-bar the top with strips of paste, or bake without cover. Eat cold, with powdered sugar strewed over it.

## LEMON PIE.

The juice and rind of one lemon, two eggs, eight heaping tablespoonfuls of sugar, one small teacupful of milk, one teaspoonful of corn starch. Mix the corn starch with a little of the milk. Put the remainder on the fire, and when boiling, stir in the corn starch. Boil one minute. Let this cool, and add the yolks of the eggs, four heaping tablespoonfuls of the sugar, and the grated rind and juice of the lemon, all well beaten together. Have a deep pie-plate lined with paste, and fill with this mixture. Bake slowly half an hour. Beat the whites of the eggs to a stiff froth, and gradually beat into them the remainder of the sugar. Cover the pie with this, and brown slowly.

## CUSTARD PIE.

Make a custard of the yolks of three eggs with milk, season to the taste; bake it in ordinary crust; put it in a quick oven, that the crust may not be heavy, and as soon as that is heated remove it to a place in the oven of a more moderate heat, that the custard may bake slowly and not curdle; when done, beat the whites to a froth; add sugar and spread over the top, and return to the oven to brown slightly; small pinch of salt added to a custard heightens the flavor; a little soda in the crust prevents it from being heavy. Very nice.

## COCOANUT PIE.

One-half pound grated cocoanut, three-quarters pound of white sugar (powdered), six ounces of butter, five eggs, the whites only, one glass of white wine, two tablespoonfuls rose-water, one tablespoonful of nutmeg. Cream the butter and sugar, and when well-mixed, beat very light, with the wine and rose-water. Add the cocoanut with as little and as light beating as possible; finally, whip in the stiffened whites of the eggs with a few skillful strokes, and bake at once in open shells. Eat cold, with powdered sugar sifted over them.

## LEMON TARTS.

Mix well together the juice and grated rind of two lemons, two cups of sugar, two eggs, and the crumbs of sponge cake; beat it all together until smooth; put into twelve patty-pans lined with puff-paste, and bake until the crust is done.

## PASTRY SANDWICHES.

Puff-paste, jam of any kind, the white of an egg, sifted sugar.

Roll the paste out thin; put half of it on a baking-sheet or tin, and spread equally over it apricot, greengage, or any preserve that may be preferred. Lay over this preserve another thin paste, press the edges together all round, and mark the paste in lines with a knife on the surface, to show where to cut it when baked. Bake from twenty minutes to half an hour; and, a short time before being done, take the pastry out of the oven, brush it over with the white of an egg, sift over pounded sugar, and put it back in the oven to color. When cold, cut it into strips; pile these on a dish pyramidically, and serve. These strips, cut about two inches long, piled in circular rows, and a plateful of flavored whipped cream poured in the middle, make a very pretty dish.

## CHERRY PIE.

Line the dish with a good crust, and fill with ripe cherries, regulating the quantity of sugar you scatter over them by their sweetness. Cover and bake.

Eat cold, with white sugar sifted over the top.

## SQUASH PIE.

Two teacups of boiled squash, three-fourths teacup of brown sugar, three eggs, two tablespoons of molasses, one tablespoon of melted butter, one tablespoon of ginger, one teaspoon of cinnamon, two teacups of milk, a little salt. Make two plate pies.

## CREAM PIE.

Pour a pint of cream upon a cup and a half powdered sugar; let stand until the whites of three eggs have been beaten to a stiff froth; add this to the cream, and beat up thoroughly; grate a little nutmeg over the mixture and bake in two pies without upper crusts.

## TARTLETS.

Puff-paste, the white of an egg, pounded sugar.

*Mode:* Roll some good puff-paste out thin, and cut it into two and a half inch squares; brush each square over with the white of an egg, then fold down the corners, so that they all meet in the middle of each piece of paste;

slightly press the two pieces together, brush them over with the egg, sift over sugar, and bake in a nice quick oven for about a quarter of an hour. When they are done, make a little hole in the middle of the paste, and fill it up with apricot jam, marmalade, or red-currant jelly. Pile them high in the centre of a dish, on a napkin, and garnish with the same preserve the tartlets are filled with.

## PEACH PIE.

Line a pie-tin with puff-paste, fill with pared peaches in halves or quarters, well covered with sugar; put on upper crust and bake; or make as above without upper crust, bake until done, remove from the oven, and cover with a meringue made of the whites of two eggs, beaten to a stiff froth with two tablespoons powdered sugar; return to oven and brown slightly. Canned peaches may be used instead of fresh, in the same way.

## TART SHELLS.

Roll out thin a nice puff-paste, cut out with a glass or biscuit cutter, with a wine-glass or smaller cup cut out the centre of two out of three of these, lay the rings thus made on the third, and bake immediately; or shells may be made by lining patty-pans with paste. If the paste is light, the shell will be fine, and may be used for tarts or oyster patties. Filled with jelly and covered with meringue (tablespoon sugar to white of one egg) and browned in oven, they are very nice to serve for tea.

## PUMPKIN PIE.

One quart of stewed pumpkin, pressed through a sieve; nine eggs, whites and yolks beaten separately; two scant quarts of milk, one teaspoonful of mace, one teaspoonful of cinnamon, and the same of nutmeg; one and a half cups of white sugar, or very light brown. Beat all well together, and bake in crust without cover.

## MINCE PIES.

Three pounds of raisins, stone and chop them a little; three pounds of currants, three pounds of sugar, three pounds of suet chopped very fine, two ounces candied lemon-peel, two ounces of candied orange-peel, six large apples grated, one ounce of cinnamon, two nutmegs, the juice of three lemons and the rinds grated, and half a pint of brandy. Excellent.

# CAKES.

### WHITE LADY-CAKE.

Beat the whites of eight eggs to a high froth, add gradually a pound of white sugar finely ground, beat quarter of a pound of butter to a cream, add a teacup of sweet milk with a small teaspoonful of powdered volatile salts or saleratus dissolved in it; put the eggs to butter and milk, add as much sifted wheat flour as will make it as thick as pound cake mixture, and a teaspoon of orange-flower water or lemon extract, then add a quarter of a pound of shelled almonds, blanched and beaten to a paste with a little white of egg; beat the whole together until light and white; line a square tin pan with buttered paper, put in the mixture an inch deep, and bake half an hour in a quick oven. When done take it from the pan; when cold take the paper off, turn it upside down on the bottom of the pan and ice the side which was down; when the icing is nearly hard mark it in slices the width of a finger, and two inches and a half long.

### MACAROONS.

One-half pound of sweet almonds, one-half pound of sifted loaf sugar, the whites of three eggs, wafer-paper. Blanch, skin, and dry the almonds, and pound them well with a little orange-flower water or plain water; then add to them the sifted sugar and the whites of the eggs, which should be beaten to a stiff froth, and mix all the ingredients well together. When the paste looks soft, drop it at equal distances from a biscuit-syringe on to sheets of wafer-paper; put a strip of almond on the top of each; strew some sugar over, and bake the macaroons in rather a slow oven, of a light brown color. When hard and set, they are done, and must not be allowed to get very brown, as that would spoil their appearance. If the cakes, when baked, appear heavy, add a little more white of egg, but let this always be well-whisked before it is added to the other ingredients. We have given a recipe for making these cakes, but we think it almost or quite as economical to purchase such articles as these at a good confectioner's.

## ALMOND ICING.

Whites of four eggs; one pound sweet almonds; one pound powdered sugar; a little rose-water. Blanch the almonds by pouring boiling water over them and stripping off the skins. When dry, pound them to a paste, a few at a time, in a Wedgewood mortar, moistening it with rose-water as you go on. When beaten fine and smooth, beat gradually into icing. Put on very thick, and, when nearly dry, cover with plain icing.

## TO MAKE ICING FOR CAKES.

Beat the whites of two small eggs to a high froth; then add to them quarter of a pound of white sugar, ground fine, like flour; flavor with lemon extract, or vanilla; beat it until it is light and very white, but not quite so stiff as kiss mixture; the longer it is beaten the more firm it will become. No more sugar must be added to make it so. Beat the frosting until it may be spread smoothly on the cake. This quantity will ice quite a large cake over the top and sides.

## LOAF CAKE.

One pound of butter beaten to a cream, two pounds of sugar rolled fine, three pounds of sifted flour, six well-beaten eggs, three teaspoonfuls of powdered saleratus, dissolved in a little hot water, one tablespoonful of ground cinnamon, and half a nutmeg grated; add one pound of currants, well washed and dried, one pound of raisins stoned and cut in two; work the whole well together, divide it in three loaves, put them in buttered basins, and bake one hour in a moderate oven.

## RICH BRIDE-CAKE.

Take four pounds of sifted flour, four pounds of sweet, fresh butter, beaten to a cream, and two pounds of white powdered sugar; take six eggs for each pound of flour, an ounce of ground mace or nutmegs, and a tablespoonful of lemon extract or orange-flower water.

## LADY FINGERS.

Take eight eggs; whip the whites to a firm snow. In the meantime, have the yolks beaten up with six ounces of powdered sugar. Each of these operations should be performed at least one hour. Then mix all together with six ounces of sifted flour; and when well incorporated, stir in half a pint of rose or orange-flower water; stir them together for some time.

Have ready some tin plates, rubbed with white wax; take a funnel with three or four tubes; fill it with the paste, and press out the cakes upon the plates, to the size and length of a finger; grate white sugar over each; let them lay until the sugar melts, and they shine; then put them in a moderate oven, until they have a fine color; when cool, take them from the tins, and lay them together in couples, by the backs. These cakes may be formed with a spoon, on sheets of writing paper. Half this quantity will be trouble enough at one time.

## QUEEN CAKE.

Beat one pound of butter to a cream, with a tablespoonful of rose-water; then add one pound of fine white sugar, ten eggs, beaten very light, and a pound and a quarter of sifted flour; beat the cake well together; then add half a pound of shelled almonds, blanched, and beaten to a paste; butter tin round basins, line them with white paper; put in the mixture an inch and a half deep; bake one hour in a quick oven.

## CHOCOLATE MACAROONS.

Put three ounces of plain chocolate in a pan and melt on a slow fire; then work it to a thick paste with one pound of powdered sugar and the whites of three eggs; roll the mixture down to the thickness of about one-quarter of an inch; cut it in small, round pieces with a paste-cutter, either plain or scalloped; butter a pan slightly, and dust it with flour and sugar in equal quantities; place in it the pieces of paste or mixture, and bake in a hot but not quick oven.

## CARAMEL CAKE.

One cup of butter, two of sugar, a scant cup milk, one and a half cups flour, cup corn starch, whites of seven eggs, three teaspoons baking powder in the flour; bake in a long pan. Take half pound brown sugar, scant quarter pound chocolate, half cup milk, butter size of an egg, two teaspoons vanilla; mix thoroughly and cook as syrup until stiff enough to spread; spread on cake and set in the oven to dry.

## POUND CAKE.

One pound of butter, one and one-quarter pounds of flour, one pound of pounded loaf sugar, one pound of currants, nine eggs, two ounces of candied peel, one-half ounce of citron, one-half ounce of sweet almonds; when liked, a little pounded mace. Work the butter to a cream; dredge in the flour; add the sugar, currants, candied peel, which should be cut into neat slices, and the almonds, which should be blanched and chopped, and mix all these well together; whisk the eggs, and let them be thoroughly blended with the dry ingredients. Beat the cake well for twenty minutes, and put it into a round tin, lined at the bottom and sides with a strip of white buttered paper. Bake it from one and one-half to two hours, and let the oven be well heated when the cake is first put in, as, if this is not the case, the currants will all sink to the bottom of it. To make this preparation light, the yolks and whites of the eggs should be beaten separately and added separately to the other ingredients. A glass of wine is added to the mixture; but this is scarcely necessary, as the cake will be found quite rich enough without it.

## COCOANUT SPONGE CAKE.

Beat the yolks of six eggs with half a pound of sugar and a quarter of a pound of flour, add a teaspoonful of salt, a teaspoonful of lemon essence, and half a nutmeg, grated; beat the whites of the eggs to a froth, and stir them to the yolks, etc., and the white meat of a cocoanut, grated; line square tin pans with buttered paper, and having stirred the ingredients well together, put the mixture in an inch deep in the pans; bake in a quick oven half an hour. cut it in squares, to serve with or without icing.

## COCOANUT POUND CAKE.

Beat half a pound of butter to a cream; add gradually a pound of sifted flour, one pound of powdered sugar, two teaspoonfuls baking powder, a pinch of salt, a teaspoonful of grated lemon-peel, quarter of a pound of prepared cocoanut, four well-beaten eggs, and a cupful of milk; mix thoroughly; butter the tins, and line them with buttered paper; pour the mixture in to the depth of an inch and a half, and bake in a good oven. When baked take out, spread icing over them, and return the cake to the oven a moment to dry the icing.

## COCOANUT CUP CAKE.

Two cups of sugar, two cups of butter, one cup of milk, one teaspoonful of essence of lemon, half a nutmeg grated, four well-beaten eggs and the white meat of a cocoanut grated; use as much sifted wheat flour as will make a rather stiff batter; beat it well, butter square tin pans, line them with white paper, and put in the mixture an inch deep; bake in a moderate oven half an hour, or it may require ten minutes longer. When cold, cut in small squares or diamonds; this is a rich cake and is much improved by a thin icing. This cake should be made with fine white sugar.

## COCOANUT DROPS.

Break a cocoanut in pieces, and lay it in cold water, then cut off the dark rind, and grate the white meat on a coarse grater; put the whites of four eggs with half a pound of powdered white sugar; beat it until it is light and white, then add to it a teaspoonful of lemon extract, and gradually as much grated cocoanut as will make it as thick as can be stirred easily with a spoon; lay it in heaps the size of a large nutmeg on sheets of white paper, place them the distance of half an inch apart; when the paper is full, lay it on a baking-tin, set them in a quick oven; when they begin to look yellowish, they are done; let them remain on the paper until nearly cold, then take them off with a thin-bladed knife.

## CITRON HEART CAKES.

Beat half a pound of butter to a cream, take six eggs, beat the whites to a froth, and the yolks with half a pound of sugar, and rather more than half a pound of sifted flour, beat these well together, add a wineglass of brandy, and quarter of a pound of citron cut in thin slips, bake it in small heart-shaped tins, or a square tin pan, rubbed over with a bit of sponge dipped in melted butter; put the mixture in half an inch deep, bake fifteen or twenty minutes in a quick oven. These are very fine cakes. Shred almonds may be used instead of citron.

## IMPERIAL CAKE.

One pound of flour, half a pound of butter, three-quarters of a pound of sugar, four eggs, half a pound of currants, well-washed and dredged, half a teaspoonful of soda dissolved in hot water, half a lemon, grated rind and juice, one teaspoonful of cinnamon. Drop from a spoon upon well-buttered paper, lining a baking-pan. Bake quickly

## PLUM CAKE.

Make a cake of two cups of butter, two cups of molasses, one cup of sweet milk, two eggs, well-beaten, one teaspoonful of powdered saleratus, dissolved with a little hot water, one teaspoonful of ground mace or nutmeg, one teaspoonful of ground allspice, a tablespoonful of cinnamon, and a gill of brandy; stir in flour to make a batter as stiff as may be stirred easily with a spoon; beat it well until it is light, then add two pounds of raisins, stoned, and cut in two, two pounds of currants, picked, washed, and dried, and half a pound of citron, cut in slips. Bake in a quick oven. This is a fine, rich cake, easily made, and not expensive.

## GOLD AND SILVER CAKE.

*Gold Part.*—Yolks of eight eggs, scant cup butter, two of sugar, four of flour, one of sour milk, teaspoon soda, tablespoon corn starch; flavor with lemon and vanilla.

*Silver Part.*—Two cups sugar, one of butter, four (scant) of flour, one of sour milk, teaspoon soda, tablespoon corn starch, whites of eight eggs; flavor with almond or peach. Put in pan, alternately, one spoonful of gold and one of silver.

## TO MAKE SMALL SPONGE CAKES.

The weight of five eggs in flour, the weight of eight in pounded loaf sugar; flavor to taste. Let the flour be perfectly dry, and the sugar well pounded and sifted. Separate the whites from the yolks of the eggs, and beat the latter up with the sugar; then whisk the whites until they become rather stiff, and mix them with the yolks, but do not stir them more than is just necesssary to mingle the ingredients well together. Dredge in the flour by degrees, add the flavoring; butter the tins well, pour in the batter, sift a little sugar over the cakes, and bake them in rather a quick oven, but do not allow them to take too much color, as they should be rather pale. Remove them from the tins before they get cold, and turn them on their faces, where let them remain until quite cold, when store them away in a closed tin canister or wide-mouthed glass bottle.

## LEMON CHEESE CAKE.

Two cups sugar, half cup butter, three-quarters cup sweet milk, whites of six eggs, three cups flour, three teaspoons baking powder.

SAUCE FOR LEMON CHEESE CAKE.—Grated rind and juice of two lemons, yolks of three eggs, half cup butter, one cup sugar; mix all together, and set on stove, and cook till thick as sponge, stirring all the time; then use like jelly between the cakes.

## SNOW CAKE.

One pound of arrowroot, half pound pounded white sugar, half pound butter, the whites of six eggs; flavoring to taste, of essence of almonds, or vanilla, or lemon.

*Mode:* Beat the butter to a cream; stir in the sugar and arrowroot gradually, at the same time beating the mixture. Whisk the whites of the eggs to a stiff froth, add them to the other ingredients, and beat well for twenty minutes. Put in whichever of the above flavoring may be preferred; pour the cake into a buttered mold or tin and bake it in a moderate oven from one to one and a half hours.

## TILDEN CAKE.

One cup butter, two of pulverized sugar, one of sweet milk, three of flour, half cup corn starch, four eggs, two teaspoons baking powder, two of lemon extract. This is excellent.

## CORN STARCH CAKE.

Whites of six eggs, one cup of butter, two cups of flour, one cup of corn starch, two cups of sugar, one cup of sweet milk, one-half teaspoonful of soda, one of cream of tartar.

## BIRTHDAY CAKE.

One pound and a half of fine sugar, one pound and a half of butter, three pounds and a half of currants, two pounds of flour, one-half pound candied peel, one-half pound almonds, two ounces spices, the grated rind of three lemons, eighteen eggs, one gill of brandy. Paper the hoops, and bake three hours. Ice when cold.

## NAPLES BISCUIT.

Beat eight eggs light; add to them one pound of fine white sugar, and one pound of sifted wheat flour; flavor with a teaspoonful of salt, and essence of lemon or orange-flower water; beat it until it rises in bubbles; bake in a quick oven.

## CAKE TRIFLE.

Bake a Naples biscuit; cut out the inside about one inch from the edge and bottom, leaving the shell. In place of the inside, put a custard made of the yolks of four eggs, beaten with a pint of boiling milk, sweetened, and flavored with half a teaspoonful of peach-water; lay on it some jelly, or jam; beat the whites of two eggs, with white ground sugar, until it will stand in a heap; put it on the jelly, and serve.

## SAVOY CAKE.

The weight of four eggs in pounded loaf-sugar, the weight of seven in flour, a little grated lemon-rind, or essence of almonds, or orange-flower water. Break the seven eggs, putting the yolks into one basin and the whites into another. Whisk the former, and mix with them the sugar, the grated lemon-rind, or any other flavoring to taste; beat them well together, and add the whites of the eggs, whisked to a froth. Put in the flour by degrees, continuing to beat the mixture for one-quarter of an hour, butter a mold, pour in the cake, and bake it from one and a quarter to one and a half hours. This is a very nice cake for dessert, and may be iced for a supper table, or cut into slices and spread with jam, which converts it into sandwiches.

## COMPOSITION CAKE.

Five cups of flour, two cups of butter, three of sugar, one of milk, five eggs, one teaspoon of soda; two of cream of tartar, fruit as you please, cinnamon, nutmeg and clove to taste.

## ALMOND CREAM CAKE.

On beaten whites of ten eggs sift one and a half goblets pulverized sugar, and a goblet of flour, through which has been stirred a heaping teaspoon cream tartar; stir very gently and do not heat it; bake in jelly-pans. For cream, take a half pint of sweet cream, yolks of three eggs, tablespoon pulverized sugar, teaspoon corn starch; dissolve starch smoothly with a little milk, beat yolks and sugar together with this, boil the cream, and stir these ingredients in as for any cream cake filling, only make a little thicker; blanch and chop fine a half pound almonds and stir into the cream. Put together like jelly cake while icing is soft, and stick in a half pound of almonds, split in two.

## ICE-CREAM CAKE.

Make good sponge cake, bake half an inch thick in jelly-pans, and let them get perfectly cold; take a pint thickest sweet cream, beat until it looks like ice-cream, make very sweet, and flavor with vanilla; blanch and chop a pound almonds, stir into cream, and put very thick between each layer. This is the queen of all cakes.

## ECONOMICAL CAKE.

One pound of flour, one-quarter pound of sugar, one-quarter pound of butter or lard, one-half pound of currants, one teaspoonful of carbonate of soda, the whites of four eggs, one-half pint of milk. In making many sweet dishes, the whites of eggs are not required, and if well beaten and added to the above ingredients, make an excellent cake, with or without currants. Beat the butter to a cream, well whisk the whites of the eggs, and stir all the ingredients together but the soda, which must not be added until all is well mixed, and the cake is ready to be put into the oven. When the mixture has been well beaten, stir in the soda, put the cake into a buttered mold, and bake it in a moderate oven for one and a half hours.

## DELICATE CAKE.

Three cups of flour, two of sugar, three-fourths cup of sweet milk, whites of six eggs, half cup butter, teaspoon cream tartar, half teaspoon of soda. Flavor with lemon.

## ORANGE CAKE.

One cup of sugar, half a cup of butter, half a cup of sweet milk, two cups of flour, three eggs, one and a half teaspoonfuls of baking powder; bake in jelly-tins.

ORANGE FROSTING FOR SAME.—One orange, grate off the outside, and mix with juice, and add sugar until quite stiff, and make like jelly cake; make four layers of the cake.

## FRIED CAKES.

One cup of sugar, two eggs, half a cup of shortening, one teaspoon of soda, one cup of sour milk, cut in rings; have your lard very hot, in which place a peeled potato to keep lard from burning, and drop in your cakes; they will come to the top of lard when light; fry a dark brown; when taken out sprinkle sugar over them.

## JELLY KISSES.

Kisses to be served for dessert at a large dinner, with other suitable confectionery, may be varied in this way: Having made the kisses, put them in a moderate oven, until the outside is a little hardened; then take one off carefully, as before directed; take out the soft inside with the handle of a spoon, and put it back with the mixture, to make more; then lay the shell down. Take another, and prepare it likewise; fill the shells with currant jelly, or jam; join two together, cementing them with some of the mixture; so continue until you have enough. Make kisses, cocoanut drops, and such like, the day before they are wanted.

## COCOANUT KISSES.

Make a kiss mixture; add to it half of a cocoanut, grated (the white meat only); finish as directed for kisses.

## FIG CAKE.

*Silver Part.*—Two cups sugar, two-thirds cup butter, not quite two-thirds cup sweet milk, whites of eight eggs, three heaping teaspoons baking powder, thoroughly sifted, with three cups flour; stir sugar and butter to a cream, add milk and flour, and last whites of eggs.

*Gold Part.*—One cup sugar, three-fourths cup butter, half

cup sweet milk, one and a half teaspoons baking powder sifted in a little more than one and a half cups flour, yolks of seven eggs thoroughly beaten, and one whole egg, one teaspoon allspice, and cinnamon until you can taste it; bake the white in two long pie-tins. Put half the gold in a pie-tin, and lay on one pound halved figs (previously sifted over with flour), so that they will just touch each other; put on the rest of the gold, and bake. Put the cakes together with frosting while warm, the gold between the white ones, and cover with frosting.

### CALIFORNIA CAKE.

Two cups of sugar, one cup butter, one cup milk, two eggs, three teaspoons baking powder, put in three cups sifted flour, flavor and add fruit. This recipe makes two cakes.

### WHITE MOUNTAIN CAKE.

One cup sugar, one-half cup of butter, one-half cup sweet milk, one-half cup corn starch, one cup flour, whites of six eggs, a little vanilla, two teaspoonfuls baking powder. Bake in layers.

FROSTING FOR ABOVE.—Whites of five eggs, twenty tablespoonfuls sifted sugar, beaten very light; a little vanilla. Spread between layers and outside of cake.

### LEMON CAKE.

One-half cup of sugar, one teaspoon butter, one tablespoonful of milk, three eggs, one cup flour, one teaspoon baking powder; bake in jelly-tins, put between two apple and one lemon, grated together with a little sugar.

### STRAWBERRY SHORTCAKE.

Make good biscuit crust; bake in two tins of same shape and size; mix berries with plenty of sugar; open the shortcake, butter well and place berries in layers, alternated with the crust; have the top layer of berries and over all put charlotte russe or whipped cream.

## MARBLE CAKE.

*White Part.*—Whites of seven eggs, three cups white sugar, one of butter, one of sour milk, four of flour, sifted and heaping, one teaspoon soda; flavor to taste.

*Dark Part.*—Yolks of seven eggs, three cups brown sugar, one of butter, one of sour milk, four of flour, sifted and heaping, one tablespoon each of cinnamon, allspice and cloves, one teaspoon soda; put in pans a spoonful of white part and then a spoonful of dark, and so on. Bake an hour and a quarter. Use coffee cups to measure. This will make one large and one medium cake. The white and dark parts are alternated, either putting in a spoonful of white, then of dark, or a layer of white and then of dark part, being careful that the cake may be nicely "marbleized."

## WHITE POUND CAKE.

One pound sugar, one of flour, half pound butter, whites of sixteen eggs, teaspoon baking powder sifted thoroughly with the flour; put in cool oven with gradual increase of heat. For boiled icing for the cake, take three cups sugar boiled in one of water until clear; beat whites of three eggs to very stiff froth, and pour over them the boiling liquid, beating all the time for ten minutes; froth while both cake and icing are warm.

## NELLY'S CHOCOLATE CAKE.

One cup of butter, two of sugar, five eggs, leaving out two of the whites, one scant cup of milk, two full teaspoons of baking powder; mix well in three cups flour; bake in two long shallow tins. Dressing: Beat the whites of two eggs to a stiff froth, add a scant cup and a half of sugar; flavor with vanilla, add six tablespoons of grated chocolate; add the dressing when the cake is cold, and cut in diamond slices.

### RICE CAKE.

One cupful of butter, two of sugar, two and one-fourth of rice flour, six eggs, the juice and rind of a lemon. Beat the butter to a cream; then gradually beat in the sugar, and add the lemon. Beat the yolks and whites separately, and add them to the beaten sugar and butter. Add also the rice flour. Pour into a shallow pan, to the depth of about two inches. Bake from thirty-five to forty-five minutes in a moderate oven.

### CREAM CAKE.

Two eggs, one cup of sugar, one cup of cream, two cups of flour, one teaspoonful of cream of tartar, and one teaspoonful of soda.

### DOUGHNUTS.

One cup of sugar, two eggs, two tablespoons of melted butter, two-thirds cup of milk, two even teaspoons of cream tartar, one even teaspoon of soda, flour enough to roll, salt and nutmeg.

### SPONGE CAKE.

One pound sugar, one of flour, ten eggs. Stir yolks of eggs and sugar till perfectly light; beat whites of eggs and add them with the flour after beating together lightly; flavor with lemon. Three teaspoons baking powder in the flour will add to its lightness, but it never fails without. Bake in a moderate oven.

## COFFEE CAKE.

Two cups brown sugar, one of butter, one of molasses one of strong coffee as prepared for the table, four eggs, one teaspoon saleratus, two of cinnamon, two of cloves, one of grated nutmeg, pound raisins, one of currants, four cups flour.

## SOFT GINGERBREAD.

Six cupfuls of flour, three of molasses, one of cream, one of lard or butter, two eggs, one teaspoonful of saleratus, and two of ginger. This is excellent.

## SPICE CAKE.

One and one-half cups of sugar, half cup butter, half of sour milk, two cups of raisins chopped, three eggs, half a nutmeg, one teaspoon cinnamon, one of cloves, one saleratus; mix rather stiff; bake in loaf tins in moderate oven.

## SWEET STRAWBERRY SHORTCAKE.

Three eggs, one cupful sugar, two of flour, one tablespoonful of butter, a teaspoonful, heaped, of baking powder. Beat the butter and sugar together, and add the eggs well-beaten. Stir in the flour and baking powder well sifted together. Bake in deep tin plates. This quantity will fill four plates. With three pints of strawberries mix a cupful of sugar. Spread the fruit between the layers of cake. The top layer of strawberries may be covered with a meringue made with the white of an egg and a tablespoonful of powdered sugar.

## GINGER NUTS.

One and three-quarter pounds of syrup, one pound of moist sugar, one pound of butter, two and three-quarter pounds of flour, one and a half ounces of ground ginger, one and a half ounces of allspice, one and a half ounces of coriander seed, sal volatile size of a bean, a little Cayenne, flour enough to roll out, but not thin, cut with a wineglass or roll between your hands into small balls, and pinch.

## RIBBON CAKE.

Two cupfuls of sugar, one of butter, one of milk, four of flour (rather scant), four eggs, half a teaspoonful of soda, one of cream of tartar. Beat the butter to a cream. Add the sugar gradually, beating all the while; then the flavoring (lemon or nutmeg). Beat the eggs very light. Add them and the milk. Measure the flour after it has been sifted. Return it to the sieve, and mix the soda and cream of tartar with it. Sift this into the bowl of beaten ingredients. Beat quickly and vigorously, to thoroughly mix, and then stop. Take three sheet pans of the same size, and in each of two put one-third of the mixture, and bake. To the other third add four teaspoonfuls of cinnamon, a cupful of currants and about an eighth of a pound of citron, cut fine. Bake this in the remaining pan. When done, take out of the pans. Spread the light cake with a thin layer of jelly, while warm. Place on this the dark cake, and spread with jelly. Place the other sheet of light cake on this. Lay a paper over all, and then a thin sheet, on which put two irons. The cake will press in about two hours.

## JELLY ROLL.

Make the sponge cake mixture as for lady-fingers, and bake in one shallow pan twenty minutes. While it is yet warm cut off the edges, and spread the cake with any kind of jelly. Roll up, and pin a towel around it. Put in a cool place until serving time. Cut in slices with a sharp knife.

## DELICATE CRULLERS.

Take four eggs, four tablespoonfuls of lard, four tablespoonfuls of sugar, a teaspoonful of salt, and half a nutmeg grated, a teaspoonful of lemon extract may be added; work into these as much sifted flour as will make a nice dough, roll it to about an eighth of an inch thickness, and fry as directed for doughnuts and crullers.

To make little baskets, cut the paste in strips an inch and a half wide, and three inches long, and with a giggling iron cut slices across it from one side to the other, within a quarter of an inch of either edge, and quarter of an inch apart; then join the two ends together in a circle, forming the basket; press it down slightly, that the strips may bulge, and so form the basket, like those made for fly-traps of paper; so soon as they are taken from the fat (five minutes will do them), grate white sugar over.

## DESSERT AND TEA DISHES.

### BOILED CUSTARD.

One quart milk, eight eggs, one-half pound of sugar; beat to a good froth the eggs and sugar. Put the milk in a tin pail and set it in boiling water; pour in the eggs and sugar and stir it until it thickens.

### LEMON CUSTARD.

Beat the yolks of eight eggs till they are white, add pint boiling water, the rinds of two lemons grated, and the juice sweetened to taste; stir this on the fire till it thickens, then add a large glass of rich wine, and one-half glass brandy; give the whole a good boil, and put in glasses. To be eaten cold. Or, put the thin yellow rind of two lemons, with the juice of three, and sugar to taste, into one pint of warm water. As lemons vary in size and juiciness, the exact quantity of sugar cannot be given. Ordinary lemons require three gills. It will be safe to begin with that quantity, more may be added if required. Beat the whites to a stiff froth, then the yolks; then beat both together, pour in gradually while beating the other ingredients; put all in a pail, set in a pot of boiling water, and stir until thick as boiled custard; strain it in a deep dish; when cool place on ice. Serve in glasses.

### SNOW CUSTARD.

Half a package of Cox's gelatine, three eggs, two cups of sugar, juice of one lemon; soak the gelatine one hour in a teacup of cold water, add one pint boiling water, stir until thoroughly dissolved, add two-thirds of the sugar and the lemon-juice; beat the whites of the eggs to a stiff froth, and when the gelatine is quite cold whip it into the whites, a spoonful at a time from half an hour to an hour. Whip steadily and evenly, and when all is stiff pour in a mold, or in a dozen egg-glasses previously wet with cold water, and set in a cold place. In four or five hours turn into a glass dish. Make a custard of one and a half pints milk, yolks of eggs, and remainder of the sugar, flavor with vanilla, and when the meringue or snowballs are turned out of the mold, pour this around the base.

## TAPIOCA PUDDING.

Three ounces of tapioca, one quart of milk, two ounces of butter, quarter of a pound of sugar, four eggs, flavoring of vanilla or bitter almonds. Wash the tapioca, and let it stew gently in the milk by the side of the stove for quarter of an hour, occasionally stirring it; then let it cool; mix with it the butter, sugar, and eggs, which should be well beaten, and flavor with either of the above ingredients. Butter a pie-dish, and line the edges with puff-paste; put in the pudding, and bake in a moderate oven for an hour. If the pudding is boiled, add a little more tapioca, and boil it in a buttered basin one and a half hours.

## BLANC-MANGE.

One quarter pound of sugar, one quart of milk, one and a half ounces of isinglass, the rind of half a lemon, four laurel leaves. Put all the ingredients into a lined saucepan, and boil gently until the isinglass is dissolved; taste it occasionally to ascertain when it is sufficiently flavored with the laurel leaves; then take them out, and keep stirring the mixture over the fire for about ten minutes. Strain it through a fine sieve into a jug, and, when nearly cold, pour it into a well-oiled mold, omitting the sediment at the bottom. Turn it out carefully on a dish, and garnish with preserves, bright jelly, or a compote of fruit.

## IVORY BLANC-MANGE.

Soak one ounce of gelatine for ten minutes in a little cold milk and pour over the gelatine, and stir it constantly until it is all dissolved; it may be placed in the dish and set on top of a boiling teakettle for a few minutes; remove it and add a small cupful of sugar and two tablespoonfuls of sherry wine. Strain into molds.

## RICE BLANC-MANGE.

One-quarter pound of ground rice, three ounces of loaf sugar, one ounce of fresh butter, one quart of milk, flavoring of lemon-peel, essence of almonds or vanilla, or laurel leaves. Mix the rice to a smooth batter with about one-half pint of milk, and the remainder put into a saucepan, with the sugar, butter, and whichever of the above flavorings may be preferred; bring the milk to the boiling point, quickly stir in the rice, and let it boil for about ten minutes, or until it comes easily away from the saucepan, keeping it well stirred the whole time. Grease a mold with pure salad oil; pour in the rice, and let it get perfectly set, when it should turn out quite easily; garnish it with jam, or pour round a compote of any kind of fruit, just before it is sent to table. This blanc-mange is better for being made the day before it is wanted, as it then has time to become firm. If laurel leaves are used for flavoring, steep three of them in the milk, and take them out before the rice is added;

about eight drops of essence of almonds, or from twelve to sixteen drops of essence of vanilla, would be required to flavor the above proportion of milk.

## APPLE TRIFLE.

Ten good-sized apples, the rind of one-half lemon, six ounces of pounded sugar, one-half pint of milk, one-half pint of cream, two eggs, whipped cream. Peel, core, and cut the apples into thin slices; and put them into a saucepan, with two tablespoonfuls of water, the sugar, and minced lemon-rind. Boil all together until quite tender, and pulp the apples through a sieve; if they should not be quite sweet enough, add a little more sugar, and put them at the bottom of the dish to form a thick layer. Stir together the milk, cream and eggs, with a little sugar, over the fire; and let the mixture thicken, but do not allow it to reach the boiling point. When thick, take it off the fire; let it cool a little, then pour it over the apples. Whip some cream with sugar, lemon-peel, etc., the same as for other trifles; heap it high over the custard, and the dish is ready for table. It may be garnished, as fancy dictates, with strips of bright apple jelly, slices of citron, etc.

## LEMON TRIFLE.

Juice of two lemons and grated peel of one, one pint cream, well sweetened and whipped stiff, one cup of sherry, a little nutmeg. Let sugar, lemon-juice and peel lie together two hours before you add wine and nutmeg. Strain through double tarlatan, and whip gradually into the frothed cream. Serve very soon, heaped in small glasses. Pass cake with this, as well as with the tea.

## FLOATING ISLAND.

Take a quart of rich cream, and divide it in half. Sweeten one pint of it with loaf sugar, and stir it into sufficient currant jelly, to color it of a fine pink. Put it into a glass bowl, and place in the centre a pile of sliced almond sponge cake, or lady cake; every slice spread thickly with raspberry jam or marmalade, and laid evenly one on another. Have ready the other pint of cream, flavored with the juice of two lemons, and beaten to a stiff froth. Heap it all over the pile of cake so as entirely to cover it. Both creams must be made very sweet.

## APPLE SNOW

Forms a showy, sweet dish, and may be made as follows. Ten or a dozen apples prepared as before, flavoring with a little lemon-juice; when reduced to a pulp let them stand to cool for a little time, meanwhile beat up the whites of ten or a dozen eggs to a froth, and stir into the apples, as also some sifted sugar, say a teacupful; stir till the mixture begins to stiffen, and then heap it up in a glass dish or serve in custard cups, ornamented with spots of red currant jelly.

Thick cream should at table be ladled out to the snow.

## TROPICAL SNOW.

Ten sweet oranges, one cocoanut, pared and grated, two glasses sherry, one cup powdered sugar, six bananas. Peel and cut the oranges small, taking out the seeds. Put a layer in a glass bowl and wet with wine, then strew with sugar. Next, put a layer of grated cocoanut, slice the bananas thin, and cover the cocoanut with them. When the dish has been filled in this order, heap with cocoanut Eat soon or the oranges will toughen.

## SWISS CREAM.

One-quarter pound of macaroons or six small sponge-cakes, one pint of cream, five ounces of lump sugar, two tablespoonfuls of arrowroot, the rind of one lemon, the juice of half lemon, three tablespoonfuls of milk. Lay the macaroons or sponge-cakes in a glass dish, and pour over them as much sherry as will cover them, or sufficient to cover them well. Put the cream into a lined saucepan, with the sugar and lemon-rind, and let it remain by the side of the fire until the cream is well-flavored, when take out the lemon-rind. Mix the arrowroot smoothly with the cold milk; add this to the cream, and let it boil gently for about three minutes, keeping it well stirred. Take it off the fire, stir till nearly cold, when add the lemon-juice, and pour the whole over the cakes. Garnish the cream with strips of angelica, or candied citron cut thin, or bright-colored jelly or preserve. This cream is exceedingly delicious, flavored with vanilla instead of lemon; when this flavoring is used, the sherry may be omitted, and the mixture poured over the *dry* cakes.

## ITALIAN CRÉAM.

Take one quart of cream, one pint of milk sweetened very sweet, and highly seasoned with sherry wine and vanilla; beat it with a whip dasher, and remove the froth as it rises, until it is all converted into froth. Have ready one box of Cox's sparkling gelatine dissolved in a little warm water; set the frothed cream into a tub of ice; pour the gelatine into it, and stir constantly until it thickens, then pour into molds, and set in a cool place.

## WHIPPED CREAM.

Mix one pint of cream with nine tablespoons of fine sugar and one gill of wine in a large bowl; whip these with the cream dasher, and as the froth rises, skim into the dish in which it is to be served. Fill the dish full to the top, and ornament with kisses or macaroons.

## TIPSY CAKE.

**One** molded sponge or Savoy cake, sufficient sweet wine or sherry to soak it, six tablespoonfuls of brandy, two ounces of sweet almonds, one pint of rich custard. Procure a cake that is three or four days old—either sponge, Savoy, or rice answering for the purpose of a tipsy cake. Cut the bottom of the cake level, to make it stand firm in the dish; make a small hole in the centre, and pour in and over the cake sufficient sweet wine or sherry, mixed with the above proportion of brandy, to soak it nicely. When the cake is well soaked, blanch and cut the almonds into strips, stick them all over the cake, and pour round it a good custard, allowing eight eggs instead of five to the pint of milk. The cakes are sometimes crumbled and soaked, and a whipped cream heaped over them, the same as for trifles.

## SNOW PYRAMIDS.

**Beat** to a stiff foam the whites of half a dozen eggs, add a small teacupful of currant jelly, and whip all together again. Fill as many saucers as you have guests half full of cream, dropping in the centre of each saucer a tablespoonful of the beaten eggs and jelly in the shape of a pyramid.

## AN EXCELLENT DESSERT.

One can or twelve large peaches, two coffeecups of sugar, one pint of water, and the whites of three eggs; break the peaches with and stir all the ingredients together; freeze the whole into form; beat the eggs to a froth.

## APPLE FRITTERS.

One teacup of sweet milk, one tablespoon sweet light dough dissolved in milk, three eggs beaten separately, one teaspoon of salt, one and a half teacups of flour, one tablespoon of sugar, and the grated peel of a lemon, peeled apples sliced without the core; drop into hot lard with a piece of apple in each one; sprinkle with powdered or spiced sugar. Let them stand after making and they will be lighter. Good.

## JELLY CAKE FRITTERS.

Some stale sponge, or *plain* cup cake, cut into rounds with a cake cutter. Hot lard strawberry or other jam, or jelly, a little boiling milk. Cut the cake carefully and fry a nice brown. Dip each slice for a second in a bowl of boiling milk, draining this off on the side of the vessel; lay on a hot dish and spread thickly with strawberry jam, peach jelly, or other delicate conserve. Pile them neatly and send around hot, with cream to pour over them. This is a nice way of using up stale cake, and if rightly prepared, the dessert is almost equal to Neapolitan pudding.

## PEACH MERINGUE.

Pare and quarter (removing stones) a quart of sound, ripe peaches, place them all in a dish that it will not injure to set in the oven and yet suitable to place on the table. Sprinkle the peaches with sugar, and cover them well with the beaten whites of three eggs. Stand the dish in the oven until the eggs have become a delicate brown, then remove and, when cool enough, set on a dish of ice, in a very cool place. Take the yolks of the eggs, add to them a pint of milk, sweeten and flavor and boil same in a custard kettle, being careful to keep the eggs from curdling. When cool, pour into a glass pitcher and serve with the meringue when ready to use.

## CHARLOTTE RUSSE.

Whip one quart rich cream to a stiff froth, and drain well on a nice sieve. To one scant pint of milk add six eggs beaten very light; make very sweet; flavor high with vanilla. Cook over hot water till it is a thick custard. Soak one full ounce Cox's gelatine in a very little water, and warm over hot water. When the custard is very cold, beat in lightly the gelatine and the whipped cream. Line the bottom of your mold with buttered paper, the sides with sponge cake or lady-fingers fastened together with the white of an egg. Fill with the cream, put in a cold place or in summer on ice. To turn out, dip the mold for a moment in hot water. In draining the whipped cream, all that drips through can be rewhipped.

## JELLIED GRAPES.

A very delicate dish is made of one-third of a cup of rice, two cups of grapes, half a cup of water, and two spoons of sugar. Sprinkle the rice and sugar among the grapes, while placing them in a deep dish; pour on the water, cover close and simmer two hours slowly in the oven. Serve warm as sauce, or cold as pudding. If served warm as pudding, increase slightly the proportion of rice and sugar.

## JELLY AND CUSTARD.

One-half package of gelatine, soaked in water enough to cover it; when soaked pour one pint of boiling water over it, then add one cup of white sugar and squeeze the juice of one large lemon into it and a little essence of lemon and set aside to stiffen.

Make a custard with a pint and a half of milk, the yolks

of three eggs, one tablespoonful of corn starch; sugar and flavoring. When the jelly is set, and just before using, cut the jelly into squares, laying them in layers at intervals in the bottom of the dish, then pour in some of the cold custard, another layer of jelly, and so on until the custard is all used. Beat the whites of the eggs to a stiff froth, adding two or three teaspoonfuls of confectioner's sugar and lay on in pieces with jelly between. All these recipes are better when prepared in a tin set inside of another in which there is a little water to prevent danger of burning.

### LEMON TOAST.

Take the yolks of six eggs, beat them well and add three cups of sweet milk; take baker's bread not too stale and cut into slices; dip them into the milk and eggs, and lay the slices into a spider, with sufficient melted butter, hot, to fry a nice delicate brown; take the whites of six eggs, and beat them to a froth, adding a large cup of white sugar; add the juice of two lemons, beating well, and adding two cups boiling water. Serve over the toast as a sauce, and you will find it a very delicious dish.

### DISH OF SNOWWHIPPED CREAM.

To the whites of three eggs beaten to a froth, add a pint of cream and four tablespoonfuls of sweet wine, with three of fine white sugar and a teaspoonful of extract of lemon or vanilla; whip it to a froth and serve in a glass dish; serve jelly or jam with it. Or lay lady-fingers or sliced sponge cake in a glass dish, put spoonfuls of jelly or jam over, and heap the snow upon it.

### OMELET FOR DESSERT.

Beat six eggs light, add a teaspoonful of salt, and four or five macaroons pounded fine, beat them well together; fry as usual; strew plentifully with sugar, and serve.

## JELLY FRITTERS.

Make a batter of two eggs, a pint of milk, and a pint bowl of wheat flour or more, beat it light; put a tablespoonful lard or beef fat in a frying or omelet-pan, add a saltspoonful of salt, make it boiling hot, put in the batter by the large spoonful, not too close; when one side is a delicate brown, turn the other; when done, take them on to a dish with a doily over it, put a dessertspoonful of firm jelly on each, and serve.

# PRESERVES, CANNED FRUITS, JELLY.

### TO PRESERVE PLUMS WITHOUT THE SKINS.

Pour boiling water over large egg or magnum bonum plums, cover them until it is cold, then pull off the skins. Make a syrup of a pound of sugar and a teacup of water for each pound of fruit, make it boiling hot, and pour it over; let them remain for a day or two, then drain it off and boil again; skim it clear and pour it hot over plums; let them remain until the next day, then put them over the fire in the syrup, boil them very gently until clear; take them from the syrup with a skimmer into the pots or jars; boil the syrup until rich and thick, take off any scum which may rise, then let it cool and settle, and pour it over the plums. If brown sugar is used, which is quite as good, except for greengages, clarify it as directed.

### TO PRESERVE PURPLE PLUMS.

Make a syrup of clean brown sugar, clarify it as directed in these recipes; when perfectly clear and boiling hot, pour it over the plums, having picked out all unsound ones, and stems; let them remain in the syrup two days, then drain it off; make it boiling hot, skim it and pour it over again; let them remain another day or two, then put them in a preserving-kettle over the fire and simmer gently until the syrup is reduced and thick or rich. One pound of sugar for each pound of plums. Small damsons are very fine, preserved as cherries or any other ripe fruit; clarify the syrup and when boiling hot put in the plums, let them boil very gently until they are cooked and the syrup rich. Put them in pots or jars; the next day secure as directed.

## PRESERVED GREENGAGES IN SYRUP.

To every pound of fruit allow one pound of loaf-sugar, one-quarter pint of water. Boil the sugar and water together for about ten minutes; divide the greengages, take out the stones, put the fruit into the syrup, and let it simmer gently until nearly tender. Take it off the fire, put it into a large pan, and, the next day, boil it up again for about ten minutes with the kernels from the stones, which should be blanched. Put the fruit carefully into jars, pour it over the syrup, and, when cold, cover down, so that the air is quite excluded. Let the syrup be well skimmed both the first and second day of boiling, otherwise it will not be clear.

## TO PRESERVE CHERRIES IN SYRUP.

Four pounds of cherries, three pounds of sugar, one pint of white-currant juice. Let the cherries be as clear and as transparent as possible, and perfectly ripe; pick off the stalks, and remove the stones, damaging the fruit as little as you can. Make a syrup with the above proportion of sugar, mix the cherries with it, and boil them for about fifteen minutes, carefully skimming them; turn them gently into a pan, and let them remain till the next day; then drain the cherries on a sieve, and put the syrup and white-currant juice into the preserving-pan again. Boil these together until the syrup is somewhat reduced and rather thick; then put in the cherries, and let them boil for about five minutes;

take them off the fire, skim the syrup, put the cherries into small pots or wide-mouthed bottles; pour the syrup over, and when quite cold, tie them down carefully, so that the air is quite excluded.

## PRESERVED PEARS.

To six pounds of pears, four pounds of sugar, two coffee-cups of water, the juice of two lemons, and the rind of one, a handful of whole ginger; boil all together for twenty minutes, then put in your pears and boil till soft, say about a quarter of an hour; take them out and boil your syrup a little longer; then put back your fruit and give it a boil; bottle while hot; add a little cochineal to give them a nice color.

## TO PRESERVE PEACHES.

Peaches for preserving may be ripe but not soft; cut them in halves, take out the stones, and pare them neatly; take as many pounds of white sugar as of fruit, put to each pound of sugar a teacup of water; stir it until it is dissolved, set it over a moderate fire, when it is boiling hot, put in the peaches, let them boil gently until a pure, clear, uniform color; turn those at the bottom to the top carefully with a skimmer several times; do not hurry them; when they are clear, take each half up with a spoon, and spread the halves on flat dishes to become cold; when all are done, let the syrup boil until it is quite thick, pour it into a large pitcher, and let it set to cool and settle. When the peaches are cold, put them carefully into jars, and pour the syrup over them, leaving any sediment which has settled at the bottom, or strain the syrup. Some of the kernels from the peach stones may be put in with the peaches while boiling. Let them remain open one night, then cover.

## TO PRESERVE CITRON.

Pare the citrons and cut them into slices about an inch and a half thick, then into strips the same thickness, leaving them the full length of the fruit; take out all the seeds with a small knife, then weigh, and to each pound of citron put a pound of white sugar, make a syrup; to ten pounds put a pint of water, and simmer gently for twenty minutes; then put in the citron and boil for one hour, or until tender; before taking off the fire put in two lemons, sliced thin, seeds taken out, and two ounces of root ginger; do not let them boil long after the lemon and ginger are put in; do not stir them while boiling. The above is very fine if carefully attended to.

## CRAB-APPLES.

To each pound of fruit allow half a pound of sugar, and a pint of water to three pounds of sugar. When the syrup is boiling hot, drop in the apples. They will cook very quickly. When done, fill a jar with the fruit, and fill it up with syrup.

## PINEAPPLE.

Pare the fruit, and be sure you take out all the eyes and discolored parts. Cut in slices, and cut the slices in small bits, taking out the core. Weigh the fruit, and put in a pan with half as many pounds of sugar as of fruit. Let it stand over night. In the morning put it over the fire and let it boil rapidly for a minute only, as cooking long discolors it. Put it in the jars as directed.

## GOOSEBERRY JAM.

To every eight pounds of red, rough, ripe gooseberries, allow one quart of red-currant juice, five pounds of loaf-sugar. Have the fruit gathered in dry weather, and set it the tops and tails. Prepare one quart of red-currant juice, the same as for red-currant jelly; put it into a preserving-pan with the sugar, and keep stirring until the latter is dissolved. Keep it boiling for about five minutes; skim well; then put in the gooseberries, and let them boil from one-half to three-quarters of an hour; then turn the whole into an earthen pan, and let it remain for two days. Boil the jam up again until it looks clear; put it into pots, and when cold cover with oiled paper, and over the jars put tissue paper, brushed over on both sides with the white of an egg, and store away in a dry place. Care must be taken in making this to keep the jam well stirred and well skimmed, to prevent it burning at the bottom of the pan, and to have it very clear.

### BLACK-CURRANT JAM.

Pick the currants carefully, and take equal quantities of fruit and sugar. Pounded loaf-sugar is best. Dissolve it over or mix it with the currants. Put in a very little water or red-currant juice, boil and skim for twenty-five minutes.

### RASPBERRY JAM.

To five or six pounds of fine red raspberries (not too ripe) add an equal quantity of the finest quality of white sugar. Mash the whole well in a preserving-kettle; add about one quart of currant juice (a little less will do), and boil gently until it jellies upon a cold plate; then put into small jars; cover with brandied paper, and tie a thick white paper over them. Keep in a dark, dry, and cool place.

### QUINCE PRESERVE.

Pare, core, and quarter your fruit, then weigh it and allow an equal quantity of white sugar. Take the parings and cores and put in a preserving-kettle; cover them with water and boil for half an hour; then strain through a hair sieve and put the juice back into the kettle and boil the quinces in it a little at a time until they are tender; lift out as they are done with a drainer and lay on a dish; if the liquid seems scarce add more water. When all are done throw in the sugar and allow it to boil ten minutes before putting in the quinces; let them boil until they change color, say one hour and a quarter, on a slow fire; while they are boiling occasionally slip a silver spoon under them to see that they do not burn, but on no account stir them. Have two fresh lemons cut in thin slices, and when the fruit is being put in jars lay a slice or two in each.

## RED-CURRANT JELLY.

Red-currants; to every pint of juice allow three-quarter pounds of loaf-sugar. Have the fruit gathered in fine weather; pick it from the stalks, put it into a jar, and place this jar in a saucepan of boiling water over the fire, and let it simmer gently until the juice is well drawn from the currants; then strain them through a jelly-bag of fine cloth, and, if the jelly is wished very clear, do not squeeze them too much, as the skin and pulp from the fruit will be pressed through with the juice, and so make the jelly muddy. Measure the juice, and to each pint allow three-quarter pounds of loaf-sugar; put these into a preserving-pan, set it over the fire, and keep stirring the jelly until it is done, carefully removing every particle of scum as it rises, using a wooden or silver spoon for the purpose, as metal or iron ones would spoil the color of the jelly. When it has boiled from twenty minutes to a half hour, put a little of the jelly on a plate, and if firm, when cool, it is done. Take it off the fire, pour it into small gallipots, cover each of the pots with an oiled paper, and then with a piece of tissue paper brushed over on both sides with the white of an egg. Label the pots, adding the year when the jelly was made, and store it away in a dry place. A jam may be made with the currants, if they are not squeezed too dry, by adding a few fresh raspberries, and boiling all together with sufficient sugar to sweeten it nicely. As this preserve is not worth storing away, but is only for immediate eating, a smaller proportion of sugar than usual will be found enough; it answers very well for children's puddings, or for a nursery preserve.

## APPLE JELLY.

Apples, water; to every pint of syrup allow three-quarters of a pound of loaf-sugar. Pare and cut the apples into pieces, remove the cores, and put them in a preserving-pan with sufficient cold water to cover them. Let them boil for an hour; then drain the syrup from them through a hair sieve or jelly-bag, and measure the juice; to every pint allow three-quarters of a pound of loaf-sugar, and boil these together for three-quarters of an hour, removing every particle of scum as it rises, and keeping the jelly well stirred, that it may not burn. A little lemon-rind may be boiled with the apples, and a small quantity of strained lemon-juice may be put in the jelly, just before it is done, when the flavor is liked. This jelly may be ornamented with preserved greengages, or any other preserved fruit, and will turn out very prettily for dessert. It should be stored away in small pots.

## BLACK-CURRANT JELLY.

Pick each currant individually, and heat the lot in a jar set in boiling water, squeeze as before, and allow a pint of juice to a pound of sugar, a little water may be added if thought proper, or a little red-currant juice. Boil for half an hour, carefully removing the skimmings. Another way: Clarify the sugar, and add the fruit to it whole, boil for twenty minutes, and strain, then boil a few minutes additional. Pot it and paper it when cool. The refuse berries may be kept as black-currant jam, for tarts, dumplings, etc.

## CRAB-APPLE JELLY.

Wash the fruit clean, put in a kettle, cover with water, and boil until thoroughly cooked. Then pour it into a sieve, and let it drain. Do not press it through. For each pint of this liquor allow one pound of sugar. Boil from twenty minutes to half an hour.

## OTHER JELLIES.

Jellies can be made from quinces, peaches and apples by following the directions for crab-apple jelly.

## WINE JELLY.

One box of Cox's gelatine, dissolved in one pint of cold water, one pint of wine, one quart of boiling water, one quart of granulated sugar, and three lemons.

## CALVES' FEET JELLY

Should be made at any rate the day before it is required. It is a simple affair to prepare it. Procure a couple of feet and put them on the fire in three quarts of water; let them boil for five hours, during which keep skimming. Pass the liquor through a hair sieve into a basin, and let it firm, after which remove all the oil and fat. Next take a teacupful of water, two wineglassfuls of sherry, the juice of half a dozen lemons and the rind of one, the whites and shells of five eggs, half a pound of fine white sugar, and whisk the whole till the sugar be melted, then add the jelly, place the whole on the fire in an enameled stewpan, and keep actively stirring till the composition comes to the boil; pass it twice through a jelly-bag, and then place in the molds.

### ORANGE MARMALADE.

Allow pound for pound. Pare half the oranges and cut the rind into shreds. Boil in three waters until tender, and set aside. Grate the rind of the remaining oranges; take off and throw away every bit of the thick white inner skin; quarter all the oranges and take out the seeds. Chop, or cut them into small pieces; drain all the juice that will come away, without pressing them, over the sugar; heat this, stirring until the sugar is dissolved, adding a very little water, unless the oranges are very juicy. Boil and skim five or six minutes; put in the boiled shreds, and cook ten minutes; then the chopped fruit and grated peel, and boil twenty minutes longer. When cold, put into small jars, tied up with bladder or with paper next the fruit, cloths dipped in wax over all. A nicer way still is to put away in tumblers with self-adjusting metal tops. Press brandied tissue paper down closely to the fruit.

### LEMON MARMALADE

Is made as you would prepare orange—allowing a pound and a quarter of sugar to a pound of the fruit, and using but half the grated peel.

### QUINCE MARMALADE.

Gather the fruit when fully ripe; pare, quarter and core it; boil the skins with as many teacupfuls of water as you have pounds of quinces; when they are soft, mash them, and strain the water from them, and put it to the quinces; boil them until they are soft enough to mash them fine; rub them through a sieve; put to the pulp as many pounds of sugar; stir them together, and set them over a gentle fire, until it will fall from a spoon, like jelly; or try some in a saucer. If it jellies when cold, it is enough.

Put it in pots or tumblers, and when cold, secure as directed for jelly.

## PEACH MARMALADE.

Peel ripe peaches, stone them, and cut them small; weigh three-quarters of a pound of sugar for each pound of cut fruit, and a teacup of water for each pound of sugar; set it over the fire; when it boils, skim it clear, then put in the peaches, let them boil quite fast; mash them fine, and let them boil until the whole is a jellied mass, and thick, then put it in small jars or tumblers; when cold, secure it as directed for jellies. Half a pound of sugar for a pound of fruit will make nice marmalade.

## APPLE BUTTER.

Boil one barrel of new cider down half, peel and core three bushels of good cooking apples; when the cider has boiled to half the quantity, add the apples, and when soft, stir constantly for from eight to ten hours. If done it will adhere to an inverted plate. Put away in stone jars (not earthen ware), covering first with writing-paper cut to fit the jar, and press down closely upon the apple butter; cover the whole with thick brown paper snugly tied down.

## LEMON BUTTER.

Beat six eggs, one-fourth pound butter, one pound sugar, the rind and juice of three lemons; mix together and set in a pan of hot water to cook. Very nice for tarts, or to eat with bread.

## PEACH BUTTER.

Take pound for pound of peaches and sugar; cook peaches alone until they become soft, then put in one-half the sugar, and stir for one-half hour; then the remainder of the sugar, and stir an hour and a half. Season with cloves and cinnamon.

## APPLE GINGER.

### (A DESSERT DISH).

Two pounds of any kind of hard apples, two pounds of loaf-sugar, one and one-half pints of water, one ounce of tincture of ginger. Boil the sugar and water until they form a rich syrup, adding the ginger when it boils up. Pare, core, and cut the apples into pieces; dip them in cold water to preserve the color, and boil them in the syrup until transparent; but be careful not to let them break. Put the pieces of apple into jars, pour over the syrup, and carefully exclude the air, by well covering them. It will remain good for some time, if kept in a dry place.

## ICED CURRANTS.

One-quarter pint of water, the whites of two eggs, currants, pounded sugar. Select very fine bunches of red or white currants, and well beat the whites of the eggs. Mix these with water; then take the currants, a bunch at a time, and dip them in; let them drain for a minute or two, and roll them in very finely-pounded sugar. Lay them to dry on paper, when the sugar will crystallize round each currant, and have a very pretty effect. All fresh fruit may be prepared in the same manner; and a mixture of various fruits iced in this manner, and arranged on one dish, looks very well for a summer dessert.

## TO BOTTLE FRESH FRUIT.

### (VERY USEFUL IN WINTER).

Fresh fruit, such as currants, raspberries, cherries, gooseberries, plums of all kinds, damsons, etc.; wide-mouthed glass bottles, new corks to fit them tightly. Let the fruit be full grown, but not too ripe, and gathered in dry weather. Pick it off the stalks without bruising or breaking the skin, and reject any that is at all blemished; if gathered in the damp, or if the skins are cut at all, the fruit will mold. Have ready some *perfectly dry* glass bottles, and some nice *new* soft corks or bungs; burn a match in each bottle, to exhaust the air, and quickly place the fruit in to be preserved; gently cork the bottles, and put them into a very *cool* oven, where let them remain until the fruit has shrunk away a fourth part. Then take the bottles out, *do not open them*, but immediately beat the corks in tight, cut off the tops, and cover them with melted rosin. If kept in a dry place, the fruit will remain good for months; and on this principally depends the success of the preparation, for if stored away in a place that is the least damp, the fruit will soon spoil.

## TO GREEN FRUIT FOR PRESERVING IN SUGAR OR VINEGAR.

Apples, pears, limes, plums, apricots, etc., for preserving or pickling, may be greened thus: Put vine-leaves under, between, and over the fruit in a preserving-kettle; put small bits of alum, the size of a pea, say a dozen bits to a kettleful; put enough water to cover the fruit, cover the kettle close to exclude all outer air, set it over a gentle fire, let them simmer; when they are tender drain off the water; if they are not a fine green let them become cold, then put vine-leaves and a bit of saleratus or soda with them, and set them over a slow fire until they begin to simmer; a bit of soda or saleratus the size of a small nutmeg will have the desired effect; then spread them out to cool, after which finish as severally directed.

## TO COLOR PRESERVES PINK.

By putting in with it a little cochineal powdered fine, then finish in the syrup.

## TO COLOR FRUIT YELLOW.

Boil the fruit with fresh skin lemons in water to cover them, until it is tender; then take it up, spread it on dishes to cool, and finish as may be directed.

## CANNED STRAWBERRIES.

After the berries are pulled, let as many as can be put carefully in the preserve kettle at once be placed on a platter. To each pound of fruit add three-fourths of a pound of sugar; let them stand two or three hours, till the juice is drawn from them; pour it in the kettle and let it come to a boil, and remove the scum which rises; then put in the berries very carefully. As soon as they come thoroughly to a boil put them in warm jars, and seal while boiling hot. Be sure the cans are air-tight.

## CANNED PEACHES.

Select some fine, free-stone peaches; pare, cut in two and stone them. Immerse in cold water, taking care not to break the fruit. See that the peaches are not over ripe. Place in the kettle, scattering sugar between the layers—the sugar should be in the proportion of a full tablespoonful to a quart of fruit. To prevent burning put a little water in the kettle. Heat slowly to a boil, then boil for three or four minutes. Can and seal the fruit.

## CANNED PEARS.

Prepare and can precisely like peaches in preceding recipe, except that they require longer cooking. When done they are easily pierced with a silver fork.

## CANNED PLUMS.

To every pound of fruit allow three-quarters of a pound of sugar; for the thin syrup, a quarter of a pound of sugar to each pint of water. Select fine fruit, and prick with a needle to prevent bursting. Simmer gently in a syrup made with the above proportion of sugar and water. Let them boil not longer than five minutes. Put the plums in a jar, pour in the hot syrup, and seal. Greengages are also delicious done in this manner.

## CANNED CURRANTS.

Look them over carefully, stem and weigh them, allowing a pound of sugar to every one of fruit; put them in a kettle, cover, and leave them to heat slowly and stew gently for twenty or thirty minutes; then add the sugar, and shake the kettle occasionally to make it mix with the fruit; do not allow it to boil, but keep as hot as possible until the sugar is dissolved, then pour it in cans and secure the covers at once. White currants are beautiful preserved in this way.

## CANNED PINEAPPLE.

For six pounds of fruit when cut and ready to can make syrup with two and a half pounds of sugar and nearly three pints of water; boil syrup five minutes and skim or strain if necessary; then add the fruit, and let it boil up; have cans hot, fill and shut up as soon as possible. Use the best white sugar. As the cans cool, keep tightening them up.

## TO CAN QUINCES.

Cut the quinces into thin slices like apples for pies. To one quart jarful of quince take a coffee-saucer and a half of sugar and a coffeecup of water; put the sugar and water on the fire, and when boiling put in the quinces; have ready the jars with their fastenings, stand the jars in a pan of boiling water on the stove, and when the quince is clear and tender put rapidly into the jars, fruit and syrup together. The jars must be filled so that the syrup overflows, and fastened up tight as quickly as possible.

## CANNING TOMATOES.

Scald your tomatoes, remove the skins, cut in small pieces, put in a porcelain kettle, salt to taste, and boil fifteen minutes; have tin cans filled with hot water; pour the water out and fill with tomatoes; solder tops on immediately with shellac and rosin melted together.

## CANNED CORN.

Dissolve an ounce of tartaric acid in half teacup water,

and take one tablespoon to two quarts of sweet corn; cook, and while boiling hot, fill the cans, which should be tin. When used turn into a colander, rinse with cold water, add a little soda and sugar while cooking, and season with butter, pepper and salt.

## ICES, ICE-CREAM, CANDY.

### CURRANT ICE.

One pint of currant-juice, one pound of sugar, and pint of water; put in freezer, and when partly frozen add the whites of three eggs well beaten.

### STRAWBERRY OR RASPBERRY ICE.

One quart of berries. Extract the juice and strain; one pint of sugar, dissolved in the juice; one lemon, juice only; half pint water.

### ORANGE AND LEMON ICES.

The rind of three oranges grated and steeped a few moments in a little more than a pint of water; strain one pint of this on a pound of sugar and then add one pint of orange or lemon-juice; pour in a freezer, and when half frozen add the whites of four eggs beaten to a stiff froth.

### ICE-CREAM.

One quart of new milk, two eggs, two tablespoons of corn starch; heat the milk in a dish set in hot water, then stir in the corn starch mixed smooth in a little of the milk; let it boil for one or two minutes, then remove from stove and cool, and stir in the egg and half a pound of sugar. If to be extra nice, add a pint of rich cream, and one-fourth pound of sugar, strain the mixture, and when cool add the flavoring, and freeze as follows: Prepare freezer in the usual manner, turn the crank one hundred times, then pour upon the ice and salt a quart of boiling water from the tea-kettle. Fill up again with ice and salt, turn the crank fifty times one way and twenty-five the other (which serves to scrape the cream from sides of freezer); by this time it will turn very hard, indicating that the cream is frozen sufficiently.

### VANILLA OR LEMON ICE-CREAM.

Take two drachms of vanilla or lemon-peel, one quart of milk, half a pound of sugar, one pint of cream, and the yolks of three eggs; beat the yolks well, and stir them with the milk, then add the other ingredients; set it over a moderate fire, and stir it constantly with a silver spoon until it is boiling hot, then take out the lemon-peel or vanilla, and, when cold, freeze it.

### STRAWBERRY ICE-CREAM.

Sprinkle strawberries with sugar, wash well and rub through a sieve; to a pint of the juice add half a pint of good cream; make it very sweet; freeze, and when beginning to set, stir lightly one pint of cream whipped, and lastly a handful of whole strawberries, sweetened. It may then be put in a mold and imbedded in ice, or kept in the freezer; or mash with a potato pounder in an earthen bowl one quart of strawberries with one pound of sugar, rub it through a colander, add one quart of sweet cream and freeze. Or, if not in the strawberry season, use the French bottled strawberries (or any canned ones), mix juice with half a pint of cream, sweeten and freeze; when partially set add whipped cream and strawberries.

## CHOCOLATE ICE-CREAM.

Take six ounces of chocolate, a pint of cream, half a pint of new milk, and half a pint of sugar. Rub the chocolate down into the milk and mix thoroughly, adding the cream and sugar. The milk should be heated almost to boiling. Heat until it thickens, stirring constantly. Strain and set aside to cool, afterwards freeze. This makes perhaps the most favorite of ice-creams.

## CREAM CANDIES.

Three and one-half pounds of sugar to one and one-half pints of water; dissolve in the water before putting with the sugar one-quarter of an ounce of fine white gum-arabic, and when added to the sugar put in one teaspoon of cream of tartar. The candy should not be boiled quite to the brittle stage. The proper degree can be ascertained if, when a small skimmer is put in and taken out, when blowing through the holes of the skimmer, the melted sugar is forced through in feather filaments; remove from the fire at this point and rub the syrup against the sides of the dish with an iron spoon. If it is to be a chocolate candy, add two ounces of chocolate finely sifted and such flavoring as you may prefer, vanilla, rolls, or orange. If you wish to make cocoanut candy, add this while soft and stir until cold.

## PINEAPPLE ICE-CREAM.

Three pints of cream, two large ripe pineapples, two pounds powdered sugar; slice the pineapples thin, scatter the sugar between the slices, cover and let the fruit stand three hours, cut or chop it up in the syrup, and strain through a hair sieve or double bag of coarse lace; beat gradually into the cream, and freeze as rapidly as possible; reserve a few pieces of pineapple unsugared, cut into square bits, and stir through cream when half frozen, first a pint of well-whipped cream, and then the fruit. Peach ice-cream may be made in the same way.

## ITALIAN CREAM.

Put one ounce of soaked isinglass, six ounces of loaf-sugar, half a stick of vanilla, and one pint of milk into a saucepan; boil slowly; and stir all the time until the isinglass is dissolved; strain the mixture, and when a little cool mix with a pint of thick cream. Beat thoroughly until it thickens. Pour into large or individual molds, and put in ice-box until wanted.

## TO MAKE BARLEY-SUGAR.

To every pound of sugar allow one-half pint of water, one-half the white of an egg. Put the sugar into a well-tinned saucepan, with the water, and when the former is dissolved, set it over a moderate fire, adding the well-beaten egg before the mixture gets warm, and stir it well together. When it boils, remove the scum as it rises, and keep it boiling until no more appears, and the syrup looks perfectly clear; then strain it through a fine sieve or muslin bag, and put it back into the saucepan. Boil it again like caramel, until it is brittle when a little is dropped into a basin of cold water; it is then sufficiently boiled. Add a little lemon-juice and a few drops of the essence of lemon, and let it stand for a minute or two. Have ready a marble slab or large dish rubbed over with salad oil, pour the sugar on it, and cut it into strips with a pair of scissors; these strips should then be twisted, and the barley-sugar stored away in a very dry place. It may be formed into lozenges or drops, by dropping the sugar in a very small quantity at a time on to the oiled slab or dish.

## TO MAKE EVERTON TOFFEE.

One pound of powdered loaf-sugar, one teacupful of water, one-quarter pound of butter, six drops of essence of lemon. Put the water and sugar into a brass pan, and beat the butter to a cream. When the sugar is dissolved, add the butter, and keep stirring the mixture over the fire until it sets when a little is poured on to a buttered dish; and just before the toffee is done add the essence of lemon. Butter a dish or tin, pour on it the mixture, and when cool it will easily separate from the dish. Butter-Scotch, an excellent thing for coughs, is made with brown, instead of white sugar, omitting the water, and flavored with one-half ounce of ginger. It is made in the same manner as toffee.

## COCOANUT DROPS.

To one grated cocoanut add half its weight of sugar and the white of one egg, cut to a stiff froth; mix thoroughly and drop on buttered white paper or tin sheets. Bake fifteen minutes.

## MOLASSES CANDY.

One cup of molasses, two cups of sugar, one tablespoon vinegar, a little butter and vanilla, boil ten minutes, then cool it enough to pull.

## CHOCOLATE CARAMELS.

Two cups of brown sugar, one cup molasses, one cup chocolate grated fine, one cup of boiled milk, one tablespoon of flour; butter the size of a large English walnut; let it boil slowly and pour on flat tins to cool; mark off while warm.

## LEMON CANDY.

Put into a kettle three and one-half pounds of sugar, one and one-half pints of water, and one teaspoon of cream of tartar. Let it boil until it becomes brittle when dropped in cold water; when sufficiently done take off the fire and pour in a shallow dish which has been greased with a little butter. When this has cooled so that it can be handled, add a teaspoon of tartaric acid and the same quantity of extract of lemon, and work them into the mass. The acid must be fine and free from lumps. Work this in until evenly distributed, and no more, as it will tend to destroy the transparency of the candy. This method may be used for preparing all other candies, as pineapple, etc., using different flavors.

# DRINKS.

### TO MAKE GREEN TEA.

Have ready a kettle of water boiling fast, pour some into the teapot, let it remain for a few minutes, then throw it out; measure a teaspoonful of tea for each two persons, put it in the pot, pour on it about a gill of boiling water, cover it close for five minutes, then fill it up; have a covered pitcher of boiling water with it; when two cups are poured from it, fill it up; you will thus keep the strength good and equal. If the company is large, it is best to have some of the tea drawn in the covered pitcher, and replenish the teapot or urn when it is exhausted.

### TO MAKE BLACK TEA.

Make as directed for green tea.

### ICED TEA.

Prepare tea in the morning, making it stronger and sweeter than usual; strain and pour into a clean stone jug or glass bottle, and set aside in the ice-chest until ready to use. Drink from goblets without cream. Serve ice broken in small pieces on a platter nicely garnished with well-washed grape-leaves. Iced tea may be prepared from either green or black alone, but it is considered an improvement to mix the two. Tea made like that for iced tea (or that left in the teapot after a meal), with sugar to taste, a slice or two of lemon, a little of the juice, and some pieces of cracked ice, makes a delightful drink. Serve in glasses.

## TO MAKE COFFEE.

Take a good-sized cupful of ground coffee, and pour into a quart of boiling water, with the white of an egg and the crushed shell. Stir well together, adding a half-cupful of cold water to clear. Put into the coffee-boiler and boil for about a quarter of an hour; after standing for a little while to settle, pour into your coffeepot, which should be well scalded, and send to the table. The coffee should be stirred as it boils. To make *coffee au lait*, take a pint each of hot *made* coffee and boiling milk; strain through thin muslin into coffeepot, to get rid of the grounds, and serve hot.

## CHOCOLATE.

Take six tablespoons scraped chocolate, or three of chocolate and three of cocoa, dissolve in a quart of boiling water, boil hard fifteen minutes, add one quart of rich milk, let scald and serve hot; this is enough for six persons. Cocoa can also be made after this receipt. Some boil either cocoa or chocolate only one minute and then serve, while others make it the day before using, boiling it for one hour, and when cool skimming off the oil, and when wanted for use, heat it to the boiling point and add the milk. In this way it is equally good and much more wholesome. Cocoa is from the seed of the fruit of a small tropical tree. There are several forms in which it is sold, the most nutritious and convenient being chocolate, the next cocoa, then cocoa nibs, and last cocoa shells. The ground bean is simply cocoa; ground fine and mixed with sugar it is chocolate; the beans broken into bits are "nibs." The shells are the shells of the bean, usually removed before grinding. The beans are roasted like coffee, and ground between hot rollers.

## LEMON SYRUP.

Take the juice of twelve lemons, grate the rind of six in it, let it stand over night, then take six pounds of white sugar, and make a thick syrup. When it is quite cool, strain the juice into it, and squeeze as much oil from the grated rind as will suit the taste. A tablespoonful in a goblet of water will make a delicious drink on a hot day, far superior to that prepared from the stuff commonly sold as lemon syrup.

## STRAWBERRY SYRUP.

Take fine ripe strawberries, crush them in a cloth, and press the juice from them; to each pint of it put a pint of simple syrup, boil gently for one hour, then let it become cold, and bottle it; cork and seal it. When served reduce it to taste with water, set it on ice, and serve in small tumblers half filled.

## RASPBERRY SYRUP.

Make as directed for strawberry.

## STRAWBERRY SHERBET.

Take fourteen ounces of picked strawberries, crush them in a mortar, then add to them a quart of water; pour this into a basin, with a lemon slic d, and a teaspoonful of orange-flower water; let it remain for two or three hours. Put eighteen ounces of sugar into another basin, cover it with a cloth, through which pour the strawberry juice; after as much has run through as will, gather up the cloth, and squeeze out as much juice as possible from it; when the sugar is all dissolved, strain it again; set the vessel containing it on ice, until ready to serve.

## RASPBERRY VINEGAR.

To four quarts red raspberries, put enough vinegar to cover, and let them stand twenty-four hours; scald and strain it; add a pound of sugar to one pint of juice; boil it twenty minutes, and bottle; it is then ready for use and will keep years. To one glass of water add a great spoonful. It is much relished by the sick. Very nice.

## LEMONADE.

Take half a pound of loaf-sugar and reduce it to a syrup with one pint of water; add the rind of five lemons and let stand an hour; remove the rinds and add the strained juice of the lemons; add one bottle of "Apollinaris" water, and a block of ice in centre of bowl. Peel one lemon and cut it up into thin slices, divide each slice in two, and put in lemonade. Claret or fine cordials may be added if desired. Serve with a piece of lemon in each glass.

## EGG-NOG.

Whip the whites and yolks of six eggs into a stiff cream, adding a half cupful of sugar. Pour into a quart of rich milk, adding a half pint of good brandy, and a little flavoring of nutmeg. Stir up and thoroughly mix the ingredients, and add the whites of three additional eggs well whipped.

## RAISIN WINE.

Take two pounds of raisins, seed and chop them, a lemon, a pound of white sugar, and about two gallons of boiling water. Pour into a stone jar, and stir daily for six or eight days. Strain, bottle, and put in a cool place for ten days or so, when the wine will be ready for use.

## CURRANT WINE.

The currants should be quite ripe. Stem, mash, and strain them, adding a half pint of water, and less than a pound of sugar, to a quart of the mashed fruit. Stir well up together and pour into a clean cask, leaving the bung-hole open, or covered with a piece of lace. It should stand for a month to ferment, when it will be ready for bottling.

## GINGER WINE.

One-half pound of cinnamon bark, four ounces of pimento, two ounces of mace, three-quarters of an ounce of capsicum, three-quarters of a pound of ginger root, five gallons of alcohol; macerate and strain or filter, after standing fifteen days. Now make syrup, thirty pounds of white sugar, half pound of tartaric acid, one and a half pounds of cream tartar, dissolved with warm water, clarify with whites of two eggs, and add soft water to make forty gallons. Color with cochineal and let it stand six months before use.

## FINE MILK PUNCH.

Pare off the yellow rind of four large lemons, and steep it for twenty-four hours in a quart of brandy or rum. Then mix with it the juice of the lemons, a pound and a half of loaf-sugar; two grated nutmegs, and a quart of water. Add a quart of rich unskimmed milk, made boiling hot, and strain the whole through a jelly-bag. You may either use it as soon as it is cold, or make a larger quantity (in the above proportion), and bottle it. It will keep several months.

## CLARET CUP.

One quart bottle of claret, one bottle of soda water, one lemon cut very thin, four tablespoons of powdered sugar, quarter of a teaspoon of grated nutmeg, one liquor glass of brandy, one wineglass of sherry wine. Half an hour before it is to be used, put in a large piece of ice, so that it may get perfectly cold.

## ROMAN PUNCH.

Grate the yellow rinds of four lemons and two oranges upon two pounds of loaf-sugar. Squeeze on the juice of the lemons and oranges; cover it, and let it stand till next day. Then strain it through a sieve, add a bottle of champagne, and the whites of eight eggs beaten to a froth. You may freeze it or not.

## CREAM NECTAR.

Dissolve two pounds of crushed sugar in three quarts of water; boil down to two quarts; drop in the white of an egg while boiling; then strain, and put in the tartaric acid; when cold drop in the lemon to your taste; then bottle and cork. Shake two or three times a day.

## RED-CURRANT CORDIAL.

To two quarts of red-currants put one quart of whiskey; let it stand twenty-four hours, then bruise and strain through a flannel bag. To every two quarts of this liquor, add one pound of loaf-sugar, add quarter of a pound of ginger well bruised and boiled; let the whole stand to settle, then strain or filter; bottle and cork, seal the corks tightly. It is an improvement to have half red-raspberry juice if the flavor is liked. The above is fit for use in a month.

## ELDERBERRY SYRUP.

Take elderberries perfectly ripe, wash and strain them, put a pint of molasses to a pint of the juice, boil it twenty minutes, stirring constantly, when cold add to each quart a pint of French brandy; bottle and cork it tight. It is an excellent remedy for a cough.

## INVALID COOKERY.

### PORT WINE JELLY.

Melt in a little warm water an ounce of isinglass; stir it into a pint of port wine, adding two ounces of sugar candy, an ounce of gum-arabic, and half a nutmeg, grated. Mix all well and boil it ten minutes; or till everything is thoroughly dissolved. Then strain it through muslin and set it away to get cold.

### TAPIOCA JELLY.

Wash the tapioca carefully in two or three waters, then soak it for five or six hours, simmer it then in a stewpan until it becomes quite clear, add a little of the juice of a lemon, wine if desired.

### ARROWROOT WINE JELLY.

One cup boiling water, two heaping teaspoons arrowroot, two heaping teaspoons white sugar, one tablespoonful brandy or three tablespoonfuls of wine. An excellent corrective to weak bowels.

### JELLIED CHICKEN.

Cook six chickens in a small quantity of water, until the meat will part from the bone easily; season to taste with salt and pepper; just as soon as cold enough to handle, remove bones and skin; place meat in a deep pan or mold, just as it comes from the bone, using gizzard, liver and heart, until the mold is nearly full. To the water left in the kettle, add three-fourths of a box of Cox's gelatine (some add juice of lemon), dissolved in a little warm water, and boil until it is reduced to a little less than a quart, pour over the chicken in the mold, leave to cool, cut with a very sharp knife and serve. The slices will not easily break up if directions are followed.

### CHICKEN BROTH.

Half fowl, or the inferior joints of a whole one, one quart of water, one blade of mace, half onion, a small bunch of sweet herbs, salt to taste, ten peppercorns. If a young one be used for this broth, the inferior joints may be put in the broth, and the best pieces reserved for dressing in some other manner. Put the fowl into a saucepan, with all the ingredients, and simmer gently for one and a half hours, carefully skimming the broth well. When done, strain, and put by in a cool place until wanted; then take all the fat off the top, warm up as much as may be required, and serve. This broth is, of course, only for those invalids whose stomachs are strong enough to digest it, with a flavoring of herbs, etc. It may be made in the same manner as beef-tea, with water and salt only; but the preparation will be but tasteless and insipid. When the invalid cannot digest this chicken broth with the flavoring, we would recommend plain beef tea in preference to plain chicken tea, which it would be without the addition of herbs, onions, etc.

### TO MAKE GRUEL.

One tablespoonful of Robinson's patent groats, two table-spoonfuls of cold water, one pint of boiling water. Mix the prepared groats smoothly with the cold water in a basin; pour over them the boiling water, stirring it all the time. Put it into a very clean saucepan; boil the gruel for ten minutes, keeping it well stirred; sweeten to taste, and serve. It may be flavored with a small piece of lemon-peel, by boiling it in the gruel, or a little grated nutmeg may be put in; but in these matters the taste of the patient should be consulted. Pour the gruel in a tumbler and serve. When wine is allowed to the invalid, two tablespoonfuls of sherry or port make this preparation very nice. In cases of colds, the same quantity of spirits is sometimes added instead of wine.

## BARLEY WATER.

Put a large tablespoonful of well-washed pearl barley into a pitcher; pour over it boiling water; cover it, and let it remain till cold; then drain off the water; sweeten to taste, and, if liked, add the juice of a lemon, and grated nutmeg.

## ARROWROOT BLANC-MANGE.

Put a quart of milk to boil, take an ounce of Bermuda arrowroot ground fine, make it a smooth batter with cold milk, add a teaspoonful of salt; when the milk is boiling hot, stir the batter into it, continue to stir it over a gentle fire (that it may not be scorched) for three or four minutes, sweeten to taste with double refined sugar, and flavor with lemon extract or orange-flower water, or boil a stick of cinnamon or vanilla bean in the milk before putting in the arrowroot; dip a mold into cold water, strain the blanc-mange through a muslin into the mold, when perfectly cold turn it out; serve currant jelly or jam with it.

## LEMONADE FOR INVALIDS.

One-half a lemon, lump sugar to taste, one pint of boiling water. Pare off the rind of the lemon thinly; cut the lemon into two or three thick slices, and remove as much as possible of the white outside pith, and all the pips. Put the slices of lemon, the peel, and lump sugar into a jug; pour over the boiling water; cover it closely, and in two hours it will be fit to drink. It should either be strained or poured off from the sediment.

## MUTTON BROTH

Is frequently ordered as a preparation for invalids. For the sick-room such broth must be made as plainly as possible, and so as to secure the juice of the meat. Boil slowly a couple of pounds of lean mutton for two hours, skim it very carefully as it simmers, and do not put in very much salt. If the doctor permits, some vegetable as seasoning may be added, and for some broths a little fine barley or rice is added.

## FLAX SEED LEMONADE.

Four tablespoons flax seed (whole), one quart boiling water poured on the flax seed, juice of two lemons, leaving out the peel. Sweeten to taste; stew three hours in a covered pitcher. If too thick, put in cold water with the lemon-juice and sugar. Ice for drinking. It is splendid for colds.

## ARROWROOT.

This is very nourishing and light, either for invalids or infants; make it with milk or water—put a pint of either into a stewpan, make it boiling hot, add a saltspoonful of salt, put a heaped teaspoonful of ground Bermuda arrowroot into a cup, make it smooth with cold milk, stir it into the stewpan, and let it simmer for two or three minutes; then turn it into a bowl, sweeten and grate nutmeg over, if liked; should it be preferred thin, use less arrowroot. This should be made only as much as is wanted at a time, as it will become as thin as water if heated over.

## STEWED RABBITS IN MILK.

Two very young rabbits, not nearly half grown; one and one-half pints of milk, one blade of mace, one dessertspoonful of flour, a little salt and Cayenne. Mix the flour very smoothly with four tablespoonfuls of the milk, and when this is well-mixed, add the remainder. Cut up the rabbits into joints, put them into a stewpan with the milk and other ingredients, and simmer them *very gently* until quite tender. Stir the contents from time to time, to keep the milk smooth and prevent it from burning. Half an hour will be sufficient for the cooking of this dish.

## SLIPPERY-ELM BARK TEA.

Break the bark into bits, pour boiling water over it, cover and let it infuse until cold. Sweeten, ice, and take for summer disorders, or add lemon-juice and drink for a bad cold.

## BEEF TEA.

One pound of *lean* beef, cut into small pieces. Put into a jar without a drop of water; cover tightly, and set in a pot of cold water. Heat gradually to a boil, and continue this steadily for three or four hours, until the meat is like white rags, and the juice all drawn out. Season with salt to taste, and, when cold, skim.

## EGG WINE.

One egg, one tablespoonful and one-half glass of cold water, one glass of sherry, sugar and grated nutmeg to taste. Beat the egg, mixing with it a tablespoonful of cold water; make the wine and water hot, but not boiling; pour it on the egg, stirring all the time. Add sufficient lump sugar to sweeten the mixture, and a little grated nutmeg; put all into a very clean saucepan, set it on a gentle fire, and stir the contents one way until they thicken, but do not allow them to boil. Serve in a glass with snippets of toasted bread or plain crisp biscuits. When the egg is not warmed, the mixture will be found easier of digestion, but it is not so pleasant a drink.

## TOAST WATER.

Slices of toast, nicely browned, without a symptom of burning. Enough boiling water to cover them. Cover closely and let them steep until cold. Strain the water, sweeten to taste, and put a piece of ice in each glassful.

## ONION GRUEL

Is excellent for cold. Slice down a few onions and boil them in a pint of new milk, stir in a sprinkle of oatmeal and a very little salt, boil till the onions are quite tender, then sup rapidly and go to bed.

## COSMETIQUES.

### COMPLEXION WASH.

Put in a vial one drachm of benzoin gum in powder, one drachm nutmeg oil, six drops of orange-blossom tea, or apple-blossoms put in half pint of rain-water and boiled down to one teaspoonful and strained, one pint of sherry wine. Bathe the face morning and night; will remove all flesh worms and freckles, and give a beautiful complexion. Or, put one ounce of powdered gum of benzoin in pint of whiskey; to use, put in water in wash-bowl till it is milky, allowing it to dry without wiping. This is perfectly harmless.

### TO CLEAR A TANNED SKIN.

Wash with a solution of carbonate of soda and a little lemon-juice; then with Fuller's earth-water, or the juice of unripe grapes.

### OIL TO MAKE THE HAIR CURL.

Olive oil, one pound; oil of organum, one drachm; oil rosemary, one and one-half drachms.

### WRINKLES IN THE SKIN.

White wax, one ounce; strained honey, two ounces; juice of lily-bulbs, two ounces. The foregoing melted and stirred together will remove wrinkles.

## PEARL WATER FOR THE FACE.

Put half a pound best Windsor soap scraped fine into half a gallon of boiling water; stir it well until it cools, add a pint of spirits of wine and half an ounce of oil of rosemary; stir well. This is a good cosmetique, and will remove freckles.

## PEARL DENTIFRICE.

Prepare chalk, one-half pound; powdered myrrh, two ounces; camphor, two drachms; orris-root powdered, two ounces. Moisten the camphor with alcohol and mix all well together.

## WASH FOR A BLOTCHED FACE.

Rose water, three ounces; sulphate of zinc, one drachm; mix. Wet the face with it, gently dry it and then touch it over with cold cream, which also gently dry off.

## FACE POWDER.

Take of wheat starch, one pound; powdered orris-root, three ounces; oil of lemon, thirty drops; oil of bergamot, oil of cloves, each fifteen drops. Rub thoroughly together.

## BANDOLINE.

To one quart of rose-water add an ounce and a half of gum tragacanth; let it stand forty-eight hours, frequently straining it, then strain through a coarse linen cloth; let it stand two days, and again strain; add to it a drachm of oil of roses; used by ladies dressing their hair, to cause it lie in any position.

## A GOOD WASH FOR THE HAIR.

One pennyworth of borax, half a pint of olive-oil, one pint of boiling water.

*Mode:* Pour the boiling water over the borax and oil; let it cool; then put the mixture into a bottle. Shake it before using, and apply it with a flannel. Camphor and borax, dissolved in boiling water and left to cool, make a very good wash for the hair; as also does rosemary water mixed with a little borax. After using any of these washes, when the hair becomes thoroughly dry, a little pomatum or oil should be rubbed in, to make it smooth and glossy.

## MISCELLANEOUS.

### AN EXCELLENT HARD SOAP.

Pour twelve quarts soft boiling water on two and one-half pounds of unslacked lime; dissolve five pounds sal soda in twelve quarts soft hot water; then mix and let them remain from twelve to twenty-four hours. Pour off all the clear fluid, being careful not to allow any of the sediment to run off; boil three and one-half pounds clean grease and three or four ounces of rosin in the above lye till the grease disappears; pour into a box and let it stand a day to stiffen and then cut in bars. It is as well to put the lime in all the water and then add the soda. After pouring off the fluid, add two or three gallons of water and let it stand with the lime and soda dregs a day or two. This makes an excellent washing fluid to boil or soak the clothes in. with one pint in a boiler of water.

### TO WASH WOOLEN BLANKETS.

Dissolve soap enough to make a good suds in boiling water, add a tablespoon of aqua ammonia; when scalding hot, turn over your blankets. If convenient, use a pounder, or any way to work thoroughly through the suds without rubbing on a board. Rinse well in hot water. There is usually soap enough from the first suds to make the second soft; if not, add a little soap and ammonia; and after being put through the wringer let two persons, standing opposite, pull them into shape; dry in the sun. White flannels may be washed in the same way without shrinking. Calicoes and other colored fabrics can, before washing, be advantageously soaked for a time in a pail of water to which a spoonful of ox gall has been added. It helps to keep the color. A teacup of lye to a pail of water will improve the color of black goods when necessary to wash them, and vinegar in the rinsing water of pink or green will brighten those colors, as will soda for purple and blue.

## FOR CLOTHES THAT FADE.

One ounce sugar of lead in a pail of rain water. Soak over night.

## LAMP-WICKS.

To insure a good light, wicks must be changed often, as they soon become clogged, and do not permit the free passage of the oil. Soaking wicks in vinegar twenty-four hours before placing in lamp insures a clear flame.

## TO MAKE OLD CRAPE LOOK NEARLY EQUAL TO NEW.

Place a little water in a teakettle, and let it boil until there is plenty of steam from the spout; then holding the crape in both hands, pass it to and fro several times through the steam, and it will be clean and nearly equal to new.

## A CEMENT FOR STOVES.

If the stove is cracked, a good cement is made for it as follows: Wood ashes and salt in equal proportions, reduced to a paste with cold water, and filled in the cracks when the stove is cool. It will soon harden.

## TO CLEAN KID GLOVES.

Rub with very slightly damp bread-crumbs. If not effectual, scrape upon them dry Fuller's earth or French chalk, when on the hands, and rub them quietly together in all directions. Do this several times. Or put gloves of a light color on the hands and wash the hands in a basin of spirits of hartshorn. Some gloves may be washed in a strong lather made of soft soap and warm water or milk; or wash with rice pulp; or sponge them well with turpentine, and hang them in a warm place or where there is a current of air, and all smell of turpentine will be removed.

## STAINS AND SPOTS.

Children's clothes, table linens, towels, etc., should be thoroughly examined before wetting, as soap suds, washing-fluids, etc., will fix almost any stain past removal. Many stains will pass away by being simply washed in pure soft water; or alcohol will remove, before the articles have been in soap-suds, many stains. Ironmold, mildew, or almost any similar spot, can be taken out by dipping in diluted citric acid; then cover with salt, and lay in the bright sun until the stain disappears. If of long standing, it may be necessary to repeat the wetting and the sunlight. Be careful to rinse in several waters as soon as the stain is no longer visible. Ink, fruit, wine, and mildew stains must first be washed in clear, cold water, removing as much of the spots as can be; then mix one teaspoonful of oxalic acid and half a pint of rain water. Dip the stain in this, and wipe off in clear water. Wash at once, if a fabric that will bear washing. A tablespoonful of white-currant juice, if any can be had, is even better than lemon. This preparation may be used on the most delicate articles without injury. Shake it up before using it, and be careful and put out of the reach of meddlers or little folks, as it is poisonous.

## TO REMOVE GREASE SPOTS.

An excellent mixture to remove grease spots from boys' and men's clothing particularly, is made of four parts alcohol to one part of ammonia and about half as much ether as ammonia. Apply the liquid to the grease spot, and then rub diligently with a sponge and clear water. The chemistry of the operation seems to be that the alcohol and ether dissolve the grease, and the ammonia forms a soap with it which is washed out with the water. The result is much more satisfactory than when something is used which only seems to spread the spot and make it fainter, but does not actually remove it. If oil is spilt on the carpet, and you immediately scatter corn meal over it, the oil will be absorbed by it. Oil may also be removed from carpets on which you do not dare to put ether and ammonia, by laying thick blotting paper over it and pressing a hot flat-iron on it. Repeat the operation several times, using a clean paper each time.

## STAINS ON MARBLE.

Iron-rust stains on marble can usually be removed by rubbing with lemon-juice. Almost all other stains may be taken off by mixing one ounce of finely-powdered chalk, one of pumice stone, and two ounces of common soda. Sift these together through a fine sieve, and mix with water. When thoroughly mixed, rub this mixture over the stains faithfully and the stains will disappear. Wash the marble after this with soap and water, dry and polish with a chamois skin, and the marble will look like new.

---

A thin coating of three parts lard melted with one part rosin applied to stoves and grates will prevent their rusting in summer.

## PAINT OR VARNISH.

Oil of turpentine or benzine will remove spots of paint, varnish, or pitch from white or colored cotton or woolen goods. After using it they should be washed in soap-suds.

## TO REMOVE INK FROM CARPETS.

When freshly spilled, ink can be removed from carpets by wetting in milk. Take cotton batting and soak up all of the ink it will receive, being careful not to let it spread. Then take fresh cotton, wet in milk, and sop it up carefully. Repeat this operation, changing cotton and milk each time. After most of the ink has been taken up in this way, with fresh cotton and clean, rub the spot. Continue till all disappears; then wash the spot in clean warm water and a little soap; rinse in clean water, and rub till nearly dry. If the ink is dried in, we know of no way that will not take the color from the carpet as well as the ink, unless the ink is on a white spot. In that case salts of lemon, or soft-soap, starch, and lemon-juice will remove the ink as easily as if on cotton.

## TO REMOVE INK FROM PAPER.

Put one pound of cloride of lime to four quarts of water. Shake well together and let it stand twenty-four hours; then strain through a clean cotton cloth. Add one teaspoonful of acetic acid to one ounce of this prepared lime water, and apply to the blot, and the ink will disappear. Absorb the moisture with blotting paper. The remainder may be bottled, closely corked, and set aside for future use.

---

An occasional feed of hard-boiled eggs made fine and mixed with cracker-crumbs is good for canary birds. Feed a couple of thimblefuls at a time.

## INK ON ROSEWOOD OR MAHOGANY.

As ink has been unfortunately spilled on mahogany, rosewood, or black walnut furniture, put half a dozen drops of spirits of nitre into a spoonful of water, and touch the stain with a feather wet in this; as soon as the ink disappears, rub the place immediately with a cloth ready wet in cold water, or the nitre will leave a white spot very difficult to remove, If after washing off the nitre the ink spot still lingers, make the mixture a little stronger and use the second time, and never forget to wash it off at once.

## COAL FIRE.

If your coal fire is low, throw on a tablespoon of salt, and it will help it very much.

## POLISH FOR BRIGHT STOVES AND STEEL ARTICLES.

One tablespoonful of turpentine; one tablespoonful of sweet oil; emery powder. Mix the turpentine and sweet oil together, stirring in sufficient emery powder to make the mixture of the thickness of cream. Put it on the article with a piece of soft flannel, rub off quickly with another piece, then polish with a little emery powder and clean leather.

## TO PREVENT PUMPS FROM FREEZING.

Take out the lower valve in the fall, and drive a tack under it, projecting in such a way that it cannot quite close. The water will then leak back into the well or cistern, while the working qualities of the pump will not be damaged.

---

To keep starch from sticking to irons rub the irons with a little piece of wax or sperm.

## TO KEEP OFF MOSQUITOES.

Rub exposed parts with kerosene. The odor is not noticed after a few minutes, and children especially are much relieved by its use.

## TO BRIGHTEN GILT FRAMES.

Take sufficient flour of sulphur to give a golden tinge to about one and one-half pints of water, and in this boil four or five bruised onions or garlic, which will answer the same purpose. Strain off the liquid, and with it, when cold, wash, with a soft brush, any gilding which requires restoring, and when dry it will come out as bright as new work.

## TO MAKE HENS LAY IN WINTER.

Keep them warm; keep corn constantly by them, but do not feed it to them. Feed them with meat scraps when lard or tallow has been tried, or fresh meat. Some chop green peppers finely, or mix Cayenne pepper with corn meal to feed them. Let them have a frequent taste of green food, a little gravel and lime, or clam-shells.

## TO PRESERVE STEEL PENS.

Steel pens are destroyed by corrosion from acid in the ink. Put in the ink some nails or old steel pens, and the acid will exhaust itself on them, and the pens in use will not corrode.

## MICE.

Pumpkin seeds are very attractive to mice, and traps baited with them will soon destroy this little pest.

## CAMPHOR

Placed in trunks or drawers will prevent mice from doing them injury.

## TO CLEAN COMBS.

If it can be avoided, never wash combs, as the water often makes the teeth split, and the tortoiseshell or horn of which they are made, rough. Small brushes, manufactured purposely for cleaning combs, may be purchased at a trifling cost; with this the comb should be well brushed, and afterwards wiped with a cloth or towel.

## FOR CLEANING INK-SPOTS.

Ink-spots on the fingers may be instantly removed by a little ammonia. Rinse the hands after washing in clear water. A little ammonia in a few spoonfuls of alcohol is excellent to sponge silk dresses that have grown "shiny" or rusty, as well as to take out spots. A silk, particularly a black, becomes almost like new when so sponged.

## FOR CLEANING JEWELRY.

For cleaning jewelry there is nothing better than ammonia and water. If very dull or dirty, rub a little soap on a soft brush and brush them in this wash, rinse in cold water, dry first in an old handkerchief, and then rub with buck or chamois skin. Their freshness and brilliancy when thus cleaned cannot be surpassed by any compound used by jewelers.

## FOR WASHING SILVER AND SILVERWARE

For washing silver, put half a teaspoonful ammonia into the suds; have the water hot; wash quickly, using a small brush, rinse in hot water, and dry with a clean linen towel;

then rub very dry with a chamois skin. Washed in this manner, silver becomes very brilliant, requires no polishing with any of the powders or whiting usually employed, and does not wear out. Silver-plate, jewelry and door-plates can be beautifully cleaned and made to look like new by dropping a soft cloth or chamois skin into a weak preparation of ammonia-water, and rubbing the articles with it. Put half a teaspoonful into clear water to wash tumblers or glass of any kind, rinse and dry well, and they will be beautifully clear.

## FOR WASHING GLASS AND GLASSWARE.

For washing windows, looking-glasses, etc., a little ammonia in the water saves much labor, aside from giving a better polish than anything else; and for general house-cleaning it removes dirt, smoke and grease most effectually.

## INSECTS AND VERMIN.

Dissolve two pounds of alum in three or four quarts of water. Let it remain over night, till all the alum is dissolved. Then, with a brush, apply, boiling hot, to every joint or crevice in the closet or shelves where Croton bugs, ants, cockroaches, etc., intrude; also to the joints and crevices of bedsteads, as bed bugs dislike it as much as Croton bugs, roaches or ants. Brush all the cracks in the floor and mop-boards. Keep it boiling hot while using.

To keep woolens and furs from moths, two things are to be observed—first, to see that none are in the articles when they are put away, and second, to put them where the parent moth cannot enter. Tin cases, soldered tight, whiskey barrels headed so that not even a liquid can get in or out, have been used to keep out moths. A piece of strong brown paper with not a hole through which even a large pin can enter, is just as good. Put the articles in a close box and cover every joint with paper, or resort to whatever will be a complete covering. A wrapper of common cotton cloth, so put around and secured, is often used. Wherever a knitting needle will pass the parent moth can enter. Carefully exclude the insect and the articles will be safe.

## MOTHS IN CARPETS.

Persons troubled with carpet moths may get rid of them by scrubbing the floor with strong hot salt and water before laying the carpet, and sprinkling the carpet with salt once a week before sweeping.

## SMOOTH SAD-IRONS.

To have your sad-irons clean and smooth rub them first with a piece of wax tied in a cloth, and afterwards scour them on a paper or thick cloth strewn with coarse salt.

## TO SWEETEN MEAT.

A little charcoal thrown into the pot will sweeten meat that is a little old. Not if it is anyway tainted—it is then not fit to eat—but only if kept a little longer than makes it quite fresh.

## STOVE POLISH.

Stove lustre, when mixed with turpentine and applied in the usual manner, is blacker, more glossy and more durable than when mixed with any other liquid. The turpentine prevents rust, and when put on an old rusty stove will make it look as well as new.

## CLEANING WHITE PAINT.

Spirits of ammonia, used in sufficient quantity to soften the water, and ordinary hard soap, will make the paint look white and clean with half the effort of any other method I ever have tried. Care should be taken not to have too much ammonia, or the paint will be injured.

## TO CLEANSE THE INSIDE OF JARS.

This can be done in a few minutes by filling the jars with hot water (it need not be scalding hot), and then stirring in a teaspoonful or more of baking soda. Shake well, then empty the jar at once, and if any of the former odor remains about it, fill again with water and soda; shake well, and rinse out in cold water.

## FURNITURE POLISH.

Equal proportions of linseed oil, turpentine, vinegar, and spirits of wine.

*Mode:* When used, shake the mixture well, and rub on the furniture with a piece of linen rag, and polish with a clean duster. Vinegar and oil, rubbed in with flannel, and the furniture rubbed with a clean duster, produce a very good polish.

---

Squeaking doors ought to have the hinges oiled by a feather dipped in some linseed oil.

---

A soft cloth, wetted in alcohol, is excellent to wipe off French plate-glass and mirrors.

---

A red-hot iron will soften old putty so that it can be easily removed.

## TO REMOVE STAINS FROM MATTRESSES.

Make a thick paste by wetting starch with cold water. Spread this on the stain, first putting the mattress in the sun; rub this off after an hour or so, and if the ticking is not clean try the process again.

## KALSOMINING.

For plain white use one pound white glue, twenty pounds English whiting; dissolve glue by boiling in about three pints of water; dissolve whiting with hot water; make the consistency of thick batter; then add glue and one cup soft soap. Dissolve a piece of alum the size of a hen's egg, add and mix the whole thoroughly. Let it cool before using. If too thick to spread nicely add more water till it spreads easily. For blue tints add five cents' worth of Prussian blue, and a little Venetian red for lavender. For peach-blow use red in white alone. The above quantity is enough to cover four ceilings, sixteen feet square, with two coats, and will not rub off as the whitewash does made of lime.

## PAPERING WHITEWASHED WALLS.

There are many ways, but we mention these that are the most reliable. Take a perfectly clean broom, and wet the walls all over with clean water; then with a small sharp hoe or scraper scrape off all the old whitewash you can. Then cut your paper of the right length, and, when you are all ready to put on the paper, wet the wall with strong vinegar. Another way is to make very thin paste by dissolving one pound of white glue in five quarts of warm water, and wash the walls with it before putting on the paper. A very good way is to apply the paste to both paper and wall. The paste may be made from either wheat or rye flour, but must be put on warm.

## HOW TO CLEAN CORSETS.

Take out the steels at front and sides, then scrub thoroughly with tepid or cold lather of white castile soap, using a very small scrubbing brush. Do not lay them in water. When quite clean let cold water run on them freely from the spigot to rinse out the soap thoroughly. Dry without ironing (after pulling lengthwise until they are straight and shapely) in a cool place.

## TO CLEAN HAIRBRUSHES.

Do not use soap, but put a tablespoon of hartshorn into the water, having it only tepid, and dip up and down until clean; then dry with the brushes down, and they will be like new ones. If you do not have ammonia, use soda; a teaspoonful dissolved in the water will do very well.

## HOW TO WASH FLANNELS.

There are many conflicting theories in regard to the proper way to wash flannels, but I am convinced, from careful observation, that the true way is to wash them in water in which you can comfortably bear your hand. Make suds before putting the flannels in, and do not rub soap on the flannel. I make it a rule to have only one piece of flannel put in the tub at a time. Wash in two suds if much soiled; then rinse thoroughly in clean, weak suds, wring, and hang up; but do not take flannels out of warm water and hang out in a freezing air, as that certainly tends to shrink them. It is better to dry them in the house, unless the sun shines. In washing worsted goods, such as men's pantaloons, pursue the same course, only do not wring them, but hang them up and let them drain; while a little damp bring in and press smoothly with as hot an iron as you can use without scorching the goods. The reason for not wringing them is to prevent wrinkles.

## CLEANING LACE.

Cream-colored Spanish lace can be cleaned and made to look like new by rubbing it in dry flour; rub as if you were washing in water. Then take it outdoors and shake all the flour out; if not perfectly clean, repeat the rubbing in a little more clean flour. The flour must be very thoroughly shaken from the lace, or the result will be far from satisfactory. White knitted hoods can be cleaned in this way; babies' socks also, if only slightly soiled.

## NEW KETTLES.

The best way to prepare a new iron kettle for use is to fill it with clean potato peelings, boil them for an hour or more, then wash the kettle with hot water; wipe it dry, and rub it with a little lard; repeat the rubbing for half a dozen times after using. In this way you will prevent rust and all the annoyances liable to occur in the use of a new kettle.

## TO KEEP FLIES OFF GILT FRAMES.

Boil three or four onions in a pint of water and apply with a soft brush.

## TO PREVENT KNIVES FROM RUSTING.

In laying aside knives, or other steel implements, they should be slightly oiled and wrapped in tissue paper to prevent their rusting. A salty atmosphere will in a short time quite ruin all steel articles, unless some such precaution is taken.

## CEMENT FOR GLASSWARE.

For mending valuable glass objects, which would be disfigured by common cement, chrome cement may be used. This is a mixture of five parts of gelatine to one of a solution of acid chromate of lime. The broken edges are covered with this, pressed together and exposed to sunlight, the effect of the latter being to render the compound insoluble even in boiling water.

## WATERPROOF PAPER.

Excellent paper for packing may be made of old newspapers; the tougher the paper of course the better. A mixture is made of copal varnish, boiled linseed oil and turpentine, in equal parts. It is painted on the paper with a flat varnish brush an inch and a half wide, and the sheets are laid out to dry for a few minutes. This paper has been very successfully used for packing plants for sending long distances, and is probably equal to the paper commonly used by nurserymen.

## RECIPE FOR VIOLET INK.

To make one gallon, take one ounce of violet analine; dissolve it in one gill of hot alcohol. Stir it a few moments. When thoroughly dissolved add one gallon of boiling water, and the ink is made. As the analine colors vary a great deal in quality, the amount of dilution must vary with the sample used and the shade determined by trial.

## PERSPIRATION.

The unpleasant odor produced by perspiration is frequently the source of vexation to persons who are subject to it. Nothing is simpler than to remove this odor much more effectually than by the application of such costly unguents and perfumes as are in use. It is only necessary to procure some of the compound spirits of ammonia, and place about two tablespoonfuls in a basin of water. Washing the face, hands, and arms with this leaves the skin as clean, sweet and fresh as one could wish. The wash is perfectly harmless and very cheap. It is recommended on the authority of an experienced physician.

## RENEWING OLD KID GLOVES.

Make a thick mucilage by boiling a handful of flax-seed; add a little dissolved toilet soap; then, when the mixture cools, put the glove on the hands and rub them with a piece of white flannel wet with the mixture. Do not wet the gloves through.

## COLOGNE WATER.

Take a pint of alcohol and put in thirty drops of oil of lemon, thirty of bergamot, and half a gill of water. If musk or lavender is desired, add the same quantity of each. The oils should be put in the alcohol and shaken well before the water is added. Bottle it for use.

## TO CLEANSE A SPONGE.

By rubbing a fresh lemon thoroughly into a soured sponge and rinsing it several times in lukewarm water, it will become as sweet as when new.

## ICY WINDOWS.

Windows may be kept free from ice and polished by rubbing the glass with a sponge dipped in alcohol.

---

To remove blood stains from cloth, saturate with kerosene, and after standing a little, wash in warm water.

## CAMPHOR ICE.

One ounce of lard, one ounce of spermaceti, one ounce of camphor, one ounce of almond oil, one-half cake of white wax; melt and turn into molds.

## STARCH POLISH.

Take one ounce of spermaceti and one ounce of white wax, melt and run it into a thin cake on a plate. A piece the size of a quarter dollar added to a quart of prepared starch gives a beautiful lustre to the clothes and prevents the iron from sticking.

## TO CLEAN FEATHERS.

Cover the feathers with a paste made of pipe-clay and water, rubbing them one way only. When quite dry, shake off all the powder and curl with a knife. Grebe feathers may be washed with white soap in soft water.

## TO TEST NUTMEGS.

To test nutmegs prick them with a pin, and if they are good the oil will instantly spread around the puncture.

## TO CLEAN MICA.

Mica in stoves, when smoked, is readily cleaned by taking it out and thoroughly washing with vinegar a little diluted. If the black does not come off at once, let it soak a little.

## TO SOFTEN HARD WATER.

Add half a pound of the best quick lime, dissolved in water to every hundred gallons. Smaller proportions may be more conveniently managed, and if allowed to stand a short time the lime will have united with the carbonate of lime and been deposited at the bottom of the receptacle. Another way is to put gallon of lye into a barrelful of water.

## TO DESTROY VERMIN IN THE HAIR.

Powdered cevadilla one ounce, powdered staves-acre one ounce, powdered panby seed one ounce, powdered tobacco one ounce. Mix well and rub among the roots of the hair thoroughly.

## TO REMOVE BRUISES FROM FURNITURE.

Wet the bruised spot with warm water. Soak a piece of brown paper of several thicknesses in warm water, and lay over the place. Then apply a warm flat-iron until the moisture is gone. Repeat the process if needful, and the bruise will disappear.

## PEARL SMELLING SALTS.

Powdered carbonate of ammonia, one ounce; strong solution of ammonia, half a fluid ounce; oil of rosemary, ten drops; oil of bergamot, ten drops. Mix, and while moist put in a wide-mouthed bottle which is to be well closed.

## POUNDED GLASS.

Pounded glass, mixed with dry corn-meal, and placed within the reach of rats, it is said, will banish them from the premises; or sprinkle Cayenne pepper in their holes.

## POLISH FOR BOOTS.

Take of ivory-black and treacle each four ounces; sulphuric acid, one ounce; best olive oil, two spoonfuls, best white-wine vinegar, three half pints; mix the ivory-black and treacle well in an earthen jar; then add the sulphuric acid, continuing to stir the mixture; next pour in the oil, and, lastly, add the vinegar, stirring it in by degrees until thoroughly incorporated.

## TO CLEAN PLATE.

Wash the plate well to remove all grease, in a strong lather of common yellow soap and boiling water, and wipe it quite dry; then mix as much hartshorn powder as will be required, into a thick paste, with cold water or spirits of wine; smear this lightly over the plate with a piece of soft rag, and leave it for some little time to dry. When perfectly dry, brush it off quite clean with a soft plate-brush, and polish the plate with a dry leather. If the plate be very dirty, or much tarnished, spirits of wine will be found to answer better than water for mixing the paste.

## TO CLEAN DECANTERS.

Roll up in small pieces some soft brown or blotting paper; wet them, and soap them well. Put them into the decanters about one-quarter full of warm water; shake them well for a few moments, then rinse with clear cold water; wipe the outsides with a nice dry cloth, put the decanters to drain, and when dry they will be almost as bright as new ones.

## SPOTS ON TOWELS AND HOSIERY.

Spots on towels and hosiery will disappear with little trouble if a little ammonia is put into enough water to soak the articles, and they are left in it an hour or two before washing; and if a cupful is put into the water in which white clothes are soaked the night before washing, the ease with which the articles can be washed, and their great whiteness and clearness when dried will be very gratifying. Remembering the small sum paid for three quarts of ammonia of common strength, one can easily see that no bleaching preparation can be more cheaply obtained.

No articles in kitchen use are so likely to be neglected and abused as the dish-cloths and dish-towels; and in washing these, ammonia, if properly used, is a greater comfort than anywhere else. Put a teaspoonful into the water in which these cloths are, or should be washed every day; rub soap on the towels. Put them in the water; let them stand a half hour or so, then rub them out thoroughly, rinse faithfully, and dry out-doors in clear air and sun, and dish-cloths and towels need never look gray and dingy—a perpetual discomfort to all housekeepers.

## CROUP.

Croup, it is said, can be cured in one minute, and the remedy is simply alum and sugar. The way to accomplish the deed is to take a knife or grater, and shave off in small particles about a teaspoonful of alum; then mix it with twice its amount of sugar, to make it palatable, and administer it as quickly as possible. Almost instantaneous relief will follow.

---

In the summer season it is not an uncommon thing for persons going into the woods to be poisoned by contact with dogwood, ivy, or the poisoned oak. The severe itching and smarting which is thus produced may be relieved by first washing the parts with a solution of saleratus, two teaspoonfuls to the pint of water, and then applying cloths wet with extract of hamammellis. Take a dose of Epsom salts internally or a double Rochelle powder.

## CONVULSION FITS.

Convulsion fits sometimes follow the feverish restlessness produced by these causes; in which case a hot bath should be administered without delay, and the lower parts of the body rubbed, the bath being as hot as it can be without scalding the tender skin.

## BURNS AND SCALDS.

A burn or scald is always painful; but the pain can be instantly relieved by the use of bi-carbonate of soda, or common baking soda (saleratus). Put two tablespoonfuls of soda in a half cup of water. Wet a piece of linen cloth in the solution and lay it on the burn. The pain will disappear as if by magic. If the burn is so deep that the skin has peeled off, dredge the dry soda directly on the part affected.

## CUTS.

For a slight cut there is nothing better to control the hemorrhage than common unglazed brown wrapping paper, such as is used by marketmen and grocers; a piece to be bound over the wound.

## COLD ON THE CHEST.

A flannel dipped in boiling water, and sprinkled with turpentine, laid on the chest as quickly as possible, will relieve the most severe cold or hoarseness.

## BLEEDING FROM THE NOSE.

Many children, especially those of a sanguineous temperament, are subject to sudden discharges of blood from some part of the body; and as all such fluxes are in general the result of an effort of nature to relieve the system from some overload or pressure, such discharges, unless in excess, and when likely to produce debility, should not be rashly or too abruptly checked. In general, these discharges are confined to the summer or spring months of the year, and follow pains in the head, a sense of drowsiness, languor or oppression, and as such symptoms are relieved by the loss of blood, the hemorrhage should, to a certain extent, be encouraged. When, however, the bleeding is excessive, or returns too frequently, it becomes necessary to apply means to subdue or mitigate the amount. For this purpose the sudden and unexpected application of cold is itself sufficient in most cases to arrest the most active hemorrhage. A wet towel laid suddenly on the back, between the shoulders, and placing the child in a recumbent posture is often sufficient to effect the object; where, however, the effusion resists such simple means, napkins wrung out of cold water must be laid across the forehead and nose, the hands dipped in cold water, and a bottle of hot water applied to the feet. If, in spite of these means, the bleeding continues, a little fine wool or a few folds of lint, tied together by a piece of thread, must be pushed up the nostril from which the blood flows; to act as a plug and pressure on the bleeding vessel. When the discharge has entirely ceased, the plug is to be pulled out by means of the thread. To prevent a repetition of the hemorrhage, the body should be sponged every morning with cold water, and the child put under a course of steel wine, have open-air exercise, and, if possible, salt water bathing. For children, a key suddenly dropped down the back between the skin and clothes, will often immediately arrest a copious bleeding.

## CHILBLAINS.

Chilblains are most irritating to children. The following is an infallible cure for unbroken chilblains: Hydrochloric acid, diluted, one-quarter ounce; hydrocyanic acid, diluted, 30 drops; camphor-water, six ounces. This chilblain lotion cures mild cases by one application. It is a deadly poison, and should be kept under lock and key. A responsible person should apply it to the feet of children. This must not be applied to broken chilblains.

## TO CURE A STING OF BEE OR WASP.

Mix common earth with water to about the consistency of mud. Apply at once.

## FOR TOOTHACHE.

Alum reduced to an impalpable powder, two drachms; nitrous spirit of ether, seven drachms; mix and apply to the tooth.

## CHOKING.

A piece of food lodged in the throat may sometimes be pushed down with the finger, or removed with a hairpin quickly straightened and hooked at the end, or by two or three vigorous blows on the back between the shoulders.

---

A very excellent carminative powder for flatulant infants may be kept in the house, and employed with advantage, whenever the child is in pain or griped, by dropping five grains of oil of aniseed and two of peppermint on half an ounce of lump sugar, and rubbing it in a mortar, with a drachm of magnesia, into a fine powder. A small quantity of this may be given in a little water at any time, and always with benefit.

## CUBEB BERRIES FOR CATARRH.

A new remedy for catarrh is crushed cubeb berries smoked in a pipe, emitting the smoke through the nose; after a few trials this will be easy to do. If the nose is stopped up so that it is almost impossible to breath, one pipeful will make the head as clear as a bell. For sore throat, asthma, and bronchitis, swallowing the smoke effects immediate relief. It is the best remedy in the world for offensive breath, and will make the most foul breath pure and sweet. Sufferers from that horrid disease, ulcerated catarrh, will find this remedy unequaled, and a month's use will cure the most obstinate case. A single trial will convince anyone. Eating the uncrushed berries is also good for sore throat and all bronchial complaints. After smoking, do not expose yourself to cold air for at least fifteen minutes.

## DIARRHŒA.

For any form of diarrhœa that, by excessive action, demands a speedy correction, the most efficacious remedy that can be employed in all ages and conditions of childhood is the tincture of kino, of which from ten to thirty drops, mixed with a little sugar and water in a spoon, are to be given every two or three hours till the undue action has been checked. Often the change of diet to rice, milk, eggs, or the substitution of animal for vegetable food, *vice versa*, will correct an unpleasant and almost chronic state of diarrhœa.

---

If it is not convenient to fill flannel bags for the sick room with sand, bran will answer the purpose very well, and will retain the heat a long time.

### BITES OF DOGS.

The only safe remedy in case of a bite from a dog suspected of madness, is to burn out the wound thoroughly with red-hot iron, or with lunar caustic, for fully eight seconds, so as to destroy the entire surface of the wound. Do this as soon as possible, for no time is to be lost. Of course it will be expected that the parts touched with the caustic will turn black.

### MEASLES AND SCARLATINA.

Measles and scarlatina much resemble each other in their early stages; headache, restlessness, and fretfulness are the symptoms of both. Shivering fits, succeeded by a hot skin; pains in the back and limbs, accompanied by sickness, and, in severe cases, sore throat; pain about the jaws, difficulty in swallowing, running at the eyes, which become red and inflamed, while the face is hot and flushed, often distinguish scarlatina from scarlet fever, of which it is only a mild form. While the case is doubtful, a dessertspoonful of spirit of nitre diluted in water, given at bedtime, will throw the child into a gentle perspiration, and will bring out the rash in either case. In measles, this appears first on the face; in scarlatina, on the chest; and in both cases, a doctor should be called in. In scarlatina, tartar-emetic powder or ipecacuhana may be administered in the meantime

### STYE IN THE EYE.

Styes are little abscesses which form between the roots of the eyelashes, and are rarely larger than a small pea. The best way to manage them is to bathe them frequently with warm water; or in warm poppy-water, if very painful. When they have burst, use an ointment composed of one part of citron ointment and four of spermaceti, well rubbed together, and smear along the edge of the eyelid. Give a grain or two of calomel with five or eight grains of rhubarb, according to the age of the child, twice a week. The old-fashioned and apparently absurd practice of rubbing the stye with a ring, is as good and speedy a cure as that by any process of medicinal application; though the number of times it is rubbed, or the quality of the ring and direction of the strokes, has nothing to do with its success. That pressure and the friction excite the vessels of the part, and cause an absorption of the effused matter under the eyelash. The edge of the nail will answer as well as a ring.

## FOR CONSTIPATION.

One or two figs eaten fastly is sufficient for some, and they are especially good in the case of children, as there is no trouble in getting them to take them. A spoon of wheaten bran in a glass of water is a simple remedy and quite effective.

## LEANNESS

Is caused generally by lack of power in the digestive organs to digest and assimilate the fat-producing elements of food. First restore digestion, take plenty of sleep, drink all the water the stomach will bear in the morning on rising, take moderate exercise in the open air, eat oatmeal, cracked wheat, Graham mush, baked sweet apples, roasted and broiled beef, cultivate jolly people, and bathe daily.

## SUPERFLUOUS HAIRS

Are best left alone. Shaving only increases the strength of the hair, and all depilatories are dangerous and sometimes disfigure the face. The only sure plan is to spread on a piece of leather equal parts of galbanum and pitch pláster, lay it on the hair as smoothly as possible, let it remain three or four minutes, then remove it with the hairs, root and branch. This is severe, but effective. Kerosene will also remove them. If sore after using, rub on sweet oil.

## THE BREATH.

Nothing makes one so disagreeable to others as a bad breath. It is caused by bad teeth, diseased stomach, or disease of the nostrils. Neatness and care of the health will prevent and cure it.

## THE QUININE CURE FOR DRUNKENNESS.

Pulverize one pound of fresh quill-red Peruvian bark, and soak it in one pint of diluted alcohol. Strain and evaporate down to one-half pint. For the first and second days give a teaspoonful every three hours. If too much is taken, headache will result, and in that case the doses should be diminished. On the third day give one-half a teaspoonful; on the fourth reduce the dose to fifteen drops, then to ten, and then to five. Seven days, it is said, will cure average cases, though some require a whole month.

## FOR SORE THROAT.

Cut slices of salt pork or fat bacon; simmer a few moments in hot vinegar, and apply to throat as hot as possible. When this is taken off, as the throat is relieved, put around a bandage of soft flannel. A gargle of equal parts of borax and alum, dissolved in water, is also excellent. To be used frequently.

## A GOOD CURE FOR COLDS.

Boil two ounces of flaxseed in one quart of water; strain and add two ounces of rock candy, one-half pint of honey, juice of three lemons; mix, and let all boil well; let cool, and bottle. *Dose:* One cupful on going to bed, one-half cupful before meals. The hotter you drink it the better.

## TO STOP BLEEDING.

A handful of flour bound on the cut.

## A HEALTHFUL APPETIZER.

How often we hear women who do their own cooking say that by the time they have prepared a meal, and it is ready for the table, they are too tired to eat. One way to mitigate this is to take, about half an hour before dinner, a raw egg, beat it until light, put in a little sugar and milk, flavor it, and "drink it down;" it will remove the faint, tired-out feeling, and will not spoil your appetite for dinner.

## TO REMOVE DISCOLORATION FROM BRUISES.

Apply a cloth wrung out in very hot water, and renew frequently until the pain ceases. Or apply raw beefsteak.

## EARACHE.

There is scarcely any ache to which children are subject so hard to bear and difficult to cure as the earache; but there is a remedy never known to fail. Take a bit of cotton batting, put upon it a pinch of black pepper, gather it up and tie it, dip in sweet oil and insert into the ear; put a flannel bandage over the head to keep it warm. It will give immediate relief. As soon as any soreness is felt in the ear, let three or four drops of the tincture of arnica be poured in and the orifice be filled with a little cotton wool to exclude the air. If the arnica be not resorted to until there is actual pain, then the cure may not be as speedy, but it is just as certain, although it may be necessary to repeat the operation. It is a sure preventive against gathering in the ear, which is the usual cause of earache.

## TO CURE TOOTHACHE.

The worst toothache, or neuralgia coming from the teeth, may be speedily and delightfully ended by the application of a bit of clean cotton, saturated in a solution of ammonia, to the defective tooth. Sometimes the late sufferer is prompted to momentary laughter by the application, but the pain will disappear.

## FOR FELON.

Take common rock salt, as used for salting down pork or beef, dry in an oven, and pound it fine and mix with spirits of turpentine in equal parts; put it in a rag and wrap it around the parts affected; as it gets dry put on more, and in twenty-four hours you are cured. The felon will be dead.

---

Coffee pounded in a mortar and roasted on an iron plate; sugar burned on hot coals, and vinegar boiled with myrrh and sprinkled on the floor and furniture of a sick room, are excellent deodorizers.

---

The skin of a boiled egg is the most efficacious remedy that can be applied to a boil. Peel it carefully, wet and apply to the part affected. It will draw off the matter, and relieve the soreness in a few hours.

## TO CURE A WHITLOW.

As soon as the whitlow has risen distinctly, a pretty large piece should be snipped out, so that the watery matter may readily escape, and continue to flow out as fast as produced. A bread and water poultice should be put on for a few days, when the wound should be bound up lightly with some mild ointment, when a cure will be speedily completed. Constant poulticing both before and after the opening of the whitlow is the only practice needed; but as the matter lies deep, when it is necessary to open the abscess, the incision must be made deep to reach the suppuration.

## TAPE-WORMS.

Tape-worms are said to be removed by refraining from supper and breakfast, and at eight o'clock taking one-third part of two hundred minced pumpkin seeds, the shells of which have been removed by hot water; at nine take another third, at ten the remainder, and follow it at eleven with strong dose of castor oil.

## FOR A CAKED BREAST.

Bake large potatoes, put two or more in a woolen stocking; crush them soft and apply to the breast as hot as can be borne; repeat constantly till relieved.

---

A good remedy for blistered feet from long walking is to rub the feet at going to bed with spirits mixed with tallow dropped from a lighted candle into the palm of the hand.

---

A lady writes that sufferers from asthma should get a muskrat skin and wear it over their lungs, with the fur side next to the body. It will bring certain relief.

## CHAPPED HANDS.

Powdered starch is an excellent preventive of chapping of the hands, when it is rubbed over them after washing and drying them thoroughly. It will also prevent the needle in sewing from sticking and becoming rusty. It is therefore advisable to have a small box of it in the work-box or basket, and near your wash-basin.

## LUNAR CAUSTIC.

Lunar caustic, carefully applied so as not to touch the skin, will destroy warts.

## CURE FOR RHEUMATISM AND BILIOUS HEADACHE.

Finest Turkey rhubarb, half an ounce; carbonate magnesia, one ounce; mix intimately; keep well corked in glass bottle. *Dose:* One teaspoonful, in milk and sugar, the first thing in the morning; repeat till cured. Tried with success.

## FEVER AND AGUE.

Four ounces galangal-root in a quart of gin, steeped in a warm place; take often.

---

For a simple fainting fit a horizontal position and fresh air will usually suffice. If a person receive a severe shock caused by a fall or blow, handle carefully without jarring. A horizontal position is best. Loosen all tight clothing from the throat, chest, and waist. If the patient can swallow, give half teaspoonful aromatic spirits of ammonia in a little water. If that cannot be procured, give whiskey or brandy and water. Apply warmth to the feet and bowels.

## TO RESTORE FROM STROKE OF LIGHTNING.

Shower with cold water for two hours; if the patient does not show signs of life, put salt in the water, and continue to shower an hour longer.

## RELIEF FOR INFLAMED FEET.

The first thing to be done is to take off and throw away tight-fitting boots, which hurt the tender feet as much as if they were put into a press. Then take one pint of wheat bran and one ounce of saleratus, and put it into a foot-bath, and add one gallon of hot water. When it has become cool enough put in the feet, soak them for fifteen minutes, and the relief will be almost immediate. Repeat this every night for a week, and the cure will be complete. The burning, prickly sensation is caused by the pores of the skin being closed up so tightly by the pressure of the boots that they cannot perspire freely.

## WARM WATER.

Warm water is preferable to cold water as a drink to persons who are subject to dyspeptic and bilious complaints, and it may be taken more freely than cold water, and consequently answers better as a diluent for carrying off bile, and removing obstructions in the urinary secretion, in cases of stone and gravel. When water of a temperature equal to that of the human body is used for drink, it proves considerably stimulant, and is particularly suited to dyspetic, bilious, gouty, and chlorotic subjects.

## CLEANING HOUSE.
### SITTING AND DINING-ROOMS.

By the time the upper part of the house is well cleaned and in good order, if it has been taken one room at a time, and leisurely, probably, the dining-room can be torn up on a warm and pleasant day, and, unless the circumstances are to be extensive, scoured and gotten to rights again before nightfall. And the sitting-room on another day. House-cleaning, unless conducted on some plan which occasions little if any disturbance in the general domestic arrangement, is a nuisance, particularly to the males of the household. Nothing can be (next to a miserable dinner) more exasperating to a tired man, than to come home and find the house topsy-turvy. And it certainly raises his opinion of his wife's executive ability to find everything freshened and brightened, and that without his having been annoyed by the odor of the soapsuds, or yet having been obliged to betake himself to the kitchen for his meals.

But if the order of work is well laid out the night beforehand, the breakfast as leisurely eaten as usual, and the family dispersed in their various ways before commencing operations, then by working with a will wonders can be accomplished in a very short time. It is not worth while to undertake a thorough cleaning of all extra china, silver and glassware, which may be stored in the china closet in addititition to the room itself. They can readily wait over until another morning, as can the examination of table-linen. In cleaning any room after the furniture and carpets have been taken out and the dust swept out with a damp broom, the proper order is to begin with the ceiling, then take the walls and windows, and lastly the floor. Kalsomining or whitewash dries most quickly when exposed to free draughts of air, the windows being thrown wide open for the purpose; this process can also be aided by lighting a fire in the room, either in the stove left for the purpose, or in the grate. These means are equally good for drying a freshly-scoured floor.

In lieu of regular carpet wadding, layers of newspapers are very good padding under a carpet, or better yet, sheets of thick brown paper will answer very well. Matting and green linen shades are delightfully cool in either sitting or dining-room for summer use, or all through the hottest weather if the dining-room can be left with a bare floor, and lightly washed off with cold water before breakfast each day it will add greatly to the coolness of the room. A fireplace can be arranged with a screen before it, or it can be left open, the fixtures taken away, and a large stone or pottery jar filled with fresh flowers daily set into it. Very showy flowers can in this way be made effective in decorating a room. Jars covered with pictures of dolcalcomania are tawdry-looking. Better far to paint them a dull black or bottle-green; or a brick-red, with a plain band or geometric design traced in some contrasting color.

In dining-room furniture oak wood with green trimmings and light paint are good contrasting colors, while black walnut or mahogany, with red carpet and shades of red predominating about the room, look well with dark paint.

In arranging a sitting-room large spaces left empty look more comfortable and are more convenient in every way than a room buddled too full of furniture. A home is not a furniture wareroom nor a fancy bazaar, but a place for people to live in, and to grow in, and to move about in.

House cleaning time presents an opportunity for disposing of many ostensibly ornamental articles which only serve to fill up place, without being either beautiful or well-made of their kind.

An empty wall looks better than one hung with daubs. Good engravings and plain cheap frames are now obtained at such a trifling cost that almost every one can afford one or two excellent ones in their sitting-room. People living at a distance can easily send to some large city for an engraving or two, or, if they prefer colored pictures, to some well-known establishment for two or three good chromos.

I have seen some of the best newspaper engravings pinned upon the sitting-room wall, framed in pressed ferns, with very good effect indeed. Once a very simple bracket held a glass bumper of unique pattern, from which was trailed cypress vines, and mingled with them, a bunch of scarlet lychnis. Against the white wall of the room they looked brilliant, and the effect was really beautiful.

When the sitting-room is torn up frequently an array of newspapers, missing books, etc., are found huddled together in some corner. In settling the room these should find their proper places, and it would be a good thing to keep them there ever after, for, no matter how thorough the cleaning process, untidiness and litter will soon make any room appear nearly as badly as before it was scoured.

## HOW TO DUST A ROOM.

**Soft** cloths make the best of dusters. In dusting any piece of furniture begin at the top and dust down, wiping carefully with the cloth, which can be frequently shaken. A good many people seem to have no idea what dusting is intended to accomplish, and instead of wiping off and removing the dust it is simply flirted off into the air and soon settles down upon the articles dusted again. If carefully taken up by the cloth it can be shaken off out of the window into the open air. If the furniture will permit the use of a damp cloth, that will more easily take up the dust, and it can be washed out in a pail of soapsuds. It is far easier to save work by covering up nice furniture while sweeping, than to clean the dust out, besides leaving the furniture looking far better in the long run. The blessing of plainness in decoration is appreciated by the thorough housekeeper who does her own work while dusting.

## GIRLS, LEARN TO COOK.

Yes, yes, learn how to cook, girls; and learn how to cook well. What right has a girl to marry and go into a house of her own unless she knows how to superintend every branch of housekeeping, and she cannot properly superintend unless she has some practical knowledge herself. It is sometimes asked, sneeringly, "What kind of a man is he who would marry a cook?" The fact is, that men do not think enough of this; indeed, most men marry without thinking whether the woman of his choice is capable of cooking him a meal, and it is a pity he is so shortsighted, as his health, his cheerfulness, and, indeed, his success in life, depend in a very great degree on the kind of food he eats; in fact, the whole household is influenced by the diet. Feed them on fried cakes, fried meats, hot bread and other indigestible viands, day after day, and they will need medicine to make them well.

Let all girls have a share in housekeeping at home before they marry; let each superintend some department by turns. It need not occupy half the time to see that the house has been properly swept, dusted, and put in order, to prepare puddings and make dishes, that many young ladies spend in reading novels which enervate both mind and body and unfit them for every-day life. Women do not, as a general rule, get pale faces doing housework. Their sedentary habits, in overheated rooms, combined with ill-chosen food, are to blame for bad health. Our mothers used to pride themselves on their housekeeping and fine needlework. Let the present generation add to its list of real accomplishments the art of properly preparing food for the human body.

## TEACH THE LITTLE ONES.

There is scarcely a busy home mother in the land who

has not at some time or other felt how much easier it would be to do all the work herself than to attempt to teach a child to assist her, whether it be in household matters or in sewing. Now, we would speak particularly of the latter. But it seems almost the right of every little girl to be taught to sew neatly, even if it does cost the mother some self-sacrifice. Very few grown women are wholly exempt from ever using a needle. On the contrary, almost every woman must take more or less care of her own wardrobe, even if she has no responsibility for that of any one's around her. Machines cannot sew up rips in gloves, replace missing buttons, or make or mend without any needlework by hand. Some stitches must be taken, and how to sew neatly is an accomplishment quite as necessary, if not more so, to the happiness of a majority of women than any other. If a little girl be early taught how to use her needle, it very soon becomes a sort of second nature to her, and very little ones can learn to thread the needle and take simple stitches. Only the mother must be patient and painstaking with them, not letting poor work receive praise or permitting the child to slight what she undertakes. The stint can be a very short one with very little children. It is usually best so, but frequent lessons should be given.

## CHILDREN LOVE GAMES.

Take advantage of this to give them physical training. Furnish them the aparatus for games which requires a good deal of muscular exercise. Those curious little affairs which require them to sit on the floor or gather about the table and remain in a cramped position, are not advisable.

It is particularly desirable that the games should call them into the open air and sunshine. In this way children lay in a stock of health and strength. Remember that, particularly in our early years, this is infinitely more important than all adornments of the person or study of books.

Let it not be forgotten that symmetrical development of the body is of the utmost importance. A child, for example, is *weak* and *round-shouldered*. It is important that he should be made strong. It is not less important that he should be made straight. Every conceivable exercise may tend to increase the strength, but only special exercises tend to draw the shoulders back, and thus secure the rectitude which is the basis of spinal and visceral tone. It is not difficult to give children such games and sports as will have this special tendency.

## TEACH YOUR OWN CHILDREN.

Some parents allow their children to acquire the very rude and unmannerly habit of breaking in upon their conversation and those of older persons with questions and remarks of their own. It is very uncivil to allow them to do so. So, even among their own brothers and sisters and schoolmates, of their own age, let them speak without interrupting. If one begins to tell a story or bit of news, teach them to let him finish it; and if he makes mistakes that ought to be corrected, do it afterwards. Don't allow them to acquire the habit of being interrupters. Most of those who allow their own children to form this disagreeable habit will be exceedingly annoyed at the same conduct in other folks' children. The fault is that of the parents in not teaching their children. If they interrupt at home, tell them to wait till they can converse without annoying, and see that they do it.

## CULTIVATING SELFISHNESS IN CHILDREN.

The mother who in the fullness of generous love runs hither and thither continually to do for the various members of the family those things which they should do themselves, comes to be regarded as a useful piece of machinery, suited to minister to their wants, but she is not regarded with one whit more of love or reverence, rather the reverse. By and by, when the mother is worn out in body and spirit, when the child, grown older, feels no need of her as its slave, it finds other more attractive playmates and companions.

The mother has necessarily far more labor, care, and anxiety than any other member of the household. She is continually occupied, and her work seems to have no end. Neither husband nor children will love her the more for sacrificing herself wholly to them, as many a sad, weary mother has learned to her cost. Let her be just to herself. Not that she should make slaves of the children any more than they should make a slave of her. But children like to be useful, like to feel that they are a real help to older persons, and if a little praise and perhaps, too, a little money is given them, they will learn to enjoy the pleasure of helping mother and of earning something for themselves, and early taught the dignity of labor as well as save their mother a little time to keep herself in advance of them in study and thought, in general information, and in spiritual growth, so as to be always reverenced as their intellectual and spiritual guide and friend and counsellor.

It has been truly said by Miss Sewell, author of an excellent work on education, that "Unselfish mothers make selfish children." This may seem startling, but the truth is, that the mother who is continually giving up her own time, money, strength, and pleasure for the gratification of her children teaches them to expect it always. They learn to be importunate in their demands, and to expect more and more. If the mother wears an old dress that her daughter may have a new one, if she work that her daughter may play, she is helping to make her vain, selfish, and ignorant, and very likely she will be ungrateful and disrespectful, and this is equally true of the husband, and other members of the family. Unselfish wives make selfish husbands.

## PACKING AWAY FURS.

All furs should be well switched and beaten lightly, free from dust and loose hairs, well wrapped in newspaper, with bits of camphor laid about them and in them, and put away in a cool dark place. If a cedar closet or chest is to be had, laid into that. In lieu of that new cedar chips may be scattered about. It is never well to delay packing furs away until quite late in the season, for the moth will early commence depredations. In packing them they should not be rolled so tightly as to be crushed and damaged.

## COURAGE.

One may possess physical courage, so that in times of danger, a railroad accident, a steamboat collision or a runaway horse, the heart will not be daunted or the cheek paled, while on the other hand, one may be morally brave, not afraid to speak a word for the right in season, though unwelcome, to perform a disagreeable duty unflinchingly or to refuse to do a wrong act, and yet be a physical coward, trembling and terrified in a thunder-storm, timid in the dark, and even scream at the sight of a mouse. Courage, both moral and physical, is one of the finest attributes of character, and both can be cultivated and gained if desired and sought after. Some girls think it interesting and attractive to be terrified at insects, and will shriek with fright if they happen to be chased a few rods by a flock of geese, but they only excite laughter and do not gain the admiration which a brave girl who tries to help herself would deserve.

## THE ART OF BEAUTY IN DRESS.

It is far easier to find fault with existing customs than to devise and put in practice other and better ones.

Ladies do not like to appear singular, and make themselves conspicuous by wearing such articles of dress as are laughed at, possibly, certainly not worn by any other persons in the city or county in which she may belong. And so the matter goes on. Manufacturers, dry goods dealers, and milliners, and dressmakers, carry the day with a high hand. Yet there is always some choice, and as, thanks to our civilized habits, a full-length mirror is obtainable by most ladies, given the resolution to make the most and best of themselves, the greater number of women can so study the art of dressing well as to produce some excellent results.

It will hardly do to copy the old masters of painting in the arrangement of drapery, at least anyways closely, for no matter how well the voluminous folds may look painted, they certainly would be very much in the way in real life, and impede any free action of the muscles somewhat, while the length of sweeping gowns certainly looks more in place on painted canvas than it can do on an ordinary walking dress. Ladies have realized this fact, however, and the short walking-skirt, at once pretty and convenient, has been the result.

In some places the common sense shoe can be found, and this permits the muscles of the foot, if not the freest, yet fair play. One great mistake in the dressing of the feet is in getting the covering too short. It will throw back the toe joints, and a bunion is only too frequently the result. If the soles of the shoes are too thin, the feet become chilled, and disease ensues. Yet in repeated instances they have been known to draw the feet and made them exceedingly tender and sore. A light cork sole sewed to a knitted worsted slipper will give a foot covering, equally light and far less injurious in its results.

There are ladies who wholly ignore woolen hosiery, preferring lisle thread, cotton or silk. Yet in winter time, particularly for children, woolen stockings are almost a necessity, particularly if woolen is worn over the rest of the body. There are some people who can not abide the feeling of woolen garments next the skin, and they are obliged to get their warmth of clothing in other than their undergarments. Heavy outside garments are not quite so graceful as those of softer and lighter material. But if they must be worn they will bear a plainer cut than such clothes as are naturally clinging, and adapt themselves to the figure.

Solid and plain colors have a greater richness than mixed shades. If combined tints are used, they should only be such as harmonize well, and in the full length figure give a good personal effect. Probably more ladies err in getting good general effects than in any other one particular. They have various garments, pretty enough, possibly, in themselves, yet which do not harmonize well together, either in material, color or cut, or possibly with their particular style of figure and shade of hair and complexion. For example, the skirt will have one style of trimming, the waist another, the bonnet may look exceedingly well with one suit, and be quite out of keeping with another. A short dumpy person will wear flounces, a tall slim one stripes, while some red-haired woman will fancy an exquisite shade of pink, while green or blue would have been much more becoming.

Black generally makes people look smaller, and white larger. A very pale person can bear a certain amount of bright red. Any delicate complexion looks well with soft ruchings or laces at neck and wrist. Lace is so expensive that it cannot be so generally worn as it might be, with excellent effect. Probably no prettier head covering has ever been designed than the veils worn by the Spanish women. Certainly they are infinitely more graceful than a modern poke bonnet.

Dress goods cut up into little bits and sewed together into fantastical shapes called trimmings, are apt if too freely used to give an air of fussiness to the dress, and be withal a source of endless annoyance in catching dust and dirt. The former ideas of a border or hem to finish has become the greater part of the garment.

Nothing is gained in grace by making any outside garment skin-tight, while much is lost in comfort by so doing. A sleeve, for instance, to be serviceable and look well, should be loose and adapt itself somewhat to the curve of the arm. Likewise a dress waist looks far better a little loose, as well as being more healthful and wearing better.

Large, stout persons can add to their appearance much by wearing all outside skirts buttoned on to fitted undergarments below the hips several inches, for gathers about the waist only add to their stoutness of look, and are uncomfortable to carry about. A yoked petticoat answers the purpose very well in lieu of the buttoned skirts.

A wrapper for a tall slim person can have a Spanish flounce, while a slashed skirt with kilt inserts is more becoming to a short figure. Large folds are always more graceful than small pleats and puckers. One very great fault of our dressmaking lies in not allowing the goods to fall in large and natural folds, but in bunching and pleating it in folding, and pressing the goods down into fantastic and inartistic shapes. Added to this, paniers, and padding, bustles, and hoops, until an ordinary woman is forced to appear like a stuffed figure instead of a living human being.

Every woman can modify, and arrange, and simplify, and that without becoming either ultra or conspicuous. It will take time. That cannot be helped, yet possibly the saving in comfort and expense may fully compensate for the few hours spent in studying her own dress with the mirror before her and with the determination to make the very best and most of herself.

## HOME DRESSMAKING.

The art of dressmaking in America has been of late years so simplified that almost anyone with a reasonable degree of executive ability can manufacture a fashionable costume by using an approved pattern and following the directions printed upon it, selecting a new pattern for each distinct style; while in Europe many ladies adhere to the old plan of cutting one model and using it for everything, trusting to personal skill or luck to gain the desired formation. However, some useful hints are given which are well worth offering after the paper pattern has been chosen.

The best dressmakers here and abroad use silk for lining, but nothing is so durable or preserves the material as well as a firm slate twill. This is sold double width and should be laid out thus folded: place the pattern upon it with the upper part towards the cut end, the selvedge for the fronts. The side pieces for the back will most probably be got out of the width, while the top of the back will fit in the intersect of the front. A yard of good stuff may be often saved by laying the pattern out and well considering how one part cuts into another. Prick the outline on to the lining; these marks serve as a guide for the tacking.

In forming the front side plaits be careful and do not allow a fold or crease to be apparent on the bodice beyond where the stitching commences. To avoid this, before beginning stick a pin through what is to be the top of the plait. The head will be on the right side, and holding the point, one can begin pinning the seam without touching the upper part of the bodice. To ascertain the size of the buttonholes put a piece of card beneath the button to be used and cut it an eighth of an inch on either side beyond. Having turned down the piece in front on the buttonhole side run a thread a sixteenth of an inch from the extreme edge, and again another the width of the card. Begin to cut the first buttonhole at the bottom of the bodice, and continue at equal distances. The other side of the bodice is left wide enough to come well under the buttonholes. The buttonholes must be laid upon it and a pin put through the centre of each to mark where the button is to be placed. In sewing on the buttons put the stitches in horizontally; if perpendicularly they are likely to pucker that side of the bodice so much that it will be quite drawn up, and the buttons will not match the buttonholes.

## A WOMAN'S SKIRTS.

Observe the extra fatigue which is insured to every woman in merely carrying a tray upstairs, from the skirts of the dress. Ask any young women who are studying to pass examinations whether they do not find loose clothes a *sine qua non* while poring over their books, and then realize the harm we are doing ourselves and the race by habitually lowering our powers of life and energy in such a manner. As a matter of fact it is doubtful whether any persons have ever been found who would say that their stays were at all tight; and, indeed, by a muscular contraction they can apparently prove that they are not so by moving them about on themselves, and thus probably believe what they say. That they are in error all the same they can easily assure themselves by first measuring round the waist outside the stays; then take them off, let them measure while they take a deep breath, with the tape merely laid on the body as if measuring for the quantity of braid to go round a dress, and mark the result. The injury done by stays is so entirely internal that it is not strange that the maladies caused by wearing them should be attributed to every reason under the sun except the true one, which is, briefly, that all the internal organs, being by them displaced, are doing their work imperfectly and under the least advantageous conditions; and are, therefore, exactly in the state most favorable to the development of disease, whether hereditary or otherwise.—*Maxmillan's Magazine.*

## TO MAKE THE SLEEVES.

As to sleeves. Measure from the shoulder to the elbow and again from elbow to the wrist. Lay these measurements on any sleeve patterns you may have, and lengthen or shorten accordingly. The sleeve is cut in two pieces, the top of the arm and the under part, which is about an inch narrower than the outside. In joining the two together, if the sleeve is at all tight, the upper part is slightly fulled to the lower at the elbow. The sleeve is sown to the armhole with no cordings now, and the front seam should be about two inches in front of the bodice.

Bodices are now worn very tight-fitting, and the French stretch the material well on the cross before beginning to cut out, and in cutting allow the lining to be slightly pulled, so that when on, the outside stretches to it and insures a better fit. An experienced eye can tell a French-cut bodice at once, the front side pieces being always on the cross. In dress cutting and fitting, as in everything else, there are failures and discouragements, but practice overrules these little matters, and "trying again" brings a sure reward in success.

A sensible suggestion is made in regard to the finish in necks of dresses for morning wear. Plain colors have rather a stiff appearance, tulle or crepe lisse frilling are expensive and frail, so it is a good idea to purchase a few yards of really good washing lace, about an inch and a half in depth; quill or plait and cut into suitable lengths to tack around the necks of dresses. This can be easily removed and cleaned when soiled. A piece of soft black Spanish lace, folded loosely around the throat close to the frillings, but below it, looks very pretty; or you may get three yards of scarf lace, trim the ends with frillings, place it around the neck, leaving nearly all the length in the right hand, the end lying upon the left shoulder being about half a yard long. Wind the larger piece twice around the throat, in loose, soft folds, and festoon the other yard and a half, and fasten with brooch or flower at the side.—*Philadelphia Times.*

## ALL ABOUT KITCHEN WORK.

A lady who for a time was compelled to do all of her own kitchen work says: "If every iron, pot, pan, kettle or any utensil used in the cooking of food, be washed as soon as emptied, and while still hot, half the labor will be saved." It is a simple habit to acquire, and the washing of pots and kettles by this means loses some of its distasteful aspects. No lady seriously objects to washing and wiping the crystal and silver, but to tackle the black, greasy, and formidable-looking ironware of the kitchen take a good deal of sturdy brawn and muscle as well as common-sense.

If the range be wiped carefully with brown paper, after cooking greasy food, it can be kept bright with little difficulty.

Stoves and ranges should be kept free from soot in all compartments. A clogged hot-air passage will prevent any 

When the draught is imperfect the defect frequently

arises from the chimney being too low. To remedy the evil the chimney should be built up, or a chimney-pot added.

It is an excellent plan for the mistress to acquaint herself with the practical workings of her range, unless her servants are exceptionally good, for many hindrances to well-cooked food arises from some misunderstanding of, or imperfection in, this article.

A clean, tidy kitchen can only be secured by having a place for everything and everything in its place, and by frequent scourings of the room and utensils.

A hand-towel and basin are needed in every kitchen for the use of the cook or house-worker.

Unless dish-towels are washed, scalded and thoroughly dried daily, they become musty and unfit for use, as also the dish-cloth.

Cinders make a very hot fire—one particularly good for ironing days.

Milk keeps from souring longer in a shallow pan than in a milk pitcher. Deep pans make an equal amount of cream.

Hash smoothly plastered down will sour more readily than if left in broken masses in the chopping bowl, each mass being well exposed to the air.

Sauce, plain, and for immediate use, should not be put into a jar and covered when warm, else it will change and ferment very quickly. It will keep some days with care in the putting up. Let it stand until perfectly cold, then put into a stone jar.

To scatter the Philadelphia brick over the scouring board on to the floor, to leave the soap in the bottom of the scrubbing pail, the sapolio in the basin of water, and to spatter the black lead or stove polish on the floor are wasteful, slatternly habits.

A clock in the kitchen is both useful and necessary.

## A NICE CLOTHES FRAME.

Our kitchen is very small; too small, in fact, to be very comfortable in, and, moreover, has to serve the double purpose of kitchen and laundry. There was no room to spare for the large clothes-horse we had been accustomed to use, nor even for a smaller clothes-screen we thought of purchasing. In this emergency we happened upon a nice frame, which consists of bars of wood secured at one end in an iron clamp, which screws on the side of a window frame. These bars move freely around, and quite a respectable sized ironing can be aired upon them. We found they were invented and made by a lady in the country who had no patent upon them, and so, of course, his sales must be limited, yet they are very convenient. The clothes are hung quite out of the way, and yet can be well aired.

## KEEP THE CELLAR CLEAN.

A great deal of the sickness families suffer could be easily traced to the cellar. The cellar and basement opens into the kitchen, the kitchen is heated, and the cellar is not. Following natural laws, the colder air of the cellar will rush to take the place of the warmer, and, therefore, lighter air of the kitchen. This would be well enough if the cellar air was pure, but often it is not; partly decayed vegetables may be there, or rotten wood, etc. A day should be taken to throw out and carry away all dirt, rotten woods, decaying vegetables, and other accumulations which have gathered there. Brush down the cobwebs, and with a bucket of lime give the walls and ceiling a good coat of whitewash. If a whitewash brush is not at hand take an old broom that the good wife has worn out, and spread the whitewash on thick and strong. It will sweeten up the air in the cellar, the parlor, and the bedrooms, and it may save the family from the afflictions of fevers, diphtheria and doctors.

## SUNLIT ROOMS.

No article of furniture should be put in a room that will not stand sunlight, for every room in a dwelling should have the windows so arranged that some time during the day a flood of sunlight will force itself into the apartments. The importance of admitting the light of the sun freely to all parts of our dwellings cannot be too highly estimated. Indeed, perfect health is nearly as much dependent on pure sunlight as it is on pure air. Sunlight should never be excluded except when so bright as to be uncomfortable to the eyes. And walks should be in bright sunlight, so that the eyes are protected by veil or parasol when inconveniently intense. A sun-bath is of more importance in preserving a healthful condition of the body than is generally understood.

A sun-bath costs nothing, and that is a misfortune, for people are deluded with the idea that those things only can be good or useful which cost money. But remember that pure water, fresh air and sunlit homes kept free from dampness, will secure you from many heavy bills of the doctors and give you health and vigor, which no money can procure. It is a well established fact that people who live much in the sun are usually stronger and more healthy than those whose occupations deprive them of sunlight. And certainly there is nothing strange in the result, since the same law applies with nearly equal force to every animate thing in nature. It is quite easy to arrange an isolated dwelling so that every room may be flooded with sunlight some time in the day, and it is possible many town houses could be so built as to admit more light than they now receive.

## PLEASANT HOMES.

Handsome furniture will not, unaided, make rooms cheerful. The charm of a cosy home rests principally with its mistress. If she is fortunate enough to have sunny rooms, her task is half done. In apartments into which the sun never shines recourse must be had to various devices to make up, so far as may be, for this grave lack. A sunless room should have bright and joyous color in its furnishings. The walls should be warmly tinted, the curtains give a roseate glow to the light that passes through them. An open fire may diffuse the sunshine but lately imprisoned in oak or hickory, or ages ago locked up in anthracite. Ferns, ice and shade-loving plants may contribute their gentle cheer to the room and suggest quiet forest nooks. An attractive room need not be too orderly. A book left lying on the table, a bit of needle-work on the window-sill, an open piano, may indicate the tastes and occupations of the inmates, without suggesting that there is not a place for everything in that room. There is such a thing as being too neat and nice to take comfort in everyday life, and this is anything but cheerful. And then there is such a thing as being so disorderly and negligent that comfort and cheer are impossible. If the house-mother cannot rest while there is a finger-mark on the paint or a spot on the window-panes, she may make a neat room, but her splint will keep it from ever being cheerful. If she has no care for the "looks of things" her failure will be equally sure. A bird singing in the window, an aquarium on the table in some corner, plants growing and blooming, domestic pets moving about as if at home, these give life and brightness to an apartment, and afford constant opportunities for the pleasantest occupation and companionship. Books people a room, and pictures on the walls, if selected with taste, are ever fresh sources of enjoyment. You may gauge the refinement and cultivation of a family by these infallible tests, unless they have been selected by some outsider. Bits of embroidery, of scroll-work, and a thousand tasteful devices may contribute to the charm of a room and make it irresistibly attractive.

## HOW TO BE HANDSOME.

Where is the woman who would not be beautiful? If such there be—but no, she does not exist. From that memorable day when the Queen of Sheba made a formal call on the late lamented King Solomon until the recent advent of the Jersey Lily, the power of beauty has controlled the fate of dynasties and the lives of men. How to be beautiful, and consequently powerful, is a question of far greater inportance to the feminine mind than predestination or any other abstract subject. If women are to govern, control, manage, influence, and retain the adoration of husbands, fathers, brothers, lovers, or even cousins, they must look their prettiest at all times.

All women cannot have good features, but they can look well, and it is possible to a great extent to correct deformity and develop much of the figure. The first step to good looks is good health, and the first element of health is cleanliness. Keep clean—wash freely, bathe regularly. All the skin wants is leave to act, and it takes care of itself. In the matter of baths we do not strongly advocate a plunge in ice-cold water; it takes a woman with some of the clear grit that Robert Collyer loves to dilate on and a strong constitution to endure it. If a hot bath be used, let it come before retiring, as there is less danger of taking cold afterwards; and, besides, the body is weakened by the ablution and needs immediate rest. It is well to use a flesh-brush, and afterwards rinse off the soap-suds by briskly rubbing the body with a pair of coarse toilet gloves. The most important part of a bath is the drying. Every part of the body should be rubbed to a glowing redness, using a coarse crash towel at the finish. If sufficient friction cannot be given, a small amount of bay rum applied with the palm of the hand will be found efficacious. Ladies who have ample leisure and who lead methodical lives take a plunge or sponge bath three times a week, and a vapor or sun bath every day. To facilitate this very beneficial practice a south or east apartment is desirable. The lady denudes herself, takes a seat near the window, and takes in the warm rays of the sun. The effect is both beneficial and delightful. If, however, she be of a restless disposition, she may dance, instead of basking, in the sunlight. Or, if she be not fond of dancing, she may improve the shining hours by taking down her hair and brushing it, using sulphur water, pulverized borax dissolved in alcohol, or some similar dressing. It would be surprising to many ladies to see her carefully wiping the separate locks on a clean, white towel until the dust of the previous day is entirely removed. With such care it is not necessary to wash the head, and the hair under this treatment is invariably good.

One of the most useful articles of the toilet is a bottle of ammonia, and any lady who has once learned its value will never be without it. A few drops in the water takes the place of the usual amount of soap, and cleans out the pores of the skin as well as a bleach will do. Wash the face with a flesh-brush, and rub the lips well to tone their color. It is well to bathe the eyes before putting in the spirits, and if it is desirable to increase their brightness, this may be done by dashing soapsuds into them. Always rub the eyes, in washing, toward the nose. If the eyebrows are inclined to spread irregularly, pinch the hairs together where thickest. If they show a tendency to meet, this contact may be avoided by pulling out the hairs every morning before the toilet.

The dash of Orientalism in costume and lace now turns a lady's attention to her eyelashes, which are worthless if not long and drooping. Indeed, so prevalent is the desire for this beautiful feature that hair-dressers and ladies' artists have scores of customers under treatment for invigorating their stunted eyelashes and eyebrows. To obtain these fringed curtains, anoint the roots with a balsam made of two drachms of nitric oxide of mercury mixed with one of leaf lard. After an application wash the roots with a camel's hair brush dipped in warm milk. Tiny scissors are used, with which the lashes are carefully but slightly trimmed every other day. When obtained, refrain from rubbing or even touching the lids with the finger-nails. There is more beauty in a pair of well-kept eyebrows and full, sweeping eyelashes than people are aware of, and a very inattractive and lustreless eye assumes new beauty when it looks out from beneath elongated fringes. Many ladies have a habit of rubbing the corners of their eyes to remove the dust that will frequently accumulate there. Unless this operation is done with little friction it will be found that the growth of hair is very spare, and in that case it will become necessary to pencil the barren corners. Instead of putting cologne water on the handkerchief, which has come to be considered a vulgarism among ladies of correct tastes, the perfume is spent on the eyebrows and lobes of the ears.

If commenced in youth, thick lips may be reduced by compression, and thin linear ones are easily modified by suction. This draws the blood to the surfaces, and produces at first a temporary and, later, a permanent inflation. It is a mistaken belief that biting the lips reddens them. The skin of the lips is very thin, rendering them extremely susceptible to organic derangement, and if the atmosphere does not cause chaps or parchment, the result of such harsh treatment will develop into swelling or the formation of scars. Above all things, keep a sweet breath.

Everybody cannot have beautiful hands, but there is no plausible reason for their being ill-kept. Red hands may be overcome by soaking the feet in hot water as often as possible. If the skin is hard and dry, use tar or oat-meal soap, saturate them with glycerine, and wear gloves in bed. Never bathe them in hot water, and wash no oftener than is necessary. There are dozens of women with soft, white hands who do not put them in water once a month. Rubber gloves are worn in making the toilet, and they are cared for by an ointment of glycerine and rubbed dry with chamois-skin or cotton flannel. The same treatment is not unfrequently applied to the face with the most successful results. If such methods are used, it would be just as well to keep the knowledge of it from the gentlemen. We know of one beautiful lady who has not washed her face for three years, yet it is always clean, rosy, sweet, and kissable. With some of her other secrets she gave it to her lover for safe keeping. Unfortunately, it proved to be her last gift to that gentleman, who declared in a subsequent note that "I cannot reconcile my heart and my manhood to a woman who can get along without washing her face."

## SOME OF THE SECRETS OF BEAUTY.

There is as much a "fashion" in complexion as there is in bonnets or boots. Sometime nature is the mode, sometimes art. Just now the latter is in the ascendant, though, as a rule, only in that inferior phase which has not reached the "concealment of art"—the point where extremes meet and the perfection of artifice presents all the appearance of artlessness. No one of an observant turn of mind, who is accustomed to the sight of English maids and matrons, can deny that making-up, as at present practiced, partakes of the amateurish element. Impossible reds and whites grow still more impossibly red and white from week to week under the unskilled hands of the wearer of "false colors," who does not like to ask for advice on so delicate a subject, for, even were she willing to confess to the practice, the imputation of experience conveyed in the asking for counsel might be badly received, and would scarcely be in good taste.

The prevalent and increasing short-sightedness of our times is, perhaps, partly the cause of the excessive use of rouge and powder. The wielder of the powder puff sees herself afar off, as it were. She knows that she cannot judge of the effect of her complexion with her face almost touching its reflection in the glass, and, standing about a yard off, she naturally accentuates her roses and lilies in a way that looks very pleasing to her, but is rather startling to any one with longer sight. Nor can she tone down her rouge with the powdered hair that softened the artificial coloring of her grandmother when she had her day. Powder is only occasionally worn with evening dress, and it is by daylight that those dreadful bluish reds and whites look their worst.

On the other hand, there are some women so clever at making up their faces that one almost feels inclined to condone the practice in admiration of the result. These are the small minority, and are likely to remain so, for their secret is of a kind unlikely to be shared. The closest inspection of these cleverly managed complexions reveals no trace of art.

Notwithstanding the reticence of these skilled artists, an occasional burst of confidence has revealed a few of their means of accomplishing the great end of looking pretty. "Do you often do that?" said one of those clever ones, a matron of 37, who looked like a girl of 19, to a friend who was vigorously rubbing her cheeks with a coarse towel after a plentiful application of cold water.

"Yes, every time I come in from a walk, ride, or drive. Why?"

"Well, no wonder you look older than you are. You are simply wearing your face out!"

"But I must wash?"

"Certainly, but not like that. Take a leaf out of my book; never wash your face just before going out into the fresh air, or just after coming in. Nothing is more injurious to the skin. Come to the glass. Do you notice a drawn look about your eyes and a general streakiness in the cheeks? That is the result of your violent assault upon your complexion just now. You look at this moment ten years older than you did twenty minutes ago in the park."

"Well, I really do. I look old enough to be your mother; but then, you are wonderful. You always look so young and fresh!"

"Because I never treat my poor face so badly as you do yours. I use rain-water, and if I cannot get that, I have the water filtered. When I dress for dinner I always wash my face with milk, adding just enough hot water to make it pleasant to use. A very soft sponge and very fine towel take the place of your terrible huckaback arrangement."

Two or three years ago a lady of Oriental parentage on her father's side spent a season in London society. Her complexion was brown, relieved by yellow, her features large and irregular, but redeemed by a pair of lovely and expressive eyes. So perfect was her taste in dress that she always attracted admiration wherever she went. Dressed in rich dark brown or dullest crimsons or russets, so that no one ever noticed much what she wore, she so managed that suggestions and hints—no more—of brilliant amber or pomegranate scarlet should appear just where they imparted brilliancy to her deep coloring, and abstract the yellow from her skin. A knot of old gold satin under the rim of her bonnet, another at her throat, and others in among the lace at her wrists, brightened up the otherwise subdued tinting of her costume, so that it always looked as though it had been designed expressly for her by some great colorist. Here rouge was unnecessary. The surroundings were arranged to suit the complexion, instead of the complexion to suit the surroundings. There can be no doubt as to which is the method which best becomes the gentlewoman.

In addition to the disagreeable sensation of making-up, it must be remembered that the use of some of the white powders eventually destroys the texture of the skin, rendering it rough and coarse. Rimmel, the celebrated perfumer, in his "Book of Perfumes," says that rouge, being composed of cochineal and saffron, is harmless, but that white cosmetics consist occasionally of deleterious substances which may injure the health. He advises actors and actresses to choose cosmetics, especially the white, with the greatest care, and women of the world, who wish to preserve the freshness of their complexion, to observe the following recipe: Open air, rest, exercise, and cold water. In another part of this pleasant book the author says that *schonada*, a cosmetic used among the Arabs, is quite innocuous and at the same time effectual. "This cream, which consists of sublimated benzoin, acts upon the skin as a slight stimulant, and imparts perfectly natural colors during some hours without occasioning the inconveniences with which European cosmetics may justly be reproached." It is a well-known fact that bismuth, a white powder containing sugar of lead, injures the nerve-centres when constantly employed, and occasionally causes paralysis itself.

In getting up the eyes, nothing is injurious that is not dropped into them. The use of *kohl* or *kohol* is quite harmless, and, it must be confessed, very effective when applied —as the famous recipe for salad dressing enjoins with regard to the vinegar—by the hand of a miser. Modern Egyptian ladies make their *kohol* of the smoke produced by burning almonds. A small bag holding the bottle of *kohol*, and a pin, with a rounded point with which to apply it, form part of the toilet paraphernalia of all the beauties of Cairo, who make the immense mistake of getting up their eyes in an exactly similar manner, thus trying to reduce the endless variety of nature to one common pattern, a mistake that may be accounted for by the fact that the Arabs believe *kohol* to be a sovereign specific against ophthalmia. Their English sisters often make the same mistake without the same excuse. A hairpin steeped in lampblack is the usual method of darkening the eyes in England, retribution following sooner or later in the shape of a total loss of the eyelashes. Eau de Cologne is occasionally dropped into the eyes, with the effect of making them brighter. The operation is painful, and it is said that half a dozen drops of whiskey and the same quantity of Eau de Cologne, eaten on a lump of sugar, is quite as effective.

## HEADACHE.

One of our English contemporaries has wisely been devoting some thought and space to the common and distressing fact that a great many English women suffer from headache. The same trouble prevails in America, and men, no matter how selfish they may be, are deeply concerned about it, for a wife with a headache cannot be companionable; the best of sweethearts with a headache is sure to be unreasonable, while a lady who has neither husband or other special cavalier to engross her attention can ruin the peace of mind of every one she meets while she has a headache of perceptible size. No amount of masculine grumbling is likely to change all this, but women themselves might change it if they would comprehend the causes of the malady, and then apply their nimble wits to the work of prevention or cure.

The trouble is that all American women who have headaches live indoors, where the best air is never good and the worst is poison, and they have none of the exercises which saves man from the popular feminine malady. Were a strong man to eat breakfast at any ordinary American table and then sit down at a work-table or even move about briskly from one room to another, he would have a splitting headache before noon, and the chatter of his innocent children would seem to be the jargon of fiends. The midday meal would increase his wretchedness, and by dusk he would be stretched in misery upon his bed, with one hand moping his forehead with ice-water, while the other would threaten with a club or pistol any one who dared to enter the room or make a noise outside. There is no reason why women should not suffer just as severely for similar transgressions of physical law. True, indoor life is compulsory for a large portion every day, but special physical exercise in a well-aired room is within the reach of almost every woman, and so is a brisk walk in garments not so tight as to prevent free respiration. There is very little complaint at summer resorts, where windows are always open and games and excursions continually tempt women who do not value complexion more than health. Girls who ride, row, sail, and shoot, seldom have headaches; neither do those unfortunate enough to be compelled to hoe potatoes or play Maud Muller in hay-fields. Let women of all social grades remember that the human machine must have reasonable treatment, and be kept at work or play, to keep it from rusting, then headaches will be rare enough to be interesting.

## HIGH-HEELED BOOTS MUST GO.

A lady looks infinitely taller and slimmer in a long dress than she does in a short costume, and there is always a way of showing the feet, if desired, by making the front quite short, which gives, indeed, a more youthful appearance to a train dress. The greatest attention must, of course, be paid to the feet with these short dresses, and I may here at once state that high heels are absolutely forbidden by fashion. Doctors, are you content? Only on cheap shoes and boots are they now made, and are only worn by common people. A good bootmaker will not make high heels now, even if paid double price to do so. Ladies —that is, real ladies—now wear flat-soled shoes and boots, a la Cinderella. For morning walking, boots or high Moliere shoes are worn.

If you wear boots you may wear any stockings you like, for no one sees them. But if you wear shoes you must adapt your stockings to your dress. Floss silk, Scotch thread, and even cotton stockings are worn for walking, silk stockings have returned into exclusively evening wear. Day stockings should be of the same color as the dress, but they may be shaded, or stripped, or dotted, just as you please. White stockings are absolutely forbidden for day wear—no one wears them—no one dares wear them under fashion's interdiction.

## DON'T STOOP.

Grandmother has noticed that some of her boys lately have acquired a very bad habit. They go about with their backs bent, as if they were fifty years old, and were bearing the responsibilities of age on their shoulders. This is all wrong. Stand up straight, boys; don't go around with a "stoop in your back," as if you had a curvature of the spine. If you do, depend upon it, you will have it sure enough long before you get to be old. Always stand erect, and when you walk, throw back your shoulders, and take that kink out of your backbone. This is easier said than done, isn't it? Grandmother will tell you just how you can do it, and remember every word she says, for she has been through it all herself, and has straightened up many a grandchild in more respects than one. Here is her rule:

"THROW UP YOUR CHIN!"

The whole secret of standing and walking erect consists in keeping the chin well away from the breast. This throws the head upward and backward, and the shoulders will naturally settle backward and in their true position. Those who stoop in walking generally look downward. The proper way is to look straight ahead, upon the same level with your eyes, or if you are inclined to stoop, until that tendency is overcome, look rather above than below the level. Mountaineers are said to be as "straight as an arrow," and the reason is because they are obliged to look upward so much. It is simply impossible to stoop in walking if you will heed and practice this rule. You will notice that all round-shouldered persons carry the chin near the breast and pointed downward. Take warning in time, and heed grandmother's advice, for a bad habit is more easily prevented than cured. The habit of stooping when one walks or stands is a bad habit and especially hard to cure.

## MAKE HOME PLEASANT.

A cheerful, happy home is the greatest safeguard against temptations for the young. Parents should spare no pains to make home a cheerful spot. There should be pictures to adorn the walls, flowers to cultivate the finer sensibilities, dominoes, checkers, and other games, entertaining books and instructive newspapers and periodicals. These things, no doubt, cost money, but not a tithe the amount that one of the lesser vices will cost—vices which are sure to be acquired away from home, but seldom there. Then there should be social pleasure—a gathering of young and old around the hearthstone, a warm welcome to the neighbor who drops in to pass a pleasant hour. There should be music and amusements and reading. The tastes of all should be consulted, until each member of the family looks forward to the hour of reunion around the hearth as the brightest one in the twenty-four. Wherever there is found a pleasant, cheerful, neat, attractive, inexpensive home there you may be sure to find the abode of the domestic virtues; there will be no dissipated husbands, no discontented or discouraged wives, no "fast" sons or frivolous daughters.

## DINNER-TABLE FANCIES.

To be thoroughly good form at dinner is the very inflorescence of civilized life. Like many other regulations of social life, dinner-table etiquette is arbitrary, but not to know certain things is to argue yourself unknown so far as society life goes. To take soup pushing the spoon from rather than toward yourself; to touch the napkin as little as possible; to accept or decline what is offered instantly and quietly; these and other trifles characterize the well-bred diner-out. The attempts to introduce too much color in dinner-table decorations are rather declining. The finest white damask still holds the preference, and the centre-piece of plush or velvet underlace is little used now. Fewer flowers, too, are seen, and those in very low forms. The dessert plates come in deep tones in Dresden china, and the doyley on which the finger-bowl rests should be immediately removed with the bowl, on reaching the guest. The latest fashion in ice-cream plates is the Bohemian glass in oval form with small handles. Menu cards, hand-painted, hold the preference, but many are seen on tinted cardboard with engraved vignette in one corner and the date in another.

## THE USE OF AMMONIA IN BAKING POWDERS.

The recent discoveries in science and chemistry are fast revolutionizing our daily domestic economies. Old methods are giving way to the light of modern investigation, and the habits and methods of our fathers and mothers are stepping down and out, to be succeeded by the new ideas, with marvelous rapidity. In no department of science, however, have more rapid strides been made than its relations to the preparation and preservation of human food. Scientists, having discovered how to traverse space, furnish heat, and beat time itself, by the application of natural forces, and to do a hundred other things promotive of the comfort and happiness of the human kind, are naturally turning their attention to the development of other agencies and powers that shall add to the years during which man may enjoy the blessings set before him.

Among the recent discoveries in this direction, none is more important than the uses to which common ammonia can be properly put as a leavening agent, and which indicate that this familiar salt is hereafter to perform an active part in the preparation of our daily food.

The carbonate of ammonia is an exceedingly volatile substance. Place a small portion of it upon a knife and hold over a flame, and it will almost immediately be entirely developed into gas and pass off into the air. The gas thus formed is a simple composition of nitrogen and hydrogen. No residue is left from the ammonia. This gives it its superiority as a leavening power over soda and cream tartar when used alone, and has induced its use as a supplement to these articles. A small quantity of ammonia in the dough is effective in producing bread that will be lighter, sweeter, and more wholesome than that risen by any other leavening agent. When it is acted upon by the heat of baking, the leavening gas that raises the dough is liberated. In this act it uses itself up, as it were; the ammonia is entirely diffused, leaving no trace of residuum whatever. The light, fluffy, flaky appearance, so desirable in biscuits, etc., and so sought after by professional cooks, is said to be imparted to them only by the use of this agent.

The bakers and baking powder manufacturers producing the finest goods have been quick to avail themselves of this useful discovery, and the handsomest and best bread and cake are now largely risen by the aid of ammonia, combined, of course, with other leavening material.

Ammonia is one of the best known products of the laboratory. If, as seems to be justly claimed for it, the application of its properties to the purposes of cooking results in giving us lighter and more wholesome bread, biscuit, and cake, it will prove a boon to dyspeptic humanity, and will speedily force itself into general use in the new field to which science has assigned it.

## LAUGHTER.

"The laughter of girls is, and ever was, among the most delightful sounds of earth." Truly there is nothing sweeter or pleasanter to the ear than the merry laugh of a happy, joyous girl, and nothing dissipates gloom and sadness quicker, and drives dull care away like a good, hearty laugh. We do not laugh enough; nature should teach us this lesson, it is true; the earth needs the showers, but if it did not catch and hold the sunshine, too, where would be the brightness and beauty it lavishes upon us? Laugh heartily, laugh often, girls; not boisterously, but let the gladness of your hearts bubble up once in a while, and overflow in a glad, mirthful laugh.

## ITEMS WORTH REMEMBERING.

A sun-bath is of more worth than much warming by the fire.

Books exposed to the atmosphere keep in better condition than if confined in a book-case.

Pictures are both for use and ornament. They serve to recall pleasant memories and scenes; they harmonize with the furnishing of the rooms. If they serve neither of these purposes they are worse than useless; they only help fill space which would look better empty, or gather dust and make work to keep them clean.

A room filled with quantities of trifling ornaments has the look of a bazar and displays neither good taste nor good sense. Artistic excellence aims to have all the furnishings of a high order of workmanship combined with simplicity, while good sense understands the folly of dusting a lot of rubbish.

A poor book had best be burned to give place to a better, or even to an empty shelf, for the fire destroys its poison, and puts it out of the way of doing harm.

Better economize in the purchasing of furniture or carpets than scrimp in buying good books or papers.

Our sitting-rooms need never be empty of guests or our libraries of society if the company of good books is admitted to them.

## THOSE UNGRACEFUL HABITS.

A public conveyance brings one awkwardly near the faces of strangers. Perhaps from sheer inanity one is apt to take undue notice of his fellow-passengers. When glances meet, the gaze is lowered to the flounces of the lady seated near, or to the trim, polished boot of a gent at the far end of the car. There are nice people everywhere, and if one is artistic in taste, there will ever be a looking for beauty of face or form, in dress, or carriage, or manner, or speech; but "why is the fresh girl face so often marred by the ugly habit of cribbing?" "A beautiful woman," whispered a friend, and the eye was attracted toward a grand looking lady with wide, white forehead, from which the brown glossy hair was smoothed away without the ghost of a crimp; there were pretty arching brows, shading lashes, shapely nose, but, alas! for the ruby lips bitten and moistened so often as to prevent the possibility of catching the outline—the profile so needful to the sketcher of beauty. A poet has somewhere said that "affectation begins with the mouth," but "who would charge the gentle sex with vanity!"

What! To redden by biting, or brighten by wetting; that folly could not be. Let us rather suppose the fair one had by some mishap forgotten to lunch, and all this is due to the gnawings of hunger. While thus seeking to palliate the fair cribber, a young man becomes noticeable by persistently pulling at the ends of his moustache, chewing them in a hungry way, now changing the exercise by twisting them to needle-like points which he seemed to be coaxing upward.

"From whence has come *this* ugly habit?" one is fain to ask. Certainly not from pride. A fine flowing beard and full moustache ought not to be a cause of folly to the owner. The hairs of the face, given to protect the throat and lungs, never to be shorn in the cold seasons, can it be that there is nutriment in them? While thus questioning, the writer's two hands were suddenly jerked from his side pockets, where they had been comfortably resting. The wife's gentle remonstrance had been brought to mind by the entrance of an awkward fellow, with hands deeply thrust in the pockets of his torn pants. A caricature of one's self is often a tacit reproof. That very morning the dear wife had said: "Those torn side-pockets are the most difficult of tears to mend. And the inward monitor asked: "From whence has come this indolent habit? From love of ease or want of mittens, which? Perhaps indifference of the patient mender's." And again the monitor asked:

"What of that habit not comparable to weeds for growth?"

"What mean you?" was meekly asked.

"That of looking well to one's own faults, that lesson the hardest and the latest learned : to know thyself." Then the writer realized that he, too, was not quite perfect.

# INDEX TO PART SECOND.

**SECRETS OF THE LIQUOR TRADE.**
  Cider without Apples; Cider Champagne; **to Neutralize** Whiskey; Port Wine; Maderia; Sherry; **to Correct** Bad Taste in Wine; to remove Ropiness; **to restore** Flat Wine; to restore Sour Wine; Ginger Wine; Brandy; French Brandy; Pale Brandy; Cognac; Bitters; Gin; Schnapps; Rum; Whiskey; Arrack; Beer; Root Beer; Ginger Beer; Spruce Beer; Old Beer; Mead; Stomach Bitters; Soda Syrup; Bead for Liquor; Coloring for Liquor; Wax Putty; Cement for Bottles. 3-11

**DRUGGISTS' DEPARTMENT.**
  Arnica Liniment; Cherry Pectoral; Balm Gilead; Blackberry Cordial; Brandreth's Pills; Bronchial Troches; Pulmonic Wafers; Candied Lemon; Camphor Balls; Camphorated Oil; Camphor Tablet; Camphor Eye-Water; Canker Cure; Cephalic Snuff; Cure for Pimples, Eruptions, Etc.; Cure for Headache, Neuralgia, Etc.; Chamomile Pills; Chlorine Pastiles; Cholera Morbus; Cholera Cure; Corn Cure; Cough Compound; Cure for Diarrhœa; Digestive Pills; Disease of Bowels; Dried Herbs; Dysentery; Anti-bilious Pills; **Pain Extractor**; Godfrey's Cordial; Female Pills; **Hydrophobia** Preventitive; Infant's Syrup; Ointments; Tincture for Wounds; Tonic, Whooping Cough; Cure for Drunkenness .................................................. 11-19

**MANUFACTURER'S DEPARTMENT.**
  Indelible Ink; Imitation Gold, Silver and Honey; **Vinegar**; Soap; Cements; Paints; Roof Composition; French Polish; Oil for Furniture; Glue; Inks; Blacking; Copying Paper; Plating Fluids; Amalgams; Bronzing; Metals, (tempering); Varnish.......................... 19-36

**TOILET, PERFUMERY, ETC.**
  Hair Restorers; Rouges; Face Washes; **Pomatum**; Tooth Paste; Cologne; Cold Cream; Cosmetics; Dandruff; Essences; Eye-Water................................... 36-43

FACE PAINTS.................................................................. 43-44

HUNTERS' AND TRAPPERS SECRETS...................... 44-46

FINE ARTS AND SCIENCES.
  Transferring; Potchiomoni; Embalming; Wax Flowers 46-48

FARMERS' DEPARTMENT.
  Potatoes; Killing Vermin; Horses............................... 48-51

CONFECTIONERS' DEPARTMENT.
  Ginger; Peppermint; Clarifying; Twist Candy; Taffy;
  Fruit; Pop Corn; Icing; Saffron; Chocolate; Lemon, 51-54

HOUSEHOLD.
  Alum; Yeast; Fire Kindlers; Insects; Lye Colors; Preserving Meats; Quick Growth of Vegetables; Drying Corn; Restoring Scorched Linen; Remove Stains; Pickling; Mending broken Ware; Preserving Milk; Vinegar; Cleaning Silver; Water-Proof Cloth; Cleaning Furniture; Washing; Burns; Smokey Chimneys; Turner's Wood; Removing Paint; Fence Posts; Milk Test; Mending Tinware; Removing Stains; Wet Feet; Moth Destroyer; the Butterfly; Poultices to remove Grease; Bleaching; Purifying Water; Chemistry of Lead; Preserving; Prevent Freezing Eggs; Fly Paper,.......................................................................... 54-73

DYES FOR CLOTHS,.................................................... 73-74

DYES FOR BONES AND IVORY................................. 74-75

MISCELLANEOUS........................................................ 75-82

PRINTING INKS,......................................................... 82-85

HORSES........................................................................ 85

GENERAL RECIPES..................................................... 86

# THE BOOK OF KNOWLEDGE,

AND

## GUIDE TO RAPID WEALTH.

---

### SECRETS OF THE LIQUOR TRADE.

*Cider Without Apples.*—To each gallon of cold water, put 1 lb. common sugar, ½ oz. tartaric acid, 1 tablespoonful of yeast, shake well, make in the evening, and it will be fit for use next day. I make in a keg a few gallons at a time, leaving a few quarts to make into next time; not using yeast again until the keg needs rinsing. If it gets a little sour make a little more in to it, or put as much water with it as there is cider, and put it with the vinegar. If it is desired to bottle this cider by manufacturers of small drinks, you will proceed as follows: Put in a barrel 5 gallons hot water, 30 lbs. brown sugar, ¾ lb. tartaric acid, 25 gallons cold water, 3 pints of hop or brewers' yeast worked into paste with ¾ lb. flour, and 1 pint water will be required in making this paste, put altogether in a barrel, which it will fill, and let it work 24 hours—the yeast running out at the bung all the time, by putting in a little occasionally to keep it full. Then bottle, putting in 2 or 3 broken raisins in each bottle, and it will nearly equal Champagne.

*Cider Champagne. No. 1.*—Good cider, 20 gallons, spirit, 1 gallon; honey or sugar, 6 lbs. Mix, and let them rest for a fortnight; then fine with skimmed milk, 1 quart. This, put up in champagne bottles, silvered and labeled, has often been sold for Champagne. It opens very sparkling.

*Cider Champagne, No. 2.*—Good pale vinous cider, 1 hogshead; proof spirit, (pale) 3 gallons; honey or sugar, 14 lbs. Mix, and let them remain together in a temperate situation for one month; then add orange-flower water 1 quart; and fine it down with skimmed milk ½ a gallon. This will be very pale; and a similar article, when bottled in champagne bottles, silvered and labeled, has been often sold to the ignorant for Champagne. It opens very brisk, if managed properly.

*British Champagne.*—Loaf sugar, 56 lbs., brown sugar (pale.) 48 lbs.; water (warm) 45 gallons; white tartar, 4 ounces. Mix, and at a proper temperature add yeast, 1 quart; afterwards add sweet cider, 5 gallons; bitter almonds (bruised,) 6 or 7 in number; pale spirit, 1 gallon; orris powder, ½ ounce.

*Cider—To Keep Sweet.*—1st. By putting into the barrel before the cider has begun to work about a half pint of whole fresh mustard seed tied up in a coarse muslin bag. 2d. By burning a little sulphur or sulphur match in the barrel previous to putting in the cider. 3d. By the use of ¾ of an ounce of the bi-sulphite of lime to the barrel. This article is the preserving powder sold at rather a high price by various firms.

*To Neutralize Whisky to make various Liquors.*—To 40 gallons of whisky, add 1½ lbs. unslacked lime; ¾ lb. alum, and ½ pint spirits of nitre. Stand 24 hours and draw it off.

*Port Wine.*—Worked cider, 42 gallons; good port wine 12 gallons; good brandy, 3 gallons; pure spirits, 6 gallons. Mix, Elderberries and sloes, and the fruit of the black hawes, make a fine purple color for wines, or use burnt sugar.

*Madeira Wine.*—To 40 gallons prepared cider, add ¼ lb. tartaric acid; 4 gallons spirits; 3 lbs. loaf sugar. Let it stand 10 days draw it off carefully; fine it down, and again rack it into another cask.

*Sherry Wine.*—To 40 gallons prepared cider, add, 2 gallons spirits; 3 lbs. of raisins; 6 gallons good sherry, and ½ ounce oil bitter almonds, (dissolved in alcohol.) Let it stand 10 days, and draw it off carefully; fine it down and again rack it into another cask.

*Port Wine.*—To 40 gallons prepared cider, add, 6 gallons good port wine; 10 quarts wild grapes, (clusters;) ½ lb. bruised rhatany root; 3 oz. tincture of kino; 3 lbs. loaf sugar; 2 gallons spirits. Let this stand 10 days, color if too light, with tincture of rhatany, then rack it off and fine it. This should be repeated until the color is perfect and the liquid clear.

*To correct a bad taste and sourness in Wine.*—Put in a bag the root of wild horse-radish cut in bits. Let it down in the wine, and leave it there two days; take this out, and put another, repeating the same till the wine is 'perfectly restored Or fill a bag with wheat; it will have the same effect.

*To remove Ropiness from Wine.*—Add a little catechu or a small quantity of the bruised berries of the mountain ash.

*To restore Flat Wine.*—Add four or five pounds of white sugar, honey, or bruised raisins, to every hundred gallons, and bung close. A little spirits may also be added.

*To restore Wine that has turned sour or sharp.*—Fill a bag with leek-seed, or of leaves or twisters of vine, and put either of them to infuse in the cask.

*Ginger Wine.*—Take one quart of 95 per cent. alcohol, and put into it one ounce of best ginger root, (bruised and not ground,) five grains of capsicum, and one drachm of tartaric acid. Let stand one week and filter. Now add one gallon of water, in which one pound of crushed sugar has been boiled. Mix when cold. To make the color boil ½ ounce of cochineal, ¾ ounces of cream tarter, ½ ounce of saleratus, and ½ ounce alum in a pint of water till you get a bright red color.

*Brandy.*—To 40 gallons of pure or neutral spirits, add 1 pound crude tartar, dissolved in 1 gallon hot water; acetic ether, ¼ pint; bruised raisins, 6 pounds; tinct. kino, 2 ounces; sugar, 3 pounds; color with sugar coloring. Stand 14 days, and draw off.

*French Brandy.*—Pure spirits, 1 gallon; best French brandy, or any kind you wish to imitate, 1 quart; loaf sugar, 2 ounces; sweet spirits of nitre, ½ ounce; a few drops of tincture of catechu, or oak bark, to roughen the taste if desired, and color to suit.

*Pale Brandy.*—Is made the same as by the above recipe, using pale instead of the French, and using only 1 ounce of tincture of kino for every five gallons.

*Cognac Brandy.*—To every 10 gallons of pure spirits add 2 quarts New-England Rum, or 1 quart Jamaica Rum, and from 30 to 40 drops of oil cognac put in half a pint of alcohol, and color with burnt sugar to suit.

*British Cognac Brandy.*—Clean spirit (17 up), 100 gallons; high flavored cognac, 10 gallons; oil of cassia, 1½ ounces; oil of bitter almonds (essential), ½ ounce; powdered catechu, 10 ounces; cream of tartar (dissolved), 16 ounces; Beaufoy's **concentrated** acetic acid, 3 pounds; coloring (sugar), 1 quart or more. Put the whole into a fresh emptied brandy piece, and let them remain a week, together with occasional agitation, then let them stand to settle.

*Brandy Bitters.*—Bruised gentian, 8 ounces; orange peel, 5 ounces; cardamoms, 3 ounces; cassia, 1 ounce; cochineal ¼ ounce; spirit 1 gallon. Digest for one week, then decant the clear, and pour on the dregs, water, 5 pints. Digest for one week longer, decant, and mix the two tinctures together.

*Gin.*—Take 100 gallons of clear, rectified spirits; add, after you have killed the oil well, 1½ ounces of the oil of English juniper, ½ ounce of angelica essence, ½ ounce of the oil bitter almonds, ½ ounce of the oil of coriander, and ½ ounce of the oil of caraway; put this into the rectified spirit and well rummage it up; this is what the rectifiers call strong gin.

To make this *up*, as it is called by the trade, add 45 pounds of loaf-sugar, dissolved; then rummage the whole well up together with 4 ounces of roche alum. For finings there may be added two ounces of salts of tartar.

*Holland Gin.*—To 40 gallons of neutral spirits, add, 2 ounces spirits nitre; 4 pounds of loaf sugar; 1 ounce oil juniper; ⅛ ounce oil caraway. The juniper and caraway to be first cut in a quart of alcohol; stand 24 hours.

*To reduce Holland Gin.*—To 25 gallons pure Holland gin, add 25 gallons pure French spirit; ½ gallon of white sugar syrup; mix thoroughly.

*Cordial Gin.*—Of the oil of bitter almonds; vitriol, turpentine, and juniper, ½ a drachm each; kill the oils in spirits of wine; 15 gallons of clean, rectified proof spirits, to which add 1 drachm of coriander seeds, 1 drachm of pulverized orris root, ½ pint of elder-flower water, with 10 pounds of sugar and 5 gallons of water or liquor.

*English Gin.*—Plain malt spirit, 100 gallons; spirits of turpentine, 1 pint; bay salt 7 pounds. Mix and distill. The difference in the flavor of gin is produced by varying the proportion of turpentine, and by occasionally adding a small quantity of juniper berries.

*Aromatic Schiedam Schnapps, to imitate.*—To 25 gallons good common gin, 5 over proof, add 15 pints strained honey; 2 gallons clear water; 5 pints white-sugar syrup; 5 pints spirit of nutmegs mixed with the nitric ether; 5 pints orange-flower water; 7 quarts pure water; 1 ounce acetic ether; 8 drops oil of wintergreen, dissolved with the acetic ether. Mix all the ingredients well; if necessary, fine with alum and salt of tartar.

*St. Croix Rum.*—To 40 gallons p. or n. spirits, add, 2 gallons St. Croix Rum; 2 oz. acetic acid; 1½ ounce butyric acid; 3 pounds loaf sugar.

*Jamaica Rum.*—To 45 gallons New-England rum, add 5 gallons Jamaica rum; 2 ounces butyric ether; ½ ounce oil of caraway, cut with alcohol; 95 per cent. Color with sugar coloring.

*Jamaica Rum, No. 2.*—To 36 gallons pure spirits, add 1 gallon Jamaica rum; 3 oz. butyric ether; 3 oz. acetic ether; ½ gallon sugar syrup. Mix the ethers and acid with the Jamaica rum, and stir it well in the spirit. Color with burnt sugar coloring.

*Santa-Cruz Rum.*—To 50 gallons pure proof spirit, add 5 gallons Santa-Cruz rum; 5 pounds refined sugar, in ½ gallon water; 3 oz. butyric acid; 2 oz. acetic ether. Color if necessary.

*Pine-Apple Rum.*—To 50 gallons rum, made by the fruit method, add 25 pine-apples sliced, and 8 pounds of white sugar. Let it stand two weeks before drawing off.

*Irish or Scotch Whiskey.*—To 40 gallons proof spirits, add 60 drops of creosote, dissolved in 1 quart of alcohol; 2 oz. acetic acid; 1 pound loaf sugar. Stand 48 hours.

*Monongahela Whiskey.*—To 40 gallons proof spirits, add 2 ounces spirits of nitre; 4 pounds dried peaches; 4 pounds N. O. sugar; 1 quart rye (burnt and ground like coffee,) ¼ pound all-spice; ½ pound cinnamon; ½ pound cloves. Put in the ingredients, and after standing 5 days, draw it off, and strain the same, if necessary.

*Batavia Arrack.*—To 12 gallons pale rum, add 2 oz. flowers of benzion; ½ ounce balsam of Tolu; 1 ounce sliced pine-apple. Digest with occasional agitation for a month; then add ½ pint raw milk agitated well for fifteen minutes, and rack in a week, a fine imitation.

*Rum Shrub.*—Tartaric acid, 5 pounds; pale sugar 100 pounds; oil lemom, 4 drs.; oil orange, 4 drs., put them into a large cask (80 gallons,) and add water, 10 gallons. Rummage till the acid and sugar are dissolved, then add rum (proof,) 20 gallons; water to make up 55 gallons in all; coloring 1 quart or more. Fine with 12 eggs. The addition of 12 sliced oranges will improve the flavor.

***Bourbon Whiskey.***—To 100 gallons pure proof spirit, add 4 ounces pear oil; 2 ounces pelargonif ether; 13 drs. oil of wintergreen, dissolved in the ether; 1 gallon wine vinegar. Color with burnt sugar.

***Strong Beer, English Improved.***—Malt, 1 peck; course brown sugar, 6 pounds; hops, 4 ounces; good yeast, 1 teacup; if you have not malt, take a little over 1 peck of barley, (twice the amount of oats will do, but are not as good,) and put it into an oven after the bread is drawn, or into a stove oven, and steam the moisture from them. Grind coarsely. Now pour upon the ground malt 3½ gallons of water at 170 or 172° of heat. The tub in which you scald the malt should have a false bottom, 2 or three inches from the real bottom; the false bottom should be bored full of gimlet holes, so as to act as a strainer, to keep back the malt meal. When the water is poured on, stir them well, and let it stand 3 hours, and draw off by a faucet; put in 7 gallons more of water at 180 to 182°; stir it well, and let it stand 2 hours and draw it off. Then put on a gallon or two of cold water, stir it well and draw it off; you should have about 5 or 6 gallons. Put the six pounds of course brown sugar in an equal amount of water; mix with the wort, and boil 1½ to 2 hours with the hops; you should have eight gallons when boiled; when cooled to 80° put in the yeast, and let it work 18 to 20 hours, covered with a sack; use sound iron hooped kegs or porter bottles, bung or cork tight, and in two weeks it will be good sound beer, and will keep a long time, and for persons of a weak habit of body, and especially females, 1 glass of this with their meals is far better than tea or coffee, or all the ardent spirits in the universe. If more malt is used, not exceeding ½ a bushel, the beer, of course, would have more spirit, but this **strength is sufficient for the use of females or invalids.**

***Cheap Beer.***—Fill a boiler with the green shells of peas, pour on water till it rises half an inch above the shells, and simmer for three hours. Strain off the liquor, and add a strong decoction of the wood sage or the hop, so as to render it pleasantly bitter, then ferment in the usual manner. The wood sage is the best substitute for hops, and being free from any anodyne property is entitled to a preference. By boiling a fresh quantity of shells in the decoction before it becomes cold, it may be so thoroughly impregnated with saccharine matter, as to afford a liquor, when fermented, as strong as ale.

*Root Beer.*—For 10 gallons beer, take 3 pounds common burdock root, or 1 ounce essence of sassafras; ½ pound good hops; 1 pint corn, roasted brown. Boil the whole in 6 gallons of pure water until the strength of the materials is obtained; strain while hot into a keg, adding enough cold water to make 10 gallons. When nearly cold, add clean molasses or syrup until palatable,—not sickishly sweet. Add also as much fresh yeast as will raise a batch of 8 loaves of bread. Place the keg in a cellar or other cool place, and in 48 hours you will have a keg of first-rate sparkling root beer.

*Root Beer, No. 2.*—For each gallon of water to be used, take hops, burdock, yellow dock, sarsaparilla, dandelion, and spikenard roots, bruised, of each ½ ounce; boil about 20 minutes, and strain while hot, add 8 or 10 drops of oils of spruce and sassafras, mixed in equal proportions, when cool enough not to scald your hand, put in 2 or 3 table-spoons of yeast; molasses, ⅛ of a pint, or white sugar, ½ pound, gives it about the right sweetness.

*Superior Ginger Beer.*—Ten pounds of sugar; 9 ounces of lemon juice; ½ a pound of honey; 11 ounces of bruised ginger root; 9 gallons of water; 3 pints of yeast. Boil the ginger half an hour in a gallon of water; then add the rest of the water and the other ingredients, and strain it when cold. Add the white of an egg, beaten, and ½ an ounce of essence of lemon. Let it stand four days, then bottle, and it will keep many months.

*Spruce Beer.*—Take of the essence of spruce half a pint; bruised pimento and ginger, of each four ounces; water, three gallons. Boil five or ten minutes, then strain and add 11 gallons of warm water, a pint of yeast, and 6 pints of molasses. Allow the mixture to ferment for 24 hours.

*To Cure Ropy Beer.*—Put a handful or two of flour, and the same quantity of hops, with a little powdered alum; into the beer and rummage it well.

*To give Beer the appearance of Age.*—Add a few handfuls of pickled cucumbers and Seville oranges, both chopped up. This is said to make malt liquor appear six months older than it really is.

*How to make Mead.*—The following is a good recipe for Mead: On twenty pounds of honey pour five gallons of boiling water; boil, and remove the scum as it rises; add one ounce of best hops, and boil for ten minutes; then put the liquor into a tub to cool; when all but cold add a little yeast spread upon a slice of toasted bread; let it stand in a warm room. When fermentation is set up, put the mixture into a cask, and fill up from time to time as the yeast runs out of the bunghole; when the fermentation is finished, bung it down, leaving a peg-hole which can afterwards be closed, and in less than a year it will be fit to bottle.

*Stomach Bitters, equal to Hostetter's, for one-fourth its cost.*—European Gentian root 1½ ounces; orange peel, 2½ ounces; cinnamon, ¼ ounce; anise seed, ½ ounce; coriander seed, ½ ounce; cardamon seed, ⅛ ounce; unground Peruvian bark, ½ ounce; gum kino, ¼ ounce; bruise all these articles, and put them into the best alcohol, 1 pint; let it stand a week and pour off the clear tincture; then boil the dregs a few minutes in 1 quart of water, strain, and press out all the strength; now dissolve loaf sugar, 1 pound, in the hot liquid, adding 3 quarts cold water, and mix with spirit tincture first poured off, or you can add these, and let it stand on the dregs if preferred.

*Soda Syrup, with or without Fountains.*—The common or more watery syrups are made by using loaf or crushed sugar, 8 pounds; pure water, 1 gallon; gum arabic, 2 ounces; mix in a brass or copper kettle; boil until the gum is dissolved, them skim and strain through white flannel, after which add tartaric acid, 5½ oz. dissolved in hot water; to flavor use extract of lemon, orange rose, pine-apple, peach, sarsaparilla, strawberry, &c., ½ ounce to each bottle, or to your taste.

*Bead for Liquor.*—The best bead is the orange-flower water bead, (oil of neroil,) 1 drop in each gallon of brandy. *Another method:*—To every 40 drops of sulphuric acid, add 60 drops purest sweet oil in a glass vessel|; use immediately. This quantity is generally sufficient for 10 gallons spirit. *Another.*—Take 1 ounce of the purest oil sweet almonds; 1 ounce of sulphuric acid; put them in a stone mortar, add by *degrees*, 2 ounces white lump sugar, rubbing it well with the pestle till it becomes a paste; then add small quantities of spirits of wine till it comes into a liquid; This quantity is sufficient for 100 gallons. The first is strongly recommended as the best.

*Coloring for Liquors.*—Take 2 pounds crushed or lump sugar, put it into a kettle that will hold 4 to 6 quarts, with ½ tumbler of water. Boil it until it is *black*, then take it off and cool with water, stirring it as you put in the water.

*Wax Putty for Leaky Cans, Bungs, etc.*—Spirits turpentine, 2 lbs.; tallow, 4 pounds; solid turpentine, 12 pounds. Melt the wax and solid turpentine together over a slow fire, then add the tallow. When melted, remove far from the fire, then stir the spirits turpentine, and let it cool.

*Cement for the Mouths of Corked Bottles.*—Melt together ¼ of a pound of rosin, a couple of ounces of beeswax. When it froths stir it with a tallow candle. As soon as it melts, dip the mouths of the corked bottles into it. This is an excellent thing to exclude the air from such things as are injured by being exposed to it.

## DRUGGISTS' DEPARTMENT.

*Arnica Liniment.*—Add to one pint of sweet oil, two tablespoonfuls of tincture of arnica; or the leaves may be heated in the oil over a slow fire. Good for wounds, stiff joints, rheumatic, and all injuries.

*Ayer's Cherry Pectoral.*—Take four grains of acetate of morphia, 2 fluid drachms of tincture of bloodroot, 7 fluid drachms each of antimonial wine and wine of ipecacuanha and three fluid ounces of syrup of wild cherry. Mix.

*Balm Gilead.*—Balm-gilead buds, bottled up in new rum, are very healing to fresh cuts or wounds. No family should be without a bottle,

*Blackberry Cordial.*—To one quart of blackberry juice, add one pound of white sugar, one tablespoonful of cloves, one of allspice, one of cinnamon, and one of nutmeg. Boil all together fifteen minutes; add a wineglass of whiskey, brandy, or rum. Bottle while hot, cork tight, and seal. This is a specific in diarrhœa. One dose, which is a wineglassful for an adult—half that quantity for a child—will often cure diarrhœa. It can be taken three or four times a day if the case is severe.

*Brandreth's Pills.*—Take two pounds of aloes, one pound of gamboge, four ounces of extract of colocynth, half a pound of castile soap, two fluid drachms of oil of peppermint; and one fluid drachm of cinnamon. Mix and form into pills.

*Brown's Bronchial Troches.*—Take one pound of pulverized extract of licorice, one and a half pounds of pulverized sugar, four ounces of pulverized cubebs, four ounces of pulverized gum arabic, and one ounce of pulverized extract of conium. Mix.

*Bryan's Pulmonic Wafers, for Coughs, Colds, &c.*—Take white sugar, 7 pounds; tincture of syrup of ipecac, four ounces; antimonial wine, two ounces; morphine, ten grains; dissolved in a tablespoonful of water, with ten or fifteen drops sulphuric acid; tincture of bloodroot; one ounce; syrop of tolu, two ounces; add these to the sugar, and mix the whole mass as confectioners do for lozenges, and cut into lozenges the ordinary size. Use from six to twelve of these in twenty-four hours. They sell at a great profit.

*Candied Lemon or Peppermint, for Colds.*—Boil one and a half pounds of sugar in a half pint of water, till it begins to candy round the sides; put in eight drops of essence; pour it upon buttered paper, and cut it with a knife.

*Camphor Balls,* for rubbing on the hands to prevent chaps, &c. Melt three drachms of spermaceti, four drachms of white wax, and one ounce of almond oil; stir in three drachms of powdered camphor. Pour the compound into small gillipots, so as to form small hemispherical cakes. They may be colored with alkanet, if preferred.

*Camphorated Oil.*—This is another camphor liniment, The proportions are the same as in the preceding formula, substituting olive oil for the alcohol, and exposing the materials to a moderate heat. As an external stimulant application it is even more powerful than the spirits; and to obtain its full influence the part treated should be also covered with flannel and oil silk. It forms a valuable liniment in chronic rheumatism and other painful affections, and is specially valuable as a counter-irritant in sore or inflamed throats and diseased bowels. Camphor constitutes the basis of a large number of valuable liniments. Thus, in cases of whooping-cough and some chronic bronchitic affections, the following liniment may be advantageously rubbed into the chest and along the spine. Spirits of camphor, two parts; laudanum, half a part; spirits of turpentine, one part; castile soap in powder, finely divided, half an ounce; alcohol, 3 parts. Digest the whole together for three days, and strain through linen. This liniment should be gently warmed before using. A powerful liniment for old rheumatic pains, especially when affecting the loins, is the following: camphorated oil and spirits of turpentine, of each two parts; water of hartshorn, one part; laudanum, one part; to be well shaken together. Another efficient liniment or embrocation, serviceable in chronic painful affections, may be conveniently and easily made as follows: Take of camphor, one ounce; cayenne pepper, in powder, two teaspoonfuls; alcohol, one pint. The whole to be digested with moderate heat for ten days, and filtered. It is an active rubificant; and after a slight friction with it, it produces a grateful thrilling sensation of heat in the pained part, which is rapidly relieved.

*Camphor Tablet for Chapped Hands, &c.*—Melt tallow, and add a little powdered camphor and glycerine, with a few drops of oil of almonds to scent. Pour in moulds and cool.

*Camphorated Eye-Water.*—Sulphate of copper, 15 grains; French bole, 15 grains; camphor, 4 grains; boiling water, 4 oz. Infuse, strain, and dilute with 2 quarts of cold water.

*Canker Cure.*—Take one large teaspoonful of water, two teaspoonfuls of honey, two of loaf sugar, three of powdered sage, two of powdered gold-thread, and one of alum. Stir up all together; put into a vessel, and let it simmer moderately over a steady fire. An oven is better. Then bottle for use. Give a teaspoonful occasionally through the day.

*Cephalic Snuff.*—Dried asarbacca leaves, three parts; marjoram, one part; lavender flowers, one part; rub together to a powder.

*Certain Cure for Eruptions, Pimples, &c.*—Having in numberless instances seen the good effects of the following precription, I can certify to its perfect remedy: Dilute corrosive sublimate with the oil of almonds, apply it to the face occasionally, and in a few days a cure will be effected.

***Certain Cure for Headache and all Neuralgic Pains.***—Opodeldoc, spirits of wine, sal ammoniac, equal parts. To be applied as any other lotion.

***Chamomile Pills.***—Aloes, 12 grains; extract chamomile, 36 grains; oil of chamomile, 3 drops; make into twelve pills; two every night, or twice a day.

***Chlorine Pastiles for Disinfecting the Breath.***—Dry chloride of lime, 2 drachms; sugar, 8 ounces; starch, 1 ounce: gum tragacanth, 1 drachm; carmine, 2 grains. Form into small lozenges.

2. Sugar flavored with vanilla, 1 ounce; powdered tragacanth, 20 grains; liquid chloride of soda sufficient to mix; add 2 drops of any essential oil. Form a paste and divide into lozenges of 15 grains each.

***Cholera Morbus.***—Take two ounces of the leaves of the bene-plant, put them in half a pint of cold water, and let them soak an hour. Give two tablespoonfuls hourly, until relief is experienced.

***Cholera Remedy.***—Spirits of wine, one ounce; spirits of lavender, quarter ounce; spirits of camphor, quarter ounce; compound tincture of benzion, half an ounce; oil of origanum, quarter ounce; twenty drops of moist sugar. To be rubbed outwardly also.

2. Twenty-five *minims* of diluted sulphuric acid in an ounce of water.

***Corn Remedy.***—Soak a piece of copper in strong vinegar for twelve or twenty-four hours. Pour the liquid off, and bottle. Apply frequently, till the corn is removed.

2. Supercarbonate of soda, one ounce, finely pulverized, and mixed with half an ounce of lard. Apply on a linen rag every night.

***Cough Compound.***—For the cure of coughs, colds, asthma, whooping cough, and all diseases of the lungs: One spoonful of common tar, three spoonfuls of honey, the yolk of three hen's eggs, and half a pint of wine; beat the tar, eggs and honey well together with a knife, and bottle for use. A teaspoonful every morning, noon, and night, before eating.

*Cough Lozenges.*—Powdered lactucarium, two drachms; extract of licorice root, twelve drachms; powdered squills, fifteen grains; refined sugar, six ounces; mucilage of tragacanth sufficient to mix. Make into two hundred and forty equal lozenges.

*Cough Mixture.*—Four drachms paregoric, with two drachms of sulphuric ether, and two drachms tincture of tolu. Dose, a teaspoonful in warm water.

*Cough Syrup.*—Put one quart hoarhound to one quart water, and boil it down to a pint; add two or three sticks of licorice and a tablespoonful of essence of lemon. take a tablespoonful of the syrup three times a day, or as often as the cough may be troublesome. The above recipe has been sold for $100. Several firms are making much money by its manufacture.

*Cure for Diarrhœa.*—The following is said to be an excellent cure for the above distressing complaint: Laudanum, two ounces; spirits of camphor, two ounces; essence of peppermint, two ounces; Hoffman's anodyne, two ounces; tincture of cayenne pepper, two drachms; tincture of ginger, one ounce. Mix all together. Dose, a teaspoonful in a little water, or a half teaspoonful repeated in an hour afterward in a tablespoonful of brandy. This preparation, it is said, will check diarrhœa in ten minutes, and abate other premonitory symptoms of cholera immediately. In cases of cholera, in has been used with great success to restore reaction by outward application.

*Digestive Pills.*—Rhubarb, 2 ounces; ipecacuanha, ½ ounce; cayenne pepper, ¼ ounce; soap, ½ ounce; ginger, ¼ ounce; gamboge, ½ ounce. Mix, and divide into four grain pills.

*Dinner Pills.*—Aloes, twenty grains; ginger, half a drachm; add syrup sufficient to mix. Divide into twenty pills. One to be taken daily, before dinner.

*Disease of the Bowels.*—Take equal parts of syrup of rhubarb, paregoric, and spirits of camphor, mix together. For an adult, one teaspoonful. If necessary, it may be repeated in 2 or 3 hours.

*Dried Herbs.*—All herbs which are to be dried should be washed, separated, and carefully picked over, then spread on a coarse paper and keep in a room until perfectly dry. Those which are intended for cooking should be stripped from the stems and rubbed very fine. Then put them in bottles and cork tightly. Put those which are intended for medicinal purposes into paper bags, and keep them in a dry place.

*Dysentery.*—In diseases of this kind, the Indians use the roots and leaves of the blackberry bush—a decoction of which in hot water, well boiled down, is taken in doses of a gill before each meal, and before retiring to bed. It is an almost infallible cure.

*Dysentery Specific,* (particularly for bloody dysentery in Adults and Children.)—Take one pound gum arabic, one ounce gum tragacanth, dissolved in two quarts of soft water, and strained. Then take one pound of cloves, half a pound of cinnamon, half a pound allspice, and boil in two quarts of soft water, and strain. Add it to the gums, and boil all together over a moderate fire, and stir into it two pounds of loaf sugar. Strain the whole again when you take it off, and when it is cool, add to it half a pint sweet tincture of rhubarb, and a pint and a half of best brandy. Cork it tight in bottles, as the gums will sour, if exposed. If corked properly it will keep for years.

*Anti-Bilious Pills.*—Compound extract of colocynth, 60 grains; rhubarb, 30 grains; soap, 10 grains. Make into 24 pills. Dose, 2 to 4.

2. Compound extract of colocynth. 2 drachms; extract of rhubarb, half a drachm; soap, 10 grains. Mix, and divide into 40 pills. Dose, 1, 2, or 3.

3. Scammony, 10 to 15 grains; compound extract of colocynth, 2 scruples; extract of rhubarb, half a drachm; soap, 10 grains; oil of caraway, 5 drops. Make into 20 pills. Dose, 1 or 2, as required.

*Great Pain Extractor.*—Spirits of ammonia, one ounce, laudanum, one ounce; oil of organum, one ounce; mutton tallow, half-pound; combine the articles with the tallow when it is nearly cool.

*Godfrey's Cordial,*—Sassafras, six ounces; seeds of coriander, caraway, and anise, of each one ounce; infuse in six pints of water; simmer the mixture till reduced to four pints; then add six pounds of molasses; boil a few minutes; when cold, add three fluid ounces of tincture of opium. For children teething.

*Hooper's Female Pills.*—Sulphate of iron, eight ounces; water, eight ounces; dissolve, and add Barbadoes aloes, forty ounces; myrrh, two ounces; make twenty pills. Dose, 2 to 6.

*Hydrophobia—to Prevent.*—Elecampane, one drachm; chalk, four drachms; Armenian bole, three drachms; alum, ten grains; oil of anise-seed, five drops.

*Infant's Syrup.*—The syrup is made thus: one pound best box raisins, half an ounce of anise-seed, two sticks licorice; split the raisins, pound the anise-seed, and cut the licorice fine; add to it three quarts of rain water, and boil down to two quarts. Feed three or four times a day, as much as the child will willingly drink. The raisins are to strengthen, the anise is to expel the wind, and the lorice as a physic.

*Basilicon Ointment.*—Good resin, five parts; lard, eight parts; yellow wax, two parts. Melt, and stir together till cool.

*Cancer Ointment.*—White arsenic, sulphur, powdered flowers of lesser spearwort, and stinking chamomile, levigated together and formed into a paste with white of egg.

*Elder Flower Ointment.*—Lard, twenty-five pounds; prepared mutton suet, five pounds; melt in an earthen vessel; add elder flower water, three gallons. Agitate for half an hour, and set it aside: the next day gently pour off the water, remelt the ointment, add benzoic acid three drachms; otto of roses, twenty drops; essence of bergamot and oil of rosemary, of each, thirty drops; again agitate well, let it settle for a few minutes, and pour off the clear into pots.

*Eruption Ointment, for Frosted Feet, &c.*—Chrome yellow and hog's lard.

*Foot Ointment.* (for all domestic animals.)—Equal parts of tar, lard and resin, melted together.

*Golden Ointment.*—Orpiment, mixed with lard to the consistence of an ointment.

*Pile Ointment.*—Powdered nutgall, two drachms; camphor, one drachm; melted wax, one ounce; tincture of opium, two drachms. Mix.

*Ointment.*—Take equal parts of yellow root or gold thread and common elder bark, and simmer them in hog's lard. No family should be without this ointment. It is good for chapped hands, chilblains, burns, scalds, sore nipples and lips.

*Swaim's Vermifuge.*—Wormseed, two ounces; valerian, rhubarb, pink-root, white agaric, of each, one and a half ounces;

boil in sufficient water to yield three quarts of decoction, and add it to thirty drops of oil of tansy, and forty-five drops of oil of cloves, dissolved in a quart of rectified spirits. Dose, one teaspoonful at night.

*For Tetter, Ringworm and Scald Head.*—One pound simple cerate; sulphuric acid, one quarter pound; mix together, and ready for use.

*Tincture for Wounds.*—Digest flowers of St. Johnswart, one handful, in half a pint of rectified spirits, then express the liquor and dissolve in it myrrh, aloes and dragon's blood, of each one drachm, with Canada balsam, half an ounce.

*Tonic.*—The following is the tonic used by reformed drunkards to restore the vigor of the stomach. Take of gentian root, half an ounce; valerian root, one drachm; best rhubarb root, two drachms; bitter orange peel, three drachms; cardamon seeds, half an ounce, and cinnamon bark, one drachm. Having bruised all the above together in a mortar (the druggist will do it if requested), pour upon it one and a half pints of boiling water and cover up close; let it stand till cold; strain, bottle and cork securely; keep in a dark place. Two tablespoonfuls may be taken every hour before meals, and half that quantity whenever the patient feels that distressing sickness and prostration so generally present for some time after alcoholic stimulants have been abandoned.

*Whooping Cough.*—Mix a quarter of a pound of ground elcampane root in half a pint of strained honey and half a pint of water. Put them in a glazed earthen pot, and place it in a stone oven, with half the heat required to bake bread. Let it bake until about the consistency of strained honey, and take it out. Administer in doses of a teaspoonful before each meal, to a child; if an adult, double the dose.

*Wild Cherry Bitters.*—Boil a pound of wild cherry bark in a quart of water till reduced to a pint. Sweeten and add a little rum to preserve, or, if to be used immediately, omit the rum. Dose, a wineglassful three times a day, on an empty stomach.

*A Certain Cure for Drunkenness.*—Sulphate of iron, 5 grains; magnesia, 10 grains; peppermint water, 11 drachms; spirits of nutmeg, 1 drachm; twice a day. This preparation acts as a tonic and stimulant, and so partially supplies the place of the accustomed liquor, and prevents that absolute physical and moral prostration that follows that sudden breaking off from the use of stimulating drinks.

## MANUFACTURERS' DEPARTMENT.

*Indelible Ink for Marking Clothing.*—Nitrate of silver, 5 scruples; gum arabic, 2 drachms; sap green, 1 scruple; distilled water, 1 ounce; mix together. Before writing on the article to be marked; apply a little of the following; carbonate of soda, one-half ounce, distilled water, four ounces; let this last, which is the mordant, get dry; then with a quill pen, write what you require.

*Imitation Gold.*—16 parts platina; 7 parts copper; 1 part zinc, put in a covered crucible, with powdered charcoal, and melt together till the whole forms one mass and are thoroughly incorporated together. Or take 4 oz. platina, 3 oz. silver, 1 oz. copper.

*Imitation Silver,*—11 oz. refined nickel; 2 oz. metalic bismuth. Melt the compositions together three times, and pour them out in lye. The third time, when melting, add 2 oz. pure silver. Or take ¼ oz. copper; 1 oz. bismuth; 2 oz. saltpeter; 2 oz. common salt, 1 oz. arsenic; 1 oz. potash; 2 oz. brass, and 3 oz. pure silver. Melt all together in a crucible.

*Recipe for Making Artificial Honey.*—To 10 pounds sugar add 3 pounds water; 40 grains cream tartar; 10 drops essence peppermint; and 3 pounds strained honey. First dissolve the sugar in water and take off the scum; then dissolve the cream of tartar in a little warm water which you will add with some little stirring; then add the honey; heat to a boiling point, and stir for a few minutes.

*Vinegar.*—Take forty gallons of soft water, six quarts of cheap molasses, and six pounds of acetic acid; put them into a barrel (an old vinegar barrel is best), and let them stand from three to ten weeks, stirring occasionally. Add a little "mother" of old vinegar if convenient. Age improves it.

*Soft Soap.*—Dissolve fifteen pounds of common cheap hard soap in fifteen gallons of hot water, and let it cool. Then dissolve fifteen pounds of sal soda in fifteen gallons of hot water; add six pounds of unslaked lime, and boil twenty minutes. Let it cool and settle, and then pour off the clear liquor very carefully and mix it with the soap solution. It improves it very much to add one quart of alcohol after mixing the two solutions. Smaller quantities can be made in the same proportions. If too strong, add water to suit.

*Babbit's Premium Soap.*—5 gallons strong lye; 5 gallons water; 5 lbs. tallow; 1 lb. potash; 2 lbs. sal soda; ½ lb. rosin; 1 pint salt; 1 pint washing fluid. Let the water boil; then put in the articles, and boil half an hour. Stir it well while boiling, and then run into moulds. It will be ready for use as soon as cold. The above preparations are for 100 pounds of soap.

*Imitation of the Ruby.*—Strass, eight parts; oxide of manganese, two parts; mix and fuse same as topaz.

*Imitation Emerald.*—Strass, five hundred parts; glass of antimony, twenty parts; oxide of cobalt, three parts; fuse with care for twenty-four hours, then cool slowly.

*Imitation Sapphire.*—Oxide of cobalt, one part; strass, eight parts. Fuse carefully for thirty-six hours.

*Paste Resembling the Diamond.*—Take white sand, nine hundred parts; red lead, six hundred parts; pearl-ash four hundred and fifty parts; nitre, three hundred parts; arsenic, fifty parts; manganese, half a part. To make it harder, use less lead, and if it should have a yellow tint, add a little more manganese.

*Imitation Topaz.*—Strass, five hundred parts; glass of antimony, twenty-one parts; purple of cassius, half a part; fuse for twenty-fore hours, and cool slowly.

*Celebrated Recipe for Silver Wash.*—One ounce of nitric acid, one ten-cent piece, and one ounce of quick silver. Put in an open glass vessel, and let it stand until dissolved; then add one pint of water, and it is ready for use. Make it into a powder by adding whiting, and it may be used on brass, copper, German silver, ect.

*Cement for Aquaria.*—Many persons have attempted to make aquariums, but have failed on account of the extreme difficulty in making the tank resist the action of water for any length of time. Below is a recipe for a cement that can be relied upon; it is perfectly free from anything that injures the animals or plants; it sticks to glass, metal, wood, stone, etc., and hardens under water. A hundred different experiments with cement have been tried, but there is nothing like it. It is the same as that used in constructing the tanks used in the Zoological Gardens, London, and is almost unknown in this country. One part, by measure, say a gill, of litharge; one gill of plaster of Paris; one gill of dry, white sand; one-third of a gill of finely-powdered resin. Sift and keep corked tight until required for use, when it is to be made into a putty by mixing in boiled oil (linseed) with a little patent dryer added. Never use it after it has been mixed (that is, with the oil) over fifteen hours. This cement can be used for marine as well as fresh water aquaria, as it resists the action of salt water. The tank can be used immediately, but it is best to give it three or four hours to dry.

*Cement for Attaching Metal to Glass.*—Take two ounces of a thick solution of glue, and mix it with one ounce of linseed-oil varnish, and half an ounce of pure turpentine; the whole are then boiled together in a close vessel. The two bodies should be clamped and held together for about two days after they are united, to allow the cement to become dry. The clamps may then be removed.

*Cement for Mending Broken China.*—Stir plaster of Paris into a thick solution of gum arabic, till it becomes a viscous paste. Apply it with a brush to the fractured edges, and draw the parts closely together.

*Cement for Mending Steam Boilers.*—Mix two parts of finely powdered litharge with one part of very fine sand, and one part of quicklime which has been allowed to slack spontaneously by exposure to the air. This mixture may be kept for any length of time without injury. In using it a portion is mixed into paste with linseed oil, or, still better, boiled linseed oil. In this state it must be quickly applied, as it soon becomes hard.

*Cheap Galvanic Battery.*—Take a cylindrical vessel, and put another of porous porcelain inside of it; fill the vessel with diluted sulphuric acid, and the space between the two with sulphate of copper (if you require to plate the article with copper); if not, a solution of the salt of gold, silver, etc., according to that which you wish it to be; put a slip of zinc in the sulphuric acid, and attach a copper wire to it, and the other end to the metal or other article you wish to plate, and immerse that in the other solution. Your battery is now complete. If you want the copper to be very thick, you must put a few solid crystals of copper in the solution; where you do not want it to come in contact, you must touch it with a little grease; if you want to take the copper off the article, you must do it over with a slight varnish.

*Cheap White House Paint.*—Take skim milk, two quarts, eight ounces fresh slaked lime, six ounces linseed oil, two ounces white Burgundy pitch, three pounds spanish white. Slake the lime in water, expose it to the air, and mix in about one-quarter of the milk; the oil, in which the pitch is previously dissolved to be added, a little at a time; then the rest of the milk, and afterwards the Spanish white. This quantity is sufficient for thirty square yards, two coats, and costs but a few cents. If the other colors are wanted, use, instead of Spanish white, other coloring matter.

*Composition for House-Roofs.*—Take one measure of fine sand, two of sifted wood-ashes, and three of lime, ground up with oil. Mix thoroughly, and lay on with a painter's brush, first a thin coat and then a thick one. This composition is not only cheap, but it strongly resists fire.

*Diamond Cement.*—Isinglass, one ounce; distilled vinegar, five and a half ounces; spirits of wine, two ounces; gum ammoniacum, half an ounce, gum mastic, half an ounce. Mix well.

*French Polish.*—To one pint of spirits of wine, add a quarter of an ounce of gum copal, quarter of an ounce of gum arabic, and one ounce of shellac. Let the gums be well bruised, and sifted through a piece of muslin. Put the spirits and the gums together in a vessel that can be closely corked; place them near a warm stove, and frequently shake them; in two or three days they will be dissolved; strain the mixture through a piece of muslin, and keep it tightly corked for use.

*Furniture Oil for Polishing and Straining Mahogany.*—Take of linseed oil, one gallon; alkanet root, three ounces; rose pink, one ounce. Boil them together ten minutes, and strain so that the oil will be quite clear. The furniture should be well rubbed with it every day until the polish is brought up, which will be more durable than any other.

*Furniture Polish.*—Take equal parts of sweet oil and vinegar, mix. add a pint of gum arabic, finely powdered. This will make furniture look almost as good as new, and can be easily applied, as it requires no rubbing. The bottle should be shaken, and the polish poured on a rag and applied to the furniture.

*Glue for ready Use.*—To any quantity of glue use common whiskey instead of water. Put both together in a bottle, cork tight, and set it away for three or four days, when it will be fit for use without the application of heat.

*A Quart of Ink for a Dime.*—Buy extract of logwood, which may be had at three cents an ounce, or cheaper by the quantity. Buy also, for three cents, an ounce of *bi-chromate of potash*. Do not make a mistake, and get the simple chromate of potash. The former is orange red, and the latter clear yellow. Now, take half an ounce of extract of logwood and ten grains of bi-chromate of potash, and dissolve them in a quart of hot rain water. When cold, pour it into a glass bottle, and leave it uncorked for a week or two. Exposure to the air is indispensable. The ink is then made, and has cost five to ten minutes' labor, and about three cents, besides the bottle. The ink is at first an intense steel blue, but becomes quite black.

*An Excellent Substitute for Ink.*—Put a couple of iron nails into a teaspoonful of vinegar. In half an hour pour in a tablespoonful of strong tea, and then you will have ink enough for a while.

*Ink, First-Rate Black.*—Take twelve pounds of bruised galls, five pounds of gum Senegal, five pounds of green sulphate of iron, and twelve gallons of rain water. Boil the galls with nine gallons of water for three hours, adding fresh water to replace what is lost by evaporation. Let the decoction settle, and draw off the clear liquor; add to it a strained solution of the gum; dissolve also the sulphate of iron separately, and mix the whole.

*Another.*—Galls, three pounds; sulphate of iron, one pound; logwood, half a pound; gum half a pound; ale, four gallons. Let it stand in loosely corked bottles in a warm place for a week or two, shaking it daily.

*Ink, Blue.*—Chinese blue, three ounces; oxalic acid, (pure,) three-quarters of an ounce; gum arabic, powdered, one ounce; distilled water, six pints. Mix.

*Ink, Blue, Easily Made.*—The soluble indigo of commerce makes a good blue ink when slightly diluted with hot water. It is incorrosive for steel pens, and flows freely.

*Ink, Cheap Black.*—Extract of logwood, two ounces; sulphate of potash, quarter of an ounce; boiling water, one gallon. Mix. This is as excellent ink, and can be made at a cost not exceeding fifteen cents a gallon.

*Ink, Cheap Printing.*—Take equal parts of lampblack and oil; mix and keep on the fire till reduced to the right consistency. This is a good ink for common purposes and is very cheap. We have used it extensively ourselves.

*Ink, Copying.*—Dissolve half an ounce of gum and twenty grains of Spanish licorice in thirteen drachms of water, and add one drachm of lamp-black, previously mixed with a teaspoonful of sherry.

*Another.*—Common black ink, three parts; sugar candy, one part.

*Ink, Indelible.*—To four drachms of lunar caustic, in four ounces of water, add 60 drops of nutgalls, made strong by being pulverized and steeped in soft water. The mordant, which is to be applied to the cloth before writing, is composed of one ounce of pearlash, dissolved in four ounces of water, with a little gum arabic dissolved in it. Wet the spot with this; dry and iron the cloth; then write.

2. Nitrate of silver, five scruples; gum arabic, two drachms; sap green, one scruple; distilled water, one ounce. Mix together. Before writing on the article to be marked, apply a little of the following: carbonate of soda. half an ounce; distilled water, four ounces; let this last, which is the mordant, get dry; then with a quill, write what you require.

*Ink, Indelible Marking.*—One and a half drachms of nitrate of silver, one ounce of distilled water, half an ounce of strong mucilage of gum arabic, three-quarters of a drachm of liquid ammonia. Mix the above in a clean glass bottle, cork tightly, and keep in a dark place till dissolved, and ever afterwards. Directions for use; Shake the bottle, then dip a clean quill in the ink, and write or draw what you require on the article; immediately hold it close to the fire (without scorching,) or pass a hot iron over it, and it will become a deep and indelible black, indestructible by either time or acids, of any description.

*Ink, Indestructible.*—On many occasions it is of importance to employ an ink indestructable by any process, that will not equally destroy the material on which it is applied. For black ink, twenty-five grains of copal, in powder, are to be dissolved in two hundred grains of oil of lavender, by the assistance of a gentle heat, and are then to be mixed with two and a half grains of lamp-black and half a grain of indigo. This ink is particularly useful for labelling phials, etc., containing chemical substances of a corrosive nature.

*Ink, for Marking Linen with Type.*—Dissolve one part of asphaltum in four parts of oil of turpentine, and lamp-black or black-lead, in fine powder, in sufficient quantity to render of proper consistency to print with type.

*Ink Powder for Immediate Use.*—Reduce to powder ten ounces of gall-nuts, three ounces of green copperas, two ounces each of powdered alum and gum arabic put, |a little of this mixture into white wine, and it will be fit for immediate use.

*Ink Stains.*—The moment the ink is spilled, take a little milk, and saturate the stain, soak it up with a rag, and apply a little more milk, rubbing it well in. In a few minutes the ink will be completely removed.

*Red Ink.*—Take of the raspings of Brazil wood, quarter of a pound, and infuse them two or three days in colorless vinegar. Boil the infusion one hour and a half over a gentle fire, and afterward filter it while hot, through paper laid in an earthenware cullender. Put it again over the fire, and dissolve in it first half an ounce of gum arabic, and afterward of alum and white sugar each half an ounce. Care should be taken that the Brazil wood be not adulterated with the Braziletto or Campeachy wood.

*Resin-oil Ink.*—Melt together thirteen ounces of resin, one pound of resin-oil, and one and a half ounces of soft soap. When cold, add lamp-black.

*Runge's Black Writing Fluid.*—Boil twenty-two pounds of logwood in enough water to yield fourteen gallons of decoction. To each one thousand parts add one part of yellow chromate of potash. Stir the mixture.

*Sympathetic Invisible Ink.*—Sulphuric acid, one part; water, ten parts; mix together and write with a quill pen, which writing can be read only after heating it.

*Sympathetic or Secret Inks.*—Mix equal quantities of sulphate of copper and sal ammoniac, and dissolve in water. Writing done with this ink is invisible until the paper is heated, when it turns a yellow color. Lemon juice, milk, juice of onions, and some other liquids become black when the writing is held to the fire.

*Transfer Ink.*—Mastic in tears, four ounces; shellac, six ounces; Venice turpentine, half an ounce; melt together, add wax, half a pound; tallow, three ounces. When dissolved further add hard tallow soap (in shavings), three ounces; and when the whole is combined, add lamp-black two ounces. Mix well, cool a little, and then pour it into molds. This ink is rubbed down with a little water in a cup or saucer, in the same way as water color cakes. In winter, the operation should be performed near the fire.

*Indian Glues.*—Take one pound of the best glue, the stronger the beter, boil it and strain it very clear; boil also four ounces of isinglass; put the mixture into a double glue pot, add half a pound of brown sugar, and boil the whole until it gets thick; then pour it into thin plates or molds, and when cold you may cut and dry them in small pieces for the pocket. The glue is used by merely holding it over steam, or wetting it with the mouth. This is a most useful and convenient article, being much stronger than common glue. It is sold under the name of Indian glue, but is much less expensive in making, and is applicable to all kinds of small fractures, etc.; answers well on the hardest woods, and cements, china, etc., though, of course, it will not resist the action of hot water. For parchment and paper, in lieu of gum or paste, it will be found equally convenient.

*Japanese Cement.*—Intimately mix the best powdered rice with a little cold water, then gradually add boiling water until a proper consistence is acquired, being particularly careful to keep it well stirred all the time; lastly, it must be boiled for one minute in a clean saucepan or earthern pipkin. This glue is beautifully white and almost transparent, for which reason it is well adapted for fancy paper work, which requires a strong and colorless cement.

*Liquid Blacking.*—Mix a quarter of a pound of ivory-black, six gills of vinegar, a tablespoonful of sweet oil, and two large spoonfuls of molasses. Stir the whole well together, and it will then be fit for use.

*Liquid Glue.*—Dissolve one part of powdered alum, one hundred and twenty parts of water; add one hundred and twenty parts of glue, ten of acetic acid, and forty of alcohol, and digest. Prepared glue is made by dissolving common glue in warm water, and then adding acetic acid (strong vinegar) to keep it. Dissolve one pound of best glue in one and a half pints of water, and add one pint of vinegar. It is then ready for use.

*Magic Copying Paper.*—To make black paper, lamp-black mixed with cold lard; red paper, Venetian red mixed with lard; blue paper, Prussian blue mixed with lard; green paper, Chrome green mixed with lard. The above ingredients to be mixed to the consistency of thick paste, and to be applied to the paper with a rag. Then take a flannel rag, and rub until all color ceases coming off. Cut your sheets four inches wide and six inches long; put four sheets together, one of each color, and sell for twenty-five cents per package. The first cost will not exceed three cents.

Directions for writing with this paper: Lay down your paper upon which you wish to write; then lay on the copying paper, and over this lay any scrap of paper you chose; then take any hard pointed substance and write as you would with a pen.

*Mahogany Stain.*—Break two ounces of dragon's blood in pieces, and put them in a quart of rectified spirits of wine; let the bottle stand in a warm place, and shake it frequently. When dissolved, it is fit for use, and will render common wood an excellent imitation of mahogany.

*Marine Glue.*—Dissolve four parts of india-rubber in thirty-four parts of coal tar naphtha, aiding the solution with heat and agitation. The solution is then thick as cream, and it should be added to sixty-four parts of powdered shellac, which must be heated in the mixture till all is dissolved. While the mixture is hot it is poured on plates of metal, in sheets like leather. It can be kept in that state, and when it is required to be used, it is put into a pot and heated till it is soft, and then applied with a brush to the surfaces to be joined. Two pieces of wood joined with this cement can scarcely be sundered.

***Parchment.***—Paper parchment may be produced by immersing paper in a concentratic solution of choloride of zinc.

***Silver Plating Fluid.***—Dissolve one ounce of nitrate of silver in crystal, in twelve ounces of soft water; then dissolve in the water two ounces cyanuret of potash, shake the whole together, and let it stand till it becomes clear. Have ready some half ounce vials, and fill half full of Paris white, or fine whiting, and then fill up the bottles with the liquor and it is ready for use. The whiting does not increase the coating power—it only helps to clean the articles, and to save the silver fluid by half filling the bottle.

***Amalgam of Gold.***—Place one part of gold in a small iron sauce-pan or ladle, perfectly clean, then add eight parts of mercury, and apply a gentle heat, when the gold will dissolve; agitate the mixture for one minute, and pour it out on a clean plate or stone slab.

For gilding brass, copper, etc. The metal to be gilded is first rubbed over with a solution of nitrate of mercury, and then covered over with a thin film of the amalgam. On heat being applied the mercury volatilizes, leaving the gold behind.

A much less proportion of gold is often employed than the above, where a very thin and cheap gilding is required, as by increasing the quantity of the mercury, the precious metal may be extended over a much larger surface. A similar amalgam prepared with silver is used for silvering.

***Amalgam for Mirrors,***—Lead and tin, each one ounce; bismuth, two ounces; mercury, four ounces; melt as before, and add the mercury. These are used to silver mirrors, glass globes, etc., by warming the glass, melting the amalgam, and applying it.

***Annealing Steel.***—1. For a small quantity. Heat the steel to a cherry red in a charcoal fire, then bury in sawdust, in an iron box, covering the sawdust with ashes. Let stay until cold.— 2. For a larger quantity, and when it is required to be very "soft." Pack the steel with cast iron (lathe or plainer) chips in an iron box, as follows: Having at least ½ or ¾ inch in depth of chips in the bottom of box, put in a layer of steel, then more chips to fill spaces between the steel, and also the ½ or ¾ inch space between the sides of box and steel, then more steel; and lastly, at least 1 inch in depth of chips, well rammed down on top of steel.

Heat to and keep at a red heat for from two to four hours. Do not disturb the box until cold.

***To make Bell Metal.***—1. Melt together under powdered charcoal, 100 parts of pure copper, with 20 parts of tin, and unite the two metals by frequently stirring the mass. Product very fine.—2. Copper 3 parts; tin 1 part; as above. Some of the finest church bells in the world have this composition.—3. Copper 2 parts; tin 1 part; as above.—4. Copper 72 parts; tin 26½ parts; iron 1½ parts. The bells of small clocks or pendules are made of this alloy in Paris.

***Brass to Make.*** 1. *Fine Brass.*—2 parts of copper to 1 part of zinc. This is nearly one equivalent each of copper and zinc, if the equivalent of the former metal be taken at 63·2; or 2 equivalents of copper to 1 equivalent of zinc, if it be taken with Liebig and Berzelius, at 31·6.

2. Copper 4 parts; zinc, 1 part. An excellent and very useful brass.

***Cleansing Solution for Brass.***—Put together two ounces sulphuric acid, an ounce and a half nitric acid, one drachm saltpetre and two ounces rain water. Let stand for a few hours, and apply by passing the article in and out quickly, and then washing off thoroughly with clean rain water. Old discolored brass chains treated in this way will look equally as well as when new. The usual method of drying is in sawdust.

***To Cover Brass with beautiful Lustre Colors.***—One ounce of cream of tartar is dissolved in one quart of hot water, to which is added half an ounce of tin salt (protochloride of tin) dissolved in four ounces of cold water. The whole is then heated to boiling, the clear solution decanted from a trifling precipitate, and poured under continual stirring into a solution of three ounces hyposulphite of soda in one-half a pint of water, whereupon it is again heated to boiling, and filtered from the separated sulphur. This solution produces on brass the various luster-colors, depending on the length of time during which the articles are allowed to stay in it. The colors at first will be light to dark gold yellow, passing through all the tints of red to an irridescent brown. A similar series of colors is produced by sulphide of copper and lead, which, however, are not remarkable for their stability; whether this defect will be obviated by the use of the tin solution, experience and time alone can show.

*Bronzing Gun-Barrels.*—The so-called butter of zinc used old for bronzing gun-barrels is made by dissolving zinc in hydrochloric acid till no more free acid is left; which is secured by placing zinc in the acid until it ceases to be dissolved. The liquid is then evaporated until a drop taken out and placed on a piece of glass solidifies in cooling, when it is mixed with two parts of olive-oil for every three parts of the liquid. The barrels must be cleansed and warmed before applying the so-called butter, which put on with a piece of linen rag.

*Bronzing Fluid.*—For brown; Iron filings, or scales, 1 lb.; arsenic, 1 oz.. hydrochloric acid, 1 lb.; metallic zinc, 1 oz. The article to be bronzed is to be dipped in this solution till the desired effect is produced.

*Bronze, Green.*—Acetic acid, diluted, 4 pounds; green verditer, 2 ounces; muriate of ammonia, 1 ounce; common salt, 2 ounces; alum ½ ounce; French berries, ½ pound; boil them together till the berries have yielded their color, and strain. Olive bronze, for brass or copper.—Nitric acid, 1 ounce; hydrochloric acid, 2 ounces; titanium or palladium, as much as will dissolve, and add three pints of distilled water.

*To Soften Cast-Iron, for Drilling.*—Heat to a cherry red, having it lie level in the fire, then with a pair of cold tongs put on a piece of brimstone, a little less in size than you wish the hole to be when drilled, and it softens entirely through the piece; let it lie in the fire until a little cool, when it is ready to drill.

*To Weld Cast-Iron.*—Take of good clear white sand, three parts; refined solton, one part; fosterine, one part; rock salt, one part; mix all together. Take two pieces of cast-iron, heat them in a moderate charcoal-fire, occasionally taking them out while heating, and dipping them into the composition, until they are of a proper heat to weld, then at once lay them on the anvil, and gently hammer them together, and, if done carefully by one who understands welding iron, you will have them nicely welded together. One man prefers heating the metal, then cooling it in the water of common beans, and heat it again for welding.

*Case-Hardening.*—The operation of giving a surface of steel to pieces of iron, by which they are rendered capable of receiving great external hardness, while the interior portion retains all the toughness of good wrought iron. Iron tools, fire-irons, fenders, keys, etc., are usually case-hardened.

1. The goods, finished in every respect put polishing, are put into an iron box, and covered with animal or vegetable charcoal, and cemented at a red heat, for a period varying with the size and description of the articles operated on.

2. Cow's horn or hoof is to be baked or thoroughly dried, and pulverized. To this add an equal quantity of bay salt; mix them with stale chamber-lye, or white wine vinegar; cover the iron with this mixture, and bed it in the same in loam, or inclose it in an iron box; lay it then on the hearth of the forge to dry and harden; then put it into the fire, and blow till the lump has a blood-red heat, and no higher, lest the mixture be burnt too much. Take the iron out, and immerse it in water to harden.

3. The iron previously polished and finished, is to be heated to a bright red and rubbed or sprinkled over with prussiate of potash. As soon as the prussiate appears to be decomposed and dissipated, plunge the article into cold water.

4. Make a paste with a concentrated solution of prussiate of potash and loam, and coat the iron therewith; then expose it to a strong red heat, and when it has fallen to a dull red, plunge the whole into cold water.

*To recut old Files and Rasps.*—Dissolve 4 ounces of saleratus in 1 quart of water, and boil the files in it for half an hour; then remove, wash, and dry them. Now have ready, in a glass or stone ware vessel, 1 quart of rain water, into which you have slowly added 4 ounces of best sulphuric acid, and keep the proportions for any amount used. Immerse the files in this preparation for from six to twelve hours, according to fineness or coarseness of the file; then remove, wash them clean, dry quickly, and put a little sweet oil on them to cover the surface. If the files are coarse, they will need to remain in about twelve hours, but for fine files six to eight hours is sufficient. This plan is applicable to blacksmiths', gunsmiths', tinners', coppersmiths' and machinists' files. Copper and tin workers will only require a short time to take the articles out of their files, as the soft metals with which they become filled are soon dissolved. Blacksmiths' and saw-mill files require full time. Files may be re-cut three times by this process. The liquid may be used at different times if required. Keep away from children as it is poisonous.

***Twist, Browning for Gun-Barrels.***—Take spirits of nitre ¾ oz.; tincture of steel, ¾ oz.; (if the tincture of steel cannot be obtained, the unmedicated tincture of iron may be used, but it is not so good) black brimstone, ¼ oz.; blue vitriol ½ oz.; corrosive sublimate ¼ oz.; nitric acid, 1 dr. or 60 drops; copperas, ¼ oz.; mix with 1½ pints of rain water, keep corked, also, as the other, and the process of applying is also the same.

***Gun Metal.***—1. Melt together 112 pounds of Bristol brass, 14 pounds of spelter, and 7 pounds of block tin.—2. Melt together 9 parts of copper and 1 part of tin; the above compounds are those used in the manufacture of small and great brass guns, swivels, etc.

***Chinese Method of Mending Holes in Iron.***—The Chinese mend holes in cast-iron vessels as follows: They melt a small quantity of iron in a crucible the size of a thimble, and pour the molten metal on a piece of felt covered with wood-ashes. This is pressed inside the vessel against the hole, and as it exudes on the other side it is struck by a small roll of felt covered with ashes. The new iron then adheres to the old.

***Common Pewter,***—Melt in a crucible 7 pounds of tin, and when fused throw in 1 pound of lead, 6 oz. of copper and 2 oz. of zinc. This combination of metal will form an alloy of great durability and tenacity; also of considerable lustre.

***Best Pewter.***—The best sort of pewter consists of 100 parts of tin, and 17 of regulus of antimony.

***Hard Pewter.***—Melt together 12 pounds of tin, 1 pound of regulus of antimony, and 4 ounces of copper.

***To Mend Broken Saws.***—Pure silver 19 parts; pure copper 1 part; pure brass 2 parts; all are to be filed into powder and intimately mixed. Place the saw level upon the anvil, the broken edges in close contact, and hold them so; now put a small line of the mixture along the seam, covering it with a large bulk of powdered charcoal; now with a spirit lamp and a jeweler's blow-pipe, hold the cold-dust in place, and blow sufficient to melt the solder mixture; then with a hammer set the joint smooth, if not already so, and file away any superfluous solder; and you will be surprised at its strength.

*Solder, to Adhere to Brass or Copper.*—Prepare a soldering solution in this way : Pour a small quantity of muriatic acid on some zinc filings, so as to completely cover the zinc. Let it stand about an hour, and then pour off the acid, to which add twice its amount of water. By first wetting the brass or copper with this preparation, the solder will readily adhere.

*Common Solder.*—Put into a crucible 2 lbs. of lead, and when melted throw in 1 pound of tin. This alloy is that generally known by the name of solder. When heated by a hot iron and applied to tinned iron with powdered resin, it acts as a cement or solder.

*Tempering Steel.*—For tempering many kinds of tools, the steel is first hardened by heating it to a cherry red, and plunging it into cold water. Afterward the temper is drawn by moderately heating the steel again. Different degrees of hardness are required for different purposes, and the degree of heat for each of these, with the corresponding color, will be found in the annexed table.

Very pale straw color, 430°—the temper required for lancets.

A shade of darker yellow, 450°—for razors and surgical instruments.

Darker straw-yellow, 470°—for penknives.

Still darker yellow, 490°—chisels for cutting iron.

A brown yellow 500°—axes and plane-irons.

Yellow, slightly tinged with purple, °520—table-knives and watch-springs.

*Tempering Liquid.*—1. To 6 quarts soft water put in corrosive sublimate, 1 oz.; common salt, 2 handfuls ; when dissolved it is ready for use. The first gives toughness to the steel, while the latter gives the hardness. Be careful with this preparation, as it is a dangerous poison.—2. Salt, ½ tea-cup ; saltpetre, ½ oz.; alum, pulverized. 1 tea-spoon; soft water, 1 gallon ; never heat over a cherry red, nor draw any temper.—3. Saltpetre, sal-ammoniac, and alum, of each 2 ounces; salt, 1½ pounds; water, 3 gallons and draw no temper.—4. Saltpetre and alum, of each 2 ounces; sal-ammoniac, ½ ounce; salt, 1½ pounds; soft water, 2 gallons. Heat to a cherry red, and plunge in, drawing no temper.

*Bayberry, or Myrtle Soap.*—Dissolve two and a quarter pounds of white potash in five quarts of water, then mix it with ten lbs. of myrtle wax, or bayberry tallow. Boil the whole over a slow fire till it turns to soap, then add a teacup of cold water; let it boil ten minutes longer; at the end of that time turn it into tin molds or pans, and let them remain a week or ten days to dry; then turn them out of the molds. If you wish to have the soap scented, stir into it an essential oil that has an agreeable smell, just before you turn it into the molds. This kind of soap is excellent for shaving, and for chapped hands; it is also good for eruptions on the face. It will be fit for use in the course of three or four weeks after it is made, but it is better for being kept ten or twelve or months.

*Chemical Soap*, (for taking Oil, Grease, etc., from Cloth.)—Take five pounds of castile soap, cut fine; one pint alcohol; one pint soft water; two ounces aquafortis; one and a half ounces lampblack; two ounces of saltpetre; three ounces potash; one ounce of camphor; and four ounces of cinnamon, in powder. First dissolve the soap, potash and saltpetre, by boiling; then add all the other articles, and continue to stir until it cools; then pour into a box and let it stand twenty-four hours and cut into cakes.

*Cold Soap.*—Mix twenty-six pounds of melted and strained grease with four pailfuls of ley made of twenty pounds of white potash. Let the whole stand in the sun, stirring it frequently. In the course of the week, fill the barrel with weak ley.

*Genuine Erasive Soap.*—Two pounds of good castile soap; half a pound of carbonate of potash; dissolve in half a pint of hot water. Cut the soap in thin slices, and boil the soap with the potash until it is thick enough to mould in cakes; also add alcohol, half an ounce; camphor, half an ounce; hartshorn, half an ounce; color with half an ounce of pulverized charcoal.

*Hard White Soap.*—To fifteen pounds of lard or suet, made boiling hot, add slowly six gallons of hot lye, or solution of potash, that will bear up an egg high enough to leave a piece big as a shilling bare. Take out a little, and cool it. If no grease rise it is done. If any grease appears, add lye, and boil till no grease rises. Add three quarts of fine salt, and boil up again. If this does not harden well on cooling, add more salt. If it is to be perfumed, melt it next day, add the perfume, and run it in moulds or cut in cakes.

***Labor-Saving Soap.*** —Take two pounds of sal-soda, two pounds of yellow bar soap, and ten quarts of water. Cut the soap in thin slices, and boil together for two hours; strain, and it will be it for use. Put the clothes in soak the night before you wash, and to every pail of water in which you boil them, add a pound of soap. They will need no rubbing, merely rinse them out, and they will be perfectly clean and white.

***To Make Good Soap.*** —To make matchless soap, take one gallon of soft soap, to which add a gill of common salt, and boil an hour. When cold, separate the lye from the crude. Add to the crude two pounds of sal soda, and boil in two gallons of soft water till dissolved. If you wish it better, slice two pounds of common bar soap and dissolve in the above. If the soft soap makes more than three pounds of crude, add in proportion to the sal soda and water.

***To make Hard Soap from Soft.*** —Take seven pounds of good soft soap; four pounds sal soda; two ounces borax; one ounce hartshorn; half a pound of resin; to be dissolved in twenty-two quarts of water, and boiled about twenty minutes.

***Whale Oil Soap.*** (for the destruction of insects.)—Render common lye caustic, by boiling it at full strength on quicklime; then take the lye and boil it with as much whale oil foot as it will saponify (change to soap), pour off into moulds, and, when cold, it is tolerably hard. Whale oil foot is the sediment produced in refining whale oil, and is worth two dollars per barrel.

***Soluble Glass.*** —Mix ten parts of carbonate of potash, fifteen parts of powdered quartz, and one pound of charcoal. Fuse well together. The mass is soluble in four or five parts of boiling water, and the filtered solution, evaporated to dryness, yields a transparant glass, permanent in the air.

***Tracing Paper.*** —In order to prepare a beautiful transparent, colorless paper, it is best to employ the varnish formed with Demarara resin in the following way: The sheets intended for this purpose are laid flat on each other, and the varnish spread over the uppermost sheet with a brush, until the paper appears perfectly colorless, without, however, the liquid thereon being visible. The first sheet is then removed, hung up for drying, and the second treated in the same manner. After being dried this paper is capable of being written on, either with chalk or pencil, or with steel pens. It preserves its colorless transparency without becoming yellow, as is frequently the case with that prepared in any other way.

*Unsurpassable Blacking.*—Put one gallon of vinegar into a stone jug, and one pound of ivory-black well pulverized, half a pound of loaf sugar, half an ounce of oil of vitriol, and seven ounces of sweet oil. Incorporate the whole by stirring.

2. Take twelve ounces each of ivory-black and molasses; spermaceti oil, four ounces; and white wine vinegar, two quarts. Mix thoroughly. This contains no vitriol, and therefore will not injure the leather. The trouble of making it is very little, and it would be well to prepare it for one's self, were it only to be assured that it is not injurious.

*Varnish for Iron Work.*—To make a good black varnish for iron work, take eight pounds of asphaltum and fuse it in an iron kettle; then add five gallons of boiled linseed oil, one pound of litharge, half a pound of sulphate of zinc (add these slowly, or it will fume over), and boil them for about three hours. Now add one and a half pounds of dark gum amber, and boil for two hours longer, or until the mass will become quite thick when cool, after which it should be thinned with turpentine to due consistency.

## THE TOILET, PERFUMERY, Etc.

*Hair Restorers and Invigorators.*—There are hundreds; Lyon's, Wood's, Barry's, Bogle's, Jayne's, Storr's, Baker's Driscol's, Phalon's, Haskel's, Allen's, Spalding's, etc. But, though all under different names, are similar in principle, being vegetable oils dissolved in alcohol, with the addition of spirit of soap, and an astringent material, such as tincture of catechu; or infusion of bark. The best is to dissolve one ounce of castor oil in one quart of 95 alcohol, and add one ounce of tincture of cantharides, two ounces of tincture of catechu, two ounces of lemon juice, two ounces of tincture of cinchona; and to scent it, add oil of cinnamon, or oil of rosemary, or both.

*To Cure Baldness.*—Take water, one pint; pearl-ash, one-half ounce; onion juice, one gill. Mix, and cork in a bottle. Rub the head night and morning, with a rough towel, dipped in the mixture.

*To Make the Hair Soft and Glossy.*—Put one ounce of castor oil in one pint of bay rum or alcohol, and color it with a little of the tincture of alkanet root. Apply a little every morning.

*Poudre Subtile for Removing Superfluous Hair.*—Take powdered quick-lime, two parts; sulphuret of arsenic, one part; starch, one part; mix into a fine powder, and keep in a close corked bottle. When required for use, take a small quantity and add two or three drops of water, and apply on the part you desire to remove the hair from—let it remain about one minute, or until it becomes red, then wash off.

*Chinese Depilatory for Removing Superfluous Hair.*—Fresh burnt lime, sixteen ounces; pearl-ash, two ounces; sulphuret of potash, two ounces. Reduce them to fine powder in a mortar, then put it into closely corked phials. For use, the part must be first soaked in warm water, then a little of the powder made into a paste must be immediately applied. Should it irritate the skin, wash it off with hot water or vinegar.

*Instantaneous Hair Dye.*—Take one drachm of nitrate of silver, and add to it just sufficient rain water to dissolve it, *and no more;* then take strong spirits of ammonia, and gradually pour on the solution of silver; until it becomes as clear as water, (*the addition of the ammonia at first makes it brown;*) then wrap around the bottle two or three covers of blue paper, to exclude the light —otherwise it will spoil. Having made this obtain two drachms of gallic acid; put this into another bottle which will contain one-half pint; pour upon it hot water, and let it stand until cold —when it is fit for use.

*Directions to Dye the Hair.*—First wash the head, beard, or mustaches with soap and water; afterwards with clean water. Dry, and apply the gallic acid solution, with a clean brush. When it is almost dry, take a small tooth comb, and with a fine brush, put on the teeth of the comb a little of the silver solution, and comb it through the hair, when it will become a brilliant jet black. Wait a few hours; then wash the head again with clean water. If you want to make a brown dye, add double or treble the quantity of water to the silver solution, and you can obtain any shade of color you choose.

***Whiskers or Mustache forced to Grow.***—Cologne, two ounces; liquid hartshorn, one drachm; tincture cantharides, two drachms; oil rosemary, twelve drops; oil nutmeg, twelve drops, and lavender, twelve drops. This is the recipe used in making the celebrated GRAHAM ONGUENT.

***To Make Hair Curl.***—At any time you may make your hair curl the more easily by rubbing it with the beaten yolk of an egg washed off afterwards with clean water.

***To Prevent Gray Hair.***—When the hair begins to change color, the use of the following pomade has a beneficial effect in preventing the disease extending, and has the character of even restoring the color of the hair in many instances; Lard 4 ounces; spermaceti, 4 drachms; oxide of bismuth, 4 drachms. Melt the lard and spermaceti together, and when getting cold stir in the bismuth; to this can be added any kind of perfume, according to choice. It should be used whenever the hair requires dressing, It must not be imagined that any good effect speedily results; it is, in general, a long time taking place, the change being very gradual.

***Liquid Rouge for the Complexion.***—Four ounces of alcohol, two ounces of water, twenty grains of carmine; twenty grains of ammonia, six grains of oxalic acid, six grains of alum, mix.

***Vinegar Rouge.***—Cochineal, three drachms; carmine lake, three drachms; alcohol, six drachms; mix, and then put into one pint of vinegar, perfumed with lavender; let it stand a fortnight, then strain for use.

***Pearl Powder for Complexion.***—Take white bismuth, one pound; starch powder, one ounce; orris powder, one ounce. Mix and sift through lawn. Add a drop of ottar of roses or neroli.

***Pearl Water for the Complexion.***—Castile soap, one pound; water, one gallon. Dissolve, then add alcohol, one quart; oil of rosemary and oil of lavender, each two drachms. Mix well.

***Complexion Pomatum.***—Mutton grease, one pound; oxide of bismuth, four ounces; powdered French chalk, two ounces; mix.

***Spanish Vermillion for the Toilette.***—Take an alkine solution of bastard saffron, and precipitate the color with lemon juice; mix the precipitate with a sufficient quantity of finely powdered French chalk and lemon juice, then add a little perfume.

*Lily White.* is nothing but purified chalk, scented.

*To Remove Freckles and Tan.*—Tincture of benzoin, one pint; tincture tolou, one-half pint; oil rosemary, one-half ounce. Put one teaspoonful of the above mixture in one-quarter pint of water, and with a towel wash the face night and morning.

*Feuchtwanger's Tooth Paste.*—Powdered myrrh, two ounces; burnt alum, one ounce; cream tartar, one ounce; cuttle fish bone, four ounces; drop lake, two ounces; honey, half a gallon; mix.

*Fine Tooth Powder.*—Powdered orris root, one ounce; peruvian bark, one ounce; prepared chalk, one ounce; myrrh, one-half ounce.

*To Make Brown Teeth White.*—Apply carefully over the teeth, a stick dipped in strong acetic or nitric acid, and immediately wash out the mouth with cold water. To make the teeth even, if irregular draw a piece of fine cord betwixt them.

*Superior Cologne Water.*—Alcohol, one gallon; add oil of cloves, lemon, nutmeg, and bergamot, each one drachm; oil neroli, three and a half drachms; seven drops of oil of rosemary, lavender and cassia; half a pint of spirits of nitre; half a pint of elder-flower water. Let it stand a day or two, then take a cullender and at the bottom lay a piece of white cloth, and fill it up, one-fourth of white sand, and filter through it.

*Smelling Salts.*—Super carbonate of ammonia, eight parts; put it in coarse powder in a bottle, and pour out lavender oil one part.

*Bandoline for the Hair.*—This mixture is best made a little at a time. Pour a tablespoonful of boiling water on a dozen quince seeds; and repeat when fresh is required.

*Oil of Roses—For the Hair.*—Olive oil, two pints; otto of roses, one drachm; oil of rosemary, one drachm, mix. It may be colored by steeping a little alkanet root in the oil (by heat) before scenting it.

*Arnica Hair Wash.*—When the hair is falling off and becoming thin, from the too frequent use of castor, Macassor oils, &c., or when permature baldness arises from illness, the arnica hair wash will be found of great service in arresting the mischief. It is thus peepared: take elder water, half a pint; sherry wine, half a pint; tincture of arnica, half an ounce; alcoholic ammonia, one drachm—if this last named ingredient is old, and has lost its strength, then two drachms instead of one may be employed. The whole of these are to be mixed in a lotion bottle, and applied every night to the head with a sponge. Wash the head with warm water twice a week, Soft brushes only must be used during the growth of the young hair.

*Ammonical Pomatum for Promoting the Growth of Hair.*—Take almond oil, quarter of a pound; white wax, half an ounce; clarified lard, three ounces; liquid ammonia, a quarter fluid ounce; otto of lavender, and cloves, of each one drachm. Place the oil, wax, and lard, in a jar, which set in boiling water; when the wax is melted, allow the grease to cool till nearly ready to set, then stir in the ammonia and the perfume, and put into small jars for use. Never use a hard brush, nor comb the hair too much Apply the pomade at night only.

*Artificial Bears' Grease.*—Bear's grease is imitated by a mixture of prepared veal suet and beef marrow. It may be scented at pleasure. The following are some of the best compounds sold by that name.

1. Prepared suets, 3 ounces; lard, 1 ounce; olive oil, 1 ounce; oil of cloves 10 drops; compound tincture of benzoin, 1 drachm. Mix.

2. Lard, 1 pound; solution of carbonate of potash, 2 ounces. Mix.

3. Olive oil, 3 pints; white wax, 3 ounces; spermaceti, 1 ounce, scent with oil of roses and oil of bitter almonds.

*Bears' Oil.*—The best description of lard oil, properly perfumed, is far preferable to any other kind of oil.

*Circassian Cream.*—One pint of olive oil: three ounces white wax; two ounces spermaceti; half an ounce alkanet root. Digest the oil with the alkanet till sufficiently colored, strain, melt the wax and spermaceti with the oil, and, when sufficiently cool, add two and a half drachms oil of lavender, one drachm of essence and of ambergies.

*Cosmetic Soap, for Washing the Hands.*—Take a pound of castile soap, or any other nice old soap; scrape it fine; put it on the fire with a little water, stir it to a smooth paste; turn it into a bowl; or any kind of essence; beat it with a silver spoon till well mixed; thicken it with Indian meal, and keep it in small pots, closely covered; exposure to the air will harden it.

*Cosmetic Wash for the Hair.*—Red wine, one pound; salt, one drachm; sulphate of iron, two drachms; boil for a few minutes, add common verdigris, one drachm; leave it on the fire two minutes; withdraw it, and add two drachms of powdered nutgall. Rub the hair with the liquid, in a few minutes dry it with a warm cloth, and afterwards wash with water.

*To Remove Dandruff.*—Take a thimbleful of powdered refined borax, let it dissolve in a teacupful of water, first brush the head well, then wet a brush and apply it to the head. Do this every day for a week, and twice a week for a few times, and you will effectually remove the dandruff.

*To make the Complexion Fair.*—Take emulsion of bitter almonds, one pint; oxymuriate of quicksilver, two and a half grains; sal ammonia, one drachm. Use moderately for pimples, freckles, tanned complexions.

*Eau de Cologne—Cologne Water.*—Oil of lavender, oil of bergamot, oil of lemon, oil of neroli, each one ounce; oil of cinnamon, half an ounce; spirit of rosemary, fifteen ounces; highly rectified spirit, eight pints. Let them stand fourteen days; then distill in a water bath.

2. Essential oils of bergamot, lemon, neroli, orangepeel and rosemary, each twelve drops; cardamon seeds, one drachm; rectified spirits, one pint. It improves by age.

*Eau de Rosieres.*—Spirits of roses, 4 pints; spirits of jessamine, one pint; spirits of orange flowers, one pint; spirits of cucumber, two and a quarter pints; spirits of celery seed, two and a quarter pints; spirits of angelica root, two and three quarter pints; tincture of benzoin, three quarters of a pint; balsam of Mecca, a few drops.

*Eau de Violettes.*—Macerate five ounces of fine orris root in a quart of rectified spirits, for some days, and filter.

*Esprit de Bouquet.*—Oil of lavender, oil of cloves and oil of bergamot, each two drachms; otto of rose, and of oil of cinnamon, each, twenty drops; essence of musk, one drachm; rectified spirits one pint. Mix.

*Essence of Ambergris.*—Spirits of wine, half a pint; ambergris

24 grains. Let it stand for three days in a warm place, and filter.

***Essence of Bergamot.***—Spirits of wine, half a pint; bergamot peel, four ounces; as above.

***Essence of Cedrat.***—Essence of bergamot, one ounce; essence of neroli, two drachms.

***Essence of Cloves.***—Spirits of wine, half a pint; bruised cloves, one ounce.

***Essence for the Headache.***—Spirits of wine, two pounds; roche alum, in fine powder, two ounces; camphor, four ounces; essence of lemon, half an ounce; strong water of ammonia, four ounces. Stop the bottle close, and shake it daily, for three or four days.

***Essence of Lavender.***Essential oil of lavender, three and a half ounces; rectified spirits, two quarts; rose water, half a pint; tincture of orris, half a pint.

***Essence of Lemon.***—Spirits of wine, half a pint; fresh lemon peel, four ounces.

***Essence of Musk.***—Take one pint proof spirit, and add two drachms musk. Let it stand a fortnight, with frequent agitation.

***Essence of Neroli.***—Spirits of wine, half a pint; orange peel cut small, three ounces; orris root in powder, one drachm; musk, two grains.

***Essence for Smelling Bottles.***—Oil of lavender and essence of bergamot, each one drachm; oil of orange peel, eight drops; oil of cinnamon, four drops; oil of neroli, two drops; alcohol and strongest water of ammonia, each two ounces.

***Essence of Verbena Leaf.***—Take rectified spirits of wine, half a pint; otto of verbena, half a drachm; otto of bergamot one drachm; tincture of tolu, quarter of an ounce. Mix them together, and it is ready for use. This sweet scent does not stain the handkerchief and is very economical.

***Essence of Violets.***—Spirits of wine, half a pint; orris root, one ounce. Other essence in the same manner.

***Eye Water,***—Take one pint of rose water, and add one teaspoonful each of spirits of camphor and laudanum. Mix and bottle. To be shaken and applied to the eyes as often as necessary. Perfectly harmless.

*Honey Water.*—Rectified spirits, eight pints; oil of cloves, oil of lavender, oil of bergamot, each half an ounce; musk, eight grains; yellow sandus shavings, four ounces; digest for eight days and add two pints each of orange flower and rose water.

*Lavender Water.*—Oil of lavender, four ounces; spirit, three quarts; rose water, one pint. Mix and filter.

*Lisbon Water.*—To rectified spirit, one gallon, add essential oils of orange peel and lemon peel, of each three ounces, and otto of roses, one quarter of an ounce.

*Odoriferous Lavender Water.*—Rectified spirit, five gallons; essential oil of lavender, twenty ounces; oil of bergamot, five ounces; essence of ambergris, half an ounce.

2. Oil of lavender, three drachms; oil of bergamot, twenty drops, nerolic, six drops; otto of roses, six drops; essence of cedrat, eight drops; essence of musk, twenty drops; rectified spirit, twenty-eight fluid ounces; distilled water, four ounces.

*Queen of Hungary's Water.*—Spirit of rosemary, four pints; orange flower water, one quarter of a pint; essence of neroli, four drops.

## FACE PAINTS.

*Almond Bloom.*—Boil one ounce of Brazil dust in three pints of distilled water, and strain; add six drachms of isinglass, two drachms of cochineal, one ounce of alum, and eight drachms of borax; boil again and strain through a fine cloth.

*Fine Carmine.*—(prepared from cochineal) is used alone, or reduced with starch, etc. And also the coloring matter of safflower and other vegetable colors, in the form of pink saucers, &c.

*Face Powder.*—Starch, one pound; oxide of bismuth, four oz.

*Face Whites.*—French chalk is one of the most innocent; finely powdered. White starch is also used.

*Rouge.*—Mix vermillion with enough gum tragacanth dissolved in water to form a thin paste; add a few drops of almond oil, place the mixture in rough pots, and dry by a very gentle heat.

*Turkish Rouge.*—Take half pint alcohol and one ounce of alkanet; Macerate ten days and pour off the liquid, which should be bottled. This is the simplest and one of the best articles of the kind.

*Caution.*—White lead, and all cosmetic powders containing it should never be applied to the skin, as it is the most dangerous article that could be used.

*Mouth Pastiles, for Perfuming the Breath.*—Extract of licorice, three ounces; oil of cloves, one and a half drachms; oil of cinnamon fifteen drops. Mix, and divide into one-grain pills, and silver them.

2. Catechu, seven drachms; orris powder, forty grains; sugar, three ounces; oil of rosemary, (or of clove, peppermint, or cinnamon,) four drops. Mix, and roll flat on an oiled marble slab, and cut into very small lozenges.

*Oil for the Hair.*—A very excellent ready-made oil for the hair which answers all common purposes, is made by mixing one part brandy with three parts of sweet oil. Add any scent you prefer.

*Oil of Roses.*—Fine olive oil, one pint; otto of roses, sixteen drops. If required red, color with alkanet root, and strain before adding the otto. For common sale essence of bergamot or of lemon is often subtituted, wholly or in part, for the expensive otto.

*Oil to make the Hair Curl*—Olive, one pound; oil of origanum, one drachm; oil of rosemary, one and a quarter drachms.

## HUNTERS AND TRAPPERS SECRETS.

The following secret applies to *all* animals, as every animal is attracted by the peculiar odor in a greater or less degree; but it is best adapted to land animals, such as Foxes, Minks, Sables, Martins, Wolves Bears, Wild Cats, etc., etc.

Take one half pound strained honey, one quarter drachm musk, three drachms oil of lavender, and four pounds of tallow, mix the whole thoroughly together, and make it into forty pills, or balls, and place one of these pills under the pan of each trap when setting it.

The above preparation will most wonderfully attract all kinds of animals, and trappers and others who use it will be sure of success.

*To Catch Foxes.*—Take oil of amber, and beaver's oil, each equal parts, and rub them over the trap before setting it. Set in the usual way.

*To Catch Mink.*—Take oil of amber, and beaver's oil, and rub over the trap. Bait with fish or birds.

*To Catch Muskrat.*—In the female muskrat near the vagina is a small bag which holds from 30 to 40 drops. Now all the trapper has to do, is to procure a few female muskrats and squeeze the contents of a bag into a vial. Now, when in quest of muskrats, sprinkle a few drops of liquid on the bushes over and around the trap. This will attract the male muskrats in large numbers, and if the traps are properly arranged, large numbers of them may be taken.

*\*\*\**In trapping Muskrats, steel traps should be used, and they should be set in the paths and runs of the animals, where they come upon the banks, and in every case the trap should be set under the water, and carefully concealed; and care should be taken that it has sufficient length of chain to enable the animals to reach the water after being caught, otherwise they are liable to escape by tearing or knawing of their legs.

*To Catch Beaver.*—In trapping for beaver, set the trap at the edge of the water or dam, at the point where the animals pass from deep to shoal water, and always beneath the surface, and fasten it by means of a stout chain to a picket driven in the bank, or to a bush or tree. A flat stick should be made fast to the trap by a cord a few feet long, which, if the animal chanced to carry away, the trap would float on the water and point out its position. The trap should then be baited with the following preparation, called

"*The Beaver Medicine.*"

This is prepared from a substance called castor, and is obtained from the glandulous pouches of the *male* animal.

The contents of five or six of these castor bags are mixed with a nutmeg, twelve or fifteen cloves and thirty grains of cinnamon in fine powder, and the whole thing well stirred together with as much whiskey as will give it the consistency of mixed mustard. This preparation must be left closely corked up, and in four or five days the odor becomes wonderful; and this medicine smeared upon the bits of wood etc., with which the traps are baited, will attract the beaver from a great distance, and wishing to make a close inspection, the animal puts its legs into the trap and is caught.

*‌*‌*The same caution in regard to length of chain should be observed for Beaver, as for Otters, Muskrats, etc., for unless they can reach the water they are liable to get out of the trap and escape.

*Chinese Art of Catching Fish.*—Take Cocculus Indicus, pulverize and mix with dough, then scatter it broadcast over the water, as you would sow seed. The fish will sieze it with great avidity, and will instantly become so intoxicated that they will turn belly up on top of the water, by dozens, hundreds, or thousands, as the case may be. All that you now have to do, is to have a boat or other convenience to gather them up, and as you gather put them in a tub of clean water and presently they will be as lively and healthy as ever.

This means of taking fish, and the manner of doing it, has, heretofore, been known to but few. The value of such knowledge admits of no question. This manner of taking fish does not injure the flesh in the least.

*Secret Art of Catching Fish.*—Put the oil of rhodium on the bait, when fishing with the hook, and you will always succeed.

*To Catch Fish.*—Take the juice of smallage or lovage, and mix with any kind of bait. As long as there remain any kind of fish within many yards of your hook, you will find yourself busy pulling them out.

*To Catch Abundance of Eels, Fish, &c.*—Get over the water after dark, with a light and a dead fish that has been smeared with the juice of stinking glawdin—the fish will gather round you in large quantities, and can easily be scooped up.

## THE FINE ARTS AND SCIENCES.

*To Transfer Engravings to Plaster Casts.*—Cover the plate with ink, polish its surface in the usual way, then put a wall of paper round; then pour on it some fine paste made with plaster of

Paris. Jerk it to drive out the air bubbles, and let it stand one hour, when you have a fine impression.

*The New and Beautiful Art of Transferring on to Glass.*—Colored or plain Engravings, Photographs, Lithographs, Water Colors, Oil Colors, Crayons, Steel Plates, Newspaper Cuts, Mezzotinto, Pencil, Writing, Show Cards, Labels,—or in fact anything.

*Directions.*—Take glass that is perfectly clear—window glass will answer—clean it thoroughly; then varnish it, taking care to have it perfectly smooth; place it where it will be entirely from dust; let it stand over night; then take your engraving, lay it in clear water until it is wet through (say ten or fifteen minutes) then lay it upon a newspaper, that the moisture may dry from the surface, and still keep the other side damp. Immediately varnish your glass the second time, then place your engraving on it, pressing it down firmly, so as to exclude every particle of air; next rub the paper from the back, until it is of uniform thickness—so thin that you can see through it, then varnish it the third time, and let it dry.

*Materials used for the above Art.*—Take two ounces balsam of fir, to one ounce of spirits of turpentine; apply with a camel's hair brush.

*The Art of Potchiomoni.*—Take plain glass jars or vases, in any shape, and clean them thoroughly; then obtain two or three sheets of figures, flowers, or views, in imitation of Chinese, Egyptian, or Swiss painting. These goods, as well as the jars, can be obtained in any of the principal cities. Now, in whatever style you determine to ornament your vase or jar in, cut out the figures from your sheet, and secure them in different parts inside your jar, with the figures looking outwards. The best material for making them adhere is, to boil a piece of parchment; this makes a good size. Having secured the prints, make a varnish of balsam of fir and turpentine, and apply all over inside with a fine brush. When the first coat is dry, give another coat; now take any color you choose—black, blue, green, yellow, white; pink, brown or red—and grind the paint fine, with the best white varnish, and apply a coat of this paint over the whole inside; let it dry, and then repeat coat upon coat, until the color is sufficiently strong to show even and bright outside. Jars and vases may be decorated in endless variety by this method. Some use cuttings from prints, silks, &c.

*New Method of Embalming.*—Mix together five pounds dry sulphate of alumine, one quart of warm water, and one hundred grains of arsenious acid. Inject three or four quarts of this mixture into all the vessels of the human body. This applies as well to all animals, birds, fishes, &c. This process supersedes the old and revolting mode, and has been introduced into the great anatomical schools of Paris.

*To Make Wax Flowers.*—The following articles will be required to commence wax work: 2 pounds white wax, ¼ pound hair wire, 1 bottle carmine, 1 ultramarine blue, 1 bottle chrome yellow, 2 bottles chrome green, No. 1, 2 bottles chrome green, No. 2, 1 bottle rose pink, 1 bottle royal purple, 1 bottle scarlet powder, 1 bottle balsam fir, 2 dozen sheets white wax. This will do to begin with. Now have a clean tin dish and pour therein a quart or two of water; then put in about 1 pound of the white wax and let it boil; when cool enough, so the bubbles will not form on top, it is ready to sheet, which is done as follows:—Take half of a window pane, 7x9, and, after having washed it clean, dip into a dish containing weak soap-suds; then dip into the wax and draw out steadily and plunge it into the suds, when the sheet will readily come off. Lay it on a cloth or clean paper to dry. Proceed in like manner until you have enough of the white; then add enough of the green powder to make a bright color, and heat and stir thoroughly until the color is evenly distributed; then proceed as for sheeting white wax. The other colors are rubbed into the leaves after they are cut out, rubbing light or heavy according to shade.

For patterns you can use any natural leaf, forming the creases in wax with the thumb nail or a needle; to put the flowers together or the leaves onto the stem, hold in the hand until warm enough to stick. If the sheeted wax is to be used in summer, put in a little balsam of fir to make it hard. If for winter, none will be required.

You can make many flowers without a teacher; but one to assist in the commencement, would be a great help; though the most particular thing about it is to get the wax sheeted. The materials I have suggested can be procured at any drug store, and will cost from $3 to $4.50.

## FARMERS' DEPARTMENT.

*How to get New Varities of Potatoes.*—When the vines are done growing and are turned brown; the seed is ripe; then take the balls and string with a large needle and strong thread; hang them in a dry place, where they will gradually dry and mature, without danger or injury from frost. In the month of April, soak the ball for several hours from the pulp, when washed and dried, they are fit for sowing in rows, in a bed well prepared in the garden; they will sprout in a fortnight; they must be attended to like other vegetables. When about two inches high, they may be thinned and transplanted into rows. As they increase in size, they should be hilled. In the autumn many of them will be the size of a walnut, and from that to a pea. In the following spring they should be planted in hills, placing the large ones together,—they will in the second season attain their full size, and will exhibit several varieties of form, and may then be selected to suit the judgment of the cultivater. I would prefer gathering the balls from potatoes of a good kind. The first crop from seeds thus obtained, will be productive, and will continue so for many years, gradually deteriorating, until they will need a renewal by the process.

*To Destroy Rats.*—Fill any deep smooth vessel of considerable capacity to within six inches of the top with water, cover the surface with bran, and set the vessel in a place most frequented by these pests. In attempting to get at the bran they will fall in and be drowned. Several dozen have been taken by this simple method at a time.

*To Kill Rats in Barn and Rick.*—Melt hogs lard in a bottle plunged in water of temperature of 150° Fahrenheit; introduced into it half an ounce of phosphorus for every pound of lard; then add a pint of proof spirits or whiskey; cork the bottle firmly after its contents have been to 150°, taking it out of the water and agitating till the phosphorus becomes uniformly diffused, making a milky looking fluid. The spirit may be poured off on the liquor cooling; and you then have a fatty compound, which after being warmed gently, may be incorporated with a mixture of wheat flower, or sugar, flavored with oil of rhodium, or oil of aniseseed, etc., and the dough, on being made into pellets, should be laid at the rat holes; being luminous in the dark and, agreeable both to the palates and noses, it is readily eaten, and proves certainly fatal. The rats issue from their holes and seek for water to quench their burning thirst, and they commonly die near the water.

*Rat Poison.*—Flour, six pounds; sugar, one pound; sulphur, four pounds; phosphorus, four pounds.

## RECIPES FOR HORSES.

*Blistering Liniment.*—Powdered Spanish flies, one ounce; spirits turpentine, six ounces. Rub on the belly for pain in the bowels, or on the surface for internal inflammation.

*Cathartic Powder.*—To cleanse out horses in the spring, making them sleek and healthy; black sulphuret of antimony, nitre, and sulphur, each equal parts. Mix well together and give a tablespoonful every morning.

*Cough Ball for Horses.*—Pulverized ipecac, three quarters of an ounce; camphor, two ounces; squills, half an ounce. Mix with honey to form into a mass, and divide into eight balls. Give one every morning.

*Diuretic Balls.*—Castile soap scraped fine, powdered resin, each three teaspoonfuls; powdered nitre, four teaspoonfuls; oil of juniper, one small teaspoonful; honey, a sufficient quantity to make into a ball.

*To Prevent Horses from Being Teased by Flies.*—Boil three handfuls of walnut leaves in three quarts of water; sponge the horse (before going out of the stable) between and upon the ears, neck and flank.

*To Prevent Botts.*—Mix a little wood-ashes with their drink daily. This effectually preserves horses against the botts.

*Liniment for Galled Backs of Horses.*—White lead moistened with milk. When milk cannot be procured, oil may be substituted. One or two ounces will last two months or more.

*Remedy for Strains in Horses.*—Take whiskey, one half pint; camphor, one ounce; sharp vinegar, one pint. Mix. Bathe the parts affected.

*Another.*—Take opodeldoc, warm it, and rub the strained part two or three times a day.

*Lotion for Blows, Bruises, Sprains, &c.*—One part laudanum, two parts oil origanum, four parts water ammonia, four parts oil of turpentine, four parts camphor, thirty-two parts spirits of wine. Put them into a bottle, and shake them until mixed.

*Fever Ball.*—Emetic tartar and camphor, each half an ounce; nitre, two ounces. Mix with linseed meal and molasses to make eight balls. Give one twice a day.

*Liniment for Sprains, Swellings, &c.*—Aqua ammonia, spirits camphor, each two ounces; oil origanum, and laudanum, each half an ounce. Mix.

*Lotion for Mange.*—Boil two ounces tobacco in one quart water; strain; add sulphur and soft soap, each, two ounces.

*Purgative Ball.*—Aloes, one ounce; cream tartar and castile soap, one quarter of an ounce. Mix with molasses to make a ball.

## CONFECTIONERS' DEPARTMENT.

*Ginger Candy.*—Boil a pound of clarified sugar until, upon taking out a drop of it on a piece of stick, it will become brittle when cold. Mix and stir up with it, for a common article, about a teaspoonful of ground ginger; if for a superior article, instead of the ground ginger add half the white of an egg, beaten up previously with fine sifted loaf sugar, and twenty drops of strong essence of ginger.

*Another.*—Take coarsely powdered ginger, two ounces; boiling water one and a quarter pints; macerate in a warm place for two hours, strain, and add seven pounds each of loaf and brown sugar.

*Ginger Drops.*—Are the same, except that they are made with all loaf sugar.

*Ginger Lozenges.*—Dissolve in one quarter of a pint of hot water half an ounce of gum arabic; when cold, stir it up with one and a half pounds of loaf sugar, and a spoonful of powdered ginger, or twelve drops of essence of ginger. Roll and beat the whole up into a paste; make it into a flat cake, and punch out the lozenges with a round stamp; dry them near the fire or in an oven.

*Peppermint Lozenges.*—Best powdered white sugar, seven lbs.; pure starch, one lb.; oil of peppermint to flavor. Mix with mucilage.

*Peppermint, Rose or Hoarhound Candy.*—They may be made as lemon candy. Flavor with essence of rose, or peppermint or finely powdered hoarhound. Pour it out in a buttered paper, placed in a square tin pan.

*To Clarify Sugar for Candies.*—To every pound of sugar, put a large cup of water, and put it in a brass or copper kettle, over a slow fire, for half an hour; pour into it a small quantity of isinglass and gum arabic, dissolved together. This will cause all impurities to rise to the surface; skim it as it rises. Flavor according to taste.

All kinds of sugar for candy, are boiled as above directed. When boiling loaf sugar, add a tablespoonful of rum or vinegar, to prevent its becoming too brittle whilst making.

Loaf sugar when boiled, by pulling and making into small rolls, and twisting a little, will make what is called little rock, or snow. By pulling loaf sugar after it is boiled, you can make it as white as snow.

*Common Twist Candy,*—Boil three pounds of common sugar and one pint of water over a slow fire for half an hour, without skimming. When boiled enough take it off; rub the hands over with butter, take that which is a little cooled, and pull it as you would molasses candy, until it is white; then twist or braid it, and cut it up in strips.

*Fine Peppermint Lozenges.*—Best powdered white sugar, seven pounds; pure starch, one pound; oil of peppermint to flavor. Mix with mucilage.

*Everton Taffee.*—To make this favorite and wholesome candy, take 1½ pounds of moist sugar, 3 ounces of butter, a teacup and a half of water and one lemon. Boil the sugar, butter, water, and half the rind of the lemon together, and when done—which will be known by dropping into cold water, when it should be quite crisp—let it stand aside till the boiling has ceased, and then stir in the juice of the lemon. Butter a dish, and pour it in about a quarter of an inch in thickness. The fire must be quick, and the taffee stirred all the time.

*Candy Fruit.*—Take 1 pound of the best loaf sugar; dip each lump into a bowl of water, and put the sugar into your preserving kettle. Boil it down and skim it until perfectly clear, and in a candying state. When sufficiently boiled, have ready the fruits you wish to preserve. Large white grapes, oranges separated into small pieces, or preserved fruits, taken out of their syrup and dried, are very nice. Dip the fruits into the prepared sugar while it is hot; put them in a cold place; they will soon become hard.

*Popped Corn.*—Dipped in boiling molasses and stuck together forms an excellent candy.

*Liquorice Lozenges.*—Extract of liquorice, 1 pound, powdered white sugar, 2 pounds. Mix with mucilage made with rose-water.

*Fig Candy.*—Take 1 pound of sugar and 1 pint of water, set over a slow fire. When done, add a few drops of vinegar and a lump of butter, and pour into pans in which split figs are laid.

*Raisin Candy.*—Can be made in the same manner, substituting stoned raisins for the figs. Common molasses candy is very nice with all kinds of nuts added.

*Scotch Butter Candy.*—Take 1 pound of sugar, 1 pint of water; dissolve and boil. When done add 1 tablespoonful of butter, and enough lemon juice and oil of lemon to flavor.

*Icing for Cakes.*—Beat the whites of two small eggs to a high froth; then add to them a quarter of a pound of white, ground or powdered sugar; beat it well until it will lie in a heap; flavor with lemon or rose. This will frost the top of a common-sized cake. Heap what you suppose to be sufficient in the centre of of the cake, then dip a broad-bladed knife in cold water, and spread the ice evenly over the whole surface.

*Saffron Lozenges.*—Finely powdered hay-saffron, one ounce; finely powdered sugar, one pound; finely powdered starch, eight ounces. Mucilage to mix.

*Chocolate Cream.*—Chocolate, scraped fine, ½ ounce, thick cream, 1 pint; sugar, (best,) 3 ounces; heat it nearly to boiling, then remove it from the fire, and mill it well. When cold add the whites of four or five eggs; whisk rapidly and take up the froth on a sieve; serve the cream in glasses, and pile up the froth on the top of them.

***Candied Lemon or Peppermint for Colds.***—Boil 1½ pounds sugar in a half pint of water, till it begins to candy round the sides; put in eight drops of essence; pour it upon buttered paper, and cut it with a knife.

## FOR THE HOUSEHOLD AND EVERY DAY REQUIREMENTS.

***Alum in Starch.***—For starching muslins, ginghams, and calicoes, dissolve a piece of alum the size of a shellbark, for every pint of starch, and add to it. By so doing the colors will keep bright for a long time, which is very desirable when dresses must be often washed, and the cost is but a trifle.

***Cider Yeast.***—Take cider from sour apples, before it ferments, scald, skim thoroughly, and pour, while hot, upon flour enough to make a stiff batter. When cool, add yeast of any kind, and let it rise, stirring it down as often as it tries to run over for several days, then put it in a cool place (where it will not freeze), and you will have something equal to the best hop yeast. It will keep until May without any further labor.

***To Destroy Cockroaches.***—The following is said to be effectual. These vermin are easily destroyed, simply by cutting up green cucumbers at night, and placing them about where roaches commit depredations. What is cut from the cucumbers in preparing them for the table answers the purpose as well, and three applications will destroy all the roaches in the house. Remove the peelings in the morning, and renew them at night.

***Fire Kindlers.***—Take a quart of tar and three pounds of resin, melt them, bring to a cooling temperature, mix with as much sawdust, with a little charcoal added, as can be worked in; spread out while hot upon a board, when cold break up into lumps of the size of a large hickory nut, and you have, at a small expense, kindling material enough for a household for one year. They will easily ignite from a match and burn with a strong blaze, long enough to start any wood that is fit to burn.

***Remedy against Moths.***—An ounce of gum camphor and one of the powdered shell of red pepper are macerated in eight ounces of strong alcohol for several days, then strained. With this tincture the furs or cloth are sprinkled over, and rolled up in sheets. Instead of the pepper, bitter apple may be used. This remedy is used in Russia under the name of the Chinese tincture of moths,

*Substitute for Yeast.*—Boil one pound of flour, one quarter pound of brown sugar and a little salt in two gallons of water for one hour. When milk-warm, bottle and cork close, and it will be ready for use in twenty-four hours.

*To Make Lye.*—Have a large tub or cask and bore a hole on one side for a tap, near the bottom; place several bricks near the hole and cover them with straw. Fill the barrel with strong wood ashes. Oak ashes are strongest, and those of apple tree wood make the whitest soap. Pour on boiling water until it begins to run, then put in the tap and let it soak. If the ashes settle down as they are wet, fill it until full.

*Tomato Wine.*—Take ripe fresh tomatoes, mash very fine, strain through a fine sieve, sweeten with good sugar, to suit the taste, set it away in an earthen or glass vessel, nearly full, cover tight, with exception of a small hole for the refuse to work off through during its fermentation. When it is done fermenting it will become pure and clear. Then bottle, and cork tight. A little salt improves its flavor; age improves it.

*To Color Brown on Cotton or Woolen.*—For ten pounds of cloth boil three pounds of catechu in as much water as needed to cover the goods. When dissolved, add four ounces of blue vitriol; stir it well; put in the cloth and let it remain all night; in the morning drain it thoroughly; put four ounces of bi-chromate of potash in boiling water sufficient to cover your goods; let it remain fifteen minutes; wash in cold water; color in iron.

*To Cleanse and Brighten Faded Brussels Carpet.*—Boil some bran in water and with this wash the carpet with a flannel and brush, using Fuller's earth for the worst parts. When dry the carpet must be well beaten to get out the fuller's earth, then washed over with a weak solution of alum to brighten the colors. Some housekeepers cleanse and brighten carpets by sprinkling them first with fine salt and then sweeping them thoroughly.

*To give Stoves a fine Brilliant Appearance.*—A teaspoonful of pulverized alum mixed with stove polish will give the stove a fine lustre, which will be quite permanent.

*Method of Keeping Hams in Summer.*—Make bags of unbleached muslin; place in the bottom a little good sweet hay; put in the ham, and then press around and over it firmly more hay; tie the bag and hang up in a dry place. Ham secured in this way will keep for years.

*How to Cause Vegetables and Fruits to Grow to an Enormous Size and also to Increase the Brilliancy and Fragrancy of Flowers.*—A curious discovery has recently been made public in France, in regard to the culture of vegetable and fruit trees. By watering with a solution of sulphate of iron, the most wonderful fecundity has been attained. Pear-trees and beans, which have been submitted to this treatment, have nearly doubled in the size of their productions, and a noticeable improvement has been remarked in their flavor. Dr. Becourt reports that while at the head of an establishment at Eughien, or the sulphurous springs, he had the gardens and plantations connected with it watered, during several weeks of the early spring, with sulphurous water, and not only the plantations prospered to a remarkable extent, but flowers acquired a peculiar brilliancy of coloring and healthy aspect which attracted universal attention.

*Drying Corn.*—With a sharp knife shave the corn from the ear, then scrape the cob, leaving one-half the hull clinging to the cob. Place a tin or earthen vessel two-thirds full of this "milk of corn" over a kettle of boiling water, stir frequently until dry enough to spread upon a firm cloth without sticking, when the wind and sun (away from dust and flies) will soon complete the process. To prepare for the table, put in cold water, set it where it will become hot, but not boil, for two hours; then season with salt and pepper, boil for ten minutes; add of butter and white sugar a tablespoonful of each just before ready to serve.

*To Destroy Lice on Chickens.*—The following will kill lice on the first application: Put six cents worth of cracked *Coculus Indicus* berries into a bottle that will hold a half pint of alcohol; fill the bottle with alcohol, and let it stand twenty-four hours. When the hen comes off with the young chickens, take the mixture, and with a small cotton rag, wet the head of each chicken enough to have it reach through the little feathers to the skin; also with the same rag, wet the hen under her wings. Be careful that no child, nor any one else, uses it, because it is a *deadly poison.*

*Cracked Wheat.*—For a pint of the cracked grain, have two quarts of water boiling in a smooth iron pot over a quick fire; stir in the wheat slowly; boil fast and stir constantly for the first half hour cooking, or until it begins to thicken and "pop up;" then lift from the quick fire, and place the pot where the wheat will cook slowly for an hour longer. Keep it covered closely, stir now and then, and be careful not to let it burn at the bottom. Wheat cooked thus is much sweeter and richer than when left to soak and simmer for hours, as many think necessary. White wheat cooks the easiest. When ready to dish out, have your moulds moistered with cold water, cover lightly, and set in a cool place. Eat warm or cold with milk and sugar.

*How to have Green Pea Soup in Winter.*—Sow peas thickly in pots and boxes, say six weeks before the soup is wanted. Place them in a temperature of 60° or so, close to the glass in a house or pit. Cut the plants as soon as they attain a height of from three to six inches, and rub them through a sieve. The shoots alone will make a fair soup. Mixed with dry peas, also passed through a sieve, no one could scarcely distinguish color or flavor from that of real green pea soup. There is, however, considerable difference in the flavor of pea leaves, as well as of the peas themselves. The best marrows, such as Ne Plus Ultra and Veitche's Perfection, yield the most piquant cuttings. Also the more light the plants receive the higher the flavor, plants drawn up or at all blanched, being by no means comparable with those well and strongly grown.

In the spring, a few patches or rows may be sown in open quarters expressly for green cuttings. These are most perfect and full flavored when four inches high. When too long the flavor seems to have run to wood, and the peculiar aroma of green peas is weaker.

There is yet another mode of making green pea soup at any season at very short notice. Chip the peas by steeping them in water and leaving them in a warm place for a few days. Then slightly boil or stew, chips and all, and pass them through a sieve. The flavor is full and good, though such pea soup lacks color. It is astonishing how much the mere vegetation of seeds develops their more active and predominant flavor or qualities;

a fact that might often be turned to useful account in the kitchen in flavoring of soups or dishes, with turnips, celery, parsley, &c.

*Composition for Restoring Scorched Linen.*—Boil, to a good consistency, in half a pint of vinegar, two ounces of Fuller's earth, an ounce of hen's dung, half an ounce of cake soap, and the juice of two onions. Spread this composition over the whole of the damaged part; and if the scorching is not quite through, and the threads actually consumed, after suffering it to dry on, and letting it receive a subsequent good washing or two, the place will appear full as white and perfect as any other part of the linen.

*To Remove Indelible Ink Stains.*—Soak the stained spot in strong salt water, then wash it with ammonia. Salt changes the nitrate of silver into chloride of silver, and ammonia dissolves the chloride.

*To Cook Cauliflower.*—Choose those that are close and white and of middle size, trim off the outside leaves, cut the stalk off flat at the bottom, let them lie in salt and water an hour before you boil them. Put them into boiling water with a handful of salt in it, skim it well and let it boil slowly till done. Fifteen minutes will suffice for a small one, and twenty will be long enough for a large one. If it is boiled a minute or two after it is done the flavor will be impaired.

*To Pickle String Beans.*—Place them in a pan with alternate layers of salt and leave them thus for twenty-four hours. Drain them and place them in a jar with allspice, cloves, pepper, and a little salt. Boil enough vinegar to cover them, pour over them and let them stand till the next day, boil the vinegar the second time, and pour it on again. The next day boil the vinegar for the last time, pour it over the beans, and when quite cold, cover the jar tightly and set in a cool closet.

*Chili Sauce.*—Twelve ripe tomatoes, four ripe peppers, two onions, two tablespoofuls of salt, two tablespoonfuls of sugar, three tea-cups of vinegar, a little cinnamon; peel the tomatoes and chop them fine, also the peppers and onions, and boil all together one hour.

*How to Cause a Baby to Thrive and Grow.*—Try the milk first drawn from a cow that is fresh, add one-quarter water, and a little sugar. If the milk constipates, sweeten it with molasses, or mix with it a small quantity of magnesia. Abjure soothing syrups, and for colic give catnip or smellage tea. Give the baby a tepid bath at night as well as in the morning, rubbing him well with the hand. After the bath, let him feed and then sleep, We find open air the best tonics for babies. Ours takes his naps out of doors in the shade during the warm weather, and his cheeks are two roses.

*To Can Gooseberries without Breaking them.*—Fill the cans with berries, and partly cover with water, set the jars into a vessel of water, and raise the temperature to the boiling point. Boil eight minutes, remove from the kettle, cover with boiling water, and seal immediately. If sugar is used, let it be pure white, and allow eight ounces to a quart of berries. Make into a syrup, and use in the cans instead of water. The glass cans with glass tops, a rubber and a screw ring, we have found the simplest and most perfect of the many kinds offered for sale in the market.

*Ready Mode of Mending Cracks in Stoves, Pipes, and Iron Ovens.*—When a crack is discovered in a stove, through which the fire or smoke penetrates, the aperture may be completely closed in a moment with a composition consisting of wood ashes and common salt, made up into paste with a little water, and plastered over the crack. The good effect is equally certain, whether the stove, etc., be cold or hot.

*Preservation of Milk and Cream.*—Put the milk into bottles, then place them in a saucepan with cold water, and gradually raise it to the boiling point; take it from the fire, and instantly cork the bottles, then raise the milk once more to the boiling point for half a minute. Finally let the bottles cool in the water in which they were boiled. Milk thus treated will remain perfectly good for six months. Emigrants, especially those having children will find the above hint add much to their comfort while on their voyage.

*To Keep Milk from Turning Sour.*—Add a little sub-carbonate of soda, or of potash. This by combining with, and neutralizing the acetic acid formed, has the desired effect, and keeps the milk from turning sooner than it otherwise would. The addition is perfectly harmless, and does not injure the taste.

*Strawberry Vinegar.*—Put four pounds of very ripe strawberries, nicely dressed, into three quarts of the best vinegar, and let them stand three or four days; then drain the vinegar through a jelly-bag, and pour it on the same quantity of fruit. Repeat the process in the days for a third time. Finally, to each pound of the liquor thus obtained, add one pound of fine sugar. Bottle, and let it stand covered, but not tightly corked, one week; then cork it tight, and set it in a cool, *dry* place, where it will not freeze. Raspberry vinegar is made the same way.

*Cider Vinegar.*—After cider has become too sour for use, set it in a warm place, put to it occasionally the rinsings of the sugar basin or molasses jug, and any remains of ale or cold tea; let it remain with the bung open, and you will soon have the best of vinegar.

*To give Lustre to Silver.*—Dissolve a quantity of alum in water, so as to make a pretty strong brine, and skim it carefully; then add some soap to it, and dip a linen rag in it, and rub over the silver.

*To make Water-Proof Porous Cloth.*—Close water-proof cloth fabrics, such as glazed oil-cloth, Indian-rubber, and guttapercha cloth are completely water-proof, put do not permit perspiration and the exhalted gases from the skin to pass through them, because they are air-tight as well as water-tight. Persons who wear air-tight garments soon become faint, if they are undergoing severe exercise, such as that to which soldiers are exposed when on march. A porous, water-proof cloth, therefore, is the best for outer garments during wet weather, for those whose duties or labor causes them to prespire freely. The best way for preparing such cloth is by the following process: Take $2\frac{1}{4}$ lbs. of alum and dissolve this in 10 gallons of boiling water; then in a separate vessel dissolve the same quantity of sugar of lead in 10 gallons of water, and mix the two solutions. The cloth is now well handled in this liquid, until every part of it is penetrated; then it is squeezed and dried in the air, or in a warm apartment, then washed in cold water and dried again, when it is fit for use. If necessary, the cloth may be dipped in the liquid and dried twice before being washed. The liquor appears curdled, when the alum and lead solutions are mixed together. This is the result of double decomposition, the sulphate of lead, which is an insoluble salt, being formed. The sulphate of lead is taken up in the pores of the cloth, and it is unaffected by rains or moisture, and yet it does not render the cloth air-tight. Such cloth is also partially non-inflammable. A solution of alum itself will render cloth, prepared as described, partially waterproof, but it is not so good as the sulphate of lead. Such cloth —cotton or woolen—sheds rain like the feathers on the back of a duck.

*To Cleanse Carpet.*—1 teaspoonful liquid ammonia in 1 gallon warm water, will often restore the color of carpets, even if produced by acid or alkali. If a ceiling has been whitewashed with carpet down, and a few drops are visible, this will remove it. Or, after the carpet is well beaten and brushed, scour it with oxgall, which will not only extract grease but freshen the colors—1 pint of gall in three gallons of warm water, will do a large carpet. Table floor-cloths may be thus washed. The suds left from a wash where ammonia is used, even if almost cold, cleanses these floor-cloths well.

*To Keep Hams.*—After the meat has been well cured by pickle and smoke, take some clean ashes from bits of coal; moisten them with a little water so that they will form a paste, or else just wet the hams a little, and rub on the dry ashes. Rubbed in thoroughly they serve as a capital insect protector, and the hams can be hung up in the smoke-house or wood-chamber without any danger of molestation.

*A Cold Cement for Mending Earthenware,* says a recent English work, reckoned a great secret among workmen, is made by grating a pound of old cheese, with a bread grater, into a quart of milk, in which it must be left for a period of fourteen hours. It should be stirred quite often. A pound of unslaked lime, finely pulverized in a mortar, is then added, and the whole is thoroughly mixed by beating. This done, the whites of twenty-five eggs are incorporated with the rest, and the whole is ready for use. There is another cement for the same purpose which is used hot. It is made of resin, beeswax, brick dust, and chalk boiled together. The substances to be cemented must be heated, and when the surfaces are coated with cement, they must be rubbed hard upon each other, as in making a glue joint with wood.

*How to Make Cucumber Vines Bear Five Crops.*—When a cucumber is taken from the vine let it be cut with a knife leaving about the eight of an inch of the cucumber on the stem, then slit the stem with a knife from the end to the vine, leaving a small portion of the cucumber on each division, and on each separate slit there will be a new cucumber as large as the first.

*White Cement.*—Take white (fish) glue, 1 lb. 10 oz., dry white lead 6 oz.; soft water 3 pints; alcohol 1 pint.

Dissolve the glue by putting it in a tin kettle or dish, containing the water, and set this dish in a kettle of water, to prevent the glue from being burned; when the glue is all dissolved, put in the lead and stir and boil until it is thoroughly mixed; remove from the fire, and when cool enough to bottle, add the alcohol, and bottle while it is yet warm, keeping it corked. This last recipe has been sold about the country for from twenty-five cents to five dollars, and one man gave a horse for it.

*To Clean Furniture.*—An old cabinet maker says the best preparation for cleaning picture frames and restoring furniture, especially that somewhat marred or scratched, is a mixture of three parts linseed oil and one part spirits of turpentine. It not only covers the disfigured surface, but restores wood to its natural color, and leaves a lustre upon its surface. Put on with a woolen cloth, and when dry, rub with woolen.

*Bruises on Furniture.*—Wet the part in warm water; double a piece of brown paper five or six times, soak in the warm water, and lay it on the place, apply on that a warm, but not hot, flat-iron till the moisture is evaporated. If the bruise be not gone repeat the process. After two or three applications the dent will be raised to the surface. If the bruise be small, merely soak it with warm water, and hold a red-hot iron near the surface keeping the surface continually wet—the bruise will soon disappear.

*To Prevent Iron Rust.*—Kerosene applied to stoves or farming implements, during summer, will prevent their rusting.

*To Color Sheep Skins.*—Unslaked lime and litharge equal parts, mixed to a thin paste with water, will color buff—several coats will make it a dark brown; by adding a little ammonia and nitrate of silver a fine black is produced. Terra japonica will impart a "tan color" to wool, and the red shade is deepened by sponging with a solution of lime and water, using a strong solution of alum water to "set" the colors; 1 part crystalized nitrate silver, 5 parts carbonate ammonia, and 1½ parts of soft water dyes brown; every additional coat darkens the color until a black is obtained.

*Remedy for Burns.*—Take one teacup of lard and the whites of two eggs; work together as much as it can be, then spread on cloths and apply. Change as often as necessary.

*How Summer Suits should be Washed.*—Summer suits are nearly all made of white or buff linen, pique, cambric, or muslin, and the art of preserving the new appearance after washing is a matter of the greatest importance. Common washwomen spoil everything with soda, and nothing is more frequent than to see the delicate tints of lawns and percales turned into dark blotches and muddy streaks by the ignorance and vandalism of a laundress. It is worth while for ladies to pay attention to this, and insist upon having their summer dresses washed according to the directions which they should be prepared to give their laundresses themselves. In the first place, the water should be tepid, the soap should not be allowed to touch the fabric; it should be washed and rinsed quick, turned upon the wrong side, and hung in the shade to dry, and when starched (in thin boiled but not boiling starch) should be folded in sheets or towels, and ironed upon the wrong side as soon as possible. But linen should be washed in water in which hay or a quart bag of bran has been boiled. This last will be found to answer for starch as well, and is excellent for pink dresses of all kinds, but a handful of salt is very useful also to set the colors of light cambrics and dotted lawns; and a little ox gall will not only set but brighten yellow and purple tints, and has a good affect upon green.

*How to Fasten Rubber to Wood and Metal.*—As rubber plates and rings are now-a-days used almost exclusively for making connections between steam and other pipes and apparatus, much annoyance is often experienced by the impossibility or imperfection of an air-tight connection. This is obviated entirely by employing a cement which fastens alike well to the rubber and to the metal or wood. Such cement is prepared by a solution of shellac in ammonia. This is best made by soaking pulverized gum shellac in ten times its weight of strong ammonia, when a slimy mass is obtained, which in three or four weeks will become liquid without the use of hot water. This softens the rubber, and becomes, after volatilization of the ammonia, hard and impermeable to gases and fluids.

*Renewing Maroon Colors on Wool.*—Wash the goods in very weak lye; then rinse thoroughly in clear water; thus you have a beautiful, *even* color, although your goods have been much faded and stained. Though the color thus obtained may not be the exact shade as when new, it is, however, a very pretty one. The above will not answer for other than all woolen goods of a maroon color.

*To make Water-Proof Cloth out of thick Ducking.*—The following French recipe is given: ' Take two pounds four ounces of alum, and dissolve it in ten gallons of water. In like manner dissolve the same quantity of sugar of lead in a similar quantity of water, and mix the two together. They form a precipitate of the sulphate of lead. The clear liquor is now withdrawn, and the cloth immersed one hour in the solution, when it is taken out and dried in the shade, washed in clean water and dried again.

*Cochineal Coloring.*—The following is a good recipe:—Cochineal, alum, cream tartar carb. potassa, each three drachms; water, eight ounces; sugar six ounces. Rub the cochineal, alum and cream tartar, with eight ounces boiling water, and, when cold, gradually add carb. potassa, and strain; pour water on the strainer sufficient to measure eight fluid ounces, then add the sugar.

*How to Stop a Pinhole in Lead Pipe.*—Take a ten-penny nail, place the square end upon the hole, and hit it two or three slight blows with s hammer, and the orifice is closed as tight as though you had employed a plumber to do it at a cost of a dollar or more.

*To Build a Chimney that Will Not Smoke.*—The *Scientific American* gives the following hints to those who would "build a chimney that would not smoke:"—The chief point is to make the throat not less than four inches broad and 12 long; then the chimney should be abruptly enlarged to double the size, and so continue for one foot or more; then it may be gradually tapered off as desired. But the inside of the chimney throughout its whole length to the top, should be plastered very smooth with good mortar, which will harden with age. The area of a chimney should be at least half a square foot, and no flues less than sixty square inches. The best shape for a chimney is circular, or many-sided, as giving less friction, (brick is the best material as it is a non-conductor,) and the higher above the roof the better.

*To Prevent Turners' Wood Splitting.*—Small pieces of valuable wood, such kinds as are used for turning, etc., are very liable to split readily—that is, outward from the centre. To prevent this, soak the pieces, when first cut, in *cold* water for twenty-four hours, then boil in hot water for two or three hours, and afterward dry slowly, and under cover. This will be found useful in making handsome mantle, toilet, and other articles from sumac, cherry, and other woods that never grow very large.

*To remove Dry Paint on Windows.*—The most economical way to remove dry paint from the panes is to make a small swab having a handle some eight inches long, dip it in a little diluted oxalic acid, and rub off the paint with a swab.

*Everlasting Fence Posts.*—I discovered many years ago that wood could be made to last longer than iron in the ground but thought the process so simple and inexpensive that it was not worth while making any stir about it. I would as soon have poplar, basswood, or quaking ash as any other kind of timber for fence posts. I have taken out basswood posts after having been set seven years, which were as sound when taken out as when they were first put in the ground. Time and weather seemed to have no effect on them. The posts can be prepared for less than two cents a piece. This is the recipe: Take boiled linseed oil and stir it in pulverized charcoal to the consistency of paint. Put a coat of this over the timber, and there is not a man who will live to see it rotten.

*How to Test the Richness of Milk.*—Procure any long glass vessel—a cologne bottle or long phial. Take a narrow strip of paper, just the length from the neck to the bottom of the phial, and mark it off with one hundred lines at equal distances; or fifty lines, and count each as two, and paste it upon the phial, so as to divide its length into a hundred equal parts. Fill it to the highest mark with milk fresh from the cow, and allow it to stand in a perpendicular position twenty-four hours. The number of spaces occupied by the cream will give you its exact precentage in the milk without any guess work.

*To Mend Tinware by the heat of a Candle.*—Take a vial about two-thirds full of muriatic acid, and put into it little bits of sheet zinc as long as it dissolves them; then put in a crump of sal-ammonias, and fill it up with water, and it is ready for use.

Then, with the cork of the vial, wet the place to be mended with the preparation; then put a piece of sheet zinc over the hole, and hold a lighted candle or spirit-lamp under the place, which melts the solder on the tin, and causes the zinc to adhere without further trouble. Wet the zinc also with the solution; or a little solder may be put on instead of the zinc, or with the zinc.

*To Remove Stains.*—The stains of ink on cloth, paper, or wood may be removed by almost all acids; but those acids are to be preferred which are least likely to injure the texture of the stained substance. The muriatic acid, diluted with five or six times its weight of water, may be applied to the spot, and after a minute or two may be washed off, repeating the application as often as may be necessary. But the vegetable acids are attended with less risk, and are equally effected. A solution of the oxalic, citric (acid of lemons), or tartareous acids in water may be applied to the most delicate fabrics, without any danger of injuring them; and the same solutions will discharge writing but not printing ink. Hence they may be applied in cleaning books which have been defaced by writing on the margin, without imparing the text. Lemon-juice and the juice of sorrels will also remove ink-stains, but not so easily as the concrete acid of lemons or citric acid.

*To Prevent Snow-water or Rain from Penetrating the Soles of Shoes or Boots in Winter.*—This simple and effectual remedy is nothing more than a little beeswax and mutton suet, warmed in a pipkin until in a liquid state. Then rub some of it lightly over the edges of the sole where the stiches are, which will repel the wet, and not in the least prevent the blacking from having the usual effect.

*An Easy Method of preventing Moths in Furs or Woolens.*—Sprinkle the furs or woolen stuffs, as well as the drawers or boxes in which they are kept, with spirits of turpentine; the unpleasant scent of which will speedily evaporate on exposure of the stuffs to the air. Some people place sheets of paper, moistened with spirits of turpentine, over, under, or between pieces of cloth, etc., and find it a very effectual mode.

*To keep Moths, Beetles, etc., from Clothes.*—Put a piece of camphor in a linen-bag, or some aromatic herbs, in the drawers, among linen or woolen clothes, and neither moth nor worm will come near them.

*To make Sea-water fit for Washing Linen at Sea.*—Soda put into sea-water renders it turbid: the lime and magnesia fall to the bottom. To make sea-water fit for washing linen at sea, as much soda must be put in it, as not only to effect a complete precipitation on these earths, but to render the sea-water sufficiently laxivial or alkaline. Soda should always be taken to sea for this purpose.

*To Destroy Insects.*—When bugs have obtained a lodgment in walls or timber, the surest mode of overcoming the nuisance is to putty up every hole is moderately large, and oil-paint the whole wall or timber. In bed-furniture, a mixture of soft soap, with snuff or arsenic, is useful to fill up the holes where the bolts or fastenings are fixed, etc. French polish may be applied to smoother parts of the wood.

*Poultice for Burns and Frozen Flesh.*—Indian-meal poultices, covered with young hyson tea; moistened with hot water, and laid over burns or frozen parts, as hot as can be borne, will relieve the pain in five minutes, and blisters, if they have not, will not arise. One poultice is usually sufficient.

*Cracked Nipples.*—Glyceine and tannin, equal weights, rubbed together into an ointment, is highly recommended, as is also mutton tallow and glycerine.

*To take the Impression of any Butterfly in all its Colors.*—Having taken a butterfly, kill it without spoiling its wings, which contrive to spread out as regularly as possible in a flying position. Then, with a small brush or pencil, take a piece of white paper; wash part of it with gum-water, a little thicker than ordinary, so that it may easily dry. Afterwards, laying your butterfly on the paper, cut off the body close to the wings, and, throwing it away, lay the paper on a smooth board with the fly upwards; and, laying another paper over that, put the while preparation into a screw-press, and screw down very hard, letting it remain under that pressure for half an hour. Afterwards take off the wings of the butterfly and you will find a perfect impression of them, with all their various colors, marked distinctly, remaining on the paper. When this is done draw between the wings of your impression the body of the butterfly, and color it after the insect itself.

*To take the Stains of Grease from Woolen or Silk.*—Three ounces of spirits of wine, three ounces of French chalk powdered, and five ounces of pipe-clay. Mix the above ingredients, and make them up in rolls about the length of a finger, and you will find a never-failing remedy for removing grease from woollen or silken goods. N. B.—It is applied by rubbing on the spot either dry or wet, and afterwards brushing the place.

*Easy and Safe Method of discharging Grease from Woollen Cloths.*—Fuller's earth and tobacco pipe-clay, being put wet on an oil-spot, absorbs the oil as the water evaporates, and leaves the vegetable or animal fibres of the cloth clean on being beaten or brushed out. When the spot is occasioned by tallow or wax, it is necessary to heat the part cautiously by an iron or the fire while the cloth is drying. In some kind of goods, blotting-paper, bran, or raw starch, may be used with advantage.

*To Take out Spots of Ink.*—As soon as the accident happens, wet the place with juice of sorrel or lemon, or with vinegar, and the best hard white soap.

*To take Iron-moulds out of Linen.*—Hold the iron-mould on the cover of a tankard of boiling water, and rub on the spot a little juice of sorrel and a little salt; and when the cloth has thoroughly imbibed the juice, wash it in lye.

*To take out Spots on Silk.*—Rub the spots with spirits of turpentine, this spirit exhaling, carries off with it the oil that causes the spot.

*To take Wax out of Velvet of all Colors except Crimson.*—Take a crumby wheaten loaf, cut in two, toast it before the fire, and, while very hot, apply it to the part spotted with wax. Then apply another piece of toasted bread hot as before, and continue this application until the wax is entirely taken out.

*To Bleach Straw.*—Straw is bleached by the vapors of sulphur, or a solution of oxalic acid or chloride of lime. It may be dyed with any liquid color.

*Windows, to Crystallize.*—Dissolve epsom-salts in hot ale, or solution of gum arabic, wash it over the window, and let it dry. If you wish to remove any, to form a border or centre-piece, do it with a wet cloth.

*Wax for Bottling.*—Rosin, 13 parts; wax, 1 part, melt and add any color. Used to render corks and bungs air-tight by *melting the wax* over them.

*Whitewash.*—Slack half a bushel of lime with boiling water, and cover the vessel to retain the steam. Strain the liquor, and add one peck of salt previously dissolved in warm water, 3 lbs. of rice boiled and ground to a paste, Spanish whiting, 8 oz.; glue, 1 pound; mix and add hot water, 5 gallons; let it stand a few days, and apply hot. It makes a brilliant wash for inside or outside works.

*To Purify Water for Drinking.*—Filter river-water through a sponge, more or less compressed, instead of stone or sand, by which the water is not only rendered more clean, but wholesome; for sand is insensibly dissolved by the water, so that in four or five years it will have lost a fifth part of its weight. Powder of charcoal should be added to the sponge when the water is foul or fetid. Those who examine the large quantity of terrene matter on the inside of tea-kettles, will be convinced all water should be boiled before drinking, if they wish to avoid being affected with gravel or stone, etc.

*To Purify the Muddy Waters of Rivers or Pits.*—Make a number of holes in the bottom of a deep tub; lay some clean gravel thereon, and above this some clean sand; sink this tub in the river or pit, so that only a few inches of the tub will be above the surface of the water; the river or pit water will filter through the sand, and rise clear through it to the level of the water on the outside, and will be pure and limpid.

*Method of Making Putrid Water Sweet in a Night's Time.*—Four large spoonfuls of unslacked lime, put into a puncheon of ninety gallons of putrid water at sea, will, in one night, make it as clear and sweet as the best spring-water just drawn; but unless the water is afterwards ventilated sufficiently to carbonize the lime, it will be lime-water. Three ounces of pure unslacked lime should saturate 90 gallons of water.

*Tree of Lead.*—Dissolve an ounce of sugar of lead in a quart of clean water, and put it into a glass decanter or globe. Then suspend in the solution, near the top, a small piece of zinc of an irregular shape. Let it stand undisturbed for a day, and it will begin to shoot out into leaves, and apparently to vegetate. If left undisturbed for a few days, it will become extremely beautiful; but it must be moved with great caution. It may appear to those unacquainted with chemistry, that the piece of zinc actually puts out leaves; but this is a mistake, for, if the zinc be examined, it will be found nearly unaltered. This phenomenon is owing to the zinc having a greater attraction for oxygen than the lead has; consequently, it takes it from the oxide of lead, which re-appears in its metallic state.

*Arbor Martis, or Tree of Mars.*—Dissolve iron filings in acqua fortis moderately concentrated, till the acid is saturated; then add to it gradually a solution of mixed alkali, commonly called oil of tartar per deliquium. A strong effervescence will ensue; and the iron, instead of falling to the bottom of the vessel, will afterwards rise so as to cover the sides, forming a multitude of ramifications heaped one upon the other, which will sometimes pass over the edge of the vessel, and extend themselves on the outside with all the appearance of a plant.

*To keep Apples from Freezing.*—Apples form an article of chief necessity in almost every family: therefore, great care is taken to keep them from frost; it being well known that they, if left unprotected, are destroyed by the first frost which occurs. They may be kept in the attic with impunity throughout the winter, by simply covering them over with a linen cloth: be sure to have *linen*, for woolen or other cloth is of *no avail*.

*To Preserve Grapes.*—Take a cask or barrel which will hold water, and put into it, first a layer of bran, dried in an oven or of ashes well dried and sifted, upon this place a layer of grapes well cleaned, and gathered in the afternoon of a dry day, before they are perfectly ripe; proceed thus with alternate layers of bran or ashes and grapes, till the barrel is full, taking care that the grapes do not touch each other, and to let the last layer be of bran or ashes, then close the barrel so that the air may not penetrate, which is an essential point. Grapes thus packed will keep for nine or even twelve months. To restore them to freshness, cut the end of the stalk of each bunch of grapes, and put it into red wine, as you would flowers into water. White grapes should be put into white wine.

*To Increase the Laying of Eggs.*—The best method is to mix with their food, every other day, about a teaspoon of ground cayenne pepper to each dozen fowl. Whilst upon this subject, it would be well to say, that if your hens lay soft eggs, or eggs without shells, you should put plenty of old plaster, egg-shells, or even oyster-shells broken up, where they can get at it.

*To Preserve Meats.*—Beef to pickle for long keeping. First, thoroughly rub salt into it, and let it remain in bulk for twenty-four hours to draw off the blood. Second, take it up, letting it drain, and pack as desired. Third, have ready a pickle prepared as follows: for every 100 pounds of beef use 7 pounds salt; saltpetre and cayenne pepper each, 1 ounce; molasses, 1 quart; and soft water, 8 gallons; boil and skim well, and when cold pour over the beef.

Another method is to use 5 pounds salt, 1 pound brown sugar, and ¼ ounce saltpetre, to each 100 pounds; dissolve the above in sufficient water to cover the meat, and in two weeks drain all off, and make more same as first. It will then keep through the season. To boil for eating, put into boiling water; for soups, into cold water.

*Flies, to Destroy.*—Boil some quassia-chips in a little water, sweeten with syrup or molasses, and place it in saucers. It is destructive to flies, but not to children.

*Walnuts to Pickle.*—Take 100 young walnuts, lay them in salt and water for two or three days, changing the water every day. (If required to be soon ready for use, pierce each walnut with a larding pin that the pickle may penetrate.) Wipe them with a soft cloth, and lay them on a folded cloth for some hours. Then put them in a jar, and pour on them sufficient of the above spiced vinegar, hot, to cover them. Or they may be allowed to simmer gently in strong vinegar, then put into a jar with a handful of mustard-seed, 1 ounce of ginger, ¼ ounce mace, 1 ounce allspice, 2 heads of garlic, and 2 split nutmegs; and pour on them sufficient boiling vinegar to cover them. Some prefer the walnuts to be gently simmered with the brine, then laid on a cloth for a day or two till they turn black, put into a jar, and hot spiced vinegar poured on them.

*To Pickle Cucumbers and Gherkins.*—Small cucumbers, but not too young, are wiped clean with a dry cloth, put into a jar, and boiling vinegar, with a handful of salt, poured on them. Boil up the vinegar every three days, and pour it on them until they become green; then add ginger and pepper, and tie them up close for use, or cover them with salt and water (as above) in a stone jar; cover them, and set them on the hearth before the fire for two or three days, till they turn yellow; then put away the water, and cover them with hot vinegar, set them near the fire, and keep them hot for eight or ten days, till they become green; then pour off the vinegar, cover them with hot spiced vinegar, and cover them close.

*Mushroom Ketchup.*—Pickled mushrooms, 4 pounds; salt, 2 pounds. Sprinkle it on the mushrooms; and, when they liquefy, remove the juice; add pimento, 6 ounces; cloves, 1 ounce; boil gently and strain; the remaining liquor, if any, may be treated with pepper, mace, and ginger for a second quality.

*Tomato Ketchup.*—Proceed as for mushroom ketchup, and add a little Chili pepper vinegar.

*Court-plaster.*—Court-plaster is made by repeatedly brushing over stretched sarcenet with a solution of 1 part of isinglass in 8 of water mixed with 8 parts of proof spirit, and finishing with a coat of tincture of benzoin, or of balsam of Peru.

*Eye-water.*—Extract of lead, 2 drachms; wine of digitalis 1 drachm tincture of opium, 2 drachms; water a pint.

*Godfrey's Cordial.*—The Philadelphia College of Pharmacy, to prevent the mischief arising from the different strengths of this compound, directs it to be prepared as follows:—Dissolve 2½ oz. of carbonate of potash in 26 pints of water, add 16 pints of treacle, heat together over a gentle fire till they simmer, remove the scum, and, when sufficiently cool, add ½ oz. of oil of sassafras dissolved in two pints of rectified spirit, and 24 fluid ounces of tincture of opium previously mixed. The old wine measure is here intended. It contains about 16 minims of laudanum, or rather more than 1 grain of opium in each fluid ounce.

*Godfrey's Smelling-salts.*—Dr. Paris says it is prepared by re-subliming volatile salt swith sub-carbonate of potash and a little spirit of wine. It is usually scented with an alcoholic solution of essential oils.

*Stoughton's Elixir.*—Gentian, 36 oz.; serpentary, 16 oz., dried orange-peel, 24 oz.; calamus aromaticus, 4 oz.; rectified spirit and water, of each 6 galls., old measure.

*Dr. Latham's Cough-linctus.*—Dover's powder, ½ dr.; compound powder of tragacanth, 2 dr.; syrup of tolu, ½ ounce; confection of hips and simple oxymel, of each 1 ounce; a teaspoonful 3 or 4 times a day.

*Morrison's Pills.*—Consist of 2 parts of gamboge, 3 of aloes, 1 of colocynth, and 4 of cream of tartar; made into pills with syrup.

## CALICO PRINTERS' FAST DYES.

*Dye-stuffs used by calico-printers for producing fast colors.*— The mordants are thickened with gum, or calcined starch, when applied with the block, rollers, plates, or pencil.

*Black.*—The cloth is impregnated with acetate of iron (iron liquor), and died in a bath of madder and logwood.

*Purple.*—The preceding mordant of iron, diluted; with the same dyeing bath.

*Crimson.*—The mordant for purple, united with a portion of acetate of alumina, or red mordant, and the above bath.

*Red.*—Acetate of alumina is the mordant, and madder is the dye-stuff.

*Pale Red of different shades.*—The preceding mordant, diluted with water, and a weak madder bath.

*Brown, or Pompadour.*—A mixed mordant, containing a somewhat larger proportion of the red than of the black, and the dye of madder.

*Orange.*—The red mordant; and a bath, first of madder, and then of quercitron.

*Yellow.*—A strong red mordant; and the quercitron bath, whose temperature should be considerably under the boiling point of water.

*Blue.*—Indigo, rendered soluble and greenish-yellow colored, by potash and orpiment. It recovers its blue color by exposure to air, and thereby also fixes firmly on the cloth. An indigo vat is also made, with that blue substance diffused in water with quicklime and copperas. These substances are supposed to deoxidize indigo, and at the same time to render it soluble.

*Golden-dye.*—The cloth is immersed alternately in a solution of copperas and lime-water. The protoxide of iron precipitated on the fiber, soon passes, by absorption of atmospherical oxygen, into the golden-colored deutoxide.

*Buff.*—The preceding substances in a more diluted state.

*Blue Vats.*—In which white spots are left on a blue ground of cloth, is made by applying to those points a paste composed of a solution of sulphate of copper and pipe-clay, and after they are dried, immersing it, stretched on frames, for a definite number of minutes, in the yellowish green vat, of 1 part of indigo, 2 of copperas, and 2 of lime, with water.

*Green.*—Cloth dyed blue, and well washed, is imbued with the aluminous acetate, dried, and subjected to the quercitron bath.

In the above cases, the cloth, after receiving the mordant paste, is dried, and put through a mixture of cow-dung and warm water. It is then put into the dyeing vat or copper.

## DYES FOR BONES AND IVORY.

*1. Red.*—Made an infusion of Cochineal in water of ammonia, then immerse the pieces therein, having previously soaked them for a few minutes in very weak aquafortis and water.

*2. Black.*—Immerse the pieces in a weak solution of nitrate of silver, for a short time, then expose them to the sunlight.

*3. Green.*—Steep in a solution of verdigris, to which a little acquafortis has been added.

*4. Yellow.*—Boil for one hour in a solution made with one pound of alum in one gallon of water, then take out the pieces and steep them in a decoction made with ½ pound of turmeric in 2 quarts of water, lastly, mix the two liquors, and boil them therein for one hour.

*5. Blue.*—Stain them green, then steep them in a hot and strong solution of pearlash.

*Remarks.*—The bones of living animals may be dyed by mixing madder with their food. The bones of young pigeons may thus be tinged of a rose-color in 24 hours, and of a deep scarlet in 3 days; but the bones of adult animals take a fortnight to acquire a rose-color. The bones nearest the heart become tinged quickest. In the same way extract of logwood will tinge the bones of young pigeons purple.

*Celebrated Washing Mixture.*—Dissolve a half pound of soda in a gallon of boiling water, and pour upon it a quarter pound of lime. After this has settled, out up to ounces of common tursoap, and strain the solution upon it, and mix perfectly. Great care must be taken that no particles of lime are poured upon the soap. Prepare the mixture the evening before washing.

*Directions.*—To 10 gallons of water and the above preparation when the water is boiling, and put the clothes in while boiling. Each lot of linen must boil half an hour, and the same liquid will answer for three batches of clothes. The white clothes must be put in soak over night, and if the collars and wristbands are soaped and rubbed lightly, so much the better, Clean cold water may be used for rincing. Some prefer boiling them for a few moments in clean blueing water, and afterwards rince in cold water. The cloths may not appear perfectly white while wet, but when dry will be clear white.

*Musk.*—Artificial Musk is made by dropping 3½ ounces of nitric acid on one ounce of rectified oil of amber. In a day or two, a black substance is produced, which smells similar to genuine musk.

*Mahogany Furniture.*—Stains and spots may be taken out of mahogany furniture by the use of a little acquafortis, or oxalic acid and water, by rubbing the part with the liquid, by means of a cork, till the color is restored, observing afterwards to well wash the wood with water, and to dry and polish as usual.

*Razor-Paste*—Levigated oxide of tin (prepared putty powder) 1 ounce; powdered oxalic acid, ¼ ounce; powdered gum, 20 grains. Make it into a stiff paste with water, and evenly and thinly spread it over the strop. With very little friction, this paste gives a fine edge to the razor, and its efficiency is still further increased by moistening it.

*Shaving-Paste.*—White Wax, Spermaceti, and Almond-Oil; melt, and while warm, beat in two square of Windsor soap, previously reduced to a paste with rose-water.

*The Hunter's Secret.*—To Catch Game—such as Mink, Musk-Rats, Weasels, Raccoons, Otter, etc.—Take one ounce of valerian, ¼ ounce of commercial musk, one pint of whiskey—mix together, and let it stand for two weeks. Put a few drops of this on your bait.

*Preservation of Hams.*—Most grocers, dealers in hams, and others, who are particular in their meat, usually take the precaution to case each one, after it is smoked, in canvas, for the purpose of defending it from the attacks of the little insect, the dermestes lardarius, which, by laying its eggs in it, soon fills it with its larvæ, or maggots. This troublesome and expensive process may be altogether superseded by the use of pyroligueous acid. With a painter's brush, dipped in the liquid, one man, in the course of a day, may effectually secure two hundred hams from all danger. Care should be taken to insinuate the liquid into all the cracks, etc., of the under surface. This method is especially adapted to the preservation of hams in hot climates.

*India-Rubber Blacking.*—(*Bryant and James' Paste.*)—Ivory black 60 pounds; treacle 45 pounds; good vinegar and oil of vitriol, of each 12 pounds; India-rubber oil, 9 pounds; mix.

2. *Liquid.*—Ivory black 60 pounds; gum (dissolved), 1 pound; vinegar (No. 24) 20 gallons; oil of vitriol 24 pounds; India-rubber oil, 9 pounds. Mix.

*Remarks.*—The India-rubber oil is made of caoutchouc 18 oz., dissolved in rape-oil, 9 pounds, by means of heat. The ingredients are mixed together in the same order and manner as common blacking.

*Alterative Syrup.*—American Sarsaparilla, Yellow Dockroot, Black Alder-bark, Prickly Ash-bark, Burdock-root, Sassafras-bark, Wintergreen, of each one ounce, make four pints of syrup. Dose, a wineglassfull, three or four times a day. This syrup is useful in all diseases where the blood or general system needs purifying.

*Bite of a Mad Dog.*—Spirits of Hartshorn is said to be a certain remedy for the bite of a mad dog. The wound should be constantly bathed with it, and three or four doses, diluted, taken inwardly, during the day. The hartshorn decomposes chemically the virus insinuated into the wound, and immediately alters and destroys its deleteriousness. The writer, who resided in Brazil for some time, first tried it for the bite of a scorpion, and found that it removed pain and inflamation almost instantly. Subsequently, he tried it for the bite of the rattlesnake, with similar success. At the suggestion of the writer, an old friend and physician tried it in cases of Hydrophobia and always with success.

*Canker Powder.*—Powdered Golden Seal, Blue Cohosh, of each one ounce. A superior remedy for canker in the mouth and stomach. Steep one teaspoonful of this powder in a gill of hot water for one hour, then strain and sweeten with loaf sugar. Gargle the throat for ten or fifteen minutes at a time with this infusion; likewise a table-spoonful may be held in the mouth for some minutes; after which drink two table-spoonfuls of it. Repeat it several times a day, until a cure is effected.

*Cough Candy.*—Cheap, Safe, and Excellent.—Take equal parts of Boneset, Spikenard, Elecampane, Comfrey, and Wild Cherry bark; make a strong decoction; to every pint of this decoction add molasses a pint; extract of liquorice, four ounces, and honey four ounces. Boil down to a proper consistence for forming a candy, when add oil of tar, one drachm; essence of sassafras, two teaspoonfuls. Work it up into a candy form by hand in the usual way. It may be en freely.

*Bronzing of Medals.*—Ornaments of copper, electrotypes, etc.— Having thoroughly cleaned and polished the surface of the specimen, with a brush apply the common crocus-powder, previously made into a paste with water. When dry, place it in an iron ladle, or on a common fire-shovel over a clear fire for about one minute; and when sufficiently cool, polish with a plate-brush. By this process a bronze similar to that on tea-urns is produced; the shade depending upon the duration of the exposure to the fire.

1. By substituting finely powdered plumbago for crocus-powder in the above process, a beautiful, deep and permanent bronze appearance is produced.

2. Rub the medal with a solution of livers of sulphur, or sulphuret of potassium, then dry. This produces the appearance of Antique bronze very exactly.

*Surface Bronzing.*—This term is applied to the process for imparting to the surfaces of figures of wood, plaster of Paris, etc., a metallic appearance. this is done by first giving them a coat of oil or size-varnish, and when this is nearly dry, applying with a dabber of cotton or a camel-hair pencil, any of the metallic bronze powders; or the powder may be placed in a little bag of muslin, and dusted over the surface, and afterwards finished off with a wad of linen. This surface must be afterwards varnished.

Paper is bronzed by mixing the powders up with a little gum and water, and afterwards burnishing.

Iron Castings may be bronzed by thorough cleaning, and subsequent immersion in a solution of sulphate of copper, when they acquire a coat of the latter metal. They must be then washed in water.

*Butter or Milk.*—To remove its Turnip Flavor. This is said to be removed by either of the following methods: When the milk is strained into the pans, put to every six gallons one gallon of boiling water. Or dissolve one ounce of nitre in a pint of spring water and put ¼ pint to every fifteen gallons of milk.

*Silver Jelly.*—Time to boil the feet, five hours and a half; to boil the jelly, twenty minutes. One set of calf's feet; one ounce of isinglass; one pint of the best gin; one pound of loaf sugar; juice of six lemons; peel of two; white of six eggs. Boil the calf's feet in four quarts of water, with the isinglass, until the feet are done to rags, and the water wasted to half the quantity; strain it, and when cold remove the feet, and the jelly from the sediment very carefully. Put the jelly into a stew-pan with the sugar, the juice of the lemons, and the peel of two; add the gin. When the flavor is thoroughly drawn from the lemon-peel, put in the whites of the eggs well beaten, and their shells broken up, place the stew-pan over the fire, and let it boil for twenty minutes, but do not stir in after the egg has been added. Dip a jelly-bag into hot water and squeeze it dry; run the jelly through it several times, until quite clear, and then pour it into the mould. If calf's feet cannot be obtained, two ounces of gelatine and one ounce of isinglass will do as well.

*Gilding of Porcelain, Glass, etc.*—This is performed by blending powdered gold with gum-water and a little borax, and applying it by means of a camel-hair pencil; the article is then heated sufficiently hot in an oven or furnace, by which means the gum is burnt, and the borax vitrifying cements the gold to the surface. When cold it is polished off with a burnisher. Names, dates, or any fancy device may thus be permanently and easily fixed on glass, china, earthenware, etc.

*Gilding of Silk, etc.*—Silks, satins, woolens, ivory bones, etc., may be readily gilded by immersing them in a solution of nitro-muriate (terchloride) of gold (1 of the salt to 3 or 4 water), and then exposing them to the action of hydrogen-gas. The latter part of the process may readily be performed by pouring some diluted sulphuric acid, or zinc or iron filings, in a bottle, and placing it under a jar or similar vessel, inverted at the top of which the articles to be gilded are to be suspended.

The foregoing experiment may be very prettily and advantageously varied as follows: paint flowers or other ornaments with a very fine camel-hair pencil, dipped in the above-mentioned solution of gold, on pieces of silk, satin, etc., and hold them over a Florence flask, from which hydrogen-gas is evolved, during the decomposition of the water by sulphuric acid and iron-filings. The painted flowers, etc., in a few minutes will shine with all the splendor of the purest gold. A coating of this kind will not tarnish on exposure to the air, or in washing.

*Gilding Varnish.*—This is oil-gilding applied to equipages, picture-frames, furniture, etc., the surface being highly varnished and polished before it receives the size or gold color; and then, after the gilding has become quite dry, a coat of spirit varnish, fumed with the chafing-dish as above, is applied, followed by two or three coats of the best copal varnish, after which the work is carefully polished with tripoli and water.

*Gilders' Varnish.*—Prep.—Beeswax, 4 ounces, verdigris and sulphate of copper, of each 1 ounce; mix.

*Fire-eating.*—The power of resisting the action of fire is given to the skin by frequently washing it with diluted sulphuric acid, until the part becomes sufficiently callous. It is said that the following mixture is very efficacious:—dilute sulphuric acid 3 parts; sal ammoniac, 1 part; juice of onions, 2 parts; mix. It is the acid, however, that produces the effect.

*Impressions from Coins.*—A very easy and elegant way of taking the impressions of medals and coins, not generally known, is as follows.—Melt a little isinglass-glue with brandy, and pour it thinly over the medal, so as to cover its whole surface; let it remain on for a day or two, till it has thoroughly dried and hardened, and then take it off, when it will be fine, clear, and as hard as a piece of Muscovy glass, and will have a very elegant impression of the coin. It will also resist the effects of damp air, which occasions all other kinds of glue to soften and bend if not prepared in this way. (Shaw.) If the wrong side of the isinglass be breathed on, and gold leaf applied, it will adhere, and be seen on the other side, producing a very pleasing effect.

Isinglass-glue, made with water **alone, will do "nearly" as well as** if brandy be used.

*Leaf-gilding.*—This term is applied to the gilding of paper, vellum, etc., by applying leaf-gold to the surface, previously prepared with a coating of gum-water, size, or white of an egg. It is usually finished with an agate burnisher.

*Letter-gilding.* The letters of signboards and similar ornamental gilding for outdoor work, is done by first covering the design with yellow or gold-color paint, then with oil gold size, and when this is nearly dry, applying the leaf-gold, observing to shield it properly from the wind, lest it be blown away or become crumpled before being properly attached. This gilding is usually varnished.

*Mahogany Stains.*—Pure Socotrine aloes, ounce, dragon's blood, ½ ounce, rectified spirit, 1 pint; dissolve and apply 2 or 3 coats to the surface of the wood, finish off with wax or oil, tinged with alkanet.

*Simple Cosmetic.*—Soft soap ½ pound; melt over a slow fire with a gill of sweet oil, add half a teacupful of fine sand, and stir the mixture together until cold. The shelly sea-sand, sifted from the shells, has been found better than that which has no shells.

*Remarks.*—This simple cosmetic, has for several years past been used by many ladies who are remarkable for the delicate softness and whiteness of their hands, which they in a great measure, attribute to the use of it. Its cheapness is a strong recommendation.

*Essence of Patchouli.*—Indian patchouli-leaves, 2 pounds; rectified spirit of wine, 9 pints; water, a gallon. Macerate for one week, frequently shaking the vessel, then distill over exactly one gallon. A very fashionable perfume.

*Essence of Roses.* (odorous)—Very fine article.—Attar of roses, 1 ounce; spirit of wine, 1 gallon. Mix in a close vessel, and assist the solution by placing it in a bath of hot water. As soon as the spirit gets warm, take it from the water and shake till quite cold. The next day filter. Unless the spirit of wine be of more than the common strength, it will not retain the whole of the attar in solution in very cold weather.

Furs may be preserved from moths and insects by placing a

little colocynth pulp (bitter apples,), or spices, as cloves, pimento, etc., wrapped in muslin among them, or they may be washed in a very weak solution of corrosive sublimate in warm water (10 or 15 grains to the pint), and afterwards carefully dried. Furs, as well as every other species of clothing, should be kept in a clean, dry place.

*Coffee Milk.*—Boil a dessert-spoonful of ground coffee in about a pint of milk a quarter of an hour; then put into it a shaving or two of isinglass and clear it; let it boil a few minutes, and set it on the side of the fire to fine. This is a very fine breakfast, and should be sweetened with real Lisbon sugar.

*Bakers' Itch-ointment.*—Mix well together one quarter ounce of ointment of nitrate of mercury and one ounce of balm-oil.

*Soap a la Rose.*—New Olive-Oil Soap 30 pounds, new tallow soap, 20 pounds; reduce them to shavings by sliding the bars along the face of an inverted plane, melt in an untinned copper pan by the heat of steam or a water-bath, add 1½ ounces of finely ground vermilion. Mix well, remove the heat, and when the mass has cooled a little, add essence of roses [attar?] 3 oz.; do. of cloves and cinnamon, of each, one ounce; bergamot 2½ ounces; mix well, run the liquid mass through a tammy-cloth, and put it into the frames. If the soaps employed are not new, one or two quarts of water must be added to make them melt easily. A very fine article.

*Soap au Bouquet.*—Best tallow soap, 30 lbs.; essence of bergamot, 4 oz.; oils of cloves, sassafras, and thyme, of each 1 ounce; pure neroli, ½ ounce; finely powdered brown ochre, 7 oz. Mix as last. Very fine.

*Soap, Bitter Almond.*—Best white tallow soap; ½ cwt.; essence of bitter almonds, 10 oz. Mix as soap a la rose. Very fine.

*Soap Cinnamon.*—Best tallow soap, 30 pounds; best balm-oil soap, 20 pounds; essence of cinnamon, 7 ounces; do. of sassafras and bergamot, of each 1¼ ounces; finely powdered yellow ochre, 1 pound. Mix as soap a la rose. Very fine.

*Soap, Musk.*—Best tallow soap, 30 pounds; palm-oil soap, 20 pounds; powdered cloves, pale roses, and gilliflowers, of each, 4½ ounces; essences of bergamot and musk, of each 3½ ounces; Spanish brown, 4 ounces. Mix as soap a la rose. Very fine.

*Soap, Orange-flower.*—Best tallow soap, 30 pounds; palm-oil soap, 20 pounds; essence of Portugal and ambergris, of each 7½ ounces, yellowish green color [ochre and indigo] 8½ ounces, vermilion, 1¼ ounce. Mix as soap a la rose. Very fine.

*Soap, Palm-oil.*—Made of palm-oil and caustic soda lye. Has a pleasant odor of violets, and a lively color.

*Almond Soap* is made from almond-oil and caustic soda, and is chiefly used for the toilet.—Cure Soap is made with tallow and soda. Mottled Soap with refuse kitchen-stuff, etc.

## PRINTING INK.

*Printing Ink.*—10 to 12 gallons of linseed-oil are set over the fire in an iron pot capable of containing at least as much more, to allow of its swelling without running over. When it boils it is kept stirred with an iron ladle, and if it does not take fire of itself soon after the smoke begins to rise, it is kindled by means of a piece of burning paper, stuck in the cleft end of a long stick. The pot is then shortly afterwards removed from the fire, and the oil is suffered to burn for about half an hour, or till a sample of the varnish cooled upon a pallet knife, may be drawn into strings of about half an inch long, between the fingers. The flame is now extinguished by the application of a close-fitting tin cover, and as soon as the froth of the ebullition has subsided, black rosin is added, in the proportion of 6 pounds, to every 6 quarts of oil thus treated; the mixture is next stirred until the rosin is dissolved, when 1¾ lbs. of brown soap, cut into slices is further added (cautiously), and the ingredients are again stirred with the spatula until united, the pot being once more placed over the fire to promote the combination. When this is effected, the varnish is removed from the heat, and after thorough stirring, covered over and set aside. It is necessary to prepare two kinds of this varnish, varying in consistence, from more or less boiling, to be occasionally mixed together as circumstances require; that which answers well in hot weather being too thick in cold, and vice versa. Large characters also require a thinner ink than small ones. A good varnish may be drawn into threads like glue, and is very thick and tenacious.

2.—Making the ink. (Black.) Finely powdered Indigo and Prussian Blue, of each 2½ ounces; best mineral lampblack, 4 pounds; best vegetable lampblack, 3½ pounds; put them into a suitable vessel and mix in gradually the warm varnish. The mixture must now be submitted to careful grinding, either in a mill or with a slab and muller. On a large scale steam power is employed for this purpose.

(An extemporaneous superfine ink). Balsam of copaiba (pure) 9 ounces; lampblack, 3 ounces; Indigo and Prussian Blue, of each, 5 drachms; Indian Red, ¾ ounces; yellow soap (dry), 3 oz., grind to an impalpable smoothness. Canada balsam may be substituted for balsam of copaiba where the smell of the latter is objectionable, but it dries quicker.

*Remarks.*—Old linseed-oil is preferable to new. Yellow rosin soap is preferred for black and dark-colored inks, and white-cure soap for light ones. Vegetable lampblack takes the most varnish. The addition of Indigo and Prussian Blue is to correct the brown color of the black. The Indian red is added to increase the body and richness of color. Some persons find much trouble in grinding up the indigo, from its running into a mass and clogging the mill; but this may be avoided by mixing it as above, or by first grinding it with sufficient quantity of Canada balsam or copaiba, and using a proportionate quantity of varnish and that of a little thicker consistence. The French employ nut-oil instead of linseed. Mr. Savage obtained the large medal of the Society of Arts for his black ink made as above. It is unrivaled. Colored inks are made in a similar way. The pigments used are, carmine, lake, vermilion, chrome red, red lead, orange red, Indian red, venetian red, orange chrome, chrome yellow, burnt terra di Siena, gallstone, Roman ochre, yellow do., verdigris, Schele's green, Schweinfurth's do., blues and yellows mixed for greens, indigo, Prussian blue, Antwerp do., cobalt do., charcoal do., luster, umber, sepia, etc., etc.

*Paper Copying.*—Make a stiff ointment with butter or lard and lampblack, and smear it thinly and evenly over soft writing-paper, by means of a piece of flannel, then wipe off the redundant portion with a piece of soft rag. Placed on paper and written on with a style, or solid pen. By repeating the arrangement, two or three copies of a letter may be obtained at once. This paper, set up in a case, forms the ordinary manifold writer.

*The Art of Inlaying and Ornamenting Papier-mache.* The articles required are a small pair of cutting nippers, a half round file, some gold size, Vegetable Black, Black Japan, two large camel's hair brushes in quills, various powder colors such as Lakes, Vermilion, Italian Pink, Prussian blue, French Ultramarine, Emerald Green, etc. Copal Varnish, Spirit of Turpentine, Gold Leaf, Pumice Stone, Pumice Powder, Putty Powder, Palette Knife and Slab, Papier-mache and Pearl. Having roughly sketched your design upon the Papier-mache, and decided upon the part to be inlaid with Pearl, take your nippers and cut or nip the pearl to your shape, which is afterwards to be finished with the file to the exact form required. You will now mix in a gallipot a small quantity of Gold Size and Vegetable Black, to the consistency of Treacle; and taking a large brush, lay a rather thick coating upon the whole of Papier-mache. You will then stick on the pieces of pearl before cut out, according to your design, and let it remain until dry, which will be 24 hours. The surface of your Papier-mache being perfectly dry, take Black Japan and give it a thick and even coating over the whole surface, not excepting the Pearl. It will require to be placed in an oven of some sort, quite free from dust, and heat about 145 degrees; but this is not particular, so long as it does not get hotter. It will be dry in 24 hours, when to test its dryness, dip a rag in spirit of turpentine, and brush the edge of the papier-mache; if it soils the rag, it is not dry, and requires to be again stoved. The articles require four coats of japan, and the above process to be repeated on each coat, the beauty of the articles entirely depending on the japan being perfectly dry and hard. A piece of pumice-stone, rubbed flat on a flag, must now be dipped in water, and rubbed on the papier-mache until it brings the whole to a level surface, and shows the pearl. Fine pumice powder and water upon a bit of list is now applied to remove the scratches made by the pumice-stone. Polish with putty powder upon a piece of wash-leather.

If your design consists of flowers, etc., color the parts as required with powder colors, mixed up with copal varnish, and diluted with turpentine, using nature as a guide. The ornamental parts, not consisting of flowers, are to be painted and gilded according to your fancy. For gilding, take gold size and mix a little chrome yellow, with which draw your design, and when partially dry in 5 or 10 minutes cut gold leaf in small pieces, apply it, and dab it on with cotton wool. In 5 or 10 minutes after rub the cotton lightly over the surface, to remove the superfluous pieces of gold. When the coloring is dry, varnish over the parts which have been painted or gilded, with copal varnish, and let it dry 24 hours, and the article is complete.

## REMEDIES FOR DISEASES OF HORSES.

*Laxative Balls* (for horses).—Aloes, ginger, and soft soap, of each 3 drachms; mix with treacle for one ball. Cordial and laxative.

*Garlic Balls* (for horses).—Garlic one ounce; liquorice-powder enough to make a ball. Use for chronic coughs.

*Mange Balls* (for horses).—Crude antimony, 2 oz.; colomel, 1 oz.; opium, ½ oz.; flowers of sulphur, 1 lb.; mix with treacle and divide into 12 balls. A piece the size of a horsebean to that of a small nut is a capital medicine for dogs.

*Stomachic Balls* (for horses).—Powdered Gentian, 4 oz.; powdered ginger and carbonate of soda, of each 2 ounces; soft soap, 8 ounces; mix and divide into 8 balls.

*Tonic Balls* (for horses).—Gentian, ½ oz.; opium, ½ drachm; cascarilla, myrrh, and carbonate of soda, of each, 1 drachm; soft soap, ½ oz. Form into one ball.

*Sulphur Balls* (for horses).—Flowers of sulphur, 1 pound; powdered antimony, 3 ounces; red sulphuret of mercury (pure), 2 ounces; powdered gum, 1 ounce; treacle to mix. For 12 balls. Said to make the coat slick; also for mange, etc.

*Strengthening Balls* (for horses).—Powdered calomba and cascarilla, of each ¼ oz.; soft soap, ¾ oz.; chalk, ½ oz.; make into a ball. For looseness.

*Worm Balls* (for horses).—Aloes, 5 drachms; castile soap, ½ oz.; calomel and ginger, of each, 1½ drachms; oil of cloves and cassia, of each, 6 drops; treacle to make a ball.

*Gripe Balls* (for horses).—Liquorice, black pepper, ginger, and prepared chalk, all in powder, of each, 4 oz.; oils of caraway, cloves and cassia, each one drachm; treacle to mix. For 12 balls.

*Influenza Balls* (for horses).—Barbadoes, aloes, nitre, and venice turpentine, of each, 1 pound; gentian, 2 pounds; ginger, ½ pound; treacle to mix. Divide into 1½ ounce balls.

*Colic Balls* (for horses).—Powdered opium, ¼ oz.; castile soap and camphor, each 1 oz.; powdered ginger and cassia, each ½ oz.; liquorice-powder, 2 oz.; treacle to make 4 balls.

*Cordial Balls.* (for horses).—Aniseed, caraway-seed, and cumin-seed, of each, 4 pounds; ginger, 2 pounds; all in powder; treacle sufficient to mix. Produce 21 pounds. To be made up in balls weighing 1¼ oz. each.

*Cough Balls* (for horses).—Cordial ball mass, 4 pounds; gum amoniacum, 4 oz.; powdered squills, 1 oz.; treacle to mix. Divide into 4 dozen balls.

*Farcy Balls* (for horses).—Corrosive sublimate, 10 grains; liquorice-powder, 1 ounce; oil of aniseed, ½ drachm; mix with treacle for one ball.

*Mercurial Balls* (for horses).—Calomel, 1 oz.; aloes, 2 oz.; rhubarb, ¾ oz.; liquorice-powder, 14 oz.; treacle to mix. Divide into 12 balls. Laxative and alterative.

*Alterative Balls* (for horses).—Calomel, sulphuret of antimony, and powdered opium, of each, ½ oz.; powdered gum guaiacum, 2½ ounces; castile soap, 12 ounces; treacle to mix. Divide into 12 balls. Use for weak horses with a bad constitution.

2. Calomel, ½ oz.; powdered aloes, 1½ oz.; starch, 6 oz.; soft soap, 8 oz. Make them into a mass, and divide into 12 balls. Use to improve the constitution.

*The Arabian Charm for Taming Horses.*—The horse castor is a wart or excrescence which grows on every horse's fore-legs, and generally on the hind-legs. It has a peculiar rank, musty smell, and is easily pulled off. For the Oil of Cumin the horse is said to have an instinctive passion, and the Oil of Rhodium possesses some very peculiar properties for animals. Produce some horse castor and grate it fine—also get some Oil of Rhodium and Oil of Cumin, and keep the three separate in air-tight bottles. Rub a little Oil of Cumin upon the hand, and approach the horse in the field on the windward side, so that he can smell the Cumin—when he approaches, immediately rub your hand gently upon the horse's nose, getting a little oil on it. Then give him a little of the castor on a piece of loaf sugar, apple, or potato. Then put eight drops of the Oil of Rhodium into a lady's silver thimble,

—Take the thimble between the thumb and middle finger of your right hand, with the forefinger stopping the mouth of the thimble, to prevent the oil from running out whilst you are opening the mouth of the horse. As soon as you have opened the horse's mouth, empty the thimble upon his tongue and he is your servant.

*Artificial Yeast.*—Honey, 5 oz.; cream of tartar, 1 oz.; malt, 16 oz.; water at 122° F. 3 pints; stir together, and when the temperature falls to 65°, cover it up and keep it at that temperature till yeast is formed.

*To Attract Rats.*—Two drachms of oil of aniseed, two drops of nitrous acid, and two grains of musk. Oil of Rhodium is also supposed to be very attractive to these vermin. Assafœtida with these oils is also used.

*Rheumatism.*—Take two eggs, one gill of vinegar, one gill of New England Rum, one teaspoonful of spirits of turpentine, one teaspoonful of sunfish-oil. Beat the eggs up well first, then add a small quantity of each article at a time, until all are mixed, stirring the mixture all the time. Bathe the affected parts with it two or three times a day.

*British Herb Tobacco.*—The principal ingredient in this compound is dried coltsfoot leaves, to which a portion of thyme, wood-betony, eyebright, and rosemary are added.

*Hair Depilatory.*—Quicklime, 16 ounces; pearlash 2 ounces; liver of sulphur, 2 ounces. Reduce to a fine powder, and keep in a close bottle. To be mixed with water, and applied to the skin, and scraped off in three or four minutes with a wooden knife. [Use caution, to prevent injury.]

*Dupuytren's Pomade.*—Beef-marrow, 6 oz.; nervine balsam, 2 oz. "This is made by melting together 4 oz. each of beef-marrow and oil of mace, and adding 2 dr. of balsam of tolu, and 1 dr. each of oil of cloves and camphor, dissolved in ½ oz. of rectified spirit." Peruvian balsam, 2 oz.; oil of almonds, 1½ oz.; extract of cantharides 16 gr. Melt the marrow and nervine balsam with the oil, strain, add the balsam of Peru, and lastly the extract, dissolved in a drachm of rectified spirit.

*Rouge.*—Rouge is prepared from carmine, and the coloring matter of safflower, by mixing them with finely levigated French chalk or talc, generally with the addition of a few drops of olive or almond oil. Sometimes fine white starch is used as the reducing ingredient.

*Hair-dye.*—Nitrate of silver, 11 drachms; nitrate acid, 1 drachm; distilled water, 1 pint; sap green, 3 drachms; gum arabic, 1 dr. Mix.

*Hair-dye.*—Litharge, 2 parts; slaked lime, 1 part; chalk, 2 parts; all finely powdered, and accurately mixed. When required for use, mix the powder with warm water, and dip a brush in the mixture, and rub the hair well with it. After two hours let the hair be washed.

*Toothache.*—Opium, 5 gr.; oil of cloves, 3 drops; extract of henbane, 5 gr.; extract of belladonna, 10 gr.; powdered pellitory sufficient to form a paste.

*Rose Tooth-paste.*—Cuttlefish-bone, 3 oz.; prepared or precipitated chalk, 2 oz.; orris, 1 oz.; lake or rose pink to give it a pale rose color, otto of rose, 16 drops; honey of roses in sufficient quantity.

*Filling for Teeth.*—Gutta-percha, softened by heat, is recommended. Dr. Rollfs advises melting a piece of caoutchouc at the end of a wire, and introducing it while warm.

*Fictitious Gold.*—Platina, 7; copper, 16; zinc, 1. Fuse together.

*Common Gold.*—Copper, 16; silver, 1; gold, 2.

*Bailey's Itch-ointment.*—Olive-oil, 1 lb.; suet, 1 lb.; alkanet-root, 2 oz. Melt, and macerate until colored; then strain, and add 3 oz. each of alum, nitre, and sulphate of zinc, in very fine powder, adding vermilion to color it, and oil of aniseed, lavender, and thyme to perfume.

*Caustic for Corns,*—Tincture of iodine, 4 dr.; iodide of iron, 12 gr.; chloride of antimony, 4 dr. Mix, and apply with a camel-hair brush, after paring the corn. It is said to cure in three times.

*Consumption.*—Rum, ½ pint; linseed-oil, honey, garlic (beaten to a pulp), and loaf sugar, of each 4 oz., yolks of 5 eggs. Mix. A teaspoonful night and morning.

*Sweet's Salve.*—Melt together 8 ounces of resin and 2 ounces of beeswax; then add the following mixture in powder; bole armenia, nitre, camphor, of each one ounce. Stir them well together, then pour the whole into cold water, and work it in the water until it can be taken out and formed into rolls or cakes.

*Opodeldoc.*—White soap, 2 ounces; camphor, 1 ounce; oil of rosemary, 2 drachms; oil of origanum, 2 drachms; strong aqua ammonia, 1 ounce; proof alcohol, 1½ pints. Dissolve together.

*Infants' Cordial.*—Pleurisy-root, scull-cap, skunk-cabbage, hops, cramp-bark, prickly-ash berries, calamus, angelica seed, sassafras, of each, in powder, one ounce; ginger, capsicum, of each two drachms. Pour on six pints of boiling water: When cold, add three pints of good Holland Gin, and two pounds of loaf-sugar. Let it stand two weeks, frequently shaking. [We have substituted this for Godfrey's, as it is far superior.]

*Milk of Roses.*—Mix one ounce of fine olive-oil with 10 drops of oil of tartar, and a pint of rose-water.

*Macassar-oil.*—The oil made by the natives in the islands is obtained by boiling the kernel of the fruit of a tree resembling the walnut, called in Malay, *Badeau.* The oil is mixed with other ingredients, and has a smell approaching to that of creosote. But the Macassar-oil sold in this country has probably no relation to the above, except in name. The following is given by Gray: Olive-oil, 1 pound; oil of origanum, 1 drachm. Others add 1¼ drachms of oil of rosemary.

*Eau d'Ange.*—Flowering tops of myrtle, 16 oz.; rectified spirit, a gallon; digest, and distill to dryness in a water-bath; or dissolve ¼ ounce essential oil of myrtle in three pints of rectified spirit. Mr. Gray gives under this name a water without spirit: water, 2 pints; benzion, 2 ounces; storax, 1 ounce; cinnamon, 1 drachm; cloves, 2 drachms; calamus, a stick; coriander-seeds, a pinch. Distill.

*Russian Tooth-powder.*—Peruvian-bark, 2 oz.; orris-root, 1 oz.; sal ammoniac, ½ ounce; catechu, 6 dr.; myrrh, 6 dr.; oil of cloves, 6 or 8 drops.

*Beetle Poison.*—Put a drachm of phosphorus in a flask with 2 ounces of water; plunge the flask into hot water, and when the phosphorus is melted pour the contents into a mortar with 2 or 3 ounces of lard. Triturate briskly, adding water, and ½ pound of flour with 1 or 2 ounces of brown sugar.

*Cockroach Poison.*—Equal parts of Plaster of Paris, with oatmeal.

*Arsenical Paste.*—Melt 2 pounds of suet in an earthen vessel over a slow fire, and add 2 pounds of wheat flower, 3 ounces of levigated white arsenic, 2½ drachms of lampblack, 15 drops of oil of aniseed. It may be used alone, or mixed with bread, crumbs, etc. For destroying rats and mice.

*Washes for Vermin in Plants.*—Infuse one pound of tobacco in a gallon of boiling water, in a covered vessel, till cold.

*For Lice in Vines.*—Boil ½ pound of tobacco in 2 quarts of water; strain, and add ½ pound of soft soap, and ¼ pound of sulphur. Mix.

*For Aphides.*—Boil 2 oz. of lime and 1 oz. of sulphur in water, and strain.

*For Red Spiders.*—A teaspoonful of salt in a gallon of water. In a few days wash the plant with pure water.

*To Mark on Glass.*—Glass may be written on for temporary purposes, by French chalk; pencils of this substance will be found convenient. Glass may be written on with ink, if the surface be clean and dry, and the pen held nearly perpendicular.

The shellac ink is the best for labels, as it resists damp, etc. "To scratch glass," a scratching diamond is used, or a piece of flint, or crystal of quartz, or the point of a small three square file. "To engrave on glass," fluoric acid is used, either in the liquid state or in vapor. The glass must be warmed, and coated with wax or engravers' cement, and the writing or design traced through the wax with a bradawl or other pointed instrument. The liquid fluoric acid is poured on it, and left to act on the uncovered portions of the glass; or the fluor-spar may be powdered and made into a paste with oil of vitriol, and laid over the prepared surface, and covered with lead-foil or tea-lead: or bruised fluor-spar is put on a Wedgewood evaporating basin, with sufficient oil of vitriol to form a thin paste, and the prepared glass laid over the basin, so that the vapors may act on the portions from which the wax has been removed. "To cut glass," (besides the usual method of dividing cut glass by a glaziers diamond), the following means may be used: To divide glass tubes or rods, form a deep mark around them with the edge of a three square file: then with a hand placed on either side of the mark, break the rod with a slightly stretching as well as bending motion. A diamond or sharp flint may be substituted for a file. Flasks, globes, and retorts, may be divided by means of iron rings, having a stem fixed in a wooden handle. Make the ring red-hot, and apply it to the flask, etc. If the vessel does not break where it came it contact with the ring, wet the part, and it will generally separate. Another method is to twist together 2 or 3 threads of cotton, such as is used for wicks: moisten them with spirit of wine, and encircle the flask with them; then, holding the flask horizontally, set fire to the wick, and turn the flask with the fingers, so as to keep the flame in the direction of the thread. If the separation does not take place the first time, the process may be repeated after the glass has cooled. By these means a common oil-flask may be divided into an evaporating dish and a funnel. By means of a stout iron rod, fixed in a wooden handle, and terminating in a blunt point and heated to redness, broken retorts, globes, and flasks, may be converted into useful evaporating dishes, etc. If any crack exists, it may easily be led in any direction, as it will follow the motion of the heated iron. If no crack exists one must be produced by applying the point of the heated rod to any convenient spot on the edge of the broken glass, touching it afterwards with a moistened finger, if necessary. The edges of glass thus divided are rendered less apt to break by heating them in the flame of a blowpipe, or grinding them smooth with emery on a flat stone.

*To Silver Glass.*—The term "silvering" is applied to the process of coating the surface of glass with amalgamated tin foil, in forming mirrors. The tinfoil is rubbed over with quicksilver, and more of the latter poured over it; the plate of glass, perfectly clean and dry, is then applied to it in such a way as to exclude all air-bubbles, and to bring the glass and foil into perfect contact. The plate, after being inclined so as to allow the superfluous quicksilver to drain off, is loaded with weights, under which it remains till the adhesion is complete. To convex and concave mirrors, the amalgamated foil is applied by accurately fitting plaster moulds. The interior of globes is silvered by introducing a liquid amalgam, and turning about the globe till every part is covered with it. But a method of literally silvering glass has lately been patented by Mr. Drayton. He mixes 1 oz. of nitrate of siver, 3 oz. of water, 1 ounce of liquid ammonia, and 3 oz. of spirit of wine, and filter the solution after it has stood 3 or 4 hours. To every ounce of solution he adds ¼ oz. of sugar (grape sugar, if possible,) dissolved in equal quantities of water and alcohol. The surface to be silvered is covered with this liquid, and a temperature of 160° F. maintained, till the deposition of the silver is complete. When quite dry, the coated surface is covered with mastic varnish.

*Cement for Steam Pipes.*—Good linseed-oil varnish, ground with equal weights of white lead, oxide of manganese, and pipeclay.

*Inks.*—The following are specimens of the most useful kinds of ink:—

*Black Writing-ink.*—Bruised Aleppo galls, 6 oz.; soft water, 6 pints. Boil together, add 4 oz. of sulphate of iron, and 4 oz. of gum arabic. Put the whole in a bottle, and keep it in a warm place, shaking it occasionally. In two months pour it off into glass bottles, and add to each pint a grain of corrosive sublimate, or 3 or 4 drops of creosote. Add one ounce of brown sugar to the above, and it will make good copying ink.

*Blue Ink.*—Prepare a solution of iodide of iron from iodine, iron, and water; add to the solution half as much iodine as first used, pour this solution into semi-saturated solution of ferro-prussiate of potash, containing nearly as much of the salt as the whole weight of iodine. Collect the precipitate, wash it, and finally dissolve it in water, to form the blue ink. The solution from which the precipitate is separated, evaporated to dryness, and the residue fused, re-dissolved and crystalized, yields pure iodide of potassium. This process is patented.

*Gold and Silver Ink.*—Fine bronze-powder, or gold, or silver leaf, ground with a little sulphate of potash, and washed from the salt, is mixed with water, and a sufficient quantity of gum.

*Ink for Marking Linen.*—Nitrate of silver, 100 grains; distilled water, 1 ounce; gum arabic, 2 drachms; sap green, a scruple. Dissolve. The linen is first to be wetted with the following "pounce," dried and rubbed smooth, then written on by a clean quill or bone pen dipped in the ink. Pounce: Subcarbonate of soda, 1 ounce; water, 8 ounces.

*Indelible Ink.*—Take 20 parts of Dantzig potash, 10 of tanned leather parings, and 5 of sulphur; boil them in an iron pot with sufficient water to dryness; then raise the heat, stirring the matter constantly, till the whole becomes soft, taking care that it does not ignite. Add sufficient water, and filter through cloth. It must be kept from the air. It resists many chemical agents.

*Cement for Glass, China, etc.*—Isinglass, one ounce; distilled water, 6 ounces; boil to 3 ounces, and add 1½ ounces of rectified spirit. Boil for a minute or two, strain, and add, while hot, first ½ ounce of a milky-emulsion of ammoniac, and then 5 dr. of tincture of mastic. [There are various kinds of this cement sold, and some of the improvements introduced have not been made public..]

*Coppersmiths' Cement.*—Powdered quicklime, mixed with bullock's blood, and applied immediately.

*Gilding.*—Leaf-gold is affixed to various surfaces, properly prepared by gold size, or other adhesive medium. Metallic surfaces are coated with gold by means of amalgam of gold and mercury, applied with a wire brush, wet with an acid solution of mercury, made by dissolving 10 parts of mercury in 11 of nitric acid, by a gentle heat, and adding 2½ parts of water. The article thus coated is heated over charcoal till the mercury is dissipated, and afterwards burnished. To give it a redder color, it is covered with gilder's wax (a compound of verdigris, ochre, alum, and yellow wax), again exposed to heat, and afterwards washed and cleaned by a scratch-brush and vinegar. An inferior kind of gilding is effected by dissolving gold, with a fifth of its weight of copper, in nitro-muriatic acid, dipping rags in the solution, drying and burning them, and rubbing the ashes on the metallic surface with a cork dipped in salt and water.

*Electro Gilding* is thus performed:—A solution of 5 oz. of gold is prepared and boiled till it ceases to give out yellow vapors; the clear solution is mixed with 4 gallons of water, 20 pounds of bicarbonate of potash added, and the whole boiled for two hours. The articles, properly cleaned, are suspended on wires, and moved about in the liquid from a few seconds to a minute, then washed, dried, and colored in the usual way. The solution used in gilding with the voltaic apparatus is made by dissolving ¼ ounce of oxide of gold with 2 ounces of cyanide of potassium, in a pint of distilled water.

*Balls for Cleaning Clothes.*—Bathbrick, 4 parts; pipeclay, 8 parts; pumice, 1; soft-soap, 1; ochre, umber, or other color, to bring it to the desired shade, sufficient ox-gall to form a paste. Make into balls, and dry them.

*To Stain Wood a Mahogany Color (dark).*—Boil one pound of

madder and 2 ounces of logwood in a gallon of water, and brush the wood well over with the hot liquor. When dry, go over the whole with a solution of 2 drachms of pearlash in a quart of water.

*To Strain Maple a Mahogany Color.*—Dragon's blood, ½ ounce; alkanet, ¼ ounce; aloes, 1 drachm; spirit of wine, 1¼ ounces. Apply it with a sponge or brush.

*Rosewood.*—Boil 8 ounces of logwood in 3 pints of water until reduced to half; apply it boiling hot two or three times, letting it dry between each. Afterwards put on the streaks with a camel-hair pencil dipped in a solution of copperas and verdigris in decoction of logwood.

*Ebony.*—Wash the wood repeatedly with a solution of sulphate of iron; let it dry, then apply a hot decoction of logwood and nutgalls for two or three times. When dry, wipe it with a wet sponge, and polish with linseed-oil.

*French Polish.*—Orange shellac, 22 ounces; rectified spirit 4 pints; dissolve.

*Etching Fluids (for steel).*—Mix 10 parts of pure hydrochloric acid, 70 of distilled water, and a solution of 2 parts of chlorate of potash in 20 of water. Dilute before using with from 100 to 200 parts of water. (*For Copper*)—Iodine, 2 parts; iodide of potassium, 5 parts; water, 5 to 8 parts.

*Silvering Compound.*—Nitrate of silver, 1 part; cyanide of potassium (Liebig's) 3 parts; water sufficient to form a thick paste.

Apply it with a rag. A bath for the same purpose is made by dissolving 100 parts of sulphate of soda, and 15 of nitrate of silver, in water and dipping the article to be silvered into it.

*Tracing Paper.*—Paper well wetted with Canada balsam and camphine, and dried.

*Shampoo Liquor.*—Rum, three quarts; spirit of wine, one pint; water, one pint; tincture of cantharides, ½ ounce; carbonate of ammonia, ½ ounce; salt of tartar, 1 ounce. Rub it on and afterwards wash with water. By omitting the salt of tartar it nearly resembles the balm of Columbia.

*Waterproof Compound.*—Suet, 8 ounces; linseed-oil, 8 ounces; yellow beeswax, 6 ounces; neatsfoot oil, 1½ ounces; lampblack, 1 oz., litharge ½ oz. Melt together, and stir till cold.

*Kittoe's Lotion for Sunburns, Freckles, etc.*—Muriate of ammonia, 1 drachm sprin water, a pint; lavender water, 2 drachms. Apply with a sponge 2 or 3 times a day.

*Virgin's Milk.*—Simple tincture of benzoin, 2 drachms; orange-flower water, 8 ounces. It may be varied by using rose or elder-flower water.

*Coloring for Brandy, etc.*—Sugar melted in a ladle till it is brown, and then dissolved in water or lime-water.

*Colors for Liquors.*—Pink is given by cochineal, yellow by saffron or safflower, violet, by litmus, blue, by sulphate of indigo, saturated with chalk; green by the last, with tincture of saffron, or by sap-green.

*To Preserve Butter.*—Powder finely, and mix together, 2 parts of the best salt, one of loaf-sugar, and one of nitre. To each pound of butter, well cleansed from the milk, add one oz. of this compound. It should not be used under a month. [Butter that has an unpleasant flavor is said to be improved by the addition of 2½ drachms of bicarbonate of soda to 3 pounds of butter. A turnipy flavor may be prevented by only feeding the cows with turnips immediately after milking them.]

*To Preserve Eggs.*—Jayne's liquid (expired patent) is thus made: Take a bushel of lime, 2 pounds of salt, ½ pound of cream of tartar, and water enough to form a solution strong enough to float an egg. In this liquid it is stated, eggs may be preserved for two years.

*How to make Fly-poison.*—A common poison for flies consists of white arsenic or king's yellow, with sugar, etc., but the use of such compounds may lead to fatal accidents. A sweetened infusion of quassia answers the same purpose, and is free from danger. Pepper, with milk, is also used; and also some adhesive compounds, by which they are fatally entangled.

*Indian Ink.*—Real lampblack, produced by combustion of linseed-oil, ground with gum, and infusion of galls. It is prepared both in a fluid and solid form, the latter being dried in the sun.

*Bedbug Poison.*—Scotch snuff mixed with soft soap.

*Sympathetic or Secret Ink.*—[The solutions used should be so nearly colorless that the writing is not seen till the agent is applied to render it visible.]

1. Digest 1 oz. of taffre, or oxide of cobalt, at a gentle heat,

with 4 oz. of nitro-muriatic acid till no more is dissolved, then add one oz of common salt, and 16 oz. of water. If this be written with and the paper held to the fire, the writing becomes green, unless the cobalt should be quite pure, in which case it will be blue. The addition of a little nitrate of iron will impart the property of becoming green. It is used in chemical landscapes for the foliage.

3. Boil oxide of cobalt in acetic acid. If a little common salt be added, the writing becomes green when heated; but with nitre it becomes a pale rose-color.

6. A solution of sulphate—or preferably, persulphate—of iron. It becomes black when washed with infusion of galls; BLUE, by prussiate of potash. [This constitutes colorless ink, which becomes visible when written with on paper containing galls, or tannin, or prussiate of potash.]

*Fattening Calves.*—Aniseed, ½ pound; fenugrec, ¼ pound; linseed meal 1 pound. Make it into a paste with milk, and cram them with it.

*Blake's Toothache Remedy.*—Finely powdered alum, 1 drachm; spirit nitric ether, 7 drachms.

*British Oil.*—Oil of turpentine, and linseed oil, of each 8 ounces; oil of amber, and oil of Juniper, of each 4 ounces; true Barbadoes tar, 3 ounces; American Petroleum, 1 ounce. Mix.

*To Preserve Milk.*—Milk the cow into glass bottles, and seal them to keep out the air.

*Armenian Cement.*—Soak isinglass in water till soft; then dissolve it in proof spirit; add a little Galbanum or gum Ammoniac, and mix it with tincture of mastic. It must be kept well stopped, and when wanted, liquefied by the phial being immersed in hot water. Used to cement jewels upon watch cases; to mend china, or to replace leaves torn out of books.

*To Prevent Flies from Setting on Pictures, Picture Frames, or other Furniture.*—Soak a large bundle of Leeks for five or six days in a pail of water, and then wash or sponge the pictures, etc., ever with it.

*To Cure Butter.*—Take 2 parts of the best common salt, 1 part of sugar, and one part of saltpetre. Beat them up, and mix well together. Take one ounce of this to every pound of butter, work it well into a mass, and close it up for use. Butter thus cured, appears of a rich marrowy consistence and fine color, and does not acquire a brittle hardness, nor taste salt. It will keep good for three years, if let stand three or four weeks before opening it.

*Wash to Whiten the Nails.*—Take diluted sulphuric acid, 2 dr.; pump water, 4 ounces; Tincture of myrrh, 1 drachm. Mix. First cleanse with white soap, and then dip the fingers into the wash.

*To join Glass together.*—Take a little isinglass, and melt it in spirits of wine. It will form a transparent glue, which will unite glass, so that the fracture will be almost imperceptible. The greatest care is necessary, that the spirits of wine shall not boil over into the fire.

*To Renovate old Apple-trees.*—Take fresh made lime from the kiln; slake it well with water, and well dress the tree with a brush, and the insects and moss will be completely destroyed.

The outer ring will fall off, and a new, smooth, clean, healthy one formed, and the trees assume a most healthy appearance, and produce the finest frui

*To prevent the Smoking of a Lamp.*—Soak the wick in strong vinegar, and dry it well before you use it. It will then burn both sweet and pleasant, and give much satisfaction for the trifling trouble in preparing it.

*To make Silvering Powder.*—Get from a drug-store 1 oz. of what is called Hydrargirum, *Cum Creta*, and mix it with 4 oz. prepared chalk. Used to give a silver polish to brass, copper, britannia ware, etc. To be rubbed on with a dry cloth.

*Nerve Ointment.*—Take half a pint of neatsfoot-oil, one gill of brandy, one gill of spirits of turpentine, and simmer them together fifteen minutes. Excellent for sprains, swellings, and rheumatism.

*To Free Plants from Leaf-lice.*—Mix 3 ounces of flowers of sulphur with a bushel of sawdust. Scatter this over the plants infested with these insects, and they will soon be freed, though a second application may possibly be necessary.

*Strawberry Jelly.*—Take of the juice of strawberries, 4 pounds; sugar, 1 pound. Boil to a jelly.

*To Avoid Injury from Bees.*—A wasp or a bee swallowed may be killed before it can do harm, by taking a teaspoonful of common salt dissolved in water. It kills the insect, and cures the sting. Salt at all times is the best cure for external stings. Sweet-oil, pounded mallows, onions, or powdered chalk made into a paste with water, are also efficacious. If bees swarm up on the head, smoke tobacco, and hold an empty hive over the head, and they will enter it.

*How to Make Rose-water.*—Take half an ounce white sugar, and drop into it 2 or 3 drops of otto of rose; then grind very fine in a mortar. After it is well ground into fine powder, pour on it half a pint of cold water; grind well for a few moments, and then mix it all with one gallon of cold water. Let it stand for 3 or 4 days, and strain through fine muslin.

*Whitewashing.*—A pint of varnish mixed with a bucket of whitewash will give it, in a great degree, the qualities of paint; and it will withstand all kinds of weather.

*Nankin Dye.*—Take arnotto and prepared Kali, equal parts, boiled in water; the proportion of Kali is altered, as the color is required to be deeper or lighter. Used to restore the color of faded nankin clothing, or to dye new goods of a nankin color.

*To make Spice Bitters.*—Golden Seal, Poplar-Bark, Bayberry, bark of the root, Sassafras, bark of the root. of each one pound; Unicorn-root, Bitter-root, Cloves, Capsicum, of each, 4 ounces, Loaf-sugar, 4 pounds. Put to one ounce of this powder, one quart of sweet wine; let it stand a week or two before using it. Dose—a wineglassful two or three times a day.

*How to make Saur Kraut.*—Take a large strong wooden vessel, or cask, resembling a salt-beef cask, and capable of containing as much as is sufficient for the winter's consumption of a family. Gradually break down or chop the cabbages (deprived of outside green leaves) into very small pieces; begin with one or two cabbages at the bottom of the cask, and add others at intervals, pressing them by means of a wooden spade, against the side of the cask, until it is full. Then place a heavy weight on top of it and allow it to stand near a warm place, for four or five days. By this time it will have undergone fermentation, and be ready for use. Whilst the cabbages are passing through the process of fermentation, a very disagreeable fetid, acid smell, is exhalted from them. Now remove the cask to a cool situation, and keep it always covered up. Strew aniseed among the layers of the cabbage during its preparation, which communicates a peculiar flavor to the Saur Kraut at an after period. In boiling it for the table, two hours is the period for it to be on the fire. It forms an excellent, nutritious, and antiscorbutic food, for winter use.

*Bedbugs.*—A strong decoction of ripe red pepper is said to be as efficacious an antidote to bedbugs as can be selected from the multitudinous recipes for the purpose.

*Burning-Fuid.*—Take four quarts of alcohol and one quart of spirits of turpentine. Mix well together.

*To Extract Paint from Cotton, Silk, and Woolen Goods.*—Saturate the spots with spirits of turpentine, and let it remain several hours; then rub it between the hands. It will crumble away, without injuring the color or texture of the article.

*To make Silver-Plating Powder.* for silvering brass, copper, etc., and for repairing worn-out parts of plated goods.—Nitrate of silver, 30 grains; common table-salt, 30 grains; cream of tartar, 3½ drachms. Mix all thoroughly, and make into a fine powder in a mortar. Moisten a soft cloth, dip into the powder, and rub over the surface to be plated for a few moments; then wash off with a solution of common salt in water, and rub dry with a cloth and chalk or whiting.

*To make Violet or Purple Ink.*—Boil 16 ounces of logwood in 3 quarts of rain water, to three pints; then add 3 ounces of clean gum arabic and 5 ounces of alum (powdered). Shake till well dissolved. It would be well to strain through a wire sieve.

*To Clean Kid Gloves.*—Add 15 drops of strongest solution of ammonia to spirits of turpentine ½ pint. Having fitted the gloves on wooden hands or pegs, apply this mixture with a brush. Follow up this application with some fine pumice powder. Rub with some flannel or sponge dipped in the mixture. Rub off the sand, and repeat the same process twice or thrice. Hang in the air to dry, and, when dry, place in a drawer with some scent.

*To make Matches without Sulphur or Phosphorus.*—Chlorate of potash, separately powdered, 6 drachms; vermilion, 1 drachm; lycopodium, 1 drachm; fine flour, two drachms. Mix carefully the chlorate with the flour and lycopodium, avoiding *much friction*, then add the vermilion, and mix the whole with a mucilage made with one drachm of powdered gum arabic, to grains of tragacanth, 2 drachms of flour, and 4 ounces of hot water. Mix. Add sufficient water to bring it into a proper consistence, and dip in the wood previously dipped in a solution of one ounce of gum camphor, in six ounces of oil of turpentine,

*To make Black Ink Powder.*—Sulphate of copper [bluestone], one ounce; gum arabic, 2 ounces; green vitriol [copperas], 8 oz.; nutgalls, powdered, 1 pound; extract of logwood, 1 pound. All are to be finely pulverized. About one ounce of this mixture will be required to make one pint of ink, to be put into boiling water. It should stand about two weeks before using.

*Baking Powder.*—Baking soda, 6 ounces; cream tartar, 8 ounces. Each should be thoroughly dry before mixing. About a teaspoonful, dissolved in warm milk or water is sufficient for a quart of flour.

*To make Syrup of Sarsaparilla,*—Take of sarsaparilla-root, 1 lb.; boiling water, 5 quarts; sugar, 1 pound. Cut or chop up the sarsaparilla-root into short pieces, the shorter the better, put it into the water, let it stand for 24 hours, then boil down to 2½ quarts, and strain the liquid *while hot.* Then add the sugar, and boil gradually for about an hour. When cool, put into bottles or a jug, and keep corked. Dose, from one to two tablespoonfuls before each meal. This is a valuable medicine to *purify the blood,* and is used with great advantage in all cases of general debility or weakness from any cause whatever: also, for disease of the liver, dyspepsia, or indigestion, scrofula, female weakness, loss of appetite, effects of syphilis or venereal disease, and in every case where the wish is to *build up* and *strengthen* the system. It should be used about two months or more at a time.

*To Make Medicated Root-beer.*—For each gallon of water to be used, take hops, burdock, yellow dock, sarsaparilla, dandelion, and spikenard roots, bruised, of each ½ ounce; boil about 20 minutes; and strain while hot; add 8 or ten drops of oils of spruce and sassafras, mixed in equal proportion. When cool enough not to scald your hand, put in two or three tablespoonfuls of yeast; molasses; two-thirds of a pint, or white sugar ½ pound, gives it about the right sweetness. Keep these proportions for as many gallons as you wish to make. You can use more or less of the roots to suit your taste, after trying it. It is best to get the dry roots, or dig them and let them dry, and of course you can add any other root known to possess medicinal properties desired in beer. After all is mixed let it stand in a jar with a cloth thrown over it, to work about two hours, then bottle and set in a cool place. This is a nice way to take alteratives, without taking medicines to operate on the bowels.

*To Make Ice Cream.*—Fresh cream, ½ gallon; rich milk, ½ gallon; white sugar one pound. Dissolve the sugar in the mixture, and flavor with extract to suit your taste; or take the peel from a fresh lemon and steep one half of it in as little water as you can, and add this. It makes the lemon flavor better than the extract, and no flavor will so universally please as the lemon. Keep the same proportion for any amount desired. The juice of strawberries or raspberries gives a beautiful color and flavor to ice-creams; or about ½ oz. of essence or extracts to a gallon, or to suit the taste. Have your ice well broke; one quart salt to a bucket of ice. About half an hour's constant stirring, and an occasional scraping down and beating together, will freeze it.

*Ice-Cream* (a cheaper kind).—Milk, 6 quarts; Oswego cornstarch, ½ pound. First dissolve the starch in one quart of the milk, and then mix all together and just simmer a little (not to boil). Sweeten and flavor to suit your taste, as above.

*Chicago Plan of making Ice-Cream.*—Irish moss, 1½ ounces; milk, one gallon. First soak the moss in a little cold water for an hour, and rinse it well to clear it of sand and a certain peculiar taste; then steep it for an hour in the milk just at the boiling point, but not to boil. It imparts a rich color and flavor without eggs or cream. The moss may be steeped *twice*. A few minutes rubbing, at the end of freezing, with the spatula against the side of the freezer, gives ice-cream a smoothness not otherwise obtained, and makes it look nice.

*To Make Fever and Ague Pills.*—Quinine, 20 grains; Dovers-powders, 10 grains; sub-carbonate of iron, 10 grains. Mix with mucilage of gum arabic, and make into 20 pills. Dose: two every hour, beginning four or five hours before the chill is expected. When the chills have been broken, take one pill night and morning for a month, to prevent a return.

*To Make Axle-Grease.*—One pound of black lead ground fine and smooth with four pounds of lard. A little powdered gum-camphor is sometimes added.

***To Tan Raw Hide.***—When taken from the animal spread it flesh side up; then put 2 parts of salt, 2 parts of saltpetre and alum combined, make it fine, sprinkle it evenly over the surface, roll it up, let it alone for a few days until dissolved; then take off what flesh remains, and nail the skin to the side of a house in the sun; stretch it tight. To make it soft like harness leather, put neatsfoot oil on it. Fasten it up in the sun again: then rub out all the oil you can with a wedge-shaped stick, and it is tanned with the hair on.

***To make Refined Oil for Watches, Sewing-machines, etc.***—Take sweet-oil, 1 pint, put into a bottle and then put into the oil 2 oz. of thin sheet-lead, in coils. Set the bottle where it will be exposed to the sun for a month (shaking it up once a week); then strain through a fine wire or cloth sieve, and keep tightly corked.

***How to Make Transparent Soap.***—Slice 6 pounds of nice bar soap into thin shavings, put into a brass, tin, or copper kettle, with 2 quarts of alcohol, and heat it gradually over a slow fire, stirring till all the soap is dissolved; then add one ounce of sassafras, and stir till all is mixed. You will then pour into pans 1½ inches deep; and, when cold, cut into bars or cakes as may be desired.

***To Make Self-raising Flour.***—This is made by adding 4 pounds of the following mixture to every 100 pounds of flour, and then mixing all completely. It must be kept perfectly dry, and, in using, mix quickly and *put into the oven at once.* Here is the mixture referred to above: carbonate of soda, 56 pounds, tartaric acid, 28 pounds, potato-flour, 112 pounds. Having used bread made from self-raising flour, we can testify that it is good.

***To make Solid Candles from common Lard.***—Dissolve ¼ lb. of alum and ¼ lb. saltpetre in ½ pint of water on a slow fire; then take 3 lbs. of lard, cut into small pieces, and put into the pot with this solution, stirring it constantly over a very moderate fire until the lard is dissolved; then let it simmer until all steam ceases to rise, and remove it at once from the fire. If you leave it too long it will get discolored. These candles are harder and better than those made from tallow.

***How to Make Oroide Gold.***—Spanish copper, 16 parts; silver, 4 parts; gold, 1 part. Melt together.

***To make Renovating Mixture, for removing grease-spots, etc.***—

Aqua-ammonia, 2 ounces; soft water, 1 quart; saltpetre, 1 teaspoonful; variegated soap, 1 ounce. Mix all, shake well, and it will be a little better to stand a few hours or days before using, which gives the soap a chance to dissolve.

*Directions.*—Pour upon the place a sufficient amount to well cover any grease or oil which may get spilled or daubed upon coats, pants, carpets, etc., sponging and rubbing well, and applying again if necessary to saponify the grease in the garment; then wash off with clear cold water.

*To make Magic Copying or Impression or Duplicating Paper.*—To make black paper, lampblack mixed with cold lard. Red paper, venetian red mixed with lard. Blue paper, prussian blue mixed with lard. Green paper, chrome green mixed with lard. The above ingredients to be mixed to the consistencey of thick paste, and to be applied to the paper with a rag or brush; then take a flannel rag and rub till the color ceases coming off. Cut your sheets 4 inches wide and 6 inches long; put 8 sheets together, 2 of each color, and sell for 25 cents per package.

*Directions for Writing with this Paper.*—Lay down your paper upon which you wish to write, then lay on the copying paper, and over this lay any scrap of paper you choose; then take any hard-pointed substance, and write as you would with a pen. To take impressions of flowers, leaves, etc., press them between this paper and a sheet of clean white paper, and then lay the leaf on another clean sheet of paper, and press the paper gently over it.

www.ingramcontent.com/pod-product-compliance
Lightning Source LLC
Chambersburg PA
CBHW020535300426
44111CB00008B/676